£2.00

Encyclopedia of

MAGIC & ANCIENT WISDOM

CASSANDRA EASON

Encyclopedia of

MAGIC & ANCIENT WISDOM

THE ESSENTIAL GUIDE TO MYTH, MAGIC AND THE SUPERNATURAL

PIATKUS

© 2000 Cassandra Eason

First published in 2000 by
Judy Piatkus (Publishers) Ltd
5 Windmill Street
London W1T 2JA
e-mail: info@piatkus.co.uk

**For the latest news and information on all our titles, visit
our website at www.piatkus.co.uk**

The moral rights of the author have been asserted
A catalogue record for this book is available from the British Library

ISBN 0 7499 2147 1

This book has been printed on paper manufactured with respect for the
environment using wood from managed sustainable resources

Design by Paul Saunders
Line illustrations by Rodney Paull

Typeset by Selwood Systems, Midsomer Norton
Printed and bound in Great Britain by
Butler & Tanner Ltd, Frome and London

CONTENTS

PART 1 Essential Wisdom

PART 2 Traditions, Myths and Folklore

PART 3 Magical, Mystical and Otherworldly Beings

Part 4 Nature Magic and Mystery

Part 5 Wisdom from Other Cultures, Other Lands

Part 6 Psychic Powers and Strange Phenomena

PART ONE

Essential Wisdom

ASTROLOGY, THE ZODIAC AND PLANETARY INFLUENCES

Astrology

'As above so below.' The opening words on the Emerald Tablet of the semi-divine 1st century Egyptian sorcerer Hermes Trismegistos sum up astrologers' belief in the influence on the lives of humankind of the movement of the stars and the planets.

Astrologers noted that the rising of certain stars seemed to regulate the seasons. For example, the ancient Egyptians set their calendar by Sirius whose first appearance of the year over the horizon signalled that the Nile was going to flood, bringing fertility to the land. Just as the stars seemed to regulate the seasons, so it was reasoned they also regulated and reflected the affairs of mankind.

Astrologers work by drawing up a horoscope. This is a chart of the heavens showing the relationships between the planets and the constellations of the zodiac, the belt of stars through which the planets of our solar system appear to move. Each of the planets and the constellations is said to have certain qualities which can influence events or indicate an individual's character.

The Western astrological tradition began with the Babylonians who were the first to divide the sky into the 12 houses of the zodiac. The Chaldeans, who lived in Mesopotamia from about 4000BC, first began to specialise in drawing up horoscopes in the 5th century BC. The Greeks then took up the idea of astrology because it accorded with their concept of the universe as a well-ordered affair. Life on earth might be confused but in the heavens everything was perfect.

Of course, one of the most striking astrological events was recorded in the Bible. The three wise men are said to have come out of the east following a great star which led them to Bethlehem and the birthplace of Christ. In around AD1600, Johannes Kepler, whose laws of planetary motion were the basis for modern astronomy, put forward the theory that the 'star' was actually a conjunction of Jupiter and Saturn. A conjunction is when two planets appear to move next to each other, in some cases appearing as a single, bright glowing object. This is a trick of perspective because in fact they are still millions of miles apart. A conjunction can be seen as favourable because the energies of the planets are working together. Some astrologers argue that the conjunction would have been an apt sign because Jupiter is the planet of kings while Saturn is said to rule the Jews. So the heavens were announcing the birth of the King of the Jews.

Kepler himself drew up horoscopes, and astrology flourished in Europe until the Renaissance despite attacks from the Christian church. In 17th century England, William Lilly published his influential textbook *Christian Astrology* and became notorious for predicting the Great Plague and the Fire of London; at one point he was even under suspicion of starting the fire in order to fulfil his prediction.

During the 18th century, the Age of Enlightenment, astrology fell out of fashion, but a revival in the 19th century was helped by astrologers like R.C. Smith who

practised under the name Raphael. Cheap astrological almanacs had been printed since the 17th century, but horoscopes only moved into the newspapers when R.H. Naylor published the horoscope of the newly born Princess Margaret of England in the *Sunday Express* in 1930. The following week, on 5 October, he published a column predicting danger to British aircraft. On that day the British airship, the R-101, crashed in northern France on its maiden voyage.

Astrology can be roughly divided into four fields:

Natal Astrology
A chart is drawn up for the moment of a person's birth. Rather than the birth or sun sign (see Zodiac, below), the ascendant – the constellation rising over the horizon at the moment of birth – is seen as the most important aspect.

Horary Astrology
This looks at how the heavens can influence a certain event at a certain time.

ESSENTIAL WISDOM

Electoral Astrology

This is used to decide the right moment to begin a venture. It is said that the astrologer Dr John Dee (1527–1608) was consulted about the best moment for the coronation of Queen Elizabeth I. If this is true, he must have chosen well considering the great achievements of her reign.

Decumbiture

This deals with matters of health, and the diagnosis and treatment of disease according to astrological precepts. The 17th-century herbalist Nicholas Culpeper assigned each of the plants in his herbal to astrological signs.

The Zodiac

The word Zodiac is derived from the Greek *zodiakos kyrklos*, meaning the circle of small animals.

The zodiac refers to the system astrologers use to mark out and name fixed constellations in the sky, as seen from earth, through which the sun, moon and other planets are observed to move in a regular pattern. The modern Western or Tropical zodiac is based on 12 constellations named after mythical characters and animals whose shapes have been observed in the night skies by astronomers or astrologers over thousands of years. These constellations have given their names and characteristics to the 12 sun or birth signs that form the root of modern popular astrology and newspaper horoscopes.

Astrological knowledge filtered to ancient Greece from Mesopotamia where the ancient Babylonians had developed a zodiac of 18 irregular signs. It is hard to date the changes, but some time after 500BC the zodiac was refined by astrologers who divided the ecliptic (the path that the sun seems to take through the skies during the earth's year-long orbit) into 12 regular 30 degree divisions. These 12 constellations are said to reflect most accurately the characteristics of those born when the sun was in that particular sign, on the principle of 'as above, so below'. Horoscopes, diagrams of the heavens at the time of an individual's birth, were known to have first been cast around 410BC, but may have existed even earlier.

Gradually the ancient Babylonian, Egyptian and Assyrian animals, heroes and deities after whom the constellations were originally called, were given Greek names and the ancient Greeks wove or adapted myths to mirror the assumed characteristics of the different constellations.

The Sun Signs

As the earth moves around the sun on its year-long journey, the background of constellations changes month by month and it appears that the sun is actually travelling through the zodiac. At night it is possible to see how these constellations of the zodiac change their positions: for example, in the northern hemisphere, at midnight in December, Gemini is high in the sky. By March at the same time Virgo is in that position.

The ancient astronomers wrongly believed that the stars revolved round the earth on giant spheres. Despite this error their observations were accurate enough to lay the foundations of astronomy and horoscopes. Watching the last stars to rise at dawn before the sun became too bright to see them, these astronomer/astrologers could tell in which constellation the sun was at that time of year.

The reason that many horoscope columns in newspapers begin with Aries is that when the first astronomical observations were made some 4,000 years ago the sun moved into that sign at the time of the spring equinox, around 21 March. This was seen as the start of the year and Aries was regarded as the birth-day of the world. However, this is no longer true, due to a phenomenon called precession. As the earth spins on its axis, it wobbles like a spinning top. The movement is slow – it takes around 25,000 years for it to wobble round in a giant circle, in addition to its daily spin. But this means that the appearance of the constellations changes.

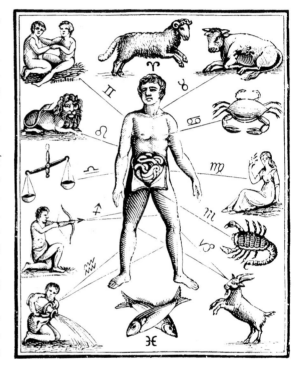

Today, at the spring equinox the sun is in the sign of Pisces, not Aries. Soon it will move into a new constellation, Aquarius. In the Indian or Vedic astrological system, a Sidereal zodiac is followed. This is based on the true position of the constellations, taking into account the precession of the equinoxes. So in effect under this system everyone's birth sign moves back a month, Arians becoming Pisceans, Taureans becoming Arians, and so on.

What is significant is that both systems work, so clearly astrology is not a matter of science, but of psychic connections. It is said that the finest astrologers are not those who can measure a chart and calculate the relationships between planets in greatest detail, but who can intuitively interpret the potentialities in a basic chart. Others argue that it is the symbolism of astrology that is important, rather than direct correspondences with the sky. This is an issue that has caused fierce argument for hundreds of years since it was first discovered that the earth revolves round the sun and not the other way round.

Whatever the arguments, astrology remains the most popular form of divination today and seems remarkably accurate. It may be that we will never understand the underlying cosmic rationale, but will continue to benefit from its guidance.

In the Western system, each of the sun signs has special qualities. Each group of three signs (starting with Aries) spans one of the seasons of the year.

Cardinal or Initiating Signs: ARIES, CANCER, LIBRA AND CAPRICORN

These are regarded as cardinal signs because when the sun moves into these signs it marks the start of a new season: spring, summer, autumn and winter. People born under a cardinal sign manifest this quality as a desire to initiate and to take command of people and situations.

Fixed Signs: LEO, TAURUS, AQUARIUS AND SCORPIO

These are called fixed signs because the sun enters them in the middle of a season. Those born under them exhibit stability and a tendency to continue in a predetermined path.

Mutable Signs: SAGITTARIUS, GEMINI, VIRGO AND PISCES

These are mutable because when the sun enters them the season is about to change. Those born under them are correspondingly versatile and ready to compromise.

Elements

The 12 sun signs are also divided into four elements, so offering more information about the characteristics of those born under each sun sign.

Fire: ARIES, LEO, SAGITTARIUS

Fire signs are volatile, full of energy and natural leaders and innovators, but may become impatient and lack perseverance.
Fire signs are best balanced by Earth signs.

Earth: TAURUS, VIRGO, CAPRICORN

Earth signs are practical, cautious and trustworthy, but may lack imagination and creativity.

Air: GEMINI, LIBRA, AQUARIUS

Air signs are intellectual, rational and good organisers, but may lack empathy and intuition.
Air signs are best balanced by Water signs.

Water: CANCER, SCORPIO, PISCES

Water signs are emotional, sympathetic and psychic, but may lack logic and focus.

Sun Sign Meanings

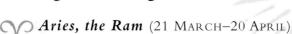

Aries, the Ram (21 MARCH–20 APRIL)
KEY WORD: *Assertiveness*

Those born under Aries are innovative, enterprising, free spirits with a strong sense of identity, energetic but self-centred.

Taurus, the Bull (21 APRIL–21 MAY)
KEY WORD: *Persistence*

Those born under Taurus are patient, reliable, practical, loyal, concerned with material comfort and security for self and loved ones, but can be possessive and materialistic.

Gemini, the Heavenly Twins (22 MAY–21 JUNE)
KEY WORD: *Communication*

Those born under Gemini are adaptable, intellectual, scientific/technologically adept, inquisitive, intelligent and adaptable, but restless and inconsistent.

Cancer, the Crab (22 JUNE–22 JULY)
KEY WORD: *Sensitivity*

Those born under Cancer are kind, home-loving and nurturing, especially towards children, creators of emotional security, but secretive and can become over-sensitive to potential criticism.

Leo, the Lion (23 JULY–23 AUGUST)
KEY WORD: *Power*

Those born under Leo are courageous, generous, noble, proud and loyal, born leaders, but need the adulation of others and can be occasionally arrogant.

Virgo, the Maiden (24 AUGUST–22 SEPTEMBER)
KEY WORD: *Perfection*

Those born under Virgo tend to be methodical, meticulous, skilful, perfectionists, modest and efficient, but can be critical of self and others and worry over details.

Libra, the Scales (23 SEPTEMBER–23 OCTOBER)
KEY WORD: *Harmony*

Those born under Libra tend to be balanced and peace-loving, harmonious, diplomatic with a strong sense of justice, but can be unwilling to make decisions and can be narcissistic.

Scorpio, the Scorpion (24 OCTOBER–22 NOVEMBER)
KEY WORD: *Intensity*

Those born under Scorpio tend to be psychic, mystical, purposeful and regenerative, but can be vengeful and overly introverted.

Sagittarius, the Archer (23 NOVEMBER–21 DECEMBER)
KEY WORD: *Expansive*

Those born under Sagittarius are visionaries, seekers after truth and meaning, flexible, open-minded, extroverted, optimistic but can be very outspoken and can lack staying power.

Capricorn, the Goat (22 DECEMBER–20 JANUARY)
KEY WORD: *Prudence*

Those born under Capricorn are cautious, quietly resolute, persistent, conventional and ambitious, with great self-discipline, but can be mean and very inflexible.

ESSENTIAL WISDOM

7

ESSENTIAL WISDOM

 Aquarius, the Water Carrier (21 JANUARY–18 FEBRUARY)
KEY WORD: *Idealism*

Those born under Aquarius are independent, idealistic, intellectual, inventive and humanitarian, but can be emotionally detached and somewhat eccentric.

Pisces, the Fish (19 FEBRUARY–20 MARCH)
KEY WORD: *Intuition*

Those born under Pisces are sensitive, sympathetic, imaginative, intuitive, impressionable and spiritual, but can be self-pitying and easily lose touch with reality.

Ascendant or Rising Sign

Each house is ruled by a sun sign, to which it bears similarities. The first house denoting self is always positioned as the segment just below the eastern horizon, a position on the wheel known as the ascendant.

The ascendant or rising sign is the same as the birth sign if a person is born at sunrise, as the sun spends two hours in each house. The ascendant sign is important because it determines the personality. It is also important because in a natal chart it determines the position of the houses in the birth chart, ie the rising sign will always mark the beginning of the first house and therefore can be as influential in explaining a person's character as the birth sign itself.

Planetary Influences

The planets have a special place in both astrology and ritual magic. As the Ancient Babylonians and Chaldeans watched the constellations of the zodiac wheel across the sky in their yearly cycle, they noticed that some of the bright objects behaved differently. While the stars that made up Aries, Taurus and others never moved out of their fixed patterns, other bright objects did. The Greeks named these *planetos* or 'wanderers', giving us the word 'planet'.

We now know that these are worlds just like the earth which also circle the sun. However, because the speeds of their orbits vary, they appear to change their positions against the backdrop of the zodiac, producing this 'wanderer' effect.

The ancients knew of only five planets – Mercury, Venus, Mars, Jupiter and Saturn. Uranus, Neptune and Pluto were discovered only after the invention of the telescope. The first astronomers also counted the sun and the moon as planets and credited them with certain qualities that have become woven into Western astrological and magical traditions.

Astrologers believe that the positions of the planets in the zodiac at the time of an individual's birth can influence or indicate that person's fate.

In magic, the planetary qualities are sometimes invoked by the use of talismans, perhaps by wearing silver or gold to draw down the powers of the moon or sun.

Today we use Roman names for the planets but the naming process began with the Babylonians. Each planet is said to rule a house of the zodiac.

The Sun (RULES LEO)

The sun represents the essential self, identity, personality and unique qualities. The sun has been worshipped by many cultures through the ages. To the Babylonians it was not an incandescent ball of gas 93 million miles away but the manifestation of the sun god Shamash. In Ancient Greece, the solar god Helios was praised each dawn as he emerged in the east and drove his chariot of winged horses around the sky.

Sun deities on the whole are male, so the sun represents mainly yang, animus or male energies in both men and women.

The sun intensifies the influence of any sign or house in which it appears, spending approximately one month in each sign. It is associated with power, creativity, vision, health and the life-force, but also arrogance.

The Moon (RULES CANCER)

The moon has traditionally been regarded as the consort of the sun; her silver to his gold. The classical goddess Diana, sister of the sun god Apollo, was worshipped as the moon in all her aspects.

In magic, the moon represents the emotional and unconscious aspects of the personality and in earlier times was the most important planet in a chart.

Since the moon spends only two and a half days a month in each sign, its influence is relatively transient and so its position is an important calculation in daily or weekly horoscopes and short-term predictions. The moon's influence is felt as unconscious urges and impulses.

Mercury (RULES GEMINI AND VIRGO)

Mercury, the planet nearest the sun, completes its orbit in only 88 days. Its swift progress through the sky has earned it the name of 'the herald of the gods': Nabu to the Babylonians, Hermes to the Greeks and Mercury to the Romans.

Mercury is associated with the mind, science, technological abilities especially computers, logic, communication and with healing, but also with sharp practice particularly in relation to money matters.

Venus (RULES TAURUS AND LIBRA)

Venus is sometimes known as the morning or evening star because it shines with a brilliant silvery hue. At its brightest it is the most brilliant object in the sky besides the sun and moon and came to represent the goddess of beauty: Ishtar to the Babylonians, Aphrodite to the Greeks and Venus to the Romans.

Venus is associated with love, beauty, the arts, all relationships, friendship and possessions, but also with excesses of love and romance.

Mars (RULES ARIES AND IS CO-RULER OF SCORPIO)

Mars has come to represent war as it has a reddish tinge to it – red being seen as a warlike colour. It represented the warrior gods Nergal to the Babylonians, Aries to the Greeks and Mars to the Romans. Mars stands for initiative, independent action and a sense of separateness from other people.

ESSENTIAL WISDOM

The planet is associated with aggression, speed, ambition, competitiveness, sexuality and passion, as well as warlike qualities. To this aspect of courage is added a nobility of spirit when angry, and warlike impulses are directed against injustice and inertia.

Jupiter (RULES SAGITTARIUS AND IS CO-RULER OF PISCES)

Jupiter is the largest of the planets and so came to be seen as the 'herdsman of the stars': Marduk, saviour of the world, to the Babylonians, Zeus to the Greeks and, to the Romans, Jupiter the sky father.

Jupiter represents the expression of the personality in the context of wider society and culture. It is known as the joy-bringer and is associated with all forms of good fortune and prosperity, compassion, ideals and altruism, higher values, wisdom and learning, expansiveness and increase, but also with extravagance and a tendency to be autocratic.

Saturn (RULES CAPRICORN AND IS CO-RULER OF AQUARIUS)

Saturn, the ringed planet, has the slowest orbit of those that can be seen with the naked eye. The Babylonians associated this planet with Ninurta, the warrior god, but the Greeks saw it as Kronos, the planet of time. To the Romans it became Saturn, the god of old age.

It represents the expression of the individual's personality and interactions within society's restrictions.

Saturn is associated with limitation, slow progress and difficulties. As the shadow side of Jupiter, Saturn is the reality factor, working within the bounds of fate, time and space. However, this can also be read as turning challenge into opportunity; Saturn's strengths are effort and perseverance.

Because it takes Saturn between 28 and 30 years to complete its orbit of the zodiac, this is the longest planetary cycle that will occur more than once in an average lifetime and so, in astrology, it represents the major stages of one human life.

Uranus (RULES AQUARIUS)

Uranus was discovered in 1781 and represents liberation from the past and the striving of individuals and organisations towards positive collective change.

Uranus is associated with sudden change, originality, inventiveness and inventions, especially telecommunications. It is also linked with sexuality and impulsiveness.

Because it takes Uranus 84 years to complete its trip around the zodiac its effects are felt through the lives of generations rather than individuals who will only experience one return of Uranus to their birth sign during their lifetime. Revolutions and breakthroughs in knowledge, especially technological, may coincide with Uranus entering a dynamic sign.

Neptune (RULES PISCES)

Neptune was discovered in 1846, the year that Darwin was developing his theory of evolution, and represents the search of the soul to find spiritual and mystical enlightenment.

ESSENTIAL WISDOM

Neptune is associated with all emotions and sensitivity, with intuition, hidden potential and with the unknown and mysterious, but also with indecisiveness.

Because it takes Neptune 165 years to complete its cycle with about 14 years in each sign, its effects are best seen in the establishment of new religions, cults and new forms of spirituality; mystical goals shared by all born in the time it spends in one particular sign.

Pluto (RULES SCORPIO)

Pluto was discovered in 1930 and represents the search for ultimate truth. It is also associated with moving towards perfection on all levels of existence through refinement of the imperfect, and the desire for mastery over self and the world.

Pluto represents endings; the removal of something redundant to herald a new beginning. It stands for hidden and unconscious powers, especially psychic ones, and the ability to start again even in difficult circumstances. It is also associated with financial astuteness and business acumen – but occasionally with a seedy lifestyle!

Psychically, its energies are experienced beyond conventional time scales. Intergalactic travel and ufology fall under its auspices.

AURAS

All living organisms are believed to have two bodies. One is the visible physical body and the other is the invisible energy or 'auric' body upon which the physical body is imposed. When we die or travel astrally this body separates from the physical, but remains linked by a silver cord. It is said that, when the silver cord is severed, this is the moment that we die. Some can see the etheric or spirit body as a silvery essence and others perceive it as a direct double, or doppelgänger, which may explain the 'living ghosts' that appear during astral travel.

When a person is not astrally travelling, the aura is generally perceived or felt around the outline of the physical body, especially around the head. Auras can extend from the body by a few inches or vast distances. The spiritual aura of the Lord Gautama Buddha was said to extend 200 miles. The aura also acts as a transmitting and receiving station for emotions and thoughts, and reveals information about the physical, mental and spiritual well-being of the individual.

References to a light or aura surrounding the human body can be found throughout Eastern and Western cultures from the beginning of recorded history.

In Western art there are many images of a glowing light or halo surrounding the heads of Jesus, the Virgin Mary and various saints. But, in even earlier times in Ancient Egypt, the aura was depicted both in tomb paintings and on papyri. One of the earliest references to auras in European literature can be found in the writings of Hildegard von Bingen (1098–1179). She was the first person to refer to *veriditas*, or 'the greening principle', and she recounts her visions of luminous objects.

In Hindu holy writings there are many references to the 'thousand-petalled lotus of light' surrounding the heads of those who achieved enlightenment, and in Eastern cultures the treatment of illness through the aura energy of the body is widely practised.

Western science began to study the human energy field from the 1800s. In 1858 Baron Karl von Reichenbach discovered an emanation coming from plants, animals, people and crystals, which he called the 'odic force'. The first visual images of the aura were created by Dr William Kilner in 1911. He used various screens and dyes to capture images of the aura on what became known as the Kilner screen. He was also the first to coin the term 'aura'. He found that the energy field varied from person to person and that it was affected by the physical and emotional condition of the subject.

Kirlian Photography

The most famous device for recording the aura is Kirlian photography, named after the Russian professor Semyon Kirlian who discovered the technique in 1939. It is a method of high frequency electronic photography that reveals beautifully patterned sparks and flares of energy emanating from the outline of living creatures. Kirlian photography can transfer the aura of the subject to film by placing the subject, such as a leaf or a human hand, directly on to the film or photographic plate and passing high-frequency electrical currents through it.

Kirlian photographic research has revealed energy fields surrounding people's physical bodies. Experiments at the Neuropsychiatric Institute at UCLA in California showed energy flares emanating from the fingertips of healers. Research has further determined that this energy is concentrated in hundreds of points all over the body that seem to correspond to Chinese acupuncture points.

Using aura photographs of the ten fingers, two palms and two feet, it is considered possible to predict incoming disorders, as disease enters the auric body long before its effects are perceived in the physical. For example, the aura rings around the fingers of healthy people are circular and complete whereas broken aura rings can indicate disorder not only in the hands but in the whole body. Similarly, aura photographs of palms and feet are clear in the case of healthy people, but black spots indicate energy blocks due to the presence of disease at the auric level.

Despite these clinical advances, most auric observations are still made by psychic methods. Recently there has been independent confirmation that this process is not all in the mind, as sceptics claim. Dr Valerie Hunt at UCLA conducted experiments in which a clairvoyant described the colour, size and energy movements of the chakras and auras of a healer and patient. Results showed that mathematical energy patterns of healer and patient corresponded to the auric colours observed by the psychics.

The Seven Layer System of the Aura

There are various ways of classifying the aura. The seven layer system helps to explain the complex interaction of mind, body and soul and their connection with the higher planes.

1. The Etheric Layer

The first auric level in this system is the etheric layer. This fits almost like a second skin, extending from just under 1cm to 5cm from the body. Lines of energy are easily seen in this section of the aura since it is most closely linked to the physical body. It usually appears initially as grey light or haze, but with more practise the red of the root or physical chakra is evident. Physical ills are seated here and a general dullness can indicate exhaustion.

2. The Emotional Body

The second layer is the emotional body. This layer deals with emotions, both within ourselves and those we experience when we come into contact with other people. These are emotions such as self-esteem, identity and the messages we are given about our worth and attractiveness that filter, sometimes incorrectly, from those around us.

The emotional layer is usually seen as a swirling mass of energy about the body and, like the etheric layer, it follows the human shape. It is not as clearly defined as the etheric layer because each layer out has less and less to do with the physical person. Its predominant colour is orange; stress and anxiety will manifest as darkness or rips, as will psychosomatic and stress-related illness.

3. The Mental Layer

The third auric level, the mental layer, is the layer of thought and ideas where concepts are fashioned into reality. It is usually most visible around the head and shoulders as a yellowish light. It is in this layer that thoughts and ideas become substantial. This is the area where depression, insomnia or racing thoughts can overload the system and is the prime candidate as a source of migraines and hypertension.

4. The Astral Layer

The fourth auric level, the astral layer, marks the division between the physical layers and the higher layers. It is concerned with interaction between people and is the layer of love and relationships. Emotional bonds are formed on this layer which has a green glow. Disturbances here can reverberate throughout the aura.

5. The Etheric Template

The fifth auric layer, the etheric template, is a copy of the physical body on a higher level. It is the master copy on which the etheric body models itself. This is a clear or navy blue colour. Breaches or dark spots here can lead to feelings of alienation and bodily perfection-related obsessions that can result in overwork, and eating or drinking disorders.

6. The Celestial Body

The sixth auric layer forms the celestial body, the emotional body on the spiritual plane. Through this layer we are able to commune personally with the cosmos and with other dimensions, whether they are perceived as spirit guides, angelic beings or the higher self. It is the level of unconditional love and trust, and is an indigo or purple colour. Disorders here can manifest in nightmares, insomnia and an inability to settle to practical tasks, as well as a concern for others and the world's problems that can paralyse rather than galvanise action.

7. The Ketheric Template

The seventh and highest auric layer, the ketheric template, is also known as the causal body. This is the highest layer of the spiritual level. Through this layer we can become one with the cosmos, with pure spirit or Divinity. This is a white or gold colour.

CANDLE MAGIC

Candles have held a magical significance since the Stone Age. Men and women used stone lamps and tapers fashioned from animal fat to illuminate not just their living quarters but also the inner caves sacred to the mother goddess.

In the 3rd century BC Egyptians used candles to seek the answers to their questions through dream. In this tradition known as 'dreaming true', the questioner went to a cave that faced south and sat in the darkness gazing at the candle flame until he or she saw a deity in it. In the sleep that followed, the god or goddess would answer their questions (see also Lucid Dreaming, p. 33).

In Mediaeval times, the Christian use of candles did not obliterate earlier beliefs. Farmers would set candles blessed by priests at Candlemas to guard livestock from danger and from the malevolence of witches (see Wicca, p. 87 and Witchcraft, p. 90).

Candles as Love Charms

Traditionally a girl would call her lover to her by piercing the wick of a lighted candle with two intertwined pins, saying:

> *Tis not these pins I wish to burn,*
> *But my lover's heart to turn,*
> *May he neither sleep nor rest,*
> *Till he has granted my request.*

She would watch the candle and if the pins remained in the wick after the candle wax had burned past the place in which they were inserted, the lover would appear at the door before the candle burned down. If the pins fell out, it was taken as an indication that her lover was faithless.

In another version, two pins were stuck in a candle for two alternative lovers and, when the candle burned down to the correct pin, the door would open and the true love – or at least a vision of him – would walk in.

Candle Curses

Although candles are neutral, they have been used for evil purpose. Bad witches would name a black candle after an enemy, let the wax fall and form a doll from it, sticking pins in it and letting the candle burn away. How much of the illness or mis-fortune was due to the malice of the curse and how much arose from the person knowing of the curse and fulfilling it unconsciously is hard to estimate.

The most infamous candle curse was the 'hand of glory'. This was the hand of a hanged man, squeezed dry, pickled for two weeks and left to dry in the sun. This then had candles attached to the fingers made from the fat of the hanged man. It was traditionally used by thieves, for it was believed that if they lit one in a house all the occupants would sleep while the burglary was taking place.

Candles and Rites of Passage

The concept of a man's life as a candle is one that has been expressed in the myths and literature of many cultures, as far back as the Vikings. This excerpt is from *Godfather Death* by the Brothers Grimm:

> *Thousands and thousands of candles were burning in countless rows, some large, some medium-sized, others small. Every instant some were extinguished, and others again burnt up, so that the flames seemed to leap hither and thither in perpetual change. See, said Godfather Death, these are the lights of men's lives. The large ones belong to children, the medium-sized ones to married people in their prime, the little ones belong to old people, but children and young folks likewise have often only a tiny candle. One must go out before a new one is lighted.*

Candles have been used by the church since the 4th century in rites of passage, beginning with baptism and ending with candles placed around the coffin at a funeral. This ritual dates back to the early belief that the dead needed the protection of light from the dark influences that lurked between the dimensions, as the deceased passed from one dimension to the other.

An external flame can be found burning in many different countries in memory of unknown warriors who died in foreign fields. In Catholic churches and some high Anglican cathedrals candles can be bought to ask for healing and comfort for the sick and in memory of those who have died.

In Ireland from mediaeval times until the beginning of the 20th century a corpse would be surrounded by 12 candles while in the Scottish lowlands, after a body had been laid out, one of the oldest women present would circle the body three times with a 'sainting' or blessing and leave the candle burning all night. The ends of these sainting candles and others used at wakes were believed to heal burns.

In Sweden candles or lanterns are placed on family graves at Christmas and on 1 November, the Day of the Dead, since All Saints Day was introduced into Sweden after 1945.

Practical Candle Magic

Wishes are often written on paper which is burned in the flame of a candle and so carried on the smoke to the cosmos. This practice dates back to the celebrations on the festival of the moon goddess Artemis when candles would be placed on cakes shaped like crescent moons and wishes made as the candles were blown out. This was the forerunner of modern birthday magic.

Another method of wishing on a candle involves engraving a symbol for the desired object, person or event on to the candle with a pin or awl. If the candle is left to burn away, the melted wax may form an image which tells how the wish might be fulfilled.

Candle Colours for Wishes and Needs

White is the colour for new beginnings and energy.

Red is the colour for change and courage.

Orange is for happiness, health, balance and identity.

Yellow is for communication, learning and travel.

Green is for love, healing and the natural world.

Blue is for power, justice and career.

Violet and **indigo** are for psychic development, spirituality and inner harmony.

Pink is for reconciliation, children and the family.

Brown is for house and home, financial matters, possessions and for older relations.

Grey is for compromise and for keeping secrets.

Silver is for secret desires.

Gold is for long-term ambitions and prosperity.

Black is for endings and banishing guilt or regrets.

Astrological Candle Associations

Each sun or birth sign is represented by a colour or colours. Each sun sign colour also represents a quality or strength and a candle of that colour can be burned if that particular strength is needed even if it is not the petitioner's own birth sign colour. It is always most potent during its own sun period (see Astrology, p. 2). The birth sign colours and strengths are listed on the opposite page.

 **Aries:** Red – Courage

Taurus: Pink – Patience

Gemini: Pale grey or yellow – Versatility

Cancer: Silver – Hidden potential

Leo: Gold or orange – Power or energy

Virgo: Green or pale blue – Desire for perfection

Libra: Blue or violet – Balance

Scorpio: Burgundy or red – Insight

Sagittarius: Yellow or orange – Clear direction

Capricorn: Brown or black – Perseverance

Aquarius: Indigo or dark blue – Independence

Pisces: White or mauve – Intuition

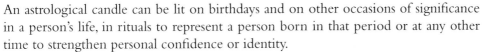

An astrological candle can be lit on birthdays and on other occasions of significance in a person's life, in rituals to represent a person born in that period or at any other time to strengthen personal confidence or identity.

Two birth candles can be lit to represent a pair of lovers and moved closer together over a three-day period until they touch. They are extinguished each day after the person lighting the candle has focused on the lover and perhaps spoken words of love. The light from the candle transmits the love to the absent lover.

CHAKRAS

What are Chakras?

The word 'chakra' is Sanskrit for wheel. Chakras, also called *padmas*, or lotuses, are energy vortexes through which spiritual energy flows through the physical body. They form part of Hindu, Tibetan Buddhist and Chinese spiritual and yogic traditions and in the West were first popularised in the late 19th century by the Theosophical movement.

However, because of different philosophical emphases, there are considerable variations in their conceptualised number and function. Modern systems usually picture chakras as whirling multi-coloured lotus petals that penetrate both the physical body and the aura, receiving and transmitting energies between the body, the earth and the cosmos.

Because they exist on a subtle rather than physical level, chakras cannot be seen or measured physically. However, Japanese experiments have demonstrated that people

ESSENTIAL WISDOM

who have worked with chakra energies over a period of years have measurably stronger chakra energies themselves than many other people.

Most traditions locate chakras vertically along the axis of the body, either on or just in front of the backbone, but they are linked with and take their name from locations on the front of the body, such as the navel, heart, throat and brow.

The universal life-force or *prana* is filtered via psychic channels or *nadis* down the chakra system, and each chakra transforms the energy into an appropriate form. Chakra energy itself is said to derive from a latent psychic root energy called *kundalini-shakti* in Hindu tantra, and *tumo* in Tibetan Buddhist tantra.

Kundalini is described as a coiled snake sleeping at the base of the spine until activated. It travels up the body through the *sushumna*, the central subtle or psychic channel, activating the various chakras along the way. Kundalini is identified with the female energy of Shakti, consort of the Hindu father god, Shiva. As well as the main chakras, some systems recognise more than 120 additional chakra points scattered across the body.

The History of Chakras

Chakras began as an esoteric concept. According to early and indeed prevailing Eastern chakra tradition, each yogi creates the chakras within the body by powerful visualisation and meditative technique, thereby attaining transcendental awareness. In Hindu tantric philosophy, references to the life-force or prana and the nadis along which it flows appear in the earliest Upanishads, or religious books, which date from about 800BC. The *Kshurika Upanishad* alone mentions 72,000 nadis centred in the heart. By meditation on the chakras, it was believed that *siddhis* or supernormal powers could be attained by dedicated yogis.

The later and influential Tibetan Buddhist theory of chakras comes from tantric Buddhism or Vajrayana, that itself stemmed from the Indian tantric tradition. In this system, the power of kundalini was replaced by the concept of red and white subtle drops of essence in the navel and head chakras.

It was the Western Theosophists who attributed an objective existence to chakras and stated that chakras could be seen or sensed clairvoyantly. Each of the seven main chakras became regarded as an energy regulator or consciousness transformer, linking the seven subtle auric bodies together. The effective functioning of each chakra therefore became associated with the physical, mental and spiritual well-being of the individual.

Finally came the rainbow theory of chakras, put forward in the early 1970s in Christopher Hill's book *Nuclear Evolution*. Hill stated that each of the chakras corresponded to one of the seven colours of the spectrum. From this point virtually every book on chakra theory has incorporated this concept.

The best of modern theories do retain connections with the ancient systems, and one of these is briefly outlined below. It is based on seven chakras, incorporating different levels of consciousness. Each of the chakras has its own element, symbolic creature, colour, sound, area and organ of the body and is linked closely with Kabbalistic symbolism.

Your Body and the Chakras

The Root or Base Chakra

This is the earth or instinctive chakra and its colour is red. Its symbolic creature is the bull. It is rooted at the base of the spine, the seat of the kundalini power. This is the energy centre of the physical level of existence, denoting survival and animal strength. It is linked with legs, feet, skeleton and the large intestine. On a psychological level, a blockage is indicated by unreasonable anger caused by trivial matters.

The Sacral Chakra

This is the moon chakra and its colour is orange. It is related to the element of water and its symbolic creature is the fish. The sacral chakra is the sphere of desire, the chakra of physical pleasure and happiness and is the home of the five senses. Though seated in the reproductive system, it focuses on all aspects of physical comfort and satisfaction. It controls the blood, the reproductive system, kidneys, circulation and bladder. On a psychological level, irritability and disorders connected with physical indulgence can result from blockages.

The Solar Plexus

This is the sun or power chakra and its colour is yellow. It relates to the element of fire and its symbolic creature is the ram. This chakra is seated around the navel. Its body parts include the digestive tract, the liver, spleen, stomach, small intestine and the metabolism. It is said to absorb the life-force from living food such as fruit, vegetables and seeds. It rules personal power, will and independence. On a psychological level, blockages can lead to obsessions and over-concern for trivial detail.

The Heart Chakra

This is the chakra of the winds. Its colour is green, its element is air and its symbol is the dove. It is situated in the centre of the chest, radiating over heart, lungs, breasts, arms and hands. In this chakra, the spiritual nature emerges, integrating mind, body and soul, balancing the male and female aspects animus and anima. This chakra controls love and emotions. On a psychological level, free-floating anxiety or depression can follow an imbalance in this area.

The Throat Chakra

This is the chakra of time and space. Its colour is blue; its element is sound and its symbolic creature is the elephant. Situated close to the Adam's apple in the centre of the neck, the throat chakra is described as the vehicle for speaking the truth. As well as the throat and speech organs, the throat chakra controls the neck and shoulders and the passages that run up to the ears. It is concerned with ideas, ideals and clear communication, and is the link between emotion and thought. On a psychological level, confusion and incoherence result from blockages here.

The Third Eye or Brow Chakra

This is the chakra of freedom and its colour is indigo. The brow chakra is situated just above the bridge of the nose in the centre of the brow. Its element is light and its

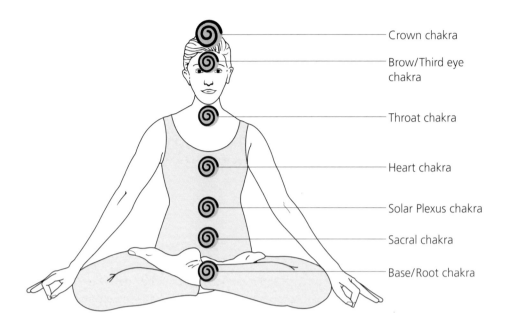

Crown chakra

Brow/Third eye chakra

Throat chakra

Heart chakra

Solar Plexus chakra

Sacral chakra

Base/Root chakra

symbolic creature the cobra. It controls the eyes, ears, both hemispheres of the brain, the psychic functions attributed to the third eye, prophetic dreams and harmony. On a psychological level, blockages can result in insomnia or nightmares.

The Crown Chakra

This is the chakra of eternity. Its colour is violet, fading to white as it moves further from the body. White, the source of pure light (all other colours combined), pours upwards and outwards into the cosmos, and downwards and inwards from the cosmos back into the crown.

The crown chakra's element is thought and its symbolic creature the serpent. It is situated at the top of the head in the centre and rules the brain, body and psyche. It connects the individual to the higher self and ultimately to the source of divinity. On a psychological level, blockages are manifest as an inability to rise above the mundane and a sense of alienation from the world.

COLOUR MAGIC

From the earliest times colour magic and healing have been inextricably linked. The Babylonians called the restorative power of light, which is made up of the spectrum of colours, the medicine of the gods. Healing colours have been used for thousands of years in China and in ayurvedic medicine, and the Ancient Egyptians wore amulets of coloured stones: red to treat disease, green for fertility, yellow for happiness and prosperity.

There is a practical basis to this idea. For example, being suffused in red light increases metabolic rate and blood pressure, hence the magical association with action and change. In contrast, pink can, in the short term, have a soothing effect especially on aggressive people or situations; in magic it is the colour for mending quarrels.

In colour magic, people drink water in which coloured crystals have been soaked, eat foods of a specific colour, and use coloured crystal spheres, coloured lights, candles or the colours of the natural world in visualisation and meditation to empower themselves. Many people regularly wear a lucky colour, which may or may not be their astrological colour, and in spells, different colours are used to represent different magical needs.

The Meaning of Colours

White

White is the colour of divinity, limitless potential and the life-force. It contains all other colours as Sir Isaac Newton proved in the 17th century when he passed a ray of white light through a prism, splitting it into a rainbow. But more than 2,000 years before this scientific proof, Pythagoras declared that white contained all sound as well as colour. In magic, white represents light, vitality and boundless energy and so is helpful when a new beginning, energy, clear vision and original ideas are needed, and for a step into the unknown. White is associated with the sun.

Black

Black is the colour not only of death, but also of regeneration. This tradition goes back to Ancient Egypt when the annual flooding of the Nile carried with it black silt which brought new life to the land each year. In magic, black is the colour of endings that carry within them the seeds of new beginnings, and it marks the boundaries of the past. Through its association with the dark primaeval waters that contained the essence of all life, it is connected with total acceptance of all people and situations. It is a colour associated with Saturn, the planet of the Greek god of fate and limitations who became Old Father Time after his own reign as father of the Greek gods ended and he was deposed by his son Zeus.

Red

Red is a magical colour in many traditions, as it represents blood and the essence of life. The runes of the Norsemen were marked in red and red was the colour of Frigga, their mother goddess, while in China the pigtails of sages would be interwoven with red threads to ward off evil influences. In magic, red is the colour of power, physical energy and determination, courage when facing opposition and for change under difficult circumstances. It is a colour associated with battle because Mars, the planet named after the Roman god of war, has a dull red glow.

Orange

Orange is another sun colour and represents the abundant fruits of the earth. An orange tree yields a vast crop each year and its white blossoms are traditionally worn by brides as a fertility symbol. Orange is therefore the colour of fertility, health and joy and also marks the boundaries between self and others.

Yellow

Traditionally the colour of the mind and communication, yellow has sometimes been associated with jealousy and treachery. In Mediaeval paintings Judas and the Devil are depicted wearing yellow, and yellow ochre is painted on the bodies of Australian Aborigines at burial ceremonies. In magic, yellow is the colour for intellectual achievement, learning and travel, or changing home and career. It is associated with Mercury, the planet named after the Roman winged messenger of the gods, who spanned the dimensions and was also the deity of healing, moneylenders and thieves. Yellow can therefore stand for business acumen and occasionally for trickery.

Green

Green is the colour of Venus, the Roman goddess of love, and so is the colour of the heart, love and emotions. Because of its association with gardens and growth it has been connected in Chinese and native North American traditions with money spells. Unlucky connotations of green stem from its association with fairy folk. In magic, it is the colour for finding new love and developing affairs of the heart.

Blue

Blue is the healing colour of the spirit. The Hindu god Vishnu is depicted with blue skin. In magic it is the colour of conventional wisdom and limitless possibilities. Blue can create confidence and so in magic it is used for idealism, dealing with officialdom and career, and when seeking justice. It is the colour of Jupiter, the planet named after the Roman supreme father god. Blue is also the colour of planet earth when seen from space.

Purple

Purple is a royal colour, worn by emperors and kings, priests and deities, and is connected with the Ancient Egyptian god Osiris. In magic, it provides a link with the higher dimensions, with nobility of spirit and with inspiration. It is also associated with wisdom, magic, religion, psychic development and spiritual strength.

Brown

Brown is the colour of the earth and the earth spirits. Rich, vibrant brown represents rooted power and instinctive wisdom. In magic, it is the colour of affinity with the natural world and acts as a protective force. It is therefore associated with all practical and financial matters, with older people, the home and with animals.

Pink

Pink is another of Venus's colours. It represents the gentler aspects of love and kindness. In magic, it is the colour of reconciliation and harmony, and can induce quiet sleep. It is also associated with family matters and children.

Grey

Grey is the shade of compromise and adaptability. In magic it is the colour of invisibility and protection against psychic attack, confrontation and secrecy. Grey is another colour ruled by Saturn.

Gold

Gold is the chief colour of the sun and its deities, such as the Egyptian god Ra and the Greek god Apollo. It represents the height of worldly achievement, wealth and recognition. In magic, it represents money, long life and great ambition.

Silver

Silver is the colour of the moon and lunar goddesses such as Isis, Selene and Diana. It represents dreams, visions and a desire for fulfilment beyond the material world. Silver in magic represents intuition, hidden potential and sudden insights, especially in dreams.

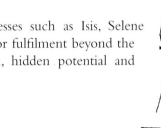

Colour and Music

Chanting a mantra is commonly believed to be one of the best aids to meditation. What is less well known is that sounds have their own colours and that beginning a colour visualisation with a particular note or humming the notes of the colours believed to be missing in your life in moments of stress can amplify your inner colour energies.

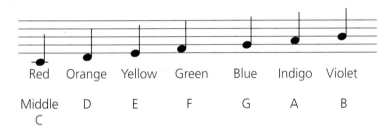

Red	Orange	Yellow	Green	Blue	Indigo	Violet
Middle C	D	E	F	G	A	B

Colour and the Days of the Week

Each day of the week is represented by a colour, so people can choose the best day to carry out a colour-based ritual. If, for example, a great deal of energy is needed on a Saturday, which is naturally a purple or brown day, the addition of red or yellow will boost the system.

Sunday	Monday	Tuesday	Wednesday	Thursday	Friday	Saturday
Yellow	White	Red	Orange	Blue	Green or pink	Purple or brown

23

CRYSTALLOMANCY

So much is true, that gems have fine spirits, and may operate, by consent, on the spirits of men, to strengthen and exhilarate them.

FRANCIS BACON (1561–1626)

The word 'crystal' is rooted in the Greek word *krystallos* from *krysos*, icy cold, because it was thought that crystals were made from ice so cold it would never melt. From the earliest times crystals and gems have been regarded as precious. Buddhists refer to clear crystal quartz as 'visible nothingness'. The Ancient Greeks believed that all quartz crystals found on earth were fragments of the archetypal crystal of truth, dropped by Hercules from Mount Olympus, home of the gods. Hence polished crystal spheres are used in divination because it is said they will never lie.

The Greek philosopher Plato (427–347BC) believed that particular stars and planets converted decayed and decaying material into the most perfect gemstones which then came under the rule of those planets and stars.

The Origins of Crystallomancy

Crystallomancy is specifically the art of crystal gazing, or scrying, to perceive images that can provide guidance to past, present and future events, but in practice the term is applied to any form of crystal work. The circle and sphere are symbols of completeness and it was believed that a crystal sphere was a microcosm of the wider universe. Within it, therefore, could be captured information about the past, present and future.

The Maya used quartz crystal which was sacred to the sun god Tezcatlipoca, and his temple walls were lined with mirrors which were also used for scrying. Apaches gazed into crystals, not only to discover if an expedition would be successful but to find the location of property and ponies stolen by other tribes.

Crystal ball divination became popular in Europe in the 15th century when it was believed that spirits or angels would appear in the glass, and rituals were long and complex.

One of the most famous scryers of the 16th century was Dr John Dee astrologer to Elizabeth I. On 21 November 1582, he bought a crystal 'as big as an egg, most bryght, clere and glorious' and through this sphere he communicated with his angels. These not only gave him all kinds of knowledge but, be believed, protected both the Queen and England. He called his crystal his 'shew-stone'. It was not a clear crystal, but an obsidian, a stone through which light can be seen when held to the sun. It is said that this crystal gave a forewarning of the Spanish Armada.

Crystals and Divination

Spheres

Modern theories attribute the knowledge gained from crystal gazing to images from within our own psyche which are projected into the glass. Crystal quartz was traditionally used because it was believed to connect heaven and earth, but crystal balls had been made from blue and yellow beryl before this. Spheres of beryl as well as round, flat beryl mirrors held in white cloth were considered a powerful focus for early Celtic visions. Beryl was used in 5th-century Ireland for scrying and is called there 'the stone of the seer'. Beryl scrying is best, it is said, during the period of the waxing moon and is especially good for finding lost objects.

Individual Crystals

As well as crystal spheres, individual crystals can be used for divination, cast like runes on to a cloth and interpreted according to their type and colour.

The hot coloured stones – red, yellow and orange, and sparkling white – contain a great deal of creative power even in their gentler shades. Any crystal in one of these colours has a natural energising force. In divination this indicates that a degree of action is desirable. They are the colours of the outer world.

The cooler colours – green, blue, pink, purple and gentle translucent white – reflect thoughts, emotions and spiritual desires. They are the colours of the inner world. Even black, which is not really a colour but a lack of one, has a place as a marker of time and earthly limitations.

The Chaldeans studied the stars for divinatory purposes and claimed that certain planets were linked to crystals, which reflected the energies and characteristics of those planets. For example, Venus rules over green stones which are therefore associated with love and all relationship matters. However, these correspondences have changed over time, especially since the discovery of the planets Uranus, Neptune and Pluto (see Colour Magic, p. 20).

Crystals and Healing

Quartz crystal balls have been used medicinally since Ancient Egyptian times to concentrate the rays of the sun upon a diseased or painful area of the body, or point them in the direction of an afflicted internal organ. The clear crystal stone has always been associated with energising power and healing and, in its spherical form, represents completeness. It is perhaps the ultimate magical healing stone.

The Russian scientist Semyon Kirlian discovered that both organic and inorganic gems were surrounded by a radiating energy field. This confirmed what people throughout the world had always believed; that stones and crystals are living entities, manifestations of the great creative spirit, having a special place in transmitting the healing energies of the earth.

ESSENTIAL WISDOM

The papyrus Ebers, dating from about 2500BC, list the healing properties of gems, including sapphires to cure eye problems, emeralds for dysentery and rubies for liver and spleen diseases. In Volume 5 of his *Materia Medica*, the Greek pharmacist Dioscorides, born in the 1st century AD, described over 2000 crystals and gems that could be used for healing.

Gems and crystals were either crushed into powders and used as ointments, soaked in water which was then drunk, placed on painful areas of the body or carried as amulets. Millennia later, the energies of crystals are still used as a natural focus for healing, and for the amplification of inner healing powers.

Rose quartz, amethyst and clear crystal quartz especially are used for virtually all forms of general healing, although stones do have their own specific healing properties, based on type and colour. For example, agates are natural balancing and soothing stones. Yellow agate assists digestion and alleviates problems with the liver and spleen, while blue lace agate soaked in water is used as a gargle to alleviate sore throats and slow down hyperactivity in children.

One of the most popular modern methods of crystal healing involves the application of a crystal to a particular chakra. Each chakra is linked to the health of a different part of the body, a different colour and different psychological and psychic functions. When a chakra becomes blocked, physical symptoms such as pain, tension or feelings of disharmony can indicate a 'dis-ease'. Many lay people as well as healers find it helpful to link particular crystal colours and types to the chakras to balance deficiencies or remove blockages in the physical and psychic body.

DOWSING

Dowsing or rhabdomancy, also sometimes called divining or water witching, is an ancient practice whereby hidden water, minerals or oil deep in the ground are detected by means of the involuntary movements of a dowsing device.

There are several suggestions for the origin of the term 'dowsing'. It may come from the old Cornish *dewsys* (goddess) and *rhodl* (tree branch). Another interpretation roots it in the Middle English *duschen* meaning 'to strike', from early German references to dowsing rods striking down towards the ground. The German and Norwegian words for the dowsing rod, *wunschelrute* and *önskekvist*, translate as 'wishing stick'.

There are four main dowsing instruments, although in practice people can dowse with almost anything. The traditional tool is a forked stick or 'Y rod', made of apple or hazel wood, which is held with both hands and usually dips downwards over its target. Another dowsing device is the wand or bobber, a flexible wire or twig, between 1 and 3ft in length, sometimes weighted at one end. Pairs of 'L rods' or 'angle rods', held parallel in each hand, will cross when they pass over a target. Each consists of a hand-held vertical section of rod 6 to 8in long, bent at a right angle, with a 10 to 18in horizontal section. Occasionally just one is used.

Pendulum dowsing using a weight on a chain, sometimes made of clear crystal quartz, has become increasingly popular in recent years. Because the pendulum is smaller than dowsing rods it offers a finely tuned method of dowsing.

As well as finding underground water and minerals, dowsing is also frequently employed to search for buried treasure, lost objects, animals and people. It is also used for making decisions, detecting health problems in the body's energy system and in identifying suitable remedies. It can locate positive and negative earth energies, the latter manifesting as 'black streams' which are believed to cause health problems for those who live or work above them. Dowsing can even be used to find archaeological remains and follow ghost paths. Some dowsers successfully practise 'remote dowsing', holding a pendulum or rod over a map to locate precisely the position of the object being sought.

The History of Dowsing

Water, the most urgent need for any settlement, has always been the first priority of the dowser. A cave drawing of a man with a forked stick in his hands was discovered in the Tassili-n-Ajjer mountains in central Algeria and has been carbon dated to around 6000BC. The Chinese and Ancient Egyptians practised the art, especially in the search for precious metals and gems, as shown by illustrations on pottery, paintings and papyri.

The first time a dowsing rod was mentioned in literature was in a 1540 German publication on mining, *De re Metallica*, by Georgius Agricola, at a time when there was a great interest in alchemy and all things magical.

Dowsing journeyed with the colonists to the US and to Australia and South Africa and proved a valuable method of locating existing wells and sources of water for their settlements.

Until Victorian times, dowsing was a natural art which was the subject of much experimentation. But because dowsing was scientifically inexplicable it was marginalised and, with the growth of urban life and municipal water systems, fell into disuse except in rural areas.

The Revival of Dowsing

After World War II, the expansion in suburban building and the rebuilding of bombed cities once more brought the talents of the water diviner to the fore, as expensive conventional methods of locating water frequently proved fruitless.

In recent years, dowsers have been employed by oil and pharmaceutical companies, as well as governments, sometimes secretly but increasingly more openly. Dr Peter Treadwell, former vitamin plant director for Hoffman La Roche, was sent all over the world to dowse water for his company's prospective factory sites. Dr Treadwell commented: 'The plain truth is that we keep finding water for our company using a method that neither physics, physiology nor psychology has even begun to explain. The dowsing method pays off. It is 100 per cent reliable.'

What is more, even military personnel are recognising the ability of dowsers to find unexploded shells and mines at sea and on land, and US marines were taught to use a

ESSENTIAL WISDOM

pendulum in Vietnam to locate underground mines and tunnels. In 1959 a dowser, Verne Cameron, successfully located by pendulum dowsing on a map every US and Soviet submarine in the world.

Scientific Evidence for Dowsing

In 1984 Professor Hans-Dieter Betz, a physicist at the University of Munich, undertook a ten-year government sponsored programme to dowse for water in arid areas such as Sri Lanka, Zaire, Kenya, Namibia and Yemen. The results showed overwhelming evidence for the validity of dowsing.

Dowsers attained an overall success rate of 96 per cent in 691 drillings in Sri Lanka against the estimated 30 to 50 per cent success rate of conventional methods in an area where finding water purely by chance is extremely unlikely. Professor Betz's most plausible hypothesis was that subtle electromagnetic gradients resulting from fissures and water flows created changes in the electrical properties of rock and soil and that dowsers sensed these gradients in what was described as a hypersensitive state.

The Forces Behind Dowsing

Scientific explanations of dowsing have varied over the centuries with new discoveries, but all seem to stop short of an explanation when they encounter the unknown factor of the human psyche.

Early accounts interpreted dowsing as signals from the aura of underground water or metal. These were followed by theories of a sympathetic attraction between specific minerals and rods cut from certain trees. Some dowsers still believe that certain substances such as flowing water, oil or gold emit a strong natural energy and that the divining tool acts as an aerial which picks up these vibrations and transmits them to the dowser. However, this does not explain how some dowsers can successfully locate oil or water by holding a divining tool over a map of the area.

Magnetic or electrical influences on dowsers and their rods also held sway as a viable rationale for a time, only recently being replaced by theories that the source is radiation or waves more akin to the electromagnetic waves emitted by television or radio stations. Another theory that has persisted over the years and which cannot be ignored is that our higher consciousness, a benign spirit or angelic guide, directs the pendulum or divining tool.

Can Anyone Dowse?

As with many intuitive arts, children are natural dowsers and many successful adult dowsers began in childhood before doubts and inhibitions entered the equation.

The American Society of Dowsers says that everyone is born with the ability to dowse and that, in any group of 25 adults, between two and five will obtain the dowsing reaction immediately, while others may have to practise for a while before they become confident dowsers. The problem with adults is not that they cannot dowse, but they think or fear that they cannot and so block the inherent ability.

DREAMS

Let us learn to dream – and then we may perhaps find the truth.
FRIEDRICH VON KEKULE, Professor of Chemistry, Ghent, Belgium, in his 1890
address to a scientific convention

For thousands of years, in all cultures, dreams were seen as the doorway to another world, offering insights into the present and future. Many indigenous people such as the Inuits of Hudson Bay retain this connection, believing that the soul leaves the body during sleep to live in a special dream world. If you wake someone who is sleeping, the Inuits say, the soul will be lost forever. In parts of Africa the dream state is as important as the waking one since it is believed that dream activities actually occur during nocturnal astral travel. Zulus interpret dream images as messages and visions sent by their ancestors.

In modern Western society many people have lost touch with the rich world of dreams that Freud called 'the royal road to the unconscious'. He believed that dreams were the key to uncovering the repressed traumas and desires of the unconscious mind that cause distress and illness. Others, such as Carl Jung, regarded dreams as a source of psychic wisdom beyond our own unconscious mind. This wisdom, he believed, derived from a universal pool of past, present and perhaps future experience. Dreams may, therefore, operate beyond the constraints of time and space and offer knowledge not yet available to the conscious mind. This could be one explanation for the accuracy of some predictive dreams.

Creative Dreaming

Access to a universal well of wisdom such as that described by Jung might also explain creative dreaming. Friedrich von Kekule, who is quoted above, was engaged in research to discover the structure of the benzene molecule, but was having no success. One evening he fell asleep in a chair and had a dream in which long rows of atoms began to twist themselves into snake-like formations. One of the snakes caught its own tail and began to spin round in a circle. Von Kekule woke and, using the closed-ring model seen in his dream, revolutionised organic chemistry.

Whether such flashes of inspiration are interpreted as psychic intervention by a higher consciousness or innate wisdom that had provided a solution from a deep, unconscious level, it remains that the vehicle of the dream has offered the elusive answer.

Dreaming True

The first recorded magical candle rituals were those of the Egyptians who, in the 3rd century, used candles to 'dream true', a method of inducing creative dreams. In this tradition, anyone of great importance or who needed an urgent answer to a question went to a south-facing cave and sat in the darkness gazing at the candle flame until he or she saw a deity in it. The god or goddess would then appear in that person's dream and provide the answer they sought (see Candle Magic, p. 14).

This method can easily be recreated in the modern world using a dark-coloured candle for quiet meditation before sleep.

Dream Interpretation

Aristotle said in his *Prophesying by Dreams* in 350BC: 'The most skilful interpreter of dreams is he who has the faculty of observing resemblances. I mean that dream presentations are analogous to the forms reflected in water.'

Dream interpretation was regarded by Aristotle as a skill akin to scrying or crystal gazing, in which the symbols of the dream were interpreted by a deeper source of wisdom of which we are not consciously aware.

Because dreams are usually highly symbolic, they can express deep-seated physical health problems and issues of mind and spirit that need resolution, revealing information that is not available to the conscious mind. They may contain symbols with a universal significance as well as images from our own minds that are unique to each of us. Jung believed symbols in dreams were of both these kinds and that the archetypal or universal symbols appeared at times of major significance or change. Both are believed to be of great importance to the psychological and psychic health of the dreamer.

Seeing Ghosts in Dreams

Unlike in African tradition, the concept of wise ancestors appearing in dreams is one that may seem strange in the Western world. Yet a significant number of people whose relations have died have told me how immensely comforting dreams of a deceased parent, grandparent or partner have proved to be. On occasions, previously unknown information given in the dream has subsequently been verified.

For example, William was in his sixties when his wife died suddenly and he became very anxious that he could not find the money she had withdrawn from the bank to pay the bills. That night, his wife came to him in a dream and told him that the money was behind the model of the Flying Scotsman he had made. In the morning William looked but could not find it, but on closer examination discovered the money, already packaged in small labelled envelopes tucked into a groove.

Whether such dreams represent psychic contact from another dimension, or are the product of our own minds recreating the love that survives death, is of less importance than the comfort the dreams provide.

Children routinely see deceased grandparents in dreams and this can be a very positive way of coming to terms with the concept of death for the whole family. Such dreams are rarely frightening to the child.

The Healing Power of Dreams

Karen Horney, the US Neo-Freudian psychoanalyst, stated that dreams expressed a level of the true self which was not available during waking consciousness and which could provide accurate information about the psyche and personality. This would allow the mind to identify hidden disease and distress during sleep.

The link between dreams and healing goes back to the time of Aristotle who believed that dreams reflected a person's bodily health and that a doctor could diagnose an illness by listening to a person's dreams. Hippocrates, the founder of modern medicine, supported this theory and it is still practised by some doctors today.

More importantly, it would seem that the dream state accesses some deeper level of awareness that can not only reveal latent problems, but suggest appropriate remedies and even activate the self-healing process.

Dream Incubation

Dream healing was practised by the Ancient Greeks, through a process known as dream incubation, which resembled the Egyptian ritual of dreaming true. The Aesculapian temples in the Classical world, which were sited at sacred wells and springs, were famous places for dream incubation. They were named after a healer who lived during the 11th century BC called Aesculapius who was later made the god of healing.

The first shrine dedicated to Aesculapius was built in Athens in the 5th century BC by Sophocles. Other shrines followed in rapid succession, the most famous at Epidaurus. Over 300 active Aesculapian healing temples still existed throughout Greece and the Roman Empire in the 2nd century AD and were visited by those seeking cures for all kinds of maladies.

The ritual involved an animal sacrifice, and the dreamer would sleep on the skin of the sacrificed animal, which was usually a ram. Evening prayers or chants were held during the 'hour of the sacred lamps' and seekers would ask Aesculapius to bring them healing dreams.

When Aesculapius appeared to the dreamers in the dream state, he would tell them the medicine and treatment they should use. Sometimes his daughter Hygeia, or Panacea, also associated with health and healing, would appear to dreamers. On occasions the god would even perform psychic surgery.

In the UK, a Roman healing dream temple was built at Lydney Park in Gloucestershire in the 1st century AD over the site of several springs. St Madron's Well in Cornwall may date back even further and it was used for more than a thousand years after the Romans left Britain as a site of dream incubation. A stone seat or bed close to the well known as St Madron's bed was also believed to have dream-incubating properties.

Cures were recorded as late as the 17th century when a local bishop reported that a severely crippled man, John Trelille, 'upon three several admonitions in his dreams, washing in St Madron's Well and sleeping afterwards in St Madron's bed, was suddenly and perfectly cured'.

ESSENTIAL WISDOM

Healing Remedies in Dreams

The necessary ingredients for a cure may also be spontaneously revealed in dreams. The Roman historian and scientist Pliny describes in *Natural History* the case of Alexander the Great and his friend Ptolemaus who was dying of an infected wound. Alexander dreamed that a great dragon appeared holding a plant in its mouth, saying that the plant would cure Ptolemaus. Soldiers were sent to find the plant which grew only in the place that had been clearly identified in Alexander's dream. Sure enough, Ptolemaus was cured.

Nowadays, treatments and herbal remedies for illnesses that have been used for centuries in popular folk tradition are being gradually reintroduced into conventional medicine. It may not be long before dream wisdom, which is believed to come from a source of collective healing knowledge similar to Jung's collective unconscious, is also given credibility.

Some people dream that physical healing has actually taken place. As a result, the illness or problem often disappears from their lives. Patricia Garfield in *The Healing Power of Dreams* describes a woman who had suffered from severe migraines for nearly 40 years. During a particularly bad attack, the woman dreamed she was taking care of an old woman who was dying. Despite the migraine, she stayed with the old lady until she died. She dreamed that after the old lady's funeral she was lying in bed with a migraine when the old lady's husband and son came to her bedside. The son placed his hand on her forehead, saying that she would never again experience a migraine because she had been so kind to his mother. When the dreamer awoke her migraine was gone and she was still free from headaches a year and a half later.

Dreams and Divination

Lovers throughout the ages have used dreams to identify a future lover or confirm that the present one will bring lasting happiness. For example, to dream of your own wedding and discover the identity of your future groom, place under your pillow a prayerbook opened at the marriage service and bound with scarlet and white ribbon and a sprig of myrtle on the page that says: 'With this ring I thee wed.' This ritual is best practised on a Wednesday or Saturday.

Traditionally, if a man places a piece of wood in a glass of water or small bowl before going to bed, he will dream of falling off a bridge into a river. Whoever rescues him will be his love. A similar ritual performed on Halloween night advises you to eat a salted herring before going to bed and in your dreams your true love will bring you a drink of water.

Rituals which involve eating Christmas or wedding cake to absorb magic can result in meaningful dreams. Sleep with wedding cake under your pillow and you are promised dreams of a future husband or wife. If you walk upstairs backwards eating a piece of Christmas cake and place the crumbs beneath your pillow, you will dream of your true love.

Dream Catchers

Dream catchers originated with the Native American clans of the Ojibwe. Legend has it that day and night the spider woman wove tiny dream catchers on the tops of cradle boards to ensure that babies slept peacefully. Bad dreams became entangled in the web and only the happy ones filtered through. The sleeping babies laughed and clapped for joy and no harm ever came to them. With the first rays of sunlight, the bad dreams broke free and returned to the place of shadows.

The day came when the Ojibwe nation grew so numerous that the tribes dispersed in different directions to new hunting grounds, and the spider woman could no longer visit all the cradle boards to keep her webs in order. So she taught her magical secret to the wise grandmothers who taught their daughters to weave magical webs for their babies, using willow hoops and sinew or cord from plants.

The tradition of dream catchers has spread worldwide, and adults as well as children sometimes hang a dream catcher above their beds, so that it catches the first light of dawn. Dream catcher webs are traditionally joined by seven or eight points to represent the Seven Great Prophesies of the Ojibwe, or the eight legs of the spider woman. The web is hung with protective feathers and crystals and a turquoise is placed in the centre. The dream catcher is said to be a great antidote against insomnia and restless nights.

Lucid Dreaming

Lucid dreaming is defined as being aware that you are dreaming. Lucidity usually begins in the midst of a dream, when the dreamer realises that the experience is not occurring in reality, but is in fact a dream. This awareness is a powerful psychic and psychological tool. Once a level of mental clarity in the dream state is sufficiently developed, the dreamer is fully aware that the experience is all in the mind and there is no real danger. The experienced lucid dreamer is then able to focus this awareness and take control of the dream.

Research suggests that accelerated physical healing often occurs after a period of creative lucid dreaming. Even nightmares have a function in bringing to the surface unwelcome but necessary issues that need to be confronted. In a nightmare in which the dreamer becomes aware that it is only a dream and they cannot be harmed, it is possible to work through the underlying problem and defeat the dream 'dragon'. The fear is real, but the danger is not. After a period of tackling the monsters of the sleeping world, the lucid dreamer's confidence begins to permeate every aspect of their life. This is in itself healing and health-restoring.

Lucid Dreams and Sleep
Lucid dreams usually occur during Rapid Eye Movement (REM) sleep, the level of sleep during which most vivid dreaming occurs. Dr Stephen La Berge at Stanford University is a pioneer in the field of lucid dream research and has founded the Lucidity Institute to research and teach lucid dreaming techniques.

The Lucidity Institute uses specific sensory stimuli as cues to help dreamers become lucid. For example, La Berge says that a tape recording of a voice saying 'You're dreaming' played while a person is in REM sleep will sometimes come through into the dream and remind the person to become lucid. La Berge found that flashing lights were an even better lucidity cue than sound because they had less tendency to wake the dreamer.

Encouraging Lucid Dreams

The aim of encouraging lucid dreams is not to dream lucidly every night, as this would prevent the spontaneous unfolding of dreams which is in itself restorative, but to dream lucidly perhaps once or twice a week. La Berge believes that lucid dreaming techniques can be improved through a series of exercises, some of which are listed below.

- Dream recall, by noting dreams at the moment of waking either during the night or early in the morning, is a valuable first step for lucid dreaming. It is also important for the process of dream interpretation, when the symbols and images in a dream are used to guide a person's actions in the real world.

- Lucid dreams can also be encouraged by creating dream scenarios immediately before sleep and, on waking, re-entering the dream you have just experienced.

- When you are relaxed, re-create in your mind former evocative dreams and consciously alter events in that dream or change the ending. This is especially valuable for a recurring dream.

- Before you go to sleep, concentrate on your intention to become aware that you are dreaming during your next significant dream.

- Visualise yourself in an exciting or positive emotive dream, either a previous one or a new scenario.

- Create a dream sign in this visualisation; something that would not readily happen in the everyday world – a talking animal, a brilliantly coloured flower or the sensation of flying.

- Say out loud: 'When this sign appears I will know I am dreaming' and continue with the scenario.

- Evoke the symbol two or three times in your fantasy, repeating each time: 'When this symbol appears, I recall that I am dreaming.'

- Let yourself drift into sleep, but keep your dream symbol and your intention to be aware of the dream in your thoughts. Recite your intention slowly and mesmerically as a mantra so that it is the last remaining thing in your mind before you fall asleep.

- If you do not see your symbol in your dreams that night, visualise it as you wake and re-enter the dream to deliberately evoke it as part of the dream. Continue this process using the same dream symbol until it finally appears of its own accord.

HERBAL WISDOM

Herbs have been used medicinally and magically in many different cultures through the ages. Indeed the two functions ran parallel until the 17th century and in the modern world they are moving closer again.

Herbs for Healing

Healing herbs have been used for at least 4,500 years in China and the *Great Herbal*, the first herbal healing book written around 2400BC, forms the basis of Chinese medicine today.

In Western medicine, the earliest written records detailing the use of herbs in the treatment of illness are Mesopotamian clay tablet writings and the Egyptian papyri. In about 2000BC, King Assurbanipal of Sumeria ordered the compilation of the first known Western medical book which contained 250 herbal drugs. The papyrus Ebers, written around 1500BC, features 876 prescriptions made up of more than 500 different substances, including many herbs.

In Rome, in the 1st century, Dioscorides wrote *De Materia Medica* which mentioned 950 curative substances, of which 600 were plant products and the rest of animal or mineral origin. Each entry consists of a drawing, a description of the plant, an account of its medicinal qualities and method of preparation, as well as possible side effects.

Herbalism has always been primarily the medicine and magic of ordinary people. In western Europe, from the 14th to the 17th century, witch burnings meant that many village wise woman died with the resulting loss of what had been mainly an oral herbal tradition. However, in remote areas of Wales, Ireland and Brittany, secret remedies have survived and are still handed down through the generations, possibly going back as far as ancient Druidic magical lore.

The most famous herbal book in publication is *Culpeper's Complete Herbal* written by Nicholas Culpeper, the 17th-century astrologer and physician, containing magico-herbal remedies that are as effective today as they were when he wrote it.

More recently, since the late 1950s, the US National Cancer Institute has tested more than 30,000 plants and found that nearly 10 per cent have positive results in anti-tumour tests. About a quarter of the prescription drugs dispensed by community pharmacies in the United States contain at least one active ingredient derived from plant material.

Herbs for Magic

The first evidence of herbs being used for magical purposes was discovered by an American anthropologist in 1960 at a 60,000-year-old Neanderthal burial site in a cave in the Zagros mountains of Iraq. Analysis of the soil in the grave around the human bones revealed large quantities of eight species of plant pollen, including yarrow and groundsel. It seems likely that the body was buried with herbs to protect and empower the person after death.

Herbs have been used in rituals and divination by men and women throughout the centuries. Infused herbs were read like tea leaves before 1885 when tea from India and Ceylon reached England.

Pots of divinatory herbs, especially parsley, sage, rosemary and thyme, were assigned the names of different lovers to see which grew fastest and strongest. Herbs were also placed in sachets which were pinned on undergarments or placed under pillows for love, prosperity or happiness; and poppets or cloth dolls were filled with rosemary to attract lovers.

In Victorian times, crushed lavender was added to the bath when young maidens soaked in front of the fire before a love tryst; herbs such as fennel were drunk as tea infusions to give courage; thyme was placed under pillows for prophetic dreams and to improve memory; and peppermint was added to hot water for mopping floors in order to remove negativity.

These herbs are still used in modern spell-casting and, as the interest in herbs has become widespread, the more fragrant of them find a place in many homes in the form of scented candles, bath essences or pot pourri. The following list gives the most common herbs and spices that still retain their magical significance today:

Herbs for Magical Empowerment and Protection

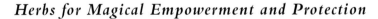

Acacia	Money; love; protection; psychic powers. Herb of Lammas, the first harvest at the beginning of August
Allspice	Money; luck; healing
Angelica	Banishes hostility from others; protection; healing; visions. Herb of Candlemas at the beginning of February and Beltane or May Day, at the beginning of the old Celtic summer
Balm, lemon	Love; success; healing
Basil	Love; exorcism; wealth; astral flying. Conquers fear of flying in the real world. One of the traditional herbs of Candlemas

Bay	Protection; psychic powers; healing; purification; strength and endurance. One of the traditional herbs of Candlemas and the mid-winter solstice
Bladderwrack	Protects against accidents or illness, especially at sea; sea rituals; wind rituals; action; money; psychic powers
Burdock	Protects against negativity; healing; love and sex magic; magical cure for coughs; hung around necks of babies in southern US
Caraway	Protection; passion; health; anti-theft; mental powers
Cascara sagrada	Legal matters; money; protection
Catnip	Cat magic; love; beauty; happiness in the home; fertility charm
Chamomile	Money; quiet sleep; affection; family
Cinnamon	Spirituality; success; healing powers; psychic powers; money; love and passion
Cinquefoil	Money; protection; prophetic dreams, especially about love; peaceful sleep; good health
Clove	Protection; banishes negativity; love; money
Clover	Protection; money; love; fidelity; banishes negativity; success
Cohosh, black	Love; courage; protection; potency
Columbine	Courage; love; the lion's herb; retrieves lost love
Comfrey	Safety during travel; money
Coriander	Love; health and healing
Cumin	Protection; fidelity; exorcism
Dill	Protection; keeps home safe from enemies and those who have envy in their hearts; also for money, passion, luck
Dittany of Crete	Contact with other dimensions; astral projection
Echinacea	Strengthens rituals and personal intuitive powers
Fennel	Protection; courage; purification
Garlic	Protection; healing; banishes negativity; passion; security from thieves
Ginger	Love; passion; money; success; power

Ginseng	Love; wishes; healing; beauty; protection; passion; increases male sexual potency. Often used as a substitute for mandrake root which is difficult to obtain
Goldenrod	Money; divination; finding buried treasure; charm against rheumatism
Heliotrope	Banishes negativity; prophetic dreams; healing; wealth; invisibility in potentially threatening situations
Juniper	Protection; anti-theft; love; banishes negativity; health; protects against accidents; increases male potency
Lavender	Love; protection, especially of children; quiet sleep; long life; purification; happiness and peace
Lemongrass	Repels spite; protects against snakes; passion; increases psychic awareness
Lucky hand root	Employment; luck; protection; money; safe travel
Maidenhair	Beauty; love
Marjoram	Protection; love; happiness; health; money
Meadowsweet	Love; divination; peace; happiness; gathered at midsummer and associated with the summer solstice
Mint	Money; love; increases sexual desire; healing; banishes malevolence; protection, especially while travelling
Moonwort	Money; love; magic associated with phases of the moon
Mugwort	Strength; psychic powers; protection; prophetic dreams; healing; astral projection
Mulberry	Protection; strength
Mullein	Courage; protection; health; love and love divination; banishes nightmares and malevolence; especially popular in India and parts of the US
Mustard	Fertility; protection; increases mental powers
Parsley	Love; protection; divination; passion; purification
Pennyroyal	Strength; protection; peace
Pepper	Protection; banishes malevolence; overcomes inertia and gives focus; positive anger for change
Peppermint	Purification; energy; love; healing; increases psychic powers
Ragweed	Courage

Ragwort	Protection; fairy magic and the ability to see fairies
Rosemary	Love; passion; increases mental powers; banishes negativity and depression; nightmares; purification; healing; quiet sleep; preserves youthfulness
Rue	Healing; protects against illnesses of all kinds and speeds recovery from surgery or wounds; increases mental powers; love enchantment; banishes regrets and redundant guilt or anger
Sage	Long life; wisdom; protection; grants wishes; improves memory; used at Halloween and Samhain, the beginning of the Celtic winter
St John's wort	Health; power; protection; strength; love and fertility; love divination; happiness; gathered on Midsummer's Eve
Sandalwood	Protection; healing; banishes negativity; spirituality; contact with guardian angels and the highest self; a herb for Lammas
Slippery elm	Prevents gossip and malice
Sweetgrass	Protection; wisdom; purification; psychic awareness
Tansy	Health; long life; invisibility against potential danger; a herb of the spring equinox
Thyme	Health; healing; prophetic dreams; increases psychic powers; improves memory; love and love divination; purification; courage
Turmeric	Purification
Valerian	Love and love divination; quiet sleep; purification; protection against outer hostility; inner fears and despair
Vanilla	Love; passion; increases mental powers
Vervain	Love; protection; transforms enemies into friends; purification; peace; money; prophecy; preserves youthfulness; peaceful sleep; healing; gathered at midsummer or when Sirius is in the ascendant
Vetivert	Love; breaks a run of bad luck; money; anti-theft; protects against all negativity
Witch hazel	Mends broken hearts and relationships; finds buried treasure and underground streams; protection
Yarrow	Courage; love; psychic powers; divination; banishes negativity; brought into house at midsummer for protection against illness and domestic strife
Yellow evening primrose	Finding what is lost
Yerba mate	Fidelity; love; passion

MYSTICISM

What is Mysticism?

Mysticism is defined as an overwhelming sense of being in complete unity or at one-ness with the deity or cosmos, whether this is interpreted as a unity with God, the Goddess, with nature, the Buddhist state of bliss or nirvana.

Mystical experiences are inevitably personal, and though the state in which a mystical experience occurs may be reached through years of contemplation, study and aestheticism, the experience itself may be a single moment of enlightenment or a series of visions, and is invariably spontaneous.

Mystical experiences have occurred in all times and all religions, usually within the framework of the existing belief system of the mystic. However, the experience may cause aspects of this system to be questioned and, as a result of the experience, the mystic may attempt to initiate changes to the system which may or may not be welcomed by the established order.

Personal Mystical Experiences

Like miracles, mystical experiences invariably cause a positive life change not only for the mystic, but for others through the writings of the mystic. However, mystical insights are by their very nature hard to explain, so the mystic may use poetry, art, music or even erotic vocabulary to convey what was felt with the heart rather than understood on an intellectual level.

Many mystics devote their lives to the hope of experiencing such a moment and, in some instances, a mystical experience can inspire the mystic to follow a life of devotion and aestheticism.

For example, Lady Juliana of Norwich, the 14th-century mystic, experienced 15 visions after a serious illness at the age of 30 and thereafter became an anchoress of the church. She moved to a small hut near the church in Norwich where she devoted the rest of her life to prayer and contemplation of the meaning of her visions, and also counselled many who came to her for advice.

Anchors of both sexes would shut themselves off from the world inside a small room, usually adjacent to a church so that they could follow the services, with a small window acting as their link to the rest of humanity.

In her work, *Revelations of Divine Love*, Juliana described seeing God holding a tiny thing in his hand, like a small brown nut, which seemed so fragile and insignificant that she wondered why it did not crumble before her eyes. She was told that it represented the entire created universe and that 'God made it, God loves it, God keeps it'. Her most memorable expression of the certainty of God's love that has endured down the centuries and has been quoted many times is the phrase 'and all shall be well, and all manner of things shall be well'.

For the 12th-century German mystic Hildegard Von Bingen, mystical experiences followed many years of gentle contemplation that began at the age of eight when she entered a Benedictine monastery run according to Celtic principles:

And it came to pass when I was 42 years and seven months old that the heavens were opened and a blinding light of exceptional brilliance flowed through my entire brain. And so it kindled my whole heart and breast like a flame, not burning but warming … and suddenly I understood.

Hildegard, an abbess at a time when women had little power, spent ten years from 1140 to 1150 recording her visions and their significance, and producing major works of theology. She wrote nine books and many songs and poems, including a play set to music called the *Ordo Virtutum* about the struggles of a human soul to find the right path.

Her special legacy to the New Age has been not only her inspirational meditative music, but also her wisdom about the healing properties of plants, animals, trees and stones. Hildegard regarded the natural world as God's creation, permeated with divine beauty and energy that was entrusted to the care of humankind. Her visionary writings have enjoyed a great revival over the past 30 years.

In contrast, the 16th-century Spanish mystics, St John of the Cross and St Teresa of Avila, followed an extreme form of aestheticism as a way of attaining enlightenment. St John followed the way of life ordained by St Teresa who believed that monks and nuns should return to a life of austerity, rather than live in comfort and gentle contemplation. Initiates went barefoot or wore sandals instead of shoes, and became known as Discalced (unshod) Carmelites, or Carmelites of the Strict Observance.

In 1577 a group of Carmelites of the Ancient Observance kidnapped John and demanded that he renounced the new way of living. When he refused, he was imprisoned completely alone, in total darkness in a Calced monastery in Toledo for about nine months, a period that led to his most profound mystical insights through suffering. His most famous poem, composed during his imprisonment, 'The Dark Night of the Soul', tells of the sense of spiritual desolation, a feeling of being abandoned by God as a way of moving through suffering to true understanding.

St John used this imagery of the love between a bride and groom in his poem 'Spiritual Canticle' to convey the idea of all-encompassing love between Christ and a Christian:

My love is hush-of-night,
Is dawn's first breathings in the heav'n above,
Still music veiled from sight,
Calm that can echoes move,
The feast that brings new strength – the feast of love.

Research into the Mystical Experience

The US psychologist Abraham Maslow (1908–1970) defined mysticism in terms of 'peak experiences' to encompass the whole spectrum of mystical states of consciousness, secular as well as religious. He said: 'Religion becomes a state of mind achievable in almost any activity of life if this activity is raised to a suitable level of perfection.'

Maslow's aim was to create a framework that would make the analysis of the peak experience scientifically possible, in terms of the frequency of occurrence and variety of experience across the population. He concluded that such experiences endowed an individual with a sense of purpose and integration and could therefore be therapeutic. By studying and determining the conditions under which peak experiences occurred, he believed that people who had not experienced these states or who had repressed them could learn to develop the necessary mind-set to follow this empowering route to personal fulfilment and integration.

The late Sir Alister Hardy (1896–1985) a biologist and Professor of Zoology at Oxford University, also wanted to understand the nature of religious and spiritual experience and, beginning in 1969, made an appeal through various national and international journals. This appeal resulted in more than 5,000 accounts of mystical experiences being sent to him from people of all cultures, creeds and walks of life over a period of more than 15 years. Although psychologists such as William James had studied religious experience within a scientific framework from around the turn of the 20th century, Sir Alister was the first to collate and analyse systematically a wide range of material over a period of years. This work has continued since his death.

For some years Dr Michael Jackson of Bangor University worked on a doctorate at the Alister Hardy Research Centre in Oxford, studying the links between mental illness and psychic or religious experience. He discovered that badly handled spiritual experiences in childhood could lead to later problems, and that the sensitivity of those who were mystical or very psychic made them especially vulnerable to the stresses of the everyday world.

In the book *Seeing the Invisible,* published in 1990, which analyses the different kinds of religious and spiritual experiences contained in records, the authors Meg Maxwell and Verna Tschudin wrote of the experiences of many men and women who had written to the Alister Hardy Research Centre about mystical moments. They speak of tapping into a universal knowledge and experiencing momentary unity with a universal source that proved life-changing and enhancing. These timeless mystical moments were described variously as:

The May sunlight was transformed into pure radiance.

I still saw the birds but instead of looking at them, I was them and they were me, I was also the sea and the sound of the sea and the grass and the sky. Everything and I were the same one.

An illuminated manuscript, 'Les très riches heures du Duc de Berry' c. 1416
depicting the zodiac signs that govern each part of the human body.

ABOVE: A Turkish miniature from the 16th century depicting the astrological sign of Pisces.

ABOVE: A 16th century illustration depicting an alchemical scene: 'Senior and Adept under the Tree of Life'.

LEFT: A 16th century painting by Ghirlandaio showing three angels.

A painting by John Simmons showing Titania, Queen of the Fairies.

A 13th century illuminated manuscript showing Hildegard von Bingen experiencing a vision of heaven.

Number Magic

The origins of Number Magic

In Ancient Egypt and among the Phoenicians from Ancient Syria, mathematics was the province of priests and scribes who, as they explored the meanings and relationships between numbers, found rules governing them which they then applied to the universe. Numbers held within them magical powers that could be invoked by using certain sacred ratios and shapes, connecting earthly and cosmic powers, and over the centuries each number acquired mystical significance. From these roots sprang the mystical arts of Hebrew gematria and Greek numerology that have formed the basis of the modern system.

0 is the symbol of time and space without limit, the external circle without beginning or end.

1 is for unity, the first manifestation of creative light that will multiply into millions of unique parts, each separate and yet containing the power of the first. In Judaism and Christianity it is associated with the One God, the All-Father, and the oneness of all mankind and the separate self.

2 is the symbol of duality, the mother/anima principle and the father/animus. The number 2 contains both complementary and opposing forces, or forces of polarity such as light and darkness, as symbolised by the waxing and waning year, which fight at the equinoxes and give way to each other. In many cultures, the Sky Father and Earth Mother come together in sacred marriage to ensure fertility of land and people.

3 is the number of trinity – father, mother and son; Father, Son and Holy Spirit; the triple goddess of the Celts; maiden, mother and crone. The sacred triangle is a form representing the external especially in Ancient Egypt. Three is the number of fertility, creation and balance.

4 is the number of the square, the physical and material world, and is said to be the most stable of all numbers, with crosses having four arms to symbolise spirit, the vertical line penetrating the horizontal.

5 is a very spiritual number, representing the quintessence, the 5th element created from and unifying the other four: earth, air, fire and water. It is itself greater than them all. The pentagram is a magical and spiritual symbol of great power, and can be seen as man extending his head or single point upwards to the heavens.

6 is the number of Venus and of love, but also of great mystical significance since it represents the six days taken to create the earth. It is also seen in the

six-pointed Seal of Solomon, a form which has pagan as well as formal religious significance as a symbol of perfection and integration. Opposites merge as complementary forces within its interconnecting triangles.

7 is the number of perfection, the most sacred of all numbers, a combination of the sacred number 3 representing spirit and the four elements of nature. To the Ancient Egyptians, 7 symbolised eternal life. The seventh day was holy because on this day God rested, hence the commandment to keep the Sabbath day holy. There were also seven ancient planets which were believed to endow a baby with their qualities as the infant's spirit descended to earth from heaven through the spheres.

8 is sometimes called 'the way of the serpent' as man weaves a figure 8 though different choices and polarities as he travels the road to wisdom. As the highest single even number, it represents balance, and is also associated with prosperity and authority, especially in matters of justice, with the emphasis on cause and effect.

9 is primarily the number of initiation, both in religious and magical rituals when actions are carried out nine times as a sign of perfection and completion. As the last of the single numbers, it brings the sequence to a close for after it there are no new numbers, only combinations.

Magical Number Squares

From early times, mathematicians have been fascinated by 'magic squares' in which numbers are laid out in grids three-by-three, four-by-four etc so that the rows, columns and diagonals all add up to the same number. Such squares were considered to have mystical significance. Magical number squares can be used in a variety of ways as a basis for candle wishes, as talismans or in rituals of empowerment.

The following is a very basic number square where the rows, columns and diagonals all add up to 15. This is the most usual and potent form of number square and is commonly used in magic.

8	3	4
1	5	9
6	7	2

The Hebrews and later the Greeks also attributed a numerical value to each of the letters of their alphabet. The system shown at the top of page 45 is the ancient Pythagorean system in which each number represents two or more letters

1	2	3	4	5	6	7	8	9
A	B	C	D	E	F	G	H	I
J	K	L	M	N	O	P	Q	R
S	T	U	V	W	X	Y	Z	

Creating a Talismanic Shape Using a Basic Number Square

This can be done by joining together the positions of the different numbers of a magic square. The shape can be used on talismans and for wishes, and drawn or painted in colours that are associated with specific needs such as red for courage and pink for mending quarrels (see Colour Magic, p. 20).

A number value can be worked out either for a personal name or for that of a desired lover or someone who needs strength or healing. This can then be drawn on a number square.

For example, for personal empowerment you could use the form of your name that you feel most comfortable with. Birth certificate names or official titles can be used just as effectively, to create a talisman shape etched on a number square. So my name, CASS EASON, in numbers becomes 3 1 1 1 5 1 1 6 5.

Use the basic number square formation and place a piece of tracing paper on top. Draw a continuous line connecting the numbers in the name or word (see illustration). If a number is repeated, draw a parallel line in the opposite direction zig-zagging as necessary.

The shape can be transferred to a thin scroll of paper and worn in a small silver tube on a chain round your neck or etched on metal or wood to serve as a protective and an empowering personal talisman.

8	3	4
1	5	9
6	7	2

which gives the sign of

Talismanic Wishes

For specific needs or wishes, a talismanic wish can be something as simple as:

M	o	n	e	y
4	6	5	5	7

or more complex, in which case it should be reduced to the key words. For example:

Joe will fall in love with me could be expressed as:

J	o	e	l	o	v	e	m	e
1	6	5	3	6	4	5	4	5

Again, the magical number shape is created by tracing over the magic square in the appropriate colour on paper, such as red for passion and yellow for communication.

Tambourine or Drum Number Ritual for Power

Drumming for power and altered states of consciousness features in the shamanic practices of almost every culture and still thrives among the shamans of Siberia and the Arctic Circle. The number square can be painted or etched on a drum or tambourine and the talismanic shape tapped out rhythmically with ever greater intensity until a climax is reached and the power is released into the cosmos.

Numerology for Divination

The Ancient Egyptians and Chinese used numbers for divination but it was the Greeks and Hebrews who developed the systems represented in modern numerology. Pythagoras regarded numbers as not just having mathematical significance but as being central to all religious and philosophical wisdom. He believed that each of the primary numbers had different vibrations and that these vibrations echoed throughout heaven and earth.

The Pythagorean system, based on the nine primary numbers representing two or more letters (see p. 45) is most commonly used in basic numerology, although the 'master numbers' of 11 and 22 are sometimes added to the system in certain aspects of numerological divination. The personal values assigned to each number are as follows:

1 *The Number of the Innovator*
Leadership, independence, personal attainment, individuality, enthusiasm, drive, assertiveness, strength, boundless energy, originality, great initiator and inspiration to others.

2 *The Number of the Negotiator*
Co-operation, adaptability, consideration of others, skill in partnerships of all kinds and in mediation, balanced opinions, desire for justice, ability to see both sides of any argument.

3 *The Number of the Creator*
Communication, both written and verbal, charisma, persuasiveness, sociability, creativity, especially in the arts, entertainment, optimism, expansion of horizons, fertility of ideas, generosity.

4 *The Number of the Realist*
Stability and common sense, practical foundation for ideas, skilled planning, loyalty, trustworthiness, ability to carry through projects, excellent organisational skills, ability to work within constraints, firm grasp on reality.

5 *The Number of the Voyager*
Expansiveness, vision, love of adventure, ability to appraise an entire situation at a glance, wide perspective, open-mindedness, eagerness for new knowledge and experiences, versatility.

ESSENTIAL WISDOM

6 *The Number of the Protector of the Weak*

Altruism, protection of the vulnerable, skilled at nurturing both close relationships and the world in general, sympathy, idealism, compassion, tolerance of others' weaknesses, wisdom concerning people.

7 *The Number of the Wise One*

Understanding of the world and connection with higher dimensions, awareness of tradition, thirst for knowledge, profound thought, spiritual nature, introspection, secrecy, powers of healing, love of beauty and harmony, seeker of truth.

8 *The Number of the Entrepreneur*

Status-orientated, power-seeking, great ambition, confidence, focused aims and energy, acumen with business and finance, efficiency and proficiency, competence in any chosen field, logical and analytical powers.

9 *The Number of the Crusader*

Courage, desire for perfection, humanitarianism, selflessness, impulsiveness, intolerance of prejudice or inaction, honesty, a refusal to be deterred no matter what the obstacle, outspokenness.

11 *The Number of the Dreamer*

Intuition, imagination, ingenuity, psychic awareness, illumination, idealism, a dreamer whose night and daytime visions may prove prophetic, mystical, insight into the unspoken motives and intentions of others, seeker of the secrets of the cosmos.

22 *The Number of the Eagle*

A master builder of society, a shaper of policy, global thinker, nobility of thought and action, the coming together of reason and intuition, logic and feeling, vision and practicality, energy and compassion.

Personal Number Combinations

There are five main personal number combinations that can reflect different facets of the personality. Studying the different numbers that make up a person's numerological chart can reveal much about the way that person regards him or herself as well as the way he or she is perceived by others. If a person wishes to alter their dominant aspect in any way, a subtle name change, altering a person's letter correspondences, often shifts the balance of power quite favourably in both working and personal life.

1 *The Birth or Life Plan (Potential Self) Number*

This number represents the possibilities that unfold throughout life. It provides an indication of what could or should be achieved, a person's predominant traits, strengths and weaknesses.

To calculate the life plan number, add together all the digits of the date of birth including the century, eg 11.11.1911, then reduce them by continually adding the sum together until the result is a number between 1 and 9. When calculating a life number, 0 is not counted so, for example, 20 or 200 is regarded simply as 2.

The only time the numbers are not reduced to a single digit is if a birth date adds up to the number 11 or 22 at any stage before its reduction to a single digit. The numbers 11 and 22 symbolise evolved states of awareness.

2 The Destiny or Fate (Manifest Self) Number

This number shows what has been made of the opportunities or challenges that have presented themselves in a person's working and personal life. It is derived by adding all the number values of all of the letters in the complete birth name. Again it is reduced to 11, 22 or a single digit.

3 The Acquired Fate Number

This is similar to the fate number, but instead of using the full birth name, the every-day, current full name is used, taking into account any variations such as using a middle name, dropping the original Christian name or any legal or informal changes. This number reflects any new persona and can replace the birth name as a benchmark of achievement. Some people still use their original full birth name, in which case the acquired fate number will be the same as the number of the manifest self.

4 The Heart or Soul Number

This is found by adding together the vowels of the full birth name. Like the birth number, it represents a person's starting point on earth. It reveals the inner private person, the secret hopes, fears and dreams, the longings of the soul, the underlying and often unconscious motivations in life. As well as a, e, i, o and u, w and y also count as vowels when used in a full name.

5 The Personality (Expression) Number

The personality or expression number, obtained by adding all the consonants together, represents the different and changing persona or faces shown to the world; the traits that others see most readily. There may be several personality numbers to reflect the names by which a person goes, for example, a Christian name, work title, nickname etc, or the name by which a person refers to themself in their thoughts. There will be several personality numbers and the relationships between them can be very revealing.

Colours and Numerology

As well as corresponding to the letters of the alphabet, each number also corresponds to a colour. The significance of this is that everyone has a primary power colour. By working out your personal number combination you can find your primary power colour, and by looking at the colour/number values of different letters in a name you can see which, if any, colours are lacking. These colours can then be introduced in rituals of empowerment, for example, when needed (see Colour Magic, p. 20, for the meanings of colours).

By adding the digits of any day – and time if a particular hour is crucial – in the same way that you would to find your personal number, it is also possible to see which colours can offer the maximum impact for success or happiness at a particular time.

The usual colour associations are shown in the table below although some systems substitute rose pink at number 8.

Red	Orange	Yellow	Green	Blue	Indigo	Violet	Silver	Gold
1	2	3	4	5	6	7	8	9

PALMISTRY

The Origins of Palmistry

Palmistry is thought by many scholars to have originated in India more than 4,500 years ago. It may have travelled from India to China via trade routes and thence west-wards to Egypt and Ancient Greece. Pythagoras wrote his *Physiognomy & Palmistry* in about 530BC, and it is recorded that Aristotle and the Roman emperors Caesar and Augustus were all skilled in palmistry. However, some schools of thought believe palmistry actually began in Ancient Egypt and Sumeria.

During the Middle Ages, palmistry was immensely popular, and gypsies and village wise women would read hands as a method of fortune-telling and character-assess-ment. By the 15th century, palmistry had been banned by the church along with other psychic arts. This only served to drive it underground, and palmistry knowledge was passed on orally, usually from the matriarch of the family to the eldest daughter and, especially in the Romany community, it continued to flourish.

The two main aspects of palmistry, chirognomy and chiromancy (sometimes spelt cheiromancy) were named after Cheiro, the Irish palm-reader and seer who was born in 1866. Cheiro read the palms of the rich and famous, including Oscar Wilde, Rasputin and Edward VII when he was Prince of Wales.

Chirognomy focuses on interpreting personality and character traits while chiromancy uses the hand to make predictions. In modern palmistry, the two are intricately interwoven.

Reading the Palm

The hand is traditionally considered to be the mirror of a person's past, present and future, containing all the achievements and failures before the time of the reading, and those to come.

The lines on the left hand reveal the abilities and weaknesses present at birth that may manifest during life, so making a person predisposed to follow certain courses rather than others, and the lines on the right hand reveal the acquired self, the self moulded by circumstance and by others. This applies if the right hand is the dominant or writing hand. If a person is left-handed, the hand meanings are reversed.

ESSENTIAL WISDOM

A more modern view sees the right hand as revealing the logical, intellectual, assertive and practical aspects of personality while the left represents the creative, intuitive and imaginative spheres. This is because physiologically the left hemisphere of the brain, the logical side, controls the right hand, and the right creative sphere of the brain controls the left hand. The texture and shape of hands, and the relative lengths of fingers are all of significance.

The Mounts

The mounts are the seven fleshy contours that appear on the palm of the hand. In general, the larger the mount is, the more powerful its characteristics are. Each mount is assigned a planet, the symbolism of which is reflected in the properties of that particular mount.

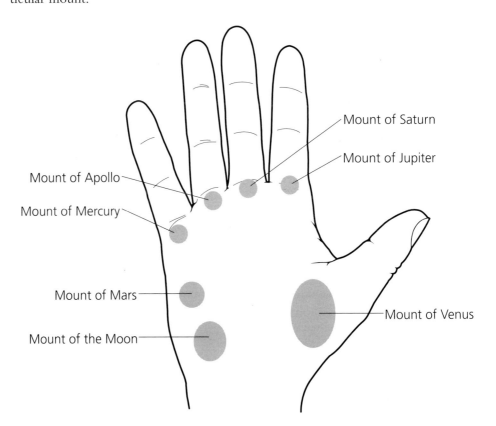

The Mount of Jupiter
The mount of Jupiter is found under the index, or Jupiter, finger and is important for assessing strength of character. It signifies ambition, idealism and wisdom.

The Mount of Saturn
The mount of Saturn is found under the second, or Saturn, finger and is concerned with life's problems and how a person copes with them. On the whole, this mount is

relatively flat compared with the others, so any prominence suggests that limitations are viewed as challenges and an impetus to change.

The Mount of Apollo or the Sun

The mount of Apollo is found under the ring, or Apollo, finger and is the area of creativity and artistic talents of all kinds, written or spoken communication skills and sensitivity.

The Mount of Mercury

The mount of Mercury is found under the little, or Mercury, finger and is the area of inventiveness, desire for travel, business and sales acumen, practical skills, intelligence, versatility and, surprisingly, psychic ability. It involves communication in a factual, as opposed to creative, sense and persuasiveness.

The Mount of Mars

Sometimes called upper Mars, it represents courage, physical energy and strength, a desire for action rather than deliberation and strong passions.

The Mount of the Moon or Luna

The mount of the moon is found under upper Mars, just above the wrist. It forms the second largest mount in the average hand and is often quite fleshy, extending to the percussion or edge of the hand. Its connection with the moon places it in the realms of imagination, dreams, fantasy and intuition.

The Mount of Venus

This mount is found under the thumb, across from the mount of the moon, and is the fount of the human personality. When there are emotional difficulties it is the one most dramatically affected by circumstances.

It is usually the largest of the mounts, covering one of the biggest blood vessels in the hand and extending from the base of the thumb to the edge of the hand and the wrist. The mount of Venus represents love, passion, affection or sentimentality and its prominence is influenced by major changes in relationships, whether romantic, formal or connected to the family.

The Plain of Mars

This is situated in the area of the palm that descends from the centre, at the level of the mount of Mars, almost to the wrist. The plain of Mars is sub-divided into middle Mars, the quadrangle (so-called because of its shape) and lower Mars, or the triangle.

The quadrangle (middle Mars): This lies between the heart line and head line. It speaks of sincerity and altruism and their mitigation of the basic warlike aspects of Mars.

The triangle (lower Mars): This is situated above the mount of Venus which is under the thumb, forming an isosceles triangle downwards from the head line to the

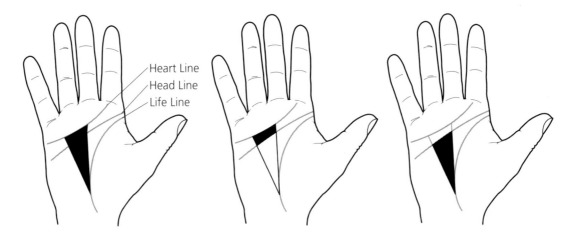

Heart Line
Head Line
Life Line

life line, joining the quadrangle at the top. This area represents intellectual achievement balancing physical energy, physical health, vigour and generosity.

The Lines

The wrinkles on the palm are called lines. Like the mounts, each line has a name and a meaning which can be positive or negative according to the application. Sometimes a challenge or setback can act as a spur for success and so a life line with breaks can be of great advantage, offering choices and unexpected opportunities.

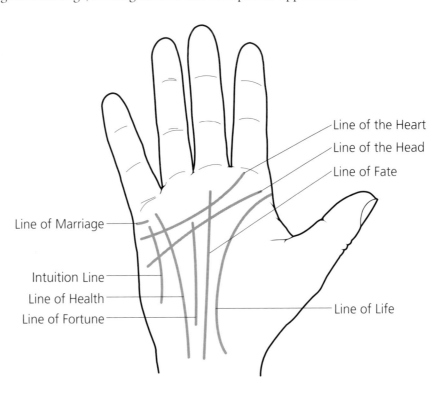

Line of the Heart
Line of the Head
Line of Fate
Line of Marriage
Intuition Line
Line of Health
Line of Fortune
Line of Life

Like the mounts, even the major lines do change and deepen, break and acquire branches and marks throughout life and, as the Chinese believe, many smaller lines linking with major lines can be relatively transient in the face of major life changes.

The Life Line

This runs in a curve from above the thumb, going between the thumb and the forefinger, to below the thumb, joining the wrist. The more impetus put into life, the stronger and deeper the life line will become.

A long, well-defined line with a broad curve is indicative of a powerful life-force, manifest both physically and mentally. It is the line of an achiever, but not necessarily a ruthless one, in success or love.

The Heart Line

The heart line begins between the mount of Mercury and the mount of Mars, and runs towards the mount of Jupiter. It is sometimes said to represent the dilemma between, or the union of, intellectual and instinctive processes. This line deals with love and relationships, and all matters concerned with emotions, the spirit and the inner world.

The Head Line

This is the line running across the palm from the area between the thumb and the forefinger to the mount of Mars or the moon area of the hand. This will give either an assertive or intuitive slant to intellectual activity. Its links with other mounts and lines are especially influential.

The head line can have several starting points, such as from the life line, whose energies reinforce the natural determination in the head line. Another beginning is at the mount of Jupiter which can indicate great authority and wisdom or, more negatively, egotism.

Secondary Lines

The Fate Line or the Line of Saturn

This line running vertically down the middle of the hand, from between the mount of the moon and the mount of Venus to the mounts of Saturn and the sun, is the fate line. It is often faint, and refers to the influence of luck or fate in one's life. It does not necessarily indicate good luck, but its prominence denotes the strength of a person's reaction – positive or negative – to good or bad challenges.

The Fortune Line or the Line of the Sun

This line, also called the Apollo line, begins around the mount of the moon and is similar to the line of fate. Sometimes, people will have one and not the other, or the two will join. The Apollo line is the line of worldly success, not necessarily in monetary terms, although the gold colour represented by the sun may be taken to mean this.

The Health Line or the Line of Mercury

This line is perpendicular to the head and heart lines and crosses the centre of the hand into the mount of Mercury or upper Mars. It is also known as the liver line, and refers to physical health, although it is also connected to mental and spiritual well-being.

The Intuition Line

This line, also known as the line of the psychic self, extends in a curve from the centre of the mount of the moon, passing through the head and heart lines almost to the marriage lines. It represents at its clearest a well-developed intuitive sense or evolved psychic abilities.

The Marriage Lines

The marriage line/lines are horizontal lines directly on the outer percussion of the hand immediately above the heart line below the finger and mount of Mercury. Their clarity, depth and number do not predict the number of permanent relationships but a desire or need to enter into a deep relationship and to relate to people on a meaningful level.

PYRAMID POWER

The Source of Pyramid Energies

It has been hypothesised that pyramids act as repositories or transformers of cosmic energy, hence their psychic and healing powers. The problem is that while experiments to demonstrate pyramid power can be carried out under laboratory conditions, the precise nature of the energies that produce the results cannot be scientifically explained.

It would seem that certain electromagnetic waves are concentrated and condensed by the particular configuration of a pyramid, for example, the Great Pyramid at Giza is aligned with magnetic north. The pyramid form seems to attract more of the earth's magnetic forces than other structures, but electromagnetic forces are not the whole secret of pyramid power.

One hypothesis is that the frequencies radiated by the earth itself (including the magnetic force lines) and cosmic or solar radiation blend within the pyramidical structure and produce a new vibrational frequency. This frequency could therefore result in a cumulative radiation that contains the power to amplify the body's natural healing and psychic powers and develop innate potential for growth within plants and animals.

Experimental and practical success in demonstrating all forms of pyramid energies is greatest when a scale model of the Great Pyramid is used. The energies are as potent in open-frame, wire and metal tubing pyramids as within enclosed ones,

ESSENTIAL WISDOM

although an open structure must have the four base sides as well as the four upright sides to be fully effective.

Experimental Evidence of Pyramid Power

Preserving Powers

During the 1930s a French radiesthesist (a person who works with human and natural energy fields), Antoine Bovis, was exploring the Great Pyramid and noticed that the bodies of animals which had become trapped in the King's Chamber had not decayed but become mummified. On his return to France he built a perfectly scaled wooden model of the pyramid and placed a dead cat in the position of the King's Chamber, about a third of the distance from the base to the apex. The cat became mummified, and so was preserved without any of the usual decaying or putrefying processes. Bovis found that he could preserve fruit and vegetables in the same way. The reason has never been found.

Two US pyramidologists, Bill Kerrell and Kathy Coggin, have also conducted numerous experiments under controlled conditions demonstrating that the taste of both fresh and frozen food can be improved by placing it under a pyramid: coffee becomes less bitter, wine more mellow and fruit juice less acidic. Milk and yoghurt packaged in a pyramid-shaped carton will keep fresh in a refrigerator for much longer than in conventional packaging, and some dairies have adopted these containers as standard.

Sharpening Powers

Bovis's work remained unnoticed until the 1950s when a Czech radio engineer, Karel Drbal, replicated his experiments and tried tests of his own. He found that a cardboard model pyramid would sharpen a blunt razor blade and keep it sharp provided that the sides of the pyramid were aligned with the earth's magnetic field and the blade also was aligned along the north–south axis. His experiments over ten years worked in pyramids of any shape and size, not just a scale model of the Great Pyramid, although this was the most effective.

Although this phenomenon is partly explained by the two-fold magnetic energy within the pyramid shape, unknown forces are still implicated.

Plant Growth

Pyramids have also been shown time and again to induce accelerated growth in plants. Indeed, plant growers have reported increases of over 150 per cent in growth under pyramids. Experiments with plants and different greenhouse shapes produced results showing that plants grew up to 8in a day in summer in a pyramid and even grew well under a pyramid frame in freezing winter weather. Tomato seeds also sprouted earlier when exposed to pyramid energy. Plants that were watered using water placed in a pyramid shape overnight showed the same accelerated growth patterns.

Psychic Pyramid Powers

According to the Egyptian Book of the Dead, the power of the pyramid awakens the god who sleeps in the soul. Dr Paul Brunton, a researcher who spent the night in the King's Chamber of the Great Pyramid in the 1930s, witnessed malformed spirit shapes floating around the chamber. After a while the evil presences departed and two Egyptian high priests appeared. Dr Brunton felt his own spirit rise from his body and found himself floating round the chamber too.

In a large number of cases studied since his experience, pyramids have served to amplify psychic powers. Sitting inside a scale model pyramid or holding a symbolic crystal one improves telepathic communication, clairaudience, clairvoyance and mediumship.

Sleeping with a scale model pyramid beneath the bed not only increases energy levels the next day in many people, but also brings to a proportion of subjects lucid and predictive dreams and out-of-body sensations, especially ones connected with past lives.

Experiments demonstrate that sitting under a pyramid measurably increases the amplitude and frequency of alpha and theta brainwaves that are naturally present in states of meditation and altered consciousness. This occurs even when subjects are blindfolded and unaware that an open pyramid structure has been lowered over them.

Many people report increased tranquillity and euphoria during meditation sessions inside a pyramid, as well as warmth and tingling sensations particularly in the upper part of the body. Children who know nothing of pyramid energies have independently described the same feelings as those reported by adults.

Healing Pyramid Powers

Pyramids also have demonstrated specific healing properties in a number of cases. By placing a pyramid beneath a bed or chair on which the subject is sitting, or directly pointing a pyramid towards the source of a pain, relief is frequently experienced within a short time. Cuts, wounds and bruises heal faster under a pyramid, and sitting under a pyramid will reduce the pain of headaches, migraine or toothache, while women who slept under a pyramid for four to 16 weeks reported that they did not suffer menstrual cramps and pains and the actual time of menstruation was reduced.

Water placed under a pyramid overnight was also found to reduce inflammation from bites and burns, and act as a natural aid to digestion. Kerrell and Coggin conducted an experiment on a nine-year-old girl who had a number of mosquito bites. One of the bites was rubbed with tap water and the other with pyramid water. The girl reported immediately that the pyramid water had stopped the itching, even when she did not know which water was being used.

ESSENTIAL WISDOM

In experiments, polluted water has been purified by placing it inside a pyramid for several days, and the taste of chlorine has also been removed.

Making a Model Pyramid

Provided that a model pyramid is constructed as nearly as possible to the scale of the Great Pyramid, it can be made of almost any material and any size, from a pyramid large enough to sit in or lie under to one small enough to hold in the hand and use as a focus for meditation.

The Great Pyramid has four sides, each measuring 755ft or 230m at the base, and 481ft or 147m from base to summit. A scale model can be made using these proportions. For example, a wigwam 4.81ft high with sides 7.77ft wide at the base could be built and kept in the garden.

RITUAL OR FORMAL MAGIC

Ritual magic can vary in formality, from a simple rite carried out by a solitary practitioner for a personal or more general need, to a full ceremony, perhaps at a handfasting or Wiccan marriage, or at a coven meeting as a healing or empowering ritual for an individual, the group or the environment.

The Magic Circle

Intrinsic to all magic is the concept of the magic circle which provides both sacred space in which magical energies are concentrated, and protection from negative forces outside the circle while the channels between the dimensions are open. The circle is symbolic of wholeness, perfection and unity, the cycle of the seasons and of life, death and rebirth.

It is cast before a ritual, in a clockwise direction beginning in the north (or in some traditions in the east) in a single, unbroken movement at floor level. It should be drawn in chalk or, if working outdoors, in the earth or sand with a ceremonial sword or *athame*, a ritual knife.

Circles can also be visualised and drawn in the air at chest or ground level using a clear, pointed quartz crystal, a wand or the forefinger of the power hand (this is the one used for writing). Again, begin in the north and continue in a unbroken circle. At the end of the ritual the circle is uncast in the reverse direction. In the southern hemisphere some practitioners follow the northern tradition. However, others adapt to their own seasonal patterns by reversing the earth and fire quadrants (see below), placing the altar in the south of the circle and moving the seasons forward six months.

The Four Elements

Earth, air, fire and water symbolise the four forces that traditionally make up life on the physical, mental and spiritual plane. In ceremonial magic they represent law, life, light and love respectively, and together they combine to form the fifth element, ether or *akasha,* that is pure spirit or perfection and allows magical working to take form.

Each element symbolises a quadrant of the circle. The powers of the ruling deva, archangel or guardian of the watchtower are invoked in turn at each of the four main compass points of the circle in the early stages of the ritual, beginning in the north (or east).

Earth

Earth is the element of order, both in nature and in institutions such as the law, politics, finance, health and education. It also represents yin, the female, nurturing goddess aspect, Mother Earth, the home and family. It is a good element to invoke when a step-by-step or practical approach is needed, and for money spells.

Earth colours are green or dark brown/black, its quarter is north, its direction is midnight and its season is winter.

Zodiacal signs: Taurus, Virgo, Capricorn

Air

Air represents life itself, logic, the mind, communication, health, new beginnings, travel, learning and healing, and the male or yang god in the form of sky deities. It is invoked when new beginnings are desired or for clearing indecision, and for spells concerning career and justice.

Air's colour is yellow, its quarter is east, its direction is dawn and its season is spring.

Zodiacal signs: Aquarius, Gemini, Libra

Fire

Fire represents light, the sun, lightning, joy, ambition, inspiration and achievement, and also destruction of what is now no longer needed.

Like air, fire represents the male or yang god in the form of the sun deities and is invoked in power and fertility rituals, as well as in banishing spells.

Fire colours are gold or orange, its quarter is south, its direction is noon and its season is summer.

Zodiacal signs: Aries, Leo, Sagittarius

Water

Water represents relationships, sympathy, intuition, healing, and the cycle of birth, death and rebirth. Like earth, water symbolises the female or yin goddess in the form of the moon goddesses and is especially potent in love spells.

Water's colour is blue, its quarter is west, its direction is dusk and its season is autumn.

Zodiacal signs: Cancer, Scorpio, Pisces

Elemental Substances

At each of the main compass points of the altar or ritual table are placed associated substances and ritual tools. The altar is either in the centre or to the north of the circle, but in some outdoor coven or collective rituals, the representatives of the guardians of the four watchtowers may hold the tools and/or substances in place of the altar.

Salt represents earth, incense represents air, orange, red or gold candles represent fire, and water represents its own element, either pure water from a sacred spring or water left for a 24-hour cycle in a crystal or clear glass container in the sun and moonlight.

Elemental Tools

Earth

The bell, an optional tool, is sounded nine times at the beginning and close of a ritual, nine being the number of completion and perfection, while standing in the south of the circle facing north, the direction associated with magic and mystery.

It is also sometimes rung in each of the four elemental quadrants when the symbol being used as a focus is taken to each quadrant in turn.

The pentacle, a female symbol, represents the Earth suit in many Tarot packs, and is used in ritual as a symbol of material possessions especially money and practical endeavour.

Crystals or herbs may be placed on the pentacle, or the symbol of the ritual carried on the pentacle round the circle. A pentacle can be created from clay, wood, wax or metal and the single point of its five-pointed star which extends upwards is seen as a conductor of positive magical power. Earth tools are placed in the north.

Air

The 'athame' is a ritual black-handled knife, usually with a double-edged blade, traditionally engraved with magical or astrological signs. It is used to direct magical air energies into a symbol and also as a conductor of energy especially in solitary rituals. It is held above the head with both hands to draw down light and energy from the cosmos into the body as part of the magical stage of raising energies. It is then brought down at the climax of the ritual, with a swift cutting movement, held with the right, or power, hand horizontally at waist level, and thrust away from the body to release this accumulated power.

The sword is rarely used in private rituals, as the black-handled knife serves the same purpose. The sword is featured in many Tarot packs as the Air suit symbol. A white-handled knife can also be substituted for the sword. Both the knife and sword are male symbols. In some magical traditions, the sword is the ritual tool of fire. Air tools are placed in the east.

Fire

The wand or fire stick, the Fire symbol in many Tarot packs, is traditionally a thin piece of wood about 21in long, narrowed at one end, rubbed smooth and usually cut from a living tree (some conservationists find this unacceptable unless the tree is being pruned). In Grail magic, the tool is called the lance or spear. Some wands have a crystal point in the end.

The wand is valuable for directing energies towards a focus and for circling in the air to raise the power, clockwise in attracting rituals and anti-clockwise for banishing ones. It is a male symbol, and in some traditions the wand is the tool of air. Fire tools are placed in the south.

Water

The chalice or ritual cup represents the water element and cups appear as the Water suit in the Tarot. The chalice used for rituals is traditionally made of silver or crystal, but stainless steel is a modern equivalent.

The cauldron, or ritual dish, is also a water tool, although occasionally it is regarded as an earth symbol. The cauldron can take many forms, from a small cast-iron pot used for brewing herbs and for scrying, to a deep dish frequently made of silver.

In indoor magic, this dish often serves as the libation bowl which holds the offering made to the cosmos or specific deities that in outdoor magic is dropped on the earth. These are female symbols. Water tools are placed in the west.

The Four Stages of Magic Ritual

The Focus

This defines the purpose of a ritual which can be as simple as coming together to greet the full moon or to celebrate the harvest, in which case the ceremony would involve quite subtle build-ups and release of power, quiet chanting, poetry and reflection within the sacred space.

Sometimes a candle, a poppet or cloth doll, or a wax image are used to represent a person. At this first vital stage the rest of the world recedes and only the need or the wish exists. Whether there is one person or a dozen present, the essence of the focus is the same.

Concentration is the key.

The Action

This is the stage where actions, either physical, mental or both, endow the focus of the ritual with magical energies. The practitioner or, in a more formal setting, the high priestess or priest, takes the symbol to the four quarters, incorporating in turn the cumulative powers of first the elemental substances and then the tools. The wish is then expressed as a magical intention in each of the four quarters.

Movement is the key.

Raising the Power

In many ways this is the most powerful part of the spell and is achieved, through the amplification of the magical energies. Tying knots in coloured cord, chanting or ritual dancing will increase in intensity and speed. The practitioner or group visualise the increasing energies as a cone of power, or spiralling coloured light that rises as this stage progresses.

The athame/s may be raised or arms extended vertically as high as possible above the head to absorb power from the cosmos, or a tight circle of power can be made by holding hands in the circle or entwining cords, interconnected to form a web.

Increase is the key.

Release of Power

At the point when the climax is reached, there is a final shout or cry, such as 'The power is free' and dancers may leap high in the air. Knots are suddenly released as the cord or web is pulled taut, and those present may see and feel the whirlwind rising into the sky from the accumulated cone of power. The released light suddenly becomes a silver fountain of pure energy, spurting into the sky to form a star or a glittering rainbow.

Release is the key.

Sacred Marriage and Sex

The sacred marriage is one that permeates all cultures, representing the union of male and female, yin and yang, animus and anima. There are many myths surrounding this coupling, linked with the creation of new life and the continuing fertility of the land and humankind. The sacred marriage between the earth and sky was celebrated in many cultures at springtime. In Ancient Babylon, for example, the sacred marriage took place each year between the god Tammuz and the goddess Ishtar. This festival of Akitu or Zag-Mug celebrated the rising of the waters of the Tigris, followed by the Euphrates, and the coming of the spring rains, to bring fertility at the spring equinox.

As the sky gods gained supremacy, they married the earth goddesses who slowly evolved into the patronesses of women, marriage and childbirth. For example, the consort of Odin the Norse All-Father was Frigga, the goddess of women, marriage and motherhood. Though such deities were far from faultless even in their own mythologies, their continuing union, consummated symbolically in annual celebrations, represented the ideal or archetypal union that is reaffirmed through every act of sacred love-making.

Sex Magic

Sex magic involves the release of sexual power in orgasm and ejaculation to give impetus to a need or wish. In the re-enactment of 'the great rite', as the culmination of a ritual, the energies of the god and goddesses are channelled into the high priest and priestess or, in a private ritual, the couple who are making love.

In some traditions, the couple engage in intercourse but, at the point of ejaculation, the man uses the semen to propel the intention of the ritual into the cosmos while the woman brings herself to climax. They then join again to end the rite. Sometimes the sexual act is symbolically performed by plunging an athame or spear into a chalice filled with wine.

Sacred Sexuality

In Hindu tantric tradition and Oriental sacred love-making, the human body is regarded as a temple, and an act of ritual sex as a means of tapping into cosmic and divine forces; a way of transcending time and space and returning to a state of undifferentiated bliss. Both cultures use the sexual energies raised during love-making, but postponed from reaching a physical climax, to unite the male/female energies in spiritual orgasm.

RUNES

The word 'rune' stems from ancient northern European languages, meaning a secret thing, or a mystery.

Runic symbols are ideographic, each representing a whole concept on many different levels of awareness, much like a Tarot card. Runes can be used for divination, magic or meditation, and when runic forms are combined as 'bind runes' they create a magical talisman of power or protection. Each runic symbol corresponds approximately to a letter and runes sometimes form a magical alphabet for encoding and thereby empowering magical wishes.

The runes have slightly different names, though similar meanings, according to the system being used. Here, I have given the Viking names.

Using the Viking Runes

The following are the 24 runes that are called the Elder Futhark, together with basic divinatory meanings. They can be used as amulets if carved on wood or drawn on stone to endow the wearer with the power within the rune meaning. You can also draw each symbol on one face of a flat stone or wooden disc and choose three runes at random. If the blank side falls uppermost these will indicate areas of your life in which change is needed. If the rune falls uppermost this indicates ways forward and strengths you possess right now to maximise opportunities and overcome obstacles. Alternatively you can put your runes in a bag and again select three, casting them on the ground. Or, by choosing a rune at random each morning, you can tune into the prevailing strengths that will help you most during the day. If the rune falls on the blank side, wait and act cautiously.

The Aett or Set of Freyja, Goddess of Fertility and Love

Fehu (Cattle): Wealth, money, financial prosperity, the price one must pay for change

Uruz (Aurochs/bison): Strength, primal power, courage, overcoming obstacles

Thurisaz (Thorn): Protection, challenges, secrecy and conflicts

Ansuz (A God): Inspiration, wisdom, aspirations and communication

Raidho (Riding): Journeys, travel, initiative, impetus and change

Kenaz (Torch): Guidance, inner voice, illumination, inner strength

Gebo (Gift): Generosity, all matters relating to exchanges, including contracts, love, marriage and sexual union

Wunjo (Joy): Personal happiness, success and recognition of worth

The Aett or Set of Hagalaz or Heimdall, Watcher of the Gods

Hagalaz (Hail): Disruption, disruption by natural events and uncontrolled forces

Naudhiz (Need): Needs that can be met by action and reaction to external events, self-reliance, the desire for achievement, passion

Isa (Ice): Blockage, a period of inactivity which can be used for good, waiting for the right moment

Jera (Year): Harvest, the results of earlier efforts realised, life cycles that can be fruitful or a repetition of old mistakes

Eihwaz (Yew): Natural endings, leading to new beginnings, banishment of what is redundant, tradition

Perthro (Gambling-cup): What is not yet known or revealed, the essential self, taking a chance

Elhaz or Algiz (Marsh Grass): The higher self, spiritual nature, duality, needing care in the approach to important matters

Sowilo (Sun): Victory, success, fulfilling potential, energy and expansion

The Aett or Set of Tiwaz

Tiwaz (The Pole or Lode Star, a Guiding Star): Justice, altruism, self-sacrifice, following a chosen path and keeping faith even in dark times

Berkano (Birch): Renewal, healing, physical or spiritual regeneration, fertility and mothering in all aspects

Ehwaz (Horse): Loyalty, harmony between people or inner and outer worlds, partnerships and friendships, moving house or career

Mannaz (Man): Power of human intelligence, seeing our lives as part of a wider pattern, compassion and acceptance of the weaknesses and strengths of self and others

Laguz (Water): Birth, beginnings, initiation into life, emotions, following the flow of life, unconscious wisdom and intuition

Ingwaz (the Fertility and Sacrifice God Ing): A time of gestation, both human and symbolic, creative withdrawal, waiting for new strength and life, the promise of better times

Othala (Homestead): Home, domestic matters, the family and family finances, stability, responsibility and duty

Dagaz (Day): Awakening, clear vision or awareness, light at the end of the tunnel, optimism

Origins of the Runes

Runes were created by the Germanic peoples: the English, German and Scandinavians who shared a common heritage and language which gradually split into different dialects. The legend that Odin, the Viking All-Father, invented the runes probably comes from an ancient tribe known as the Volsungr who originated from the far north with the last ice age. They were a priest/magician tribe who were said to guard the ancient forests and trackways, helping any in need and using an early form of runes known as the 'Ur runes'.

The Volsungr spread their wisdom, including their sacred incantations associated with magical runic symbols, and eventually disappeared back into the northern forests. These early runic symbols relied on images from the natural world, such as the six-pointed snowflake or star and the sun wheel, the rune of action, and holy signs from the Bronze Age associated with the Mother Goddess, such as the lozenge for fertility.

The runic systems that are used today date from the 2nd and 3rd centuries BC, when the Germanic peoples of the Middle Danube came into contact with the Mediterranean Etruscan alphabet system. The runes followed the trade routes across Europe, their usage spread by the traders who cast lots to discover propitious times for journeys and negotiations.

Norse rune staves have been found in many parts of the world where the early Vikings penetrated, from Iceland, which they colonised in about 815AD, to America, which was discovered in about 992AD by Leif, son of the famed Erik the Red. The Vikings voyaged from Russia to what is now Turkey and Greece and even North Africa, as shown by stone monuments, graves and artefacts marked with runes. However, runic symbols were not used in formal writing, which did not appear until the 11th-century when Christian monks reached Scandinavia and recorded what were until then oral legends and lays.

Wisdom of the Runes

Much of the current rune lore is based on a series of rune poems which were written down by these monks from oral poems and stories. They reflect the Christian viewpoint of the scribes, but still capture much of the early dangers and hardships of the pioneers and warriors who first adopted the runes as a guide.

The three main poems are the Anglo-Saxon or Old English Rune Poem, the Old Norse Rune Poem and the Icelandic Rune Poem.

There are many accounts of the discovery of runes and their inherent wisdom by Odin or his Anglo-Saxon counterpart, Woden, suggesting that runes contained knowledge and wisdom beyond even that possessed by the gods. This knowledge was thought to stem from the depths of time, from the roots of the Norse world trees or Yggdrassil, which contained the nine worlds, inhabited by gods and mortals alike.

ESSENTIAL WISDOM

This extract from an early Icelandic poem describes the wisdom of the Yggdrassil:

Wounded I hung on Yggdrassil
For nine nights long
Pierced by a spear
Consecrated to Odin,
Sacrifice to myself
Upon that tree
The wisest know not the roots
of ancient times whence it sprang.
None brought me bread
None gave me mead
Down to the depths I searched
I took up the Runes …
And from that tree I fell
Screaming

Casting the Runes

Runes were cast or thrown for divination and to invoke higher powers that might influence the fortune of humankind. They were still publicly cast by tribes and individuals for divinatory purposes until the 11th century and the last true rune-masters and mistresses did not die out until about 300 years ago. In his *Germania*, written in about 98AD, the Roman author Tacitus described the custom of the ancient Germanic people of throwing rune staves on to a white cloth to then be interpreted by the runemaster.

Tacitus recounted that a branch would be cut from a nut-bearing tree and etched with markings known as 'rune slips'. These staves were cast and interpreted either by a priest or the father of the family or clan, who 'offered a prayer to the gods and, looking up to the sky, picked up three strips, one at a time and read their meaning from the signs previously scored on them'.

He records that women were involved in augury of all kinds. Rune mistresses, for it was often the women who learned the lore while the men were away at battle, were described as follows by the thirteenth-century author of Erik the Red:

'She wore a cloak set with stones along the hem. Around her neck and covering her head she wore a hood lined with white catskins. In one hand she carried a staff with a knob on the end and on her belt, holding together her long dress, hung a charm pouch.'

Demonisation of the Runes

Like the Tarot, runes have negative connotations. These dark associations stem from early Mediaeval times in northern Europe when priests, unable to read runic inscriptions and magical charges, believed them to be dark spells capable of unlocking the powers of evil.

With the coming of Christianity to Scandinavia, pagan gods became demonised, the goddesses became witches and even the black cats, who in Norse mythology pulled the chariot of Freyja or Frea, the goddess of love and fertility, were regarded as witches' familiars.

During the late 1930s and 1940s, the Nazis in Germany used runes in their military insignia and propaganda and further increased their dark reputation, showing that runes, like any other form of magic or indeed any form of learning, can be used for good or evil purposes alike, depending on the intent of the user.

SACRED GEOMETRY

What is Sacred Geometry?

Sacred geometry is the enclosure of a sacred space with geometric shapes and principles that have spiritual as well as mathematical significance. Though sacred geometry has been used for secular purposes, its prime importance is in its spiritual symbolism, as a connection between the human and the divine.

The simplest form might be a temporary enclosure of scaled-down proportions, marked by thread or drawn on the ground. In the northern magical tradition the sacred plot is traditionally square, with each side facing one of the cardinal directions.

For example, the 'sacred grid of nine' was an ancient Scandinavian magical device, drawn in the earth in front of a shaman's hut. It was also created on a specially erected square platform which acted as a protective magical area between earth and sky. The nine squares were thus contained within a larger outer protective square, thereby further focusing the energies of time and space.

The History of Sacred Geometry

The Great Pyramid is aligned to the magnetic north. Until very recently it was thought that the pyramid was slightly off this true north–south axis, but with the development of more sophisticated measuring systems, the accuracy of the ancient Egyptian mathematicians was vindicated. The position of the Great Pyramid is also in the exact centre of the earth's land mass. It is built on the mathematical ratio of pi 3.14159, the ratio of a circle's circumference to its diameter, all the more remarkable in that the true value of pi was not discovered until 600 years ago.

The Ancient Greeks, influenced by Platonic and Pythagorean principles, also believed that certain geometrically-derived ratios and shapes had spiritual significance. Pythagoras regarded both numbers and geometrical shapes as being central to religious and philosophical wisdom.

ESSENTIAL WISDOM

For example, the cube symbolised kingship and earthly foundations and so royal buildings were constructed using cubic geometry.

Even today, the creation of Hindu religious structures, whether a wayside shrine or a great temple, involves prayer and ritual. Having aligned east and west, the architect constructs a square on the earth on which the whole projected structure is set out, according to sacred measurements. This act physically inscribes the sacred form upon the earth.

Christian sacred geometry based buildings on the emblem of the cross and this was elaborated upon during Mediaeval times to become the form of an unfolded cube, as a symbol of the Kingdom of God on earth. Chartres Cathedral in France is said to be the most perfect example of Christian sacred geometry. It is aligned so that the altar and nave are lit by the midsummer sun and has a complex labyrinth in classical design set in the floor of the nave.

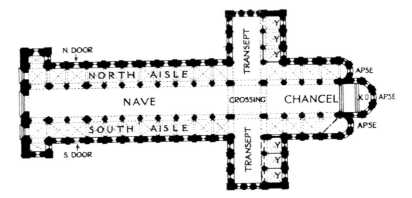

Why Sacred Geometry Declined

During the Dark Ages, ancient geometric principles became the province of the trade guilds who preserved the tradition. This knowledge, known only to the guilds, therefore became secret. This increased its mystery but also resulted in the loss of its wider dissemination. During the Renaissance, interest in the Classical world rekindled, but the adoption of the Arabic numbering system meant that numbers became biased towards arithmetic with the emphasis on absolute numbers. More complex geometrical ratios and proportional measurements therefore became less appealing when buildings could be constructed quickly and accurately with less effort.

During the 19th century, the standardisation of building materials by mass manufacture meant that complex mathematical skills were no longer necessary in carpentry and construction, and it was not until 1925 when Jay Hambidge wrote *The Parthenon and Other Greek Temples: Their Dynamic Symmetry*, that interest in the sacred geometric ratios of ancient buildings and their artefacts was revived. This led to an awareness that ancient peoples without technological aids had an astounding knowledge of geometry and astronomy; with their structures, linked to the movement of the stars and the seasons, they had created sacred places where mankind could experience the power of the divine.

The Golden Mean

The golden rectangle is one of the most significant forms in sacred geometry. It is based on the golden mean, a measure that was discovered by Pythagoras and is represented by the Greek letter phi or mathematically as 1.6180339887499 recurring. In the natural world, golden mean ratios occur in the growth patterns of plants such as the sunflower and creatures like the mollusc nautilus which, in its shell construction, grows larger on each spiral using the phi ratio of the golden mean. The ancient Greeks constructed their temples to fit the golden mean; the Parthenon in Athens, for example, forms a perfect golden mean square.

During the Renaissance, the golden mean ratio was used by Italian painters to create perspective in their art.

Labyrinths

The labyrinth is a universal symbol of transformation, created to represent the search by humankind for his or her core of divinity.

The oldest known full-scale labyrinth dates from 1230BC and was created in King Nestor's Palace in Phylos, Greece. But the most famous labyrinth is that connected with the fertility cult of Crete. Here the labyrinth held the Minotaur and, in Greek legend, a complex myth of fertility, sacrifice, redemption and the triumph of the willing sacrifice over the forces of humankind's brute instincts, is woven around it.

The Minotaur, who had the head of a bull and the body of a man, was created when Poseidon enchanted Pasiphaë, Queen of Crete, to mate with the snow-white bull that Poseidon had sent to her husband King Minos. This was because Minos had angered Poseidon by refusing to sacrifice the animal, and commanded a skilled architect to construct such an intricate labyrinth in which to keep the Minotaur that escape was impossible. Every nine years the Athenians were forced to send seven virgin youths and seven maidens as sacrifices to the Minotaur. Theseus, the Greek hero, offered himself as a willing sacrifice, but Ariadne, the King's daughter who had fallen in love with Theseus, gave him a ball of thread, which he fastened to the door of the labyrinth and unwound as he went deeper in. Having killed the Minotaur, Theseus led the victims out and claimed Ariadne as his prize.

In Scandinavia there are hundreds of large stone labyrinths, some dating from the Bronze Age. In parts of Sweden and Finland, between the spring equinox and midsummer, labyrinth games are held in which a maiden stands in the centre and youths compete to rescue her. Traditionally, Swedish seafarers would build labyrinths near the shore to ensure a good wind. If they were becalmed, they would row to an island and construct one.

Megaliths and Sacred Geometry

Magic circles are the most basic form of sacred geometry and have been used throughout history. Stone circles were created with precision and set out according to Pythagorean geometric principles. The unit of measure used was the megalithic yard of 2.72ft which, along with the megalithic mile, is found in the distances and angles along ley lines between ancient sites. Stone circles were aligned to mark significant positions in the path of the moon or sun, especially the equinoxes and solstices.

The 56 holes dug inside the bank at Stonehenge, known as the Aubrey holes, are positioned at precise regular intervals around a concentric circle about 285ft in diameter. It has been hypothesised that the cycle of the moon, which takes 27.3 days, was tracked by the megalith builders by moving a marker by two holes each day to complete a circuit in 28 days. What is more, by moving the marker by three holes per year to complete a full circuit in 18.67 years, it would be possible to keep track of the nodes, the points where the paths of the sun and the moon apparently intersect to produce an eclipse. Thus both lunar and solar eclipses could be predicted. Since many of the festivals were based on the passage of the sun and moon and became formalised in the Celtic eightfold wheel of the year, the circles themselves provided a microcosm in which the cosmic cycles were celebrated and linked with the lives of the people and their agricultural year.

Mandalas

A mandala is a geometric pattern that represents the sacred sphere, the union of the self and the universe. It features in the rituals and meditative practices of Hinduism, and many forms of Buddhism, especially Tibetan. Indeed the form was originally created by Tibetan Buddhists who were influenced by Hindu traditions.

Mandalas are said to be the formal geometrical expression of sacred vibrations or sound and are created in many art forms as a way of expressing the path to the infinite. The mandala has also entered the Western mystical tradition, especially in more recent years, to express the relationships between the sacred symbols of the Kabbalah or alchemy, for example.

They are primarily used for meditation either as an actual reproduction on a scroll or created in the mind by visualisation. They are also drawn to create a temporary sacred space in which rituals and initiations can take place. For ritual purposes, the mandala may be drawn in the earth or sand and is always completely destroyed after the ceremony.

The Sanskrit words from which 'mandala' is derived mean 'the sphere of the essence'. Mandala also means circle in Sanskrit and it has a perfect symmetrical form, concentrated around a central axis.

From this central axis, the mandala is usually divided into four equal sections. Each of these divisions is itself made up of concentric circles and squares, the centres of which coincide with the centres of all the circles, thus creating an intricate design that contains the geometric forms symbolising time, space and eternity.

The mandala design is intended to guide an initiate into an altered state of awareness through contemplation, inwards to the sacred centre, the heart of silence. It is also used in the construction of palaces or monasteries in the Far East.

SACRED SOUND

What is Sacred Sound?

Throughout the ages, in almost every religion, both formal and natural, chanting, singing and rhythm have offered a pathway to raise consciousness and enter mystical trance states. The ancients understood the spiritual qualities of sound and vibration. Sound was regarded as sacred, and music as a microcosm of the order of the universe, reflecting the harmonious movement of the heavenly bodies. Music was seen to be the way to the ultimate perfect silence at the heart of sound and the cosmos. This is the archetypal sound of which all earthly chants and songs were a reflection. Pythagoras called the harmony of the different levels of cosmic existence 'the music of the spheres'. He also believed that each level had a specific numerical vibration.

Since only a small proportion of the vibrations of the universe can be heard by the human ear, the purpose of chant and song was to attune the spirit of the chanter or musician to the more subtle sounds on higher levels. In doing so, it was said the soul would move closer to harmony and finally unity with the cosmic rhythms, and the 'sound of silence'.

Sound is believed to have brought the world into being by many different religions. According to the Book of Genesis, 'In the beginning was the Word, and the Word was with God and the Word was God'. In Hindu tradition 'om' is the first, the primal or sacred sound and is probably the best known mantra in Eastern faiths, signifying 'that which has no beginning or end' and is central to both Buddhist and Hindu meditative practices. The Hindu creator god is call Nada Brahma, a name made up of words which mean 'he who creates all' and 'sound'.

A Scientific Basis

During the 1930s, Hans Jenny, a Swiss researcher, demonstrated that sound could not only cause matter to move, but create specific forms and shapes from it. By vibrating sand, powders and liquids on metal discs or drumheads at certain audible frequencies or by playing the violin, Jenny caused the substances to form many complex geometric shapes that are found in nature, such as snowflakes, honeycombs, or markings like those on the tortoise shell.

A change in the sound frequency resulted in a corresponding alteration in the shape and forms of the substances. What is most significant is that as higher sound frequencies were introduced, the forms became more ethereal. Complex tones increased the complexity of shapes and specific frequencies produced the same patterns on every occasion that particular sound was made. If sound frequencies stopped, so would the movement.

This new discipline was called cymatics. Jenny also investigated sacred sounds. When he chanted 'om' into a device called a tonoscope, it produced first a circle, then a mandala pattern (see p. 70).

Mantras

A mantra is the repetition of sacred words, phrases or syllables in religious and ceremonial rituals in Judaism, Islam and Christianity and also in ritual and meditation in the Vedic faiths of the Far East. It is said to be a manifestation of *shabda*, or sacred sound. Chanting out loud or meditating silently on mantras, either enunciating the words without voice or repeating them in the mind, forms a path to altered states of consciousness, in which it is possible for an adept to connect with his or her own divine nature, the source of divinity, or, in Buddhism, nirvana or cosmic bliss.

Adepts can also use the power generated through reciting mantras to attain psychokinetic powers. However, these powers can be used for good or evil in the same way that sound can either be used harmoniously for healing or as loud, discordant noise that can be damaging to humans, animals and plant life.

Chanting

The continuous recitation aloud or singing of mantras is called chanting. When chanting is part of a religious ceremony or a ritual in which many voices are joined, great spiritual and psychic power can be generated and participants and onlookers can feel themselves losing their individual boundaries and merging in collective worship or ecstasy.

Through repetitively chanting, many ordinary Catholics learned the sounds of the Latin Mass in earlier times, its deeper significance without ever understanding the actual words. Gregorian chants, still used in monasteries, have entered the wider musical field as a consciousness-raising tool. These chants are a single-line melody, known as plainchant or plainsong. They have also been called prayer on pitch.

In some Evangelical churches, singing, especially of Gospel music, raises the collective consciousness sufficiently for some members of the congregation to give ministry, to speak in tongues and even to be spontaneously healed.

Among indigenous peoples, shamans augment or replace chants with repetitive and regular drum and rattle rhythms as a way of reaching other worlds. Native Americans have also traditionally chanted in preparation for hunting, war and in such ceremonies as the Winter Dance that marks the coming of winter by singing with channelled spirit voices to call back the light.

Sound Magic

The Native American Navajos have many ceremonies of *hatal*, a word that literally translated means 'sings', and elaborate songs and chants are an essential part of the rituals. They are used for healing, to herald the changing seasons or to bring an abundant harvest.

If a person is taken ill, a rite is chosen by the diviner, and a singer, who will be expert in the precise order and detail of the chants, will be appointed. The *hogan* or home of the sick person is then swept and cleansed, and healing herbs and necessary materials for the ritual will be brought in. Up to a hundred people can attend a healing on the final night of the 'chantway'.

'Hailway' and 'waterway' chants treat illnesses caused by cold or rain while the 'shooting chant' is used to cure burns from lightning, arrows or snake-bites.

The 'night chant' or *Yeibichai*, is a major ceremony and lasts for nine days, carried out only between the first frost and first thunderstorm. It is a ritual of winter renewal and rebirth and may be held in a ceremonial hogan.

In Ancient Greece, howling incantations were made by female seers and in Mediaeval times by sorcerers and magicians who sang complex lists of angelic and demonic hosts and used Hebrew invocations to summon spirits. The 20th-century occultist Aleister Crowley also used chants as a way of connnecting with cosmic powers.

Wiccans sometimes use chants in group rituals to raise and create a cone of power, using the various names of the gods and goddesses in cycles of increasing speed and intensity until the power is released on the final utterance.

Healing Sounds

In the Classical world, Aristotle believed the flute was a powerful instrument of healing, while Pythagoras taught his students to transform emotions of worry, fear, sorrow and anger through singing and playing a musical instrument.

Aaron Watson, an archaeology research student at Reading University, and Dr David Keating of the university's cybernetics department, studied such ancient sites as Camster Round, a passage grave in Caithness, Maes Howe in Orkney and Newgrange in Ireland. They found that monuments were able to bounce sound around according to a principle known to physicists as Helmholtz resonance. This gave rise to speculation that stone circles and passage graves were actually used for rituals of sound healing.

The French ear, nose and throat specialist, Dr Alfred Tomatis, who has developed methods of treating autism and hyperactivity using sound, was called to a monastery where an outbreak of ill health among the monks could not be explained. Dr Tomatis pinpointed the cause as a change in the monastic tradition; the monks had stopped singing Gregorian chants. When chanting was resumed, the monks' health immediately improved.

Music and Colours

Colours have their own sounds that correspond with their particular vibration. By beginning a colour visualisation with a particular note or notes of colours that are needed for empowerment, protection or healing, with the name of the colour sung as a mantra, it is possible to amplify inner colour energies and attract them from the natural world at large.

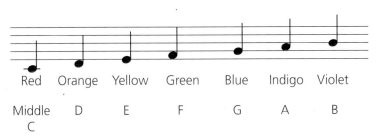

Red	Orange	Yellow	Green	Blue	Indigo	Violet
Middle C	D	E	F	G	A	B

SHAMANISM

Shamans are magician-priest-healers found in the diverse communities of India, Australia, Japan, China, Siberia, Mongolia, Africa, among the Bedouins in the Middle East and in North, Central and South America. In fact, shamanism may be the oldest continuing spiritual practice in the world.

It is said that the shaman, who could travel in the upper and lower worlds, and meet both demons and the masters and mistresses of all living things, was the first communicator of religion and that priests of later faiths have lost the ability to see and enter the realms of spirit of which they tell their congregations.

The word 'shaman' means 'to heat up; to burn; to work with heat and fire' and the shaman's essential characteristic is a mastery of energy and fire as a medium of transformation. In some parts of Siberia and Mongolia, the blacksmith was regarded as a superior shaman, for it was the mastery of fire that enabled mankind to survive even in inhospitable conditions. A lantern or fire forms the focal point of many shamanic ceremonies.

Shamanism is the oldest 'green' spirituality, maintaining balance and harmony in society, and within the individual. It also connects with the essences of fish, birds, animals, rocks and trees in this world, in the lower realms and in the upper realms where wise ancestors may reside.

The Origins of Shamanism

Some geographical links can be made between shamans of different lands that would explain the similarity of practices and beliefs. For example, the almost identical shamanic practices and legends of the Inuit or Eskimo people in the very north of the

American continent and of those living in north-eastern Siberia may have been connected by the land bridge that crossed the Baring Straits thousands of years ago. However, there are remarkable similarities in ritual and belief between shamans in areas where there was no such physical connection. This suggests that shamanism is an archetypal form of spirituality, addressing the fundamental needs and tapping into the universal powers, of the human psyche.

The key to the parallel development of ritual may lie in the common needs of the early hunter-gatherer societies. Shamanism still survives in places such as the Arctic Circle and Siberia where hunting is the main supporter of life.

The most important function of the shaman was to negotiate with the master or mistress of the herds or fish either in the underworld, under the sea or in the upper realms so that hunting might be fruitful and the tribes know where to look for animals. He or she would obtain a promise of herds and foreknowledge of their whereabouts from the master or mistress of the hunt, from helper spirits and even from animal spirits, in

return for sacrifices, rituals and high standards of moral behaviour, which would ensure the continuing plentiful supply of food for the tribe.

One of the earliest recorded examples of shamanism is the Dancing Sorcerer. Painted in black and found on the cave walls of Les Trois Frères in the French Pyrennees, this shamanic figure, who may be a man in animal skins, dates from about 14,000BC and stands high above the animals that throng the walls. Only his feet are human and he possesses the large round eyes of an owl or lion, the antlers and ears of a stag, the front paws of a lion or bear, the genitals of a feline and the tail of a horse or wolf.

More traditionally, the shaman is pictured as a skeleton since he is ritually dismembered and reassembled or reborn, having either married a spirit of noble caste or been suckled by a spirit mother or animal. The tradition of the ancient Bone Woman who dismembers and reassembles the shaman in a new enlightened form is one that underpins many ancient sacrifice myths, such as the dismembering of the Egyptian Osiris and the reassembling of his body by Isis.

The Upper and Lower Worlds

The lower world is sometimes called the world of myth and fairy tale. It can be beneath the sea, under the ground, or accessed through a hole in the ground such as a mineshaft, a well, a tree or a doorway. It offers practical help, guidance and sometimes a confrontation with the terrors within our own psyches, and may look like a surreal version of an ordinary landscape.

In the lower realms, action is often in the form of an adventure, the hero or heroine rescuing a trapped soul or overcoming a monster, aided by helpful animals, or mythological or archetypal figures. The 'trickster' may be encountered here sometimes as a coyote or raven (the finest shamans are tricksters who confront others with alternative views and their own hypocrisy). The animal helpers offer the explorer the necessary qualities to complete the journey successfully, and these strengths may be brought back to the material world.

The upper world is that of spirit guides, guardian angels and wise ancestors whose festival fires are seen as the Aurora Borealis or Northern Lights. Here too reside the sun and moon deities. This realm can be reached by climbing a tree, ascending a rope or, in the case of the *mekigar* or Aborigine clever men or shamans in Australia, ascending the cord that unwinds from the testicles, which was given in initiation by the All-Father, and finding a hole in the sky. Most frequently in many shamanic societies, the shaman travels upwards by flight on the back of a bird. Many shamans' costumes have a bird's head or wings.

The realms are not rigid, for in Siberian mythology the deities concerned with the earth reside in the lower realms. Neither upper nor lower realm is superior but, like yin and yang in Oriental philosophy, are part of the ever-changing pattern.

Shamanic Healing

A shaman has to seek a lost soul to restore a patient's health – in traditional cultures a person has up to four souls representing different aspects of their personality – either in the upper or lower realms, in the underworld or in high trees. A loss of soul might lead to infertility, illness or misfortune to the individual or community and the shaman would negotiate symbolically doing battle with spirits who might represent the negativity of others or unresolved conflicts from past or present. The shaman would travel in either a spirit canoe or ride his or her horse, whose hoofbeats were heard in the drum.

Rhythmic Stimulation

Music and Song

Many shamanic ceremonies are accompanied by music and song. The patient and audience hear the drumming and singing that the shaman uses to enter an altered state and might enter a lesser trance themselves. Traditional shamans use a pentatonic scale – one of five notes instead of the eight in today's standard notation. The basic rhythm, perhaps focused on the repetition of a single phrase, increases in speed and intensity, until the shaman is carried astrally out of his body. The physical body then becomes inert or may communicate in different voices or languages.

Drums and Rattles

Shamans keep up a steady 240 drumbeats a minute, beating one hand in time to the passing seconds while beating four beats with the other. This rhythm aids the lower vibrations of the ear and is considered the single most effective tool for raising consciousness and allowing healing to take place.

Other shamans use a rattle which addresses the higher vibrations, frequently made with a gourd and often decorated with symbols of flight or power animals.

Dancing

The shaman's feet and body move with increasing speed and intensity so that the shaman can dance him or herself out of the body.

All these techniques – music, dancing, drumming and using a rattle – have been carried through to neo-shamanism, and are also often used to stimulate astral projection.

THE TAROT

The Cards of the Tarot

The Tarot pack comprises 78 highly illustrated cards: 22 major cards, or trumps as they were traditionally called, 40 numbered cards in four suits and 16 court cards. The first 22 cards form the Major Arcana (arcana means hidden wisdom). Many people use these alone, since they represent the main archetypes known to mankind in all times and places: the father, the mother, the wise man, the fool or child, the trickster, the divine sacrifice, the judge, the hero and the virgin, as well as fate, the sun and the moon. They also represent the eternal quest to confront the basic human dilemmas of finiteness and being ultimately alone (except in the mother's womb or when pregnant).

The 16 court cards have four more cards than the usual playing deck because the Jack takes on two aspects: the Page and the Knight (sometimes the Page is regarded as the feminine side of youthfulness). The court cards can have different names such as Princess and Prince, Daughter and Son, even Priestesses and Shamans instead of the traditional Queens and Kings. These cards usually refer to personalities or aspects of personalities and, as such, focus on relationship issues.

The Minor Arcana includes 40 numbered cards from Ace (or one) to ten in each of the four suits. Pentacles, coins or discs, Cups or chalices, Wands, spears or staves, and Swords correspond with the four traditional playing card suits: Diamonds, Hearts, Clubs and Spades. These suits also represent the four basic elements earth, water, fire and air and the spiritual qualities associated with these elements. In a reading, these number cards tend to refer to specific issues and courses of action (see Alchemy, p. 94 and Formal Magic, p. 57).

Pentacles (Earth)

Cups (Water)

Wands (Fire)

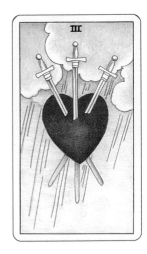

Swords (Air)

Pentacles (EARTH)

The Pentacles represent the dish from which Jesus ate the paschal lamb. In Celtic tradition it represented the ancient Stone of Fal, on the sacred hill Tara on which the High Kings of Ireland stood to be crowned.

Cups (WATER)

The Cups are symbolic of the Grail cup from which Jesus drank at the Last Supper, and the Cauldron of the Dagda, the Celtic father god, that was never empty and had great healing powers.

Wands (FIRE)

The Wands symbolise the sacred lance that pierced Jesus's side. In Celtic tradition the wand is the spear of Lugh, who slew his own grandfather, the old solar god Balor, with it and so brought about the new order.

Swords (AIR)

The Swords stand for the sword of King David and, in Celtic tradition, the sword of Nuada of the Silver Hand whose sword hand was cut off in battle, but who had one fashioned of silver and went on to lead his people to victory.

More than any other form of divination, the Tarot has been unfairly regarded as dark magic, the stuff of malevolent clairvoyants in B horror movies because of the erroneously literal interpretation of the Death, Devil and Tower of Destruction cards.

The Origins of the Tarot

Theories on the origins of the Tarot vary greatly. Tarot cards in their present form seem to be a Mediaeval creation, although the images and themes are much older. The Bibliothèque Nationale in Paris has 17 ornate cards, 16 of them Tarot trumps, originally believed to have been made for Charles VI of France around 1392, but now thought to be Italian, dating from about 1470.

One suggestion is that Tarot cards sprang from northern Italy, in the valley of the Taro River which is a tributary of the River Po. This could have influenced the Italian name for the cards *Tarrochi* and the French name Tarot. The modern Tarot pack comes directly from an Italian version, the Venetian or Piedmontese Tarot, which has 22 trumps. The same form is found in the French pack called the Tarot of Marseilles that is still sold. Both designs were in popular use by about 1500 in northern Italy and France. The four suits each represented a different strata of society: the swords as the aristocracy, cups or chalices as the clergy and monastic orders, coins for the merchants and batons for the peasants.

Another theory claimed that gypsies brought the Tarot with them in their long trek to Europe from India via the Middle East. In 1781, a time when Egypt was seen as the source of all knowledge, Antoine Court de Gebelin, a French Protestant clergyman who became fascinated by the occult, found some friends playing with Tarot cards. He believed the cards contained the secrets of the priests of Ancient Egypt, the lost Egyptian magical wisdom written by Thoth, the Egyptian god of inspired written knowledge, encoded in Tarot symbolism to protect this wisdom from invading barbarians.

The Arabic word *Tariqua* (the way of wisdom) bears some resemblance to Tarot and the Ancient Egyptian word *Ta-rosh* means 'the royal way'. Some believe that the Tarot was named after Taueret, the Great One. Taueret was the Egyptian hippopotamus goddess who was the protective deity of childbirth. It was said she gave birth to Tarot wisdom.

A fourth root was seen in the Kabbalah, the source of Hebrew esoteric wisdom. *Torah* is the Hebrew name for the first books of the Old Testament. The mystical Golden Dawn group attaches much significance to the Latin word *rota* meaning wheel which is engraved on the Wheel of Fortune card. When reversed it gives Tora(h), and can be rearranged as Taro. By learning the Tarot wisdom, one can step off the wheel of unremitting fate.

In 1856 Eliphas Levi made the first connections between the Tarot and the Kabbalah, linking the 22 Major Arcana cards with the 22 letters of the Hebrew alphabet that each possessed inherent esoteric significance. Eliphas Levi Zahed, usually shortened to Eliphas Levi, was the pseudonym for Alphonse Louis Constant, born in 1810 and originally a Catholic priest who became interested in the study of magic and coined the word occult. He strongly believed that it was still possible to acquire a great deal of knowledge through the Tarot packs including wisdom associated with the Kabbalah and the Bible.

Other explanations link the origin of the name with the Celtic Tara, the sacred Hill of the High Kings of Ireland, which was in use until the 6th century. This view was given credence by Robert Graves, the historian and novelist, who believed that the 22 Tarot trumps were derived from the 22-symbol Celtic tree alphabet.

The greatest influence on modern Tarot reading is Arthur Edward Waite who, in 1891, joined the Order of the Golden Dawn, a mystical group whose members included the poet W.B. Yeats. The Tarot was important to the Golden Dawn which traced its traditions back to the mysterious Rosicrucians of the 17th century (see p. 86) who in turn drew on alchemical and Kabbalistic traditions, traceable, it is said, back to Moses. The Rider Waite Tarot pack with its richly illustrated Minor Arcana was intended to promote visions as well as be used for divination, and this pack has influenced countless others, especially with Minor Arcana meanings. It was Waite who associated the four suits with the four sacred objects of the Holy Grail quest, namely the Pentacles, Cups, Wands and Swords.

Some Tarot practitioners do identify the Tarot journey with the quest for the Holy Grail. The Emperor is seen as the Fisher King whose wounds have caused the land to become barren, the High Priestess is the female guardian of the Grail and the Fool himself is the seeker. The Hermit, Charioteer and Lovers also feature in early Grail legends.

THEOSOPHY

What is Theosophy?

Theosophy has been one of the most formative spiritual influences upon the modern Western magical tradition and upon many New Age practices, both by introducing Eastern spirituality to the West and by reviving the magical and spiritual traditions of ancient civilisations.

The term theosophy is derived from the Greek *theos* (god) and *sophia* (wisdom) and is rooted in the belief that all major religions are derived from one original universal religion, like branches on a tree, although expressed through different myths and symbols. Modern theosophy draws on theosophical thought from China, India and Egypt, from the works of the Gnostics, Neoplatonists and Kabbalists, and from the philosophy of Plato, Plotinus, Apollonius of Tyana, and Mediaeval mysticism and magic.

The ideas of karma and reincarnation from the East, which offered alternative views of heaven and hell and emphasised personal redemption and natural laws of justice, contributed significantly to the beliefs of the Theosophists. They also developed the concept that chakras, psychic energy points within the body, were permanent and personal energy sources, rather than temporary manifestations of universal energies, attained during altered states of consciousness, which is the Eastern interpretation.

Theosophy maintains that spiritual power and wisdom are within the reach of everyone, regardless of race, creed or background. The great teachers, such as Buddha and Christ, are among those who have reached this goal and whose evolved wisdom guides others on the path. The true teachers of theosophical wisdom were thought to be the *Mahatmas*, the old souls or masters of wisdom as they were known in India, who had completed their own cycles of earthly incarnations, and returned to teach those who might understand and disseminate their message.

Theosophical Beliefs

The Nature of the Soul

Theosophists believe that there exists an omnipresent, eternal, unknowable, boundless and immutable principle. The human soul, like the universe itself, emanates from this divine source and is immortal and indestructible.

The soul reincarnates into successive lives, evolving from the mineral kingdom, through the plant and animal realms. Once the soul has reached the human level and attained self-consciousness, it does not regress back into animal form, but embarks on a long journey, evolving towards perfection on the physical, mental and spiritual planes, and ultimately returning to the highest spiritual sphere.

Humankind possesses a seven-fold constitution, extending from the physical plane to the plane of pure spirit. The three higher planes form the higher self, or essential soul, that reincarnates from life to life and is refined through the accumulation of virtues and experience on the lower mental and physical planes. The higher levels or higher self can be reached through dream interpretation of messages from the higher realms, and by developing intuitive powers through meditation, studying myths, from the wisdom of the great teachers who come periodically to impart this knowledge to humankind, through moving towards harmony with nature and by compassion and altruism towards others.

Karma

The law of karma operates throughout the universe and within individual lives, ensuring natural justice whereby people cause their own joys and sorrows. On the higher planes, it is believed that thought is tangible and so every thought as well as every action affects others and the environment, so having karmic consequences.

The Akashic Records

At the highest level of consciousness, the super-conscious level, a person can gain access to the akashic records. These are tangible expressions of the tribal mind or collective unconscious, universal chronicles of everything that has ever been thought, said or done by everybody who has ever lived. According to Helena Blavatsky, the founder of the Theosophical Society, all knowledge of the past is imprinted on a subtle substance called akasha or soniferous ether.

These records can be reached by those who are less spiritually evolved through dreams, astral projection, meditation or channelling. A wider knowledge of past and future is therefore available to us all if only we are able to access it.

Helena Blavatsky and the Theosophical Society

The 19th century mystic and medium, Helena Petrova Blavatsky, was the inspiration behind the Theosophical Society. She was interested in magic and the occult from her childhood in Russia. Being born in the seventh month of the year, she was called a *sedmitchka*, which meant she was able to control supernatural beings. On the night of her birthday the servants would carry her around the house and stables, sprinkling holy water and repeating magical incantations to appease the *domovoy* goblin who lived behind the stove and might bring bad luck.

As an adult, Madame Blavatsky spent two years in Tibet studying with the Lama. Here, in 1856, she is said to have witnessed evidence for reincarnation, in the form of a four-month-old baby who was placed on a carpet in the centre of the ceremonial hall in front of the Lama. The infant stood up and walked up and down, chanting: 'I am Buddha, I am the old Lama, I am his spirit in a new body'.

On her return to Russia, Madame Blavatsky discovered that Russian intellectuals were beginning to take an interest in the paranormal and she made a great impression with her powers of mediumship. Her cousin Sergei Witte wrote: 'On one occasion she caused a closed piano in an adjacent room to emit sounds as if invisible hands were playing upon it. This was done in my presence, at the insistence of one of the guests.'

Madame Blavatsky was eventually guided by her 'mysterious Hindu' to travel to America. In New York, she met Henry Olcott, a middle-aged lawyer, who became fascinated by psychic phenomena and by Madame Blavatsky herself. In 1875, together with William Q. Judge, they founded the Theosophical Society, originally to study such subjects as Egyptian mysteries and the Kabbalah. The society was organised under conditions of great secrecy, with members writing F.T.S. (Fellow, Theosophical Society) after their names, and acknowledging one another by secret signs, mainly derived from Egyptian occultism. However, accusations of fraud were made against Madame Blavatsky, concerning alleged communications from the Mahatmas in letters to society members, which appeared to be in her own handwriting. It may be that, as with some channellers, Madame Blavatsky used the medium of automatic writing in trance without being aware she was doing so.

During December 1884, Richard Hodgson of the Psychical Research Society in London went to the Theosophical Society headquarters in Adyar, India, to investigate the society. The following spring, he condemned Madame Blavatsky and her associates as frauds. It was not until 1986 that the Psychical Research Society published an article in its journal admitting that Hodgson had ignored all the favourable evidence concerning Madame Blavatsky and that the Theosophists were owed an apology.

Certainly the prolific nature of Madame Blavatsky's writings would indicate some truth in her claim that the Mahatmas dictated the wisdom that appeared in her books, lectures and articles, by impressing thoughts in her mind which she later wrote down.

In 1877 she produced *Isis Unveiled* which contained over 1,300 pages, followed by the *Secret Doctrine* in 1888 which was 'dictated' by the Mahatmas and included material on the creation of the universe, the evolution of humankind, and the traditions underlying various religions, mythologies and philosophies. During 1889 Madame

Blavatsky completed two more books, *The Key to Theosophy* which is an introduction to theosophical thought and philosophy, and *The Voice of the Silence*, a mystical and poetic work on the subject of enlightenment.

After her death on May 8, 1891, which Theosophists commemorate with White Lotus Day, Annie Wood Besant continued her work, converting her London home into the society headquarters. By the 1970s there were theosophical organisations in more than 60 countries.

THE WESTERN MAGICAL TRADITION

Different Kinds of Magic

Magic, either in the form of folk customs or more formal ceremonies, can be categorised under the following headings. These types of magic are true of all kinds of magic around the world at all times.

Sympathetic Magic

Sympathetic magic involves performing a ritual that imitates what is actually desired. For example, in some states in America's midwest money is incubated by adding copper coins to a jar kept in the warmth of the kitchen.

Contagious Magic

Contagious magic involves acquiring the power of a symbolic object or animal. For example, hunters might wear the pelt of a lion to bring them to the beast's courage and ferocity. A couple wanting a baby would make love on top of an ancient fertility earth symbol, such as the phallus of the chalk figure of the Cerne Abbas Giant in Dorset, to absorb concentrated fertility energies from the earth. The magic can also work the other way round, for instance when young couples made love in the fields on May Day Eve to encourage the earth to be fertile.

Attracting Magic

Attracting Magic embraces both sympathetic and contagious magic to bring about a desired result. For example, in one of the oldest floral spells, a lover would strew five red roses along the pathway between his or her own and the lover's house, calling the loved one's name. Then, from a sixth rose, five red rose petals were burned in the flame of a pure beeswax candle at dusk, one after the other, while the spell caster chanted:

> *Burn a pathway to my door, five rose petals now are four.*
> *Four to three in candle fire, bringing closer my desire*
> *Three to two, I burn the rose, love no hesitation shows*
> *Burn two to one, till there are none, the spell is done*
> *Come lover, come.*

The remaining rose was placed in a vase of water at an uncurtained window and the candle left to burn so that its light was cast on the rose.

Banishing and Protective Magic

This involves driving away bad feelings and fears by casting away or burying a focus of the negativity. For example, a word or symbol for an unhappy memory or unresolved anger would be cast into fast-flowing water or etched on a bone that would be buried and left to decay. This is the origin of the saying 'to bury the bone'. An ancient ritual involves tangling threads to represent negative feelings and shutting them away in a jar with a lid, saying with each thread:

> *Tangle the anger,*
> *Tangle the pain*
> *By this knot*
> *Make me free again.*

When full of threads, the bottle was buried.

The Origins of the Western Magical Tradition

Magic itself goes back to the first efforts of Palaeolithic people to influence the hunt through sympathetic or contagious magical means by donning antlers and animal skins and re-enacting the kill. However, the origins of formal magic can be dated from the Magi, the wise men from the Assyro-Babylonian culture more than 4,000 years ago, who manipulated fire and lightning and were said to have been the first to discover electricity. It was the same priestly caste who took gold, frankincense and myrrh to the infant Jesus after following the star that had been predicted would lead to a new prophet and saviour. The Magi also invented the zodiac with its 12 signs and the 360° circle that is still used in horoscopes in modern astrology.

During the 7th and 6th centuries BC the legendary prophet Zarathustra, or Zoroaster in Greek, taught that fire (*asha*) was the divine energy of Ahura Mazda, the god of goodness or the sage god. He believed that the rotation of the celestial bodies, the waxing and the waning of the moon, the seasons and the rise and fall of tides were all due to the Law of Asha (cosmic fire) through which the universe was slowly being refined towards perfection. There was also a constant battle between good and evil both in the cosmos and in the hearts of people. In modern zoroastrianism, the sacred fire still burns continually from those early days and is ritually fuelled at least five times a day.

Zoroaster's writings have given him the title of the Father of Magic, in the rituals he set forth, in his concepts of the duality of equally matched good and evil forces, and the central role of fire in magic. Fire is still one of the alchemists' and magicians' most powerful tools and manifests in the great seasonal fire festivals, fire magic and all forms of candle magic.

Another important influence on modern Westernised magic that has filtered from Egypt through Hermetic magic (see below) is the belief in names and words, ie, that everyone, whether human, spirit or deity, has a true but secret name. If a magician could discover this name, he or she could command the person or spirit to obey every command. This belief underpinned Mediaeval and Renaissance angelology and demonology and has survived in modern incantations and use of the deity names in Wiccan ritual. However, this is not used to command a deity, but to tap into the archetypal power.

The Hermetic Tradition

The Hermetic tradition of Western magic was a root influence on modern magic, as well as forming the foundations for alchemical practices over many centuries. It is named after the semi-divine 1st-century Egyptian sorcerer Hermes Trismesgistos, whose Emerald Tablet was said to contain the secrets of all magic.

Its key principle 'As above, so below', the opening words on the Emerald Tablet, established the most important occult principle; that through the connection between cosmic and earthly realms, anything might be achieved through magical manipulation of this connection in ritual and by mastery of the mind.

Hebrew Magic

Much Hebrew magic may have come from Egyptian sources. The greatest mystical system, the Kabbalah, was said to be dictated by God to Moses. It is the secret or esoteric wisdom that was subsequently encoded in the early books of the Bible.

The second major influence on Hebrew magic is attributed to Solomon, the son of David, who was a powerful magician, possessing a ring that enabled him to summon and control every spirit in the cosmos. His name was given to the magical books whose theories were known as Solomonic magic. The most famous magical work bearing his name is called *The Key*

of Solomon, and gives details of magical hours, summoning spirits, ritual tools, invisibility, binding incantations, talismans, archangels, colours and metals. It formed the main source of Mediaeval ceremonial magic and was regarded by A.E. Waite, creator of the influential Waite Tarot system and a prominent member of the Order of the Golden Dawn, as the ultimate source of magical knowledge.

The Golden Dawn and Modern Magic

The actual birth of modern magic is often calculated from the creation in 1887 of the mystical and secret Order of the Golden Dawn. Though it was not a magical order itself, the Golden Dawn was responsible for the collation and teaching of ancient magical practices and, through the publication of material by disaffected former members, was connected with the wider dissemination of ritual magic and the Western magical tradition.

The society is said to have been initiated when Dr William Wynn Westcott, a London coroner and a Rosicrucian (a member of the secret German mystical order) discovered part of an ancient manuscript, written in brown-ink cipher. This revealed fragments of mystical rituals of the Golden Dawn, a mysterious organisation which, unusually for the time, admitted women as well as men. Westcott contacted Fraulein Anna Sprengel, a Rosicrucian adept living in Germany, whose name was found with the manuscript, and she gave permission for the society to be established in England. The aim of the Golden Dawn was 'to obtain control of the nature and power of [one's] own being'.

It has been suggested that Westcott invented the mysterious German woman to authenticate the secret society, in the same way that Madame Blavatsky gave authenticity to the Theosophical Society with the writings of the Mahatmas she claims to have channelled.

The society taught through a series of progressive stages many of the subjects that now form the core of New Age wisdom. These disciplines included alchemy, astral projection, astrology, clairvoyance and scrying, geomancy, the Hebrew alphabet, Kabbalistic correspondences and practice, Tarot divination and, after the initial stages of learning, ceremonial magic and ritual.

Although the Golden Dawn exists today in various forms on both sides of the Atlantic, the original society survived for less than 20 years. It is said that, although the knowledge and practices were profound, its members did not follow the aesthetic lifestyles of Eastern practitioners. This is thought to have caused many of the schisms and power struggles that occurred. However, the dissemination of what were hitherto secret and elitist rituals and knowledge by Aleister Crowley on his defection, published in his own journal *Equinox*, prepared the way for the New Age movement.

WICCA

What is Wicca?

Wicca is not modern witchcraft *per se*, but a contemporary neo-pagan religion. Neo-paganism regards the divine life source as a part of nature, not a force beyond creation. *Paganus* is the Latin word for country dweller, and so *neo* or new paganism looks back to the old nature religions and the many deities that embodied different aspects of the natural world. This divine source of life is manifest as the god and goddess within us all, male, female, animal, bird, tree and flower.

Some Wiccans do call themselves witches, a link with the men and women who, throughout the ages, have preserved what is sometimes regarded as the oldest religion in the world. Many Wiccans cast spells for healing, happiness and the environment as well as to empower personal or group projects. But for others, their connection with and awareness of the sanctity of the earth is expressed through ritual, dance, song, celebration and invocation without directing natural energies through specific magical channels.

Most Wiccans worship some form of the Earth Goddess and her consort, the Horned God. Along with other earlier deities, the Horned God became demonised with the advent of Christianity and so was incorrectly associated with the forces of darkness.

ESSENTIAL WISDOM

Wiccans do not recognise any demonic figures in their religion. The Horned God and the Goddess are the creative male and female principles, not in opposition with each other but complementary and necessary parts of the whole. There are variations within Wicca; some traditions emphasise the Goddess while others regard them as equal, but assuming different aspects according to the season and ritual. For example, the Goddess is seen as the earth or moon deity, and the Horned God is connected with the sun or corn.

The Origins of Wicca

One powerful school of thought links Wicca with the earliest forms of religious and magical ritual, namely the evolution of the Horned God from the earlier God of the Herds who, like his prey, was depicted with horns and wearing animal skins. According to this view, ritually honouring the earth began when early men and women lit juniper twig tapers in inner caves to honour the Earth Mother in whose cave (or womb) they found shelter. The 'magic man' of these early tribes wore antlers and animal skins in order to bring about a successful hunt through dance and chant.

Goddess worship evolved from the concept of the Earth and Moon Mothers as sources of fertility, birth, death and rebirth and came to incorporate the role of the Goddess of the Grain. In the evolving agrarian societies, the Goddess ruled over the summer, while her horned son or consort became God of Vegetation, the deity of the winter and, by association with the death of the crops and the leaves, also of death and the afterlife. These core functions, and the ritual coupling in spring to create new life, formed the basis of many religions but kept its purest form in the unbroken tradition of Wicca. Even in Wiccan tradition, however, the male and female god forms have assumed many names and different functions as society becomes more complex.

In this tradition, the old ways were handed down through the generations, often in secret to avoid persecution by a suspicious society. The Book of Shadows, the name for the collection of herb lore, ritual, mythology and seasonal celebrations, is the most treasured possession of a coven or individual Wiccan; the reference to shadows merely demonstrating that the knowledge within it was secret. In the days before widespread literacy, ritual and herb lore were handed down orally through the family, especially the female line. Some witches had their personal Book of Shadows burned after their death as it was considered to contain so much of the witch's essence that it might hold her back.

Another theory traces the origins of modern Wicca, which began to re-emerge with the repeal of the Witchcraft Act in 1951, in part to the research of the Victorian Charles Leland whose books revealed that witches were still practising in Italy during the 19th century. These witches, he wrote, were still worshipping Diana in a tradition that began in 500BC in Ancient Greece. Diana is still a major goddess form beloved by significant numbers of Wiccans who, because of her strong association with the moon in all its phases, is an icon of fertility, love, the hunt, the earth and, though a virgin goddess, as protector of women in childbirth.

Leland is regarded as a major influence on Gerald Gardner, the retired civil servant who established modern Wicca. Sir James Frazer's *The Golden Bough*, written in 1890, also provided a valuable source of knowledge on magic and ritual through-out the world, especially in the 1950s and 1960s during the formative years of modern Wicca, though in recent years some people have disputed its accuracy.

Wiccan Rituals and Ethics

The chief moral codes are the Wiccan Rede and the Threefold Law. The Wiccan Rede states: 'An [if] it harm none, do what you will'. This deceptively simple statement refers to the self as well as others. Its positive intent, the Threefold Law, states that whatever you do or send to others will be returned threefold, a great incentive to positive thought and action.

Rituals are held at Wiccan *sabbats* and *esbats*. The eight sabbats are described in Seasonal Magic (p. 209) and celebrate the Celtic eightfold year on the solstices, the equinoxes and the old fire festivals to mark the passing of the seasons. Esbats are ceremonies traditionally held at the full moon but can mark any moon phases and are occasions when a coven meets formally. There are also many ceremonies to mark transitions in the life cycle, such as handfastings or weddings and rites of passage to welcome a recently deceased Wiccan to the familiar circle whenever he or she wishes to draw near.

Wiccan covens or groups, which can be of any number and do not have to be the mythical 13, vary in organisation and formality. Dedication of a new member usually ceremonially marks the beginning of the path to learning about Wicca. Initiation, perhaps after a year and a day or a similar recognised magical period, will confer formal entry in a coven or tradition, or may mark the transition of an existing member to a different level of knowledge and responsibility. The section on Formal Magic (p. 57) describes some of the more formal rituals and tools used.

Being a Hedge Witch or Solitary Practitioner

The term 'hedge witch' comes from the old practice of a witch planting hawthorns round her home as a sacred boundary. Many Wiccans begin as solitary practitioners and a number prefer to continue in that fashion. Other people who follow the old ways do not subscribe to any tradition but use herbs and divination in a way often passed down by older family members. Indeed, many of our grandmothers and great-grandmothers who possessed a remarkable intuition, read the tea leaves or made herbal concoctions were called witches as a joke by their own families – and were just that!

WITCHCRAFT

Throughout history and in literature, witchcraft has been endowed with negative connotations, for example, the hags in Shakespeare's *Macbeth* or the biblical Witch of Endor, who raised the spirit of King Samuel at the demand of King Saul. Samuel told Saul that his army would be defeated by the Philistines and his kingdom taken by David, which came to pass, because of Saul's own weaknesses rather than the intervention of black magic, although the witch was blamed.

The positive side of witchcraft and the practice of white magic is becoming more acceptable in the modern world, although there is still a great deal of prejudice especially in the UK even against witches who practise only empowering and healing magic. The word 'witch' is itself neutral, implying knowledge of magic without reference to its intent. However, one theory says that the word is derived from the old English word *wita* meaning wise. In fact, the Wiccans were the wise ones and their name has been adopted by one of the most popular neo-pagan religions (see p. 87).

Though the Wiccan religion is, for example, recognised by the US army, pagan chaplains are found in some hospitals and universities in the UK and books on spells sell in great numbers, the media are still ambivalent about witchcraft, with the cosy Disney witch at one end of the spectrum and X-movie devil worship at the other. The Hampshire witch Sybil Leek was invited on the US *NBC Today* show in the late 1960s apparently for a serious discussion on her craft. On arrival she was presented with a cauldron and asked to recite the *Macbeth* 'Double, double' witches' speech. On my first appearance on a top UK show in 1998 I was greeted by a set containing a cauldron, broomstick, flying bats and mock Gothic castle – and I was discussing ghosts.

The Origins and History of Witchcraft

It is said that witchcraft goes back more than 20,000 years to Palaeolithic times.

After the formation of the Christian church, the worship of the old gods was forbidden and nature festivals supplanted by religious ones. However, in 597AD, Pope Gregory acknowledged that it was better to try to graft the new festivals on to the existing solstices and equinoxes, and, for example, Easter is now celebrated close to the spring equinox. Churches and abbeys were erected on the sites of old pagan temples and were rededicated with holy water.

The builders of the new shrines were the creators or descended from the creators of the former edifices and so images of the green man, the early god of vegetation, fauns and satyrs were introduced into the design of cathedrals and churches.

The old ways continued in country places until the time of the Reformation and even priests would join in pagan seasonal celebrations. However, the tide was turning. In 1450, two German Inquisitors, Henrich Institoris Kramer and Jakob Sprenger, wrote and published the *Malleus Maleficarum* or *Hammer of the Witches*, which pre-scribed the application of torture to extract confessions and offered justification for the persecution of those who followed the old religion, and by 1484, Pope Innocent VIII had produced his Bull Against Witches.

Shakespeare endeared himself to James I by making his witches evil because the King himself had written a book condemning witchcraft called *Daemonologie*. In 1604 James I passed his harsh Witchcraft Act, which was not repealed until 1736. James was drawn to study the subject by the 1590–92 trials of the Scottish North Berwick witches. Agnes Sampson, a local and respected wise woman, was implicated along with many others in an alleged coven, by the confession under hideous torture of a maidservant Gillie Duncan, herself accused for displaying apparently miraculous healing powers she could not explain. Agnes, also cruelly tortured, confessed to James himself, who became involved in the case, that the witches had created terrible storms to drown him, by casting a cat into the ocean, its paws bound with the limbs of a corpse, on the instructions of the Devil. In spite of her confessions, which she hoped would save her, Agnes was strangled and burned. She obviously did have clairvoyant or telepathic powers for she had repeated to James a private conversation he and his bride, Anne of Denmark, had shared in Norway on the first night of their marriage.

Healing and mediumistic abilities were regarded as the work of the Devil at the time of the witch trials, though true Devil worshippers are believed by recent researchers to have been disaffected Christians in the Middle Ages. They were thought to be rebelling against the structures of a faith where wealthy abbots lived like lords and corrupt churchmen demanded tithes for the church to finance war and politics while the poor starved.

The ancient Horned God of the countryside, originally God of the Hunt and Herds was very different from the Horned Devil of the Christian church. The gatherings around fires at full moon derived not from occult practices, but were circle dances when villagers danced on the lightest day of the month for pleasure and to connect with the powerful energies of the land. Under torture and the promptings of the Inquisitors, the old ways were given a more sinister interpretation.

The worst period for witch burnings and hangings in Europe and Scandinavia was between the mid-15th and early 18th centuries. Matthew Hopkins, the Witchfinder General who died in 1647, brought about the executions of at least 236 accused witches, mainly in the eastern counties of England, and often upon flimsy charges because accusers were paid a bounty – as was Hopkins himself for any successful prosecutions.

The number of witches officially executed during this period is generally accepted as about a quarter of a million, although many more were illegally lynched or hanged by mobs eager to blame bad harvests or dying cattle on a scapegoat.

About three-quarters of all killed as witches were women, mainly lower-class older women, also healers and village herbalists, wise women and midwives. The latter were especially vulnerable in times of high mortality, because of the superstition that witches needed unbaptised babies that they could sacrifice to the Devil.

In the colonies of America where witches were hanged, the most notorious trials were those at Salem between 1692 and 1693. During this mass hysteria, 141 people from the town and immediate area were arrested, 19 were hanged and a landowner,

ESSENTIAL WISDOM

Giles Corey, an innocent spectator, was pressed to death by heavy stones; an execution that took three days. Even a dog was hanged for witchcraft!

The hysteria began with accusations by teenage girls who had been dabbling with the occult and whose experiments went wrong. A four-year-old child, Dorcas Good, was the youngest victim to be accused of witchcraft and imprisoned. Dorcas was released on bail after her mother was hanged, but her younger sibling died in prison. Dorcas was driven insane by her experience.

Although the last execution for witchcraft in England was Alice Molland in Exeter in 1712, it was not until 1951 that the later Witchcraft Act of 1736 was repealed and replaced with the Fraudulent Mediums Act.

The old ways were still practised in remote places until Victorian times and beyond, covens being mainly family affairs, and the poet Rudyard Kipling makes reference to them in his poem 'Oak and Ash and Thorn'.

After the repeal of the Witchcraft Act in 1951, witches slowly came out of hiding. In 1954, Gerald Gardner wrote his first book *Witchcraft Today*, opening the way for people who had no family connections to learn about witchcraft. This led to the formation of the Wiccan religion through which modern witchcraft has evolved, although not all Wiccans practise magic or use the term witch in connection with their religion.

PART TWO

Traditions,
Myths
& Folklore

ALCHEMY

The word 'alchemy' comes from *chyma*, Greek for the casting or fusing of metals. Alchemy was also known as 'theurgy', the Divine or Great Work. The fundamental aim of alchemy in the Western world was to create the Philosopher's Stone that would transform base metal into gold. The Philosopher's Stone was a powder or elixir rather than an actual stone, just as the Holy Grail was a spiritual icon as well as a physical object. The discovery of this stone would bring the key to knowledge, enlightenment and healing, for if it could elevate base metal, it was believed it might also heal physical ills, slow or even reverse the ageing process and, on a spiritual level, restore the divine connection man lost with the fall of Adam.

The emphasis of Eastern alchemy was to make a perfect elixir of gold that, when consumed, would enable a person to use celestial knowledge for human benefit and gain immortality.

It is difficult with the modern divisions between religion, philosophy and science to accept what was, until the 17th century, the interconnectedness of wisdom. Not only were alchemists the predecessors of the later modern chemists and biologists, but were skilled in medicine and herbalism, and many were also great magicians. Magical, astrological, symbolic and Kabbalistic knowledge were a vital part of an apprentice's training.

In alchemy the three kingdoms, mineral, plant and animal, correspond with the three alchemical elements, salt, mercury and sulphur. These elements, which were concepts and processes rather than actual substances of that name, represented the body, soul and spirit awakened and refined during the alchemical process. When purified and integrated in the right way, it was believed they would form the Philosopher's Stone or quintessence, the fifth and greatest element formed by the synthesis of the other four. The four traditional elements, Earth, Air, Fire and Water, also vital for the processes, were contained in the *prima materia* or 'first matter' that was the

source material for alchemical processes. Salt related to Earth, mercury was both Air and Water and sulphur was Fire.

The Great Work could take months, years or even decades to execute and the alchemist would need to be pure in soul and action to be fit to undergo the task. As the work progressed, so he or she advanced spiritually.

The problem of researching and writing about alchemy is that the art was shrouded in secret, not least because a man or woman who was attempting to make gold out of base metals was regarded as a political threat as well as a challenge to established religion in attempts to change the order of the universe.

The History of Alchemy

Western and also perhaps Eastern alchemy was influenced by Ancient Egypt which was famed for its skilled metal work, creation of alloys and metal tinting.

Alchemy was, according to myth, created in Egypt by the god Thoth. Like many conquering races, the Ancient Greeks, who invaded Egypt, combined Egyptian native deities with their own. For example, Thoth, god of letters and science, became Thoth-Hermes, Hermes being the Greek god of writing, medicine and communication.

The invention of alchemy is usually attributed to Hermes Trismesgistos (thrice-blessed Hermes) who was probably a 1st century powerful Egyptian sorcerer who, after his death, became worshipped as a god. It is claimed that the legendary Emerald Tablet, said to contain all magical knowledge and the principles of alchemy, was discovered by Alexander the Great in the mummified hands of Hermes Trismegistos. This, plus other books attributed to Hermes Trismegistos, forms the foundations of the mystical tradition Hermeticism that is closely associated with alchemy.

Others say that alchemical knowledge dates from about 200AD and comes from the Gnostic community in Alexandria, an area of alchemical expertise. Certainly, during the Alexandrian period (4th to 7th centuries AD), alchemy flourished, influenced by the Gnostics and by Hermetic groups in the Mediterranean.

Although alchemical wisdom flourished in the Greek and Arabic worlds, it did not reach western Europe until the late 10th century, and the flow of knowledge increased throughout the early Middle Ages, as the Crusades began to open the East culturally. It is said that in the 14th century, Nicholas Flamel did transmute mercury into silver or gold three times, either by magic, science or a mixture of both.

The Emerald Tablet that was engraved on many alchemists' walls did not reach the West until 1460, when both Classical and Middle Eastern documents were brought to Florence from Constantinople after its fall. The translation of the Emerald Tablet in 1471 opened the floodgates to other magical and alchemical tracts and the creation of many that were attributed to ancient sources.

With the Renaissance and the interest in all matters classical, many famous magicians or 'mages', wise men and alchemists emerged throughout the 15th and 16th centuries, including Paracelsus, Agrippa and Count Saint-Germain. Theophrastus Bombastus von Hohenheim, or Paracelsus, was a 16th century philosopher and physician of extraordinary learning who worked within the alchemical tradition to create a holistic system of medicine.

Alchemy remained popular until it was discredited only in the early 19th century with the discovery of oxygen and the composition of water. Sadly, much of its wisdom was also lost and the validity of some of this knowledge, especially the herbal wisdom, is only just being rediscovered.

Alchemical societies still meet on astrologically important days, but the majority of modern alchemists operate secretly as solitary practitioners and have just a single apprentice. In recent years the spiritual aspects of alchemy have become predominant and the ancient symbols and processes have been incorporated into systems for development of the psyche, both formally using the alchemical stages of initiation and informally for meditation and visualisation work.

The Application of Alchemy

The number and stages of the Great Work vary in different accounts and are clothed in secrecy. But there are generally considered to be either seven stages to represent the seven days of creation or 12 stages for the 12 signs of the zodiac.

The Prima Materia

Originally, Egyptian black silt, a source of fertility, was used as the prima materia or basic unrefined matter. Prima materia was considered by some alchemists to contain the embryo of the Philosopher's Stone which might be released by a variety of processes and transmutations.

The prima materia was symbolised by the *ouroboros*, the world serpent that swallowed its own tail and so nourished itself in an ongoing cycle. This is not unlike the concept of ritual dismemberment and recreation of a shaman by the ancient Bone Goddess, which is a feature of surviving hunter-gatherer societies today.

Colour was also attributed special powers and the alchemical process followed a series of colour changes that marked the different stages from prima materia to Philosopher's Stone. According to the Golden Treatise of Hermes, the alchemical sequence was black, white, green, red and gold, but other systems added yellow and purple. The following is an inevitably simplified version of the basic processes and images.

Symbolism in Alchemy

Dreams and visions were considered important vehicles for the transmission of knowledge from a divine source to the alchemist. Each process was described by animal or bird images that encapsulated the spiritual significance of the alchemical quest. Mercury, which represented the process of transformation, was symbolised by the green dragon, which was released from the prima materia and ultimately transformed into the stone.

Earth, the ouroboros, was depicted as a deer or unicorn, water as a fish, fire as the mythical salamander called from his cave and air as the realm of the birds.

The prima materia, formed through putrefaction, representing natural, physical decay and spiritual death of the body and ego, was first destroyed by fire or acidic processes. This was described as setting two dragons against each other to release the male and female elements. Then took place the sacred marriage of male and female, King Sol (the sun) and Queen Luna (the moon) by mixing the sulphur (male) and mercury (female). The union was rooted in salt, sustainer of life. Further treatment of the substance by heat led to *nigredo* or blackening, symbolised by the black raven. The fertilised soul of the materia remained in a hermetically sealed vessel, leading to the resurrection, announced by the appearance of iridescent colours known as the Peacock's Tail.

The product of the union, the Divine Hermaphrodite, was nurtured by adding liquid condensed from the vessel during the previous process. The concept of feeding back an essence to its offspring for nourishment is likened to the pelican who was said to feed her young with the blood of her breast. So the Hermaphrodite grew and whitened to form the elixir or White Stone as it is known, which, if correctly made, could transform base metals into silver. This female tincture was equivalent to the moon. To create the gold-giving tincture, further processes and refinements followed until the Red Rose or red stone, as it was symbolically called, was obtained. This was the final result of the process. Hermes said of this fruition: 'The Son is invested with the red garment and the purple is put on.'

Gold, the final colour, spiritual if not actual, could be obtained if a true Philosopher's Stone was applied to base metals as this might reconnect humanity with the godhead. However, almost every alchemist spent many years, some an entire lifetime, in the elusive quest to find the correct formula for the physical transformation – though they may have gained the spiritual enlightenment through the search that some argue is the true purpose of alchemy.

AMULETS AND TALISMANS

These are charms, either carried or placed in a house, to offer protection against danger and illness. Technically, an amulet is protective, warding off illness or danger, but when charged with healing energies, it becomes a talisman and is said to attract health and good fortune. In practice the terms are interchangeable. Particular symbols have been associated with luck and protection over many centuries and so the individual charm seems to share in the cumulative energies stored in the archetypal symbol of good fortune that is drawn or carved upon it.

The first amulets were probably small painted stones. Examples have been discovered at the foot of rock painting sites in western Canada and date from prehistoric times. From ancient times people also crafted amulets and talismans of tiny figures representing gods, sacred animals, arrows and tools. Indeed it was suggested that jewellery originated as the wearing of amulets, made of lucky or healing stones (see Crystallomancy, p. 24).

Chinese parents still give their children jade amulets to protect them and keep them healthy, and in many countries coral jewellery is worn by young children to prevent falls. Coral and bell teething rings were given at christenings and naming ceremonies in both the Eastern and Western worlds to ward off negativity and nightmares.

In mediaeval Europe, holy relics carried by pilgrims – sometimes the bones of saints or what were believed to be fragments of the true cross – were believed to cure ills and even transport murderers straight to heaven on execution (see Arthur Conan Doyle's *The White Company* for a graphic example). Amulets would also be made from an animal part, for example a mole's foot; because it had a very cramped appearance, it was worn as an antidote to cramp.

The most popular amulets have been made of natural substances that were readily available to poorer people and yet still regarded as magical.

Clover

It was believed that Eve took the clover from Eden with her. According to legend the trefoil or shamrock became an emblem of Ireland in 433AD when St Patrick used it as a symbol of the Holy Trinity. But its use is much older. It was used by the Druids as a charm against evil and to attain clairvoyant powers, and was considered a powerful charm in Ancient Greece where it was said to be the food of Zeus's horse. It was also found on Roman coins, and painted in Egyptian tombs.

The rarer four-leaf clover is said to be found growing where a white mare has given birth to her first foal. Who finds one, it is said, will find treasure. According to a Sussex rhyme:

*T*he first leaf is for fame,
The second for wealth,
The third a glorious lover
and the fourth for health.

Placed under a pillow it induced dreams of a future lover. The two-leaf clover worn in the right shoe by a young unmarried woman on a journey was said to ensure that the first young man she met would become her husband.

Horseshoe

Made of protective iron and in a sacred shape, horseshoes were considered lucky in Greek and Roman times, ten times more so if found rather than bought. Some finders of cast-off horseshoe nails made them into lucky rings.

Legend says that St Dunstan, the 10th century English saint, was a gifted smith and that the Devil entered his forge at Glastonbury Abbey and demanded to be shod. The saint seized him by the nose with a pair of tongs and refused to free him until Satan promised never to enter a house or forge again that had a horseshoe nailed to the wall.

Nailing an iron horseshoe over a door with the convex side pointing up is said to offer protection against sorcery, bad luck and the evil eye. For good luck, the horseshoe should be nailed with the convex side pointing down. Horseshoe charms in a charm bag or worn on a bracelet also attract fertility.

In mediaeval Britain three horseshoes were nailed to the end of a sick person's bed head with a hammer laid across them to the chant of: '*One for God, one for Wod and one for Lok.*' God represented the Christian element but where the old ways lingered, Wod was Woden, the Anglo-Saxon All-Father, Lok, which give us our expression 'one for luck' was Loki, the god of evil who must be appeased. The hammer represented *Mjollnir*, the magical invincible hammer of Thor, the thunder god who was also associated with fire and the forge.

Lucky Coins

Coins were believed to be lucky because they were engraved originally with the image of a god and then royalty, who were supposed to have magical powers that were transferred to the token.

The most famous remarkable coin was the Lee Penny, said to have accumulated healing energies powerful enough to cure whole cities. It began as a magical stone, said to have been used by Saladin, the Saracen king, to cure Richard the Lionheart of a deadly fever by giving him water in which the talisman had been dipped three times.

The stone reached the Lee family in Scotland after Sir Simon Lockart captured a powerful emir, or Muslim ruler, in Palestine during the 14th century. Part of the emir's ransom was the stone, by now credited with the power to stop bleeding and heal wounds. It was passed on through the family and set in the reverse side of an Edward IV groat, regarded as an especially sainted king. Water in which the coin had been steeped according to the ancient ritual was sent throughout the UK. Whenever a town was afflicted by plague, the Lee Penny would be requested. In the reign of Charles I, the city of Newcastle paid a bond of £6,600, an enormous amount, to save the city from the plague – and apparently its success rate was very high.

Coins with holes are considered especially lucky and in northern Europe gold coins are believed to give protection against drowning because they were prized by the Viking sea goddess Ran who was said to love gold above all things.

A silver, gold or bronze holed coin worn around the neck is said to ensure the owner will never be without money. In Ancient China copper was used to produce coins with holes in the middle through which a string was passed. Since *tong* means 'together' as well as being the word for pure copper, copper coins were placed in the bridal bed to ensure a lasting union.

The US had a strong tradition of 20th century lucky coins. For example, coins known as 'pocket pieces' are usually bronze or gold-plated created in the same sizes as the US quarter, half-dollar and silver dollar. They augur good luck and financial prosperity and bear traditionally lucky symbols such as the horseshoe, four-leaf clover, wishbone or rabbit foot. Not surprisingly they were incredibly popular during the Great Depression in the 1930s. On the reverse side of the coins were images such as the flying eagle, and they bear messages like 'Take me for luck'.

Magical Bags

Until Victorian times, when country folk moved to a new home or when a couple set up home for the first time together, they would fill a little red bag with symbols of love, health, wealth and happiness: a pinch of salt, a piece of cloth, a tiny lump of coal, a silver heart or piece of silk cut into the shape of a heart, a silver sixpence and a piece of bread. The bag would be sewn up in red thread or tied with a red drawstring thread and the following words chanted nine times:

This bag I sew [or carry] for me
And also for my family,
Let it keep through every day,
Trouble, ills and strife away,
Flags, flax, food and Frey.

The last line referred to flagstones for a home, flax for clothing, food and Frey, the old northern European god of fertility. Sometimes the bag would be replenished on New Year's Eve at midnight.

The Native American Indian medicine bag held an assortment of objects with magical and healing powers, often dictated by dreams and visions. Many tribes believe in *manitou*, whereby if, on finding a particular object, a person has a psychic sensation, sometimes described as a sense of sudden excitement or awareness, the object takes on great magical and healing significance. All tribes possessed such a bag which would be opened before a special event or ritual, symbolising the release of the power. The medicine bundles were passed down by their guardians, and personal bags were buried with their owners or bequeathed to a chosen relative.

Abracadabra

In earlier times, this popular cry by magicians was considered a powerful talisman, which was used by the Gnostics in Rome for invoking the aid of good spirits as protection against disease, misfortune and death. It may have been the name of an ancient god, lost in time or disguised, because to speak the name of a god was often regarded as evoking misfortune, especially among the Kabbalists, an esoteric sect of the 2nd century Hebrew world, who used Abracadabra as a protective charm to invoke the Holy Trinity (see Kabbalah, p. 262).

Abracadabra remained a popular charm and was used in Europe during the Middle Ages. It was also sold as a talisman, often wreathed with lavender during the Great Plague of London in 1665 to offer guard against infection. It was recited nine times to offer protection and banish negative forces, beginning with the full word and ending with the single A sound. The chant was then reversed to attract good luck and prosperity, ending with the full word Abracadabra.

ABRACADABRA
BRACADABR
RACADAB
ACADA
CAD
A

Sammonicus, a Gnostic physician, used this magical triangle shape for curing agues and fevers. He believed that the letters should be written down on paper, folded into the shape of a cross and worn round the neck for nine days. Then, before sunrise, the charm should be cast behind the patient into an east-flowing stream.

CURSES

What are Curses?

Curses are deliberate malevolence directed towards another person by magical means, whether by spells, incantations or by sending evil in a symbolic form. Not only witches and sorcerers, but ordinary people and even priests, have in all cultures and all times inflicted a deliberate psychic attack on enemies. In the case of professional magicians and witches, this can sometimes be done on behalf of someone else for a fee. Malevolent attack is different from the evil eye, which tends to stem from unconscious envy or jealousy.

Mary ann evand

I act thise fell apon your grong my
ball heart wishing for you to never
rest no reat non sffep the rester
part of your life I hope your
flesh will waste away

and I hope you will never
spend another penny of
aught to have

Wishing this from
my whole heart

Deathbed curses were considered most potent, since not only did the final surge of the life-force go into the curse, but the damning words could not be reversed by the perpetrator.

Cursing was in earlier times – and is still by some indigenous magicians – also used for the protection of homes, treasure stores and burial places. Burial place curses may remain unactivated until the site is disturbed by grave robbers or unwitting archaeologists.

Priests in mediaeval times would perform a version of the forbidden Black Mass. This was held in a ruined church, beginning at 11pm and finishing at midnight. The Mass was said backwards, and the Communion wafer was black and had three points, rather than the conventional circular shape. Instead of consecrated wine, water from a well into which the corpse of an unbaptised child had been thrown was used. The sign of the cross was made by the ministering priest on the ground with the left foot. This ceremony was said to cause the cursed person who was the focus of the ceremony to waste away.

Even within the established church of the time, boundaries between natural prohibitions and curses were blurred. For example the Bell, Book and Candle Excommunication ritual was close to a curse in words and form, condemning the excommunicated person to eternal fire with Satan; a candle representing the cursed soul being extinguished. In mediaeval sorcery too there was no clear division between black and white magic, and the great magicians, who included Popes, would summon and bid demons as well as angels to do their will.

The most common method of cursing a person in black magic involves using an effigy such as that described in Candle Magic, p. 14. The effigy is created from the melted wax of a black candle, representing the victim, and pins are stuck into it. Curse images were used from early times in India, Persia, Ancient Egypt, Africa and Europe – and the practice continues in parts of Africa, India, the Middle East, the West Indies and Central and South America.

The last attested candle curse in England was in 1843 when, during a prosecution for assault in a Norwich court, Mr and Mrs Curtis declared that a certain Mrs Bell had bewitched Mr Curtis by lighting a black candle, sticking pins in it and muttering curses over an oyster shell filled with dragon's blood.

Poppets or dolls were also made from clay, wood or cloth and used. An effigy would be painted or embroidered to resemble the victim, and hair clippings, nail parings and even pubic hair from the victim were attached to the doll. The doll was then harmed or destroyed and, in the case of a faithless lover, the heart and genital area would be pierced with a pin. The intention was to transfer the pain to the victim by a process of sympathetic magic. This negative use of cloth poppets has detracted from their healing properties when they are filled with health or love-bringing herbs.

Animal or human hearts or eggs were buried, often close to the victim's boundaries, so that as they decayed, so would the cursed person.

Stone and Crystal Curses

Gems, bones, shells, crystals and even ordinary stones were, and still are in some indigenous cultures, believed to contain living energies that could be manipulated to absorb negative as well as positive powers. Diamonds were said to carry a special curse if they were originally stolen or given for the wrong reasons, a belief dating from an Indian legend of a goddess who cursed diamonds after her diamond eyes were stolen by looters. The Hope Diamond purchased by Louis XVI in 1668, has, it is said, brought misfortune to many of its owners. For example, at one stage, it was bought by the Russian Prince Kanitovski who gave it to his French mistress, a dancer, to wear for her performance at the Folies-Bergère. He became suddenly mad with jealousy that others were sharing her beauty and shot her dead while she was on stage. Two days later Russian revolutionaries stabbed the prince to death.

I have come across cases of such curses in my own research. Carol, who lives in Berkshire, received a cowrie shell from her future mother-in-law who lived in the West Indies. When Carol put it to her ear, tendrils of black smoke came out and the walls and ceiling of the room closed in on her. Then a ball of fire burst from the shell.

Carol took the shell to the river and threw it in, but was plagued by voices in her head and negative shadowy forms for weeks afterwards and eventually admitted herself to a psychiatric clinic. Years later, a friend of the family admitted that her prospective mother-in-law had gone to a practitioner in an outlying village in the West Indies and had had the shell cursed. This practice is called a 'sending'.

Protective Curses

The tomb of Tutankhamen was said to be protected by a curse upon all who opened it, as were other ancient tombs throughout Egypt and Asia. Howard Carter and the Earl of Carnarvon were the first to enter Tutankhamen's burial chamber in 1922 and found its treasures undisturbed by earlier grave robbers. Legend has it that in an antechamber they found an inscribed tablet which read: 'Death shall come on swift wings to him who disturbs the peace of the king.'

Whether or not this was true, six of the seven people present at the opening of the tomb met strange deaths within a relatively short time. A few months after entering the tomb, Lord Carnarvon, who was only 57, became ill and died in Cairo of an infection from an insect bite. It is said that when he died all the lights in Cairo went out, and back in England his dog howled and died at the same moment. When the mummy of Tutankhamen was unwrapped in 1925, it was found to have a wound on the left cheek in the same position as Carnarvon's fatal insect bite. By 1929 the total of strange deaths had risen to 11 among those connected with the discovery of the tomb.

In 1999 a German microbiologist, Gotthard Kramer, from the University of Leipzig, suggested that potentially dangerous mould spores may have been released that would have survived in the tomb for thousands of years – and so those who opened ancient tombs activated what was a natural, rather than a magical curse.

Modern Witchcraft and Curses

Cursing is against the Wiccan rede that forbids harm and the Threefold Law that says all actions return threefold to the sender. However, some witches among the Italian *Striga*, Mexican *Bruja* and some covens of Dutch Pennsylvanian witches do believe that cursing or 'hexing' is justifiable in order to stop harm being done to children or the vulnerable, whether human or animal, for example. A compromise among more liberal witches is to return the pain inflicted to the sender.

Cursing Wells

Water was also regarded as a powerful transmitter of curse energies. The most famous source of curse water is the Roman baths in Bath, Avon. Though they are healing springs dedicated to Sulis Minerva, the Celtic-Romano Goddess, they may also contain an ancient Roman curse.

Lead tablets, used because the metal was easy to inscribe, were engraved with curses by the Romans against known and unknown persons who stole property, harmed reputations or seduced wives. Some also demanded on the tablets that the unknown perpetrator of a crime might be unmasked. The tablets were then cast into the water, and unknowingly cursed those who were poisoned by the seepage of lead, not known by the Romans to be physically harmful.

Healing wells were also used for curses and in some cases this function became more important than the restorative properties. For example, St Elian's Well in Llanalian yn Rhos in Clwyd, Wales, was used until the late 19th century as a curse well, the well custodian casting a stone into the well on which the victim's initials were inscribed.

Repelling Curses

The unanswered question is whether a curse is more effective or indeed only possible if the victim knows of it, thereby activating the self-fulfilling prophecy or making the psychic connection. Pointing either a bone in some African nations, or a dagger such as the *kris* in Malaysia, at the victim can make that person lose the will to live, and he or she may be shunned by his or her fellow tribespeople.

My research suggests that a curse cannot be activated unless it is known about and those who approached ancient tombs would have known of the curse mythology, even if it was not written explicitly on the tomb. Carol feared her future mother-in-law and had been warned that there was great opposition to the union – and so she may have been subconsciously expecting negative magic in the gift, as the older woman was known to be involved in voodoo.

If the curse *is* known about, its removal traditionally involved seeking the help of a magic practitioner to reverse it or, in modern magic, redirecting the curse back to its sender, thereby bringing into action the Threefold Law. Folk remedies include filling a poppet with nettles and burning or burying it. Burning purple candles, on which the uttered curse is written backwards, is also believed to repel negativity.

The evil eye is said to be different to a curse in that its negativity is effective even when the person it is directed against is unaware of it.

Dice Divination

The Origins of Dice Magic

Dice magic was popularised by travelling people, especially those in fairs and circuses, because it was a very portable method of divination and one that crossed language barriers easily. The same set of dice was frequently used for gaming and for magic.

Dice of ivory, wood, metal and glass have been discovered among the relics of Ancient Egypt, Greece and Rome, marked with dots like modern-day dice. Robert Graves recorded that the Roman emperor Claudius felt safe to embark on his invasion of Britain because a dice roll promised success. The Druids used wooden dice, carved with *coelbrenn* (secret letters) on each face. These were cast like conventional dice and were used not only for telling the future, but also for passing secret messages.

Casting the Dice

Dice are not usually cast on a Monday, a Wednesday or in stormy weather. The best time for dice divination is said to be two hours after sunset on a calm night. Nineteenth century Western systems developed a fortune-telling method with lists of 30 or more questions linked to common dilemmas, for example, whether or not it was safe to travel. Two dice were rolled and, rather than being added up, different number combinations, such as a three and a two or a four and a three, directed the questioner to the appropriate answer from a large number of options. For example in answer to the question: 'Where will I find a missing item?', a roll of one–one might proclaim 'in the closet' while three–three would suggest that a child has it. Six–six would indicate the missing item was hidden in a box. Though such methods tended to concentrate on specifics, they were, according to contemporary sources, surprisingly accurate.

In another method also dating from the 19th century, three dice were cast into a chalk circle that was drawn on a board or table. The dice were shaken in a box or in the palm of the hand in total silence. Any dice that fell outside the circle were not read and if no dice fell in the circle the reading was abandoned, as conditions were said not to be propitious. The numbers of the uppermost face on each dice were added together. This form of divination was mainly surface fortune-telling. In more recent years dice divination has come to rely increasingly on numerological interpretations and uses the dice roll as an indicator of possible courses of action, rather than a fixed future.

Although the literal and clear-cut nature of the answers suggested a simple solution, people often read more into the solutions offered, and related them to their own personal lives. For example, the number might highlight unspoken fears about a person's lifestyle or temporary difficulties and offer reassurance, such as in the stereotypical phrase 'an illness soon to be past'. The ubiquitous 'travel over water' or 'news from overseas' beloved by Victorian diviners, often betrayed a restlessness in the questioner that demanded, if not a passage to India, then an expansion of mental horizons. If a dice fell on the floor while being cast, it was said to herald quarrels, and more than one of the same number cast indicated important news from abroad. If one dice landed on top of the other it warned a woman of a deceitful lover and a man of the need to take care in his ventures. Today, this translates in the first case as the need to address fears about a relationship, and in the second case, warns about taking unnecessary risks.

There is surprising consistency of meaning in the numbers in conventional dice divination over several traditional systems. The common interpretations are:

1   A new arrival, a baby or an unexpected sum of money.
2   A road that forks two ways, but the longest is best.
3   A pleasant surprise and the granting of wishes.
4   A disappointment.
5   A stranger coming soon bringing happiness.
6   There may be a material loss, but an increase in spiritual or emotional wealth.
7   Gossip and spite should be ignored.
8   An unwise course that will bring censure.
9   Joy in love, even a wedding.
10 Family happiness, leading to a meeting that will bring new opportunity in the business world.
11 Illness or unhappiness in someone close will be resolved.
12 A letter needing a quick decision – seek advice.
13 Tears and sorrow.
14 A new admirer who will soon become close.
15 The need to avoid being drawn into intrigue or trouble by others.
16 A pleasant and profitable journey, but delays must be avoided.

An Egyptian relief from the Temple of Seti I showing Seti making an incense offering to Horus.

A 17th century French sculpture of the Black Madonna

A 14th century illuminated manuscript depicting the Wheel of Fortune.

ABOVE: A 17th century Indian miniature depicting the crowning of the Great Goddess Devi.

LEFT: Ivory Figure of the Hindu Goddess, Kali.

17 Journeys overseas or dealings with those from overseas will be advantageous.

18 A great profit or promotion within a short period.

Tibetan Dice Divination

In the Far East dice were made of gems or crystals such as sacred green jade to add to their potency. In Tibet, as recently as the 19th century, dice were used purely for fore-telling events and not for gambling. Even today Tibetan Buddhist lamas cast the dice and interpret the oracle for devotees.

One system, invoking the Buddhist protectress Palden Lhamo, uses three dice offering 15 possible answers, with each answer broken down further to relate to different areas such as money or health. A number from one to six is indicated by dots on each face of the three dice. Diviners visualise their personal deity who will influence the roll of the dice. Some do refer to a divination book, of which there are many, written by different lamas. However, eventually the diviner moves beyond the texts and interprets the wisdom given directly by the spirit guide. The dice are made of bone, wood or conch shell.

A second system, sacred to the Buddhist saint of wisdom, Manjushri, uses only one dice. On its six faces are inscribed the last six of the seven syllables of a mantra, the sacred chant of Manjushri. This system requires devotees to visualise Manjushri in the sky while reciting his mantra and asking his blessing. Then the dice is thrown twice and the oracle consulted.

For a divination to be successful, it is said that the diviner should have a pure moti-vation and the person seeking advice should believe in the diviner.

Dice are used for resolving many spiritual and religious issues. For example, in June 1995, dice divination was used to identify from 20 boys the true reincarnation of the Panchen Lama. The divination dice were cast while pronouncing each young child's name three times.

DRUIDS

Druids were the Celtic high priests, and wise men and women, who provided a unifying force for the disparate Celtic tribes, so preserving a common culture, religion, history, laws, scholarship, healing, magic and science. Indeed the Roman writer Diogenes considered the Druids as equal to the Magi of Persia or the Chaldeans, the Babylonian wise men and priests with their mathematical, astronomi-cal and philosophical skills. There is historical evidence of Druids in Ireland, England, Wales and Gaul and it would seem that they also held sway in the Celtic settlements of Spain, Italy, Galatia and the Danube Valley, although under a different name.

Druidic knowledge of astronomy and sacred geomancy may have come from the priests of earlier megalithic times who built the great stones circles and standing stones. Though the earliest surviving classical references to Druids date from the 2nd century BC, there is now evidence of Celtic culture existing in Britain from the 2nd millennium BC, much earlier than previously thought – Druids may after all have connections with Stonehenge.

According to the Roman writer Pliny the Elder the origin of the term 'Druid' comes from the Greek *drus*, or 'oak' which was the Druidic sacred tree. *Duir* is the Celtic name for oak tree and *wid* means to know or see and is similar to the Sanskrit *vid*. *Dru-wid* was therefore he or she who possessed the knowledge or wisdom of the long-living oak. He or she who had gained such wisdom over many years might even control the elements.

Female Druids were highly respected, for Celtic society was certainly in earlier stages matrilineal. Being a Druid involved a lifelong training that began when a child was selected for their spiritual nature or early wisdom. It took 12 years or more to reach the first level, that of a Bard. The Bards were said to be the memory of the tribe. They preserved its history by learning hundreds of poems, stories and the secret tree alphabet, and creating new songs and poetry to record new events. Though many Druids knew Greek, to write things down was believed to diminish the power of the cultural memory, thus dishonouring the sanctity of the knowledge. Even the Romans would send their sons for druidic training in oratory.

The next stage in the training was that of the Ovate which took a further ten years or more. The Ovate studied natural medicine, divination and prophecy and passed between the dimensions. It was he or she who contacted Annwyn, the Otherworld, especially at Samhain, and travelled to the Realm of the Ancestors to seek their wisdom. Annwyn was believed to be either beneath the earth or a floating fortified island to the west of this world, associated with Avalon, the land of apples. It was thought to be a place full of light and joy.

Finally, after a further ten years of study, the novice became a Druid; a judge, philosopher, high priest of the tribe and adviser to kings and tribal chiefs, over whom they had authority.

After the formal druidic religion was wiped out in Wales by Julius Caesar during his conquest of Britain, the wisdom went underground and many minstrels travelled round carrying this knowledge and passing it on to secret converts as they sang the old songs for entertainment. Others fled to Ireland where the tradition lasted much longer.

Trees and the Tree Alphabet

The Celtic tree alphabet was like the songs and legends, used by the Druids to carry arcane knowledge of the Celts through times of persecution. It consisted of angular markings, signed out using different joints of the fingers, and incorporated a complex grammar for transmitting secret wisdom and lore. It was not used in formal writing except for inscriptions or markers and there are many disagreements about the definitive form of the symbols and even which trees are included in the alphabet.

Trees were sacred to the Druids because they acted as bridges between the realms of land and sky, transmitting water between these realms. Trees therefore created great power because, through them, the sacred triad of land, water (sea) and sky met, hence the central role of the tree in worship and divination. Mistletoe from the sacred oak was called the all-healer and was harvested on the midwinter solstice and also on the sixth day of the moon by a Druid in a white robe with a golden sickle and caught by virgins in a pure white cloth. The white berries were potent fertility symbols and regarded as the semen of the gods because they grew on the sacred tree upon which the gods bestowed their blessings.

The yew tree was also a special tree for the Druids because when it died, a new trunk grew within the old. It was therefore seen as a symbol of death and rebirth in the cycle of life.

The Wisdom of the Druids

Modern knowledge of the Druids comes mainly from classical writers. Julius Caesar, who regarded the Druids as a force of resistance to be crushed, nevertheless wrote of them: '*They know much about the stars and celestial motions, and about the size of the earth and universe, and about the essential nature of things, and about the powers and authority of the immortal gods; and these things they teach to their pupils.*'

Though popular literature associates their ceremonies with the great stone circles, Druids worshipped mainly in sacred oak groves, close to sacred springs and wells, and in places of natural power that long predated the stone circles. However, the great stone temples may have been used for the large festivals of the solstices and equinoxes, the rising and setting of which the stones marked (see Megaliths, p. 196).

Druidic Festivals

The Druids presided over the eight celebrations that marked the passing of the Wheel of the Year (see Seasonal Magic, p. 209). There were four great fire festivals when bonfires were lit in high places to strengthen the power of the sun, for fire was a potent symbol of cleansing and renewal to the Druids, transmitting magical energies as it flamed upwards to the sky. The fire festivals were interspersed with the solstices and equinoxes, the Druidic festivals of light. The Wheel of the Year marked not only the changing seasons and the planting, growing, reaping and laying fallow cycle but also the passing of the life of man in a continuing cycle of birth, maturity, death and rebirth.

The festival for which they are best known in modern times, mainly because of the controversy in recent years over access to Stonehenge, is Alban Heruin, the Light of the Shore or longest day. This is celebrated around 21 June when the Druids still hold three ceremonies: at midnight on the eve of the solstice, at dawn and at noon on the solstice to welcome the sun at its full power.

The Powers of the Druids

According to historical accounts, Druids possessed, through their long training, magical powers of divination and prophesy, healing and levitation. They were also able to shape-shift into the forms of animals and birds, especially owls or crows, and also into oak trees. They divined using water, cloud shapes, fire and haruspicy, the study of the entrails and flowing blood of a dying victim.

Druids believed that the soul was immortal and the souls of men resided in the Otherworld until they chose to be reborn and take with them the accumulated wisdom they had acquired.

A white bull, which was sacred to the Druids, was sacrificed on the midwinter solstice. A druid would then sit against the magical and protective rowan tree within the bloody skin, and a trance-like state was induced in which prophecies were made in answer to the questions of the tribe or individuals.

THE EVIL EYE

The evil eye operates on an unconscious level, transmitting negativity to another person. It is not a deliberate curse, but envy, jealousy or resentment towards some-one considered more fortunate, or directed at an object belonging to another, which provokes an intense desire to possess it.

This desire, whether focused on property, wealth, health or fertility, was traditionally believed to affect infants and children especially because they were vulnerable and open to psychic influences. The evil eye could also, it was said, be cast upon grazing animals, fruit trees and crops with which wealth was frequently bound. Houses might burst into flames, and ploughs break as a result of covetousness. Ironically, the influence was believed to be passed on by overt 'praise' of, for example, a pretty or healthy child, a fine animal or an orchard with trees in blossom, and so in more superstitious times and places, even a genuine compliment was feared. So a bad harvest, a sick child or a blighted fruit crop might unfairly be blamed on a stranger or someone who appeared different from the community and had tried to be friendly by admiring a newborn infant or a well-tended garden. In the Middle East, Italy and

Spain, Central America and Mexico even today, belief in the evil eye remains strong, especially in remote areas. Blue-eyed people are particularly under suspicion.

The History of the Evil Eye

The first references to the evil eye appear in the cuneiform texts of the Assyro-Babylonians, around 3000BC and it was referred to in many incantations such as the Assyrian chant:

Thou man, son of his God,
The eye which hath looked upon thee for harm,
The eye which hath looked upon thee for evil . . . .

The Ancient Egyptians also feared the eye and Egyptian women used eye shadow made from powdered lapis lazuli and also painted their lips to prevent the evil eye from penetrating their eyes or mouths.

Roman men, women and children so feared the eye that they carried phallus-shaped charms (to counter the oval female shape of the eye) in gold, silver and bronze as antidotes.

Professor Alan Dundes, of the University of California, Berkeley, who is author of *The Evil Eye: A Casebook*, says that evil-eye beliefs are Semitic and Indo-European in origin. China, Korea, Burma, Taiwan, Indonesia, Thailand, Sumatra, Vietnam, Cambodia, Laos, Japan, Aboriginal Australia, Maori New Zealand, Native North and South America and Africa south of the Sahara, do not have this belief as part of their indigenous culture. In these regions the concept was introduced by colonists and traders from Europe and the Middle East. My own theory is that the evil eye emerged when the system of land and property ownership was rigid and there was a sharp division between rich and poor.

Methods of Averting the Evil Eye

Because belief in the evil eye was relatively widespread and its powers did not seem to depend on the perpetrator possessing special psychic powers, fears of psychic attack were common – and still are in some locations. Therefore if a person did genuinely want to admire an infant or animal, he or she would afterwards spit or touch the infant to remove the eye.

If this was not done, the mother or owner would either offer a prayer or mediate the praise by pointing out a defect in the infant or coveted object. A child might even be smeared with dirt before being taken out and bells were hung from cradles and prams for the same reason. Horse brasses were also protective and would be handed down by carters and ostlers from father to son. Touching wood was another form of appeasement.

TRADITIONS, MYTHS & FOLKLORE

Detecting the Evil Eye and Mitigating its Effects

If a child or animal became sick, household accidents occurred or crops became blighted, the evil eye was a prime suspect, along with deliberate witchcraft. Water, oils or other liquids were used to remove the evil eye since it was thought that the eye caused the natural, sustaining fluids of life to dry up. One theory is that the origin of the evil eye was in desert regions where water was precious. In Eastern Europe charcoal, coal or burnt match heads were dropped into a bowl of water. If they floated, the evil eye had been cast. A local wise woman would be sought who knew the secret words to take away the influence – these formulae were passed down through the matriarchs of large families and communities. Holy water would sometimes be sprinkled on a victim – human, animal or blighted tree – at the same time.

In Italy, olive oil was dripped into water, a single drop at a time, while the matriarch recited her secret mantras. If the drops formed an eye shape, prayers would be said over the victim while oil was continuously dripped until a series of shapes appeared, but the eye formation was no longer there.

In Mexico, an egg was rolled across the supposed victim's body and then cracked to see if an eye formed in the yolk. If it did, a cross was drawn on the forehead with the egg while incantations were made. Afterwards the eggs were thrown away in a shady place or buried to prevent a second attack. Holy water was also sprinkled over the victim.

Charms Against the Evil Eye

Carrying charms, especially eye charms like the Eye of Horus, Horus being the Egyptian sun god, was regarded as a potent method of repelling attack. From Assyrian times, camels were traditionally protected by wearing a stone with a hole around their necks and horses in many cultures carried blue beads, sometimes made of turquoise, in their manes and bridles.

In Greece and Turkey a blue glass eye charm was said to mirror back the evil eye and thus confound it. In India, cord charms from which hang a blue bead are still worn by newborn babies. Once the cord breaks, the child is thought to be old enough to resist attack.

The most common protective symbol in India, Israel and in the Arab lands is an engraved eye within a palm, covered with magical symbols. This has become Christianised as the Hand of God or *manopoderosa*.

A Scientific View of the Evil Eye: The Staring Experiments

Modern researchers are moving away from the physical aspect of 'evilling' to an awareness that negative feelings can be carried telepathically when a person spontaneously visualises a cause of envy or resentment. So too is scientific research discovering that people are aware of being stared at even if they cannot see the person who is looking at them. The Cambridge biologist Dr Rupert Sheldrake is carrying out ongoing research into this subject and has discovered that a person's mind can reach out and affect someone they are thinking about, albeit benignly in experiments.

During the late 1980s scientists William Brand and Sperry Andrews conducted experiments at the Mind Science Foundation in San Antonio, Texas, using close-circuit television, in which subjects were asked to sit in a room for 20 minutes, letting their thoughts flow freely. Each individual was observed indirectly by the experimenters from a viewing room in a series of 30-second trials with rest periods in between. The sequence of whether a subject was or was not looked at followed an entirely random sequence. The subjects' unconscious bodily responses were monitored electronically and the results showed significant differences in skin resistance when the subjects were being looked at, even though they were not asked to try to pinpoint the times they were being viewed. Other experiments have also found significant correlation between subjects being secretly observed from another building and consciously identifying times when they believed someone was 'staring' at them.

If people are then aware of being the subject of resentment or envy, it is possible to invoke psychic protection from this unconscious malevolence, either by using protective crystals, creating psychic barriers around the home and self or calling upon angelic or spirit guides for protection. It is also possible, as with more deliberate curses, to reverse the energy and send it back to the perpetrator.

FATE

The concepts of fixed fate and free will are crucial to the processes behind divination and for the interpretation of information given by clairvoyance, mediumship and other psychic channels. They also have implications for the belief in reincarnation and the afterlife. I have also covered the issue of fate in the sections on clairvoyance, mediumship, precognition, prophecy and reincarnation, for if the future is entirely predetermined, then any divinatory process becomes entirely passive and to know what cannot be changed may be in a sense counterproductive.

The goddesses of fate, usually three sisters who are weavers or spinners of the web of destiny, appear in many cultures. Always above and beyond the power of even the Sky Fathers and the parameters of accepted time, they represent unanswerable questions that lie at the heart of spirituality.

The Hand of Fate

*F*IRST WITCH: *All hail, Macbeth! Hail to thee, thane of Glamis!*
SECOND WITCH: *All hail, Macbeth! Hail to thee, thane of Cawdor!*
THIRD WITCH: *All hail, Macbeth, that shalt be King hereafter*

Macbeth by William Shakespeare

TRADITIONS, MYTHS & FOLKLORE

The three witches or weird sisters on the stormy heath who greeted Macbeth with a prophecy of his future greatness are representations of the three fates. Yet the witches were not foretelling a fixed future, but one which depended on the decisions made by Macbeth and the thane of Cawdor. Macbeth was already thane of Glamis. His elevation to Cawdor resulted because the former thane committed an act of treachery, thereby forfeiting his life and title. Macbeth, as a favourite of King Duncan, was a likely candidate for elevation.

As for becoming King, the seeds of ambition were already within Macbeth, as was the cruelty necessary to kill Duncan. The hags were merely revealing one potential path, which Macbeth could have rejected.

Fate can change the lives of any of us in an instant: a lottery win, an unexpected promotion, a redundancy, illness or bereavement or falling in love. Yet many acts of 'blind fate' depend not on external forces, but are results, direct or indirect, of the acts and omissions of self and others.

Even illness may be caused by a genetic or personal physical weakness or the anti-social habits of others, such as pollution.

The Runic Concept of Fate

The Teutonic concept of destiny was a forerunner of the modern idea that humankind influences his or her fate by what he or she is, does and has been – so destiny is not fixed but constantly changing. The concept of the web is crucial to an interpretation of the future that seems to explain how clairvoyance is possible without denying free will.

Under one of the roots of Yggdrassil, the world tree of the Vikings and other Teutonic peoples, was the Well of Urd or Wyrd (fate), guarded by the three Norns, the goddesses of destiny. Here the gods held their daily council, and the Norns nourished the tree with water.

These three sisters, not unlike Macbeth's weird or 'wyrd' sisters, wove the web of the world and the fate of individual beings, mortal and gods. They wove, not according to their own desires, but according to *Orlog*, the eternal law of the universe.

The first Norn, Urdhr, the oldest of the sisters, always looked backwards and talked of the past which in Viking tradition influences a person's own present and future and that of his or her descendants. The second Norn, Verdhandi, a young vibrant woman, looked straight ahead and talked of present deeds which also influenced the future. Skuld, the third Norn, who tore up the web as the other two created it, was closely veiled and her head was turned in the opposite direction from Urdhr. She held a scroll which had not been unrolled, telling what would pass as a result of the intricate connection of past and present interaction.

In this tradition, personal 'wyrd' or fate could be affected by good and bad deeds and in turn could affect family and kinsfolk, who could then influence others in the family by their own fate. By personal interconnections, towns, states and even nations could build up a collective fate, implying that individual actions and decisions have a shaping influence far beyond the personal sphere.

Morphic Resonance

This is the belief that the fluttering of the wings of a butterfly can change the course of the world and that if someone smiles in London, by evening the smile will have reached Hong Kong or Los Angeles. Experimentally, the biologist Rupert Sheldrake has demonstrated that as animals of a given species learn a new pattern of behaviour, other animals in the species will subsequently tend to learn the same thing more readily all over the world, as a result of morphic resonance. The more that learn it, the easier it should become for others.

So personal fate is, in this view, like that of the wyrd, an interactive concept.

Fate in Different Cultures

In Ancient Greece, the fates were called the *Moerae* or *Moirai*: Clotho wove the thread of life, Lachesis measured it out and Atropos cut it off with her scissors of death.

The Roman fates were very similar, called the *Parcae*, three very old women who spun the fate of mortal destiny. They were Nona, Decuma and Morta. Nona spun the thread of life, Decuma assigned it to a person and Morta cut it, ending that person's life.

In Russia, the goddess of fate was said to live behind the stove. When she was happy, she appeared in the form of a tiny old lady, Dolya, who brought good luck, but when she was angry she became Nedolya, the shabbily dressed crone of bad fortune. Like the Albanian Fatit, who appeared at the side of a crib three days after a baby's birth and ordained a child's fortune, Dolya manifested either as a grey-haired old woman or a beautiful young one at the birth of a child. The Norns too would appear at christenings, leading to variations of the sleeping beauty legend in which the benign fate or fairy mitigated the curse of the malevolent one.

Fortuna

This Roman goddess is the most intriguing of all the fate goddesses, since she is blind or blindfolded. This implies that good fortune is a random affair, or perhaps even beyond the understanding of the goddess herself who may administer it according to dictates that are given by a higher power. She has given her name to fortune-telling and is depicted holding a rudder and a cornucopia, which is a symbol of potential wealth.

The Nexus Effect

It can be very dangerous and misleading when unscrupulous clairvoyants predict disaster or death, or even a golden future that results in the enquirer making no effort of his or her own in the real world. People can actually make a predicted result come true by unconsciously changing their behaviour or becoming overanxious, a mechanism known as the self-fulfilling prophecy. For this reason, traffic collisions do increase on Friday the 13th. A study of accident figures by Dr Thomas Scanlon, Public Health Registrar on the southern section of the M25 in 1995, revealed that although there were fewer people using the stretch of road on six consecutive Friday the 13ths, there were more injuries from accidents and the risk of an accident was increased by 52 per cent.

The nexus effect, rather than focusing on a fixed unchangeable fate, explains the future as a web. Throughout this web are nexuses or change points where the threads cross and open out into a variety of courses. What clairvoyants 'see' may be these change points that lie ahead where decisions can be made to affect the future course of events. This information can also be gained through personal divination and enables the questioner to identify alternative routes that can be taken at these nexus points, thereby gaining control over the future.

THE GRAIL

What is the Grail?

The Grail is usually represented as the chalice that Christ used at the Last Supper, in which His blood was collected after the Crucifixion. As such it signifies not only a source of healing and spiritual sustenance, but offers direct access to the godhead through the sacred blood it once contained. According to Roman Catholic doctrine, the wine in the chalice is transformed into the blood of Christ during Mass through the mystical process of transubstantiation. In other Christian religions the sacrament is seen as a symbolic representation of the holiness of Christ. The Grail legend is then an allegory for humankind's spiritual quest for enlightenment, a pathway to reach the heart of divinity.

Carl Jung regarded the Grail quest as a search for the essential self. To him, the restoration of the wasteland that results from finding the Grail represents an individual's progression towards the integration of mind, body and soul through experience. This universal theme may help to explain why there are so many different versions of the Grail legend, giving alternatives for the origin of, the search for and the location of the Grail, and even what it looks like.

Some legends identify the Grail as a small stone drinking vessel, others a larger silver cup. However, the most popular interpretation is that the original Grail cup was fashioned by Roman craftsmen into a gold and jewelled chalice called the Marian chalice, named after Mary Magdalene. There is the possibility that there were two Grail cups, one obtained by Mary Magdalene and one by Joseph of Arimathea, the wealthy merchant who cared for Christ's body after death. It has also been suggested that the Grail was the dish from which Christ ate the Paschal lamb with his disciples, which passed into the possession of Joseph of Arimathea, and was then used to gather Christ's blood.

The Grail was also regarded in another tradition as the alchemist's Philosopher's Stone, a precious stone brought down by the angels, or an emerald from Lucifer's crown as he fell to earth; whatever the origin, this stone was endowed with miraculous powers, and was the key to immortality.

TRADITIONS, MYTHS & FOLKLORE

The Origins of the Grail

In pagan times the Grail icon was known as the *Graal*, the sacred cauldron of creation and nourishment that symbolised the womb of the Earth Mother. Indeed cauldrons or cups of inspiration and rebirth have featured in Vedic, Egyptian, Classical and Celtic traditions from early times. The first Grail or Graal legend was told by the 6th century Welsh bard Taliesin, though like many of the Celtic myths it was not written down for several centuries, and was then Christianised by the monks who did finally record it. The legend speaks of the magic cauldron in Annwyn, the Celtic Otherworld. Its guardians were nine maidens and in some mediaeval stories a Grail maiden appears, carrying the Grail and offering sustenance from it, maintaining links with this older world.

In mediaeval times the legend of the Christianised Grail or sacred chalice became the focus of a quest by King Arthur's knights who themselves were transformed to represent the idealistic, courtly values of the Middle Ages, rather than those of King Arthur himself. The original Arthur was an ancient British king of Celtic origin who united parts of Britain in the 5th century against hostile forces after the collapse of the Roman Empire. In 496AD, under the command of Arthur, the Britons defeated the Saxons at the Siege of Mount Badon, the last of 12 battles which resulted in a generation of peace.

Grail Legend and Tradition

Most of the Grail stories were written between 1180 and 1240, mainly in French, as the Celtic influence was strong especially around Brittany, but they also appeared in German, English, Norwegian, Italian and Portuguese literature. There are two kinds of legend, the first centred around the quest for the Grail and the second dealing with the origins and history of the Grail vessel itself. It is the latter that has given rise to the most speculation and there is still a belief that the Grail may exist.

There is a strong tradition that the Grail and other sacred treasures actually came to England, though both date and location are uncertain. The following accounts are an amalgamation of the most consistent factors from the myriad stories of what is a multi-layered allegory.

Joseph of Arimathea

In this version of events, the Grail cup used in the Last Supper was obtained from Pilate by the rich merchant Joseph of Arimathea and used to collect drops of blood from the wounds of Christ's crucified body as he was prepared for burial. But when the body of Christ was missing after the Resurrection, Joseph was imprisoned by the Jews, accused of stealing it. The cup was confiscated or simply disappeared. However, Christ brought the Grail cup to Joseph in prison, making him its guardian, and each day a dove dropped a wafer into it – this is the same dove that can be seen in the Rider Waite Tarot Ace of Cups. Thus the Grail sustained Joseph for 42 years until he was released by Vespasian. Joseph brought the Grail cup to Avalon, identified as Glastonbury in Somerset, and founded a church on the spot where he planted his thorn staff, which instantly flowered, though it was mid-winter.

Bron, his sister's husband, came with Joseph to England (in some versions Bron came to England with the chalice after Joseph's death). Certainly after Joseph died, Bron became the Rich Fisher who fed many from the cup with a single fish, like the ever-nourishing cauldron of Dagda, the Irish Father God. The Grail was housed in a temple or castle, guarded by an order of Grail knights.

Bron was said in some legends to be immortal (explaining how he could live from the time of Christ until the time of Arthur), but was wounded in the genitals or thighs by a spear. As a result, the kingdom also withered and could only be restored when the true successor came and the Fisher was allowed to die. No one knew where the castle of the Fisher King was, not even Perceval or Perseval, the grandson of the Fisher King, and so the sacred guardianship remained uninherited. In many of the old myths the successor had to overcome or be more worthy and purer than the old deity/king in order for an imperfect order to be replaced by natural spiritual evolution.

At Pentecost, the Grail appeared floating on a sunbeam to the Knights of the Round Table who pledged to find it. Perseval, known as the fool, another link with the Tarot, went in search of the Grail, but had to undergo many experiences and much suffering before he obtained sufficient wisdom to be worthy of his sacred task. Merlin was his mentor (and secret adversary to test the youth). Perseval could only cure his grandfather, and so paradoxically allow him to die, by asking the correct ritual question: 'What is it that the Grail has served and what is it that the Grail serves?'

Perseval could then be told or read the secret words of Christ in a book – which has since been identified as the true Grail – written by Didymus, a disciple of Christ. Perseval was successful, the Fisher King died and the wasteland was restored. Perseval then took the Fisher King's place as the Grail keeper.

Mary Magdalene

A second explanation is that the Grail cup was used by Mary Magdalene to collect the drops of the blood at the crucifixion. In this tradition the Grail cup was discovered in the early 4th century after Emperor Constantine was converted to Christianity and his mother the Empress Helena ordered an excavation of Christ's tomb in Jerusalem. The 5th century Greek historian Olympiadorus claims that the cup was taken to Britain when Rome was sacked by the Visigoths, possibly passing to Arthur at his stronghold near Shrewsbury for safe keeping in a specially erected chapel, along with other sacred treasures.

In his book *The Search for the Grail*, Graham Phillips locates Arthur's kingdom at the Roman city of Viroconium, which was the most important Dark Age settlement, now a ruin five miles south-east of Shrewsbury.

The Crusaders

In several Grail legends, the Grail knights are identified as the Knights Templar. Constantinople in Turkey (now Istanbul) was said by the Crusaders to possess more holy relics than the rest of the Christian world put together and that its rulers searched Europe for the treasures. In Scotland, the Templars, specifically the Clairs, were the traditional guardians of various holy relics brought back from the Crusades. One suggestion is that the Grail is hidden within the Apprentice Pillar in the St Clair's Rosslyn Chapel, near Edinburgh. Other locations vary from Glastonbury to the most recent discoveries in Shropshire. There may be in fact several cups associated with the old legends, or the original may have been lost or destroyed. Though people will continue the search for the *true* Grail, its meaning has moved far beyond an actual and historical form to represent the search for the unattainable and perfect through which humankind can move towards personal perfection. The search for the Grail will, therefore, always be a pervading theme of spiritual development.

HEALING

Healing Energies

There are a number of different methods of transferring healing energies from healer to patient. For example, Mental Healing involves healing through mind power using telepathic channels and psychokinetic energies. This is an especially effective method of triggering the self-healing powers of the patient and involves visualisation, for example surrounding a person with a specific healing colour that may be missing or weak in their aura or may be associated with a specific illness (a dull or murky yellow may indicate problems with the digestive system, for example).

Magnetic healing also involves mind power, but because it transfers the energy between the magnetic field or aura of the healer and the aura of the patient, it is very energy intensive. Repeated treatments may leave the healer feeling exhausted or ill as a result of absorbing part of the patient's pain. In everyday life this method is adopted unconsciously by mothers when soothing away the pain of a sick child.

In all forms of healing, energies can either be transferred directly to the patient or focused on the sick person wherever he or she may be (even if they are hundreds of miles away). The former method, contact healing, channels the healing rays through personal contact between healer and the person or animal seeking healing, either by touch or through a crystal or pendulum. Absent healing is usually carried out either by speaking the name of the sick person or animal or by focusing on a photograph, an appropriately coloured candle or a poppet/doll (to represent the person) and directing the healing energies to wherever they are needed. This is the method by which healing can be sent into the environment and involves strong visualisation processes as well as psychokinetic energies.

Channelled Healing

Channelled healing is the most common and most traditional method of spiritual healing and does not cause a loss of energy in the healer, since the power is being transmitted from a higher source.

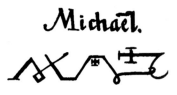

This form of spiritual healing calls upon a higher force of positive energy, whether interpreted as the Divine Healing Powers of God or an Archangel, the Mother Goddess or the life-force, known as *prana* in the Vedic tradition and ch'i in Chinese medicine. The healing process involves either mental or physical mediumship to channel healing energies through the healer into the person who is ill or distressed. Many churches have special services for healing, sometimes involving the laying on of hands in the tradition of Christ. Spiritualists ask for healing from Spirit as the highest form of energy and source of life, while neo-pagans ask for healing from the Goddess/God energies, who are sometimes personified as healing deities or directly channelled through ritual into the vehicle of the healer's body. The power of prayer is well attested in effecting cures, even when a person does not know he or she is being prayed for.

Healing Hands

Some people have a natural gift for healing which science cannot explain, though this gift may take months or years of training to develop. Simply by laying their hands on a sufferer, they can effect an improvement or even a cure for mental and physical conditions, and the person being healed may speak of warmth or heat flowing through the fingertips of the healer. In experiments at the Neuropsychiatric Institute at UCLA in California, energy flares emanating from the fingertips of healers were recorded by Kirlian photographic techniques. Research has determined that this healing energy is especially concentrated in those points on the body that correspond to Chinese acupuncture points. Hippocrates, after whom the medical Hippocratic Oath is named, wrote of 'the force which flows from many people's hands'. Franz von Mesmer, the father of hypnotism, carried out cures using a force he referred to as 'animal magnetism'.

Today, this force is often referred to as the biofield, the energy that permeates a human body. Some practitioners see this biofield extending past the human body to form the aura itself. At present, the biofield is seen as something existing outside the material world and therefore untestable. Indeed, it may never be measurable in terms of conventional science, since it would seem to emanate from the world of spirit. However, some modern physicians are exploring such less tangible forms of healing to supplement conventional methods.

Different Forms of Healing

Pranic Healing

This form of energy healing makes direct use of prana, or vital energy, in the treatment of a wide variety of ailments. Prana, it is believed, is obtained from direct sunlight and by drinking water that has absorbed solar energies. Such water is also used in magical rituals. Seasonal Affective Disorder (SAD) is thus regarded as a natural result of lack of solar prana, a fact now accepted by conventional medicine (although it can be dangerous if too much solar power is allowed to enter the body).

Ozone prana comes from the Air and is naturally absorbed through deep, slow, rhythmic or pranic breathing, and through the energy chakras of the inner and outer aura.

Ground prana emanates from the Earth and enters the body through the soles of the feet and so can be absorbed in natural places, such as beaches and hillsides, especially when walking barefoot.

Trees and plants are natural pranic transmitters since they absorb so much prana from the natural world. This can be absorbed by humans through tree hugging and sitting under trees, and from plants by eating raw, unprocessed foods such as nuts and seeds and through visualisation and meditation on flowers and fruit.

Pranic healing is therefore a method that can be used for self-healing, or via the evolved and focused pranic energies of a healer who removes unhealthy energies from the patient's invisible or etheric energy body and transfers fresh unpolluted prana via his or her hands into the aura.

TRADITIONS, MYTHS & FOLKLORE

Reiki Healing

Reiki is a Japanese word meaning universal (*Rei*) life-force energy (*Ki*), and known as *Ki* in Japan. Reiki healing energy flows naturally to the parts of the body and mind where it is most needed, with the healer acting as the channel through which this power is manifest. The energies are channelled via the Reiki practitioner's higher energy centres, the heart and throat chakras, the Third Eye and the crown chakra, through the healer's hands to the recipient, so increasing the body's natural ability to restore itself.

Though Reiki has a long history in Tibet, China and India, the method was rediscovered during the late 19th century by Dr Mikao Usui, a Christian Theologian, who had spent years searching for the secrets of ancient healing. In a Tibetan monastery, he was shown ancient manuscripts which contained healing symbols. After a 21-day period of purification, fasting and meditation on a Japanese mountain top, he received enlightenment and the power of healing, using the mystical knowledge that was encoded in the healing glyphs.

Reiki training involves progression through three degrees, the second divided into two stages, to become a full Reiki Master and teacher of others. Reiki healing is used for animals, to cleanse food and living areas and for spiritual evolvement through self-healing, as well as for healing the mind, body and spirit of those who are ill or distressed.

Native North American Healing

Jamie Sams, a Native American shaman of Cherokee and Seneca descent, explained his native healing tradition: 'When we look at the idea of medicine, we have to embrace the total person: the body, the heart, the mind, and the spirit. When any of these part are out of balance, then there is a need for healing.'

Dry Paintings or Sand Paintings

Sand paintings are an integral part of healing and regeneration ceremonies in the Navajo traditions. More than fifty paintings may be created during a ritual. Each of these rituals has over generations assumed a specific form in which certain paintings are created and specific chants uttered in order to effect a cure. The precise composition of the paintings is secret. Because of the sacred nature of the ceremonies the paintings are started, finished, used and destroyed within twelve hours. They are made with sand, or sometimes on cloth or buckskin using sand, corn meal, flower pollen, powdered roots, charcoal stone and bark. The finished pictures are credited with powerful healing powers. A patient sits on the picture – an embodiment of the Holy Ones – and thereby absorbs their power.

In one version of the ritual, Father Sky and Mother Earth are depicted so they can recreate the Earth and thus heal the patient. The place from which the first humans are said to have emerged is shown by a small bowl of water buried in the sand or the earth. Once the picture is completed, a line of corn pollen is drawn between Sky Father and Earth Mother to show the path of harmony to be taken by the patient.

Natural Healing

Natural Healing Methods

Colour, herbs, crystals and flowers can all act as a focus for a trained healer's innate healing powers. However, in the folk tradition these natural sources of healing were also used by ordinary people. Before the Industrial Revolution most families knew the healing powers of different herbs and flowers. Even after the formalisation of medical practices, healing was commonly performed by the village wise man or woman, usually an older person whose family had been especially gifted in the healing arts since time immemorial. Animals as well as people were healed by folk remedies, as in pre-industrial times they were both a source of food and power, being essential to pull carts and ploughs to work the fields.

Many mediaeval practitioners used a mixture of Christian and pagan charms and, until after the Second World War and the establishment of the health system in the UK, mothers and grandmothers of poorer families would resort to the old ways in the case of a domestic accident or minor illness, making herb poultices and reciting ancient charms. In Somerset, for example, the remedy for a burn was to blow over the injury three times after thrice reciting:

*T*here were three Angels came out from East and West
One brought fire and another brought frost
And the third it was the Holy Ghost
Out fire and in frost.

Magnetic Energies

As early as 200BC the Greek doctor Galena reported having successfully used natural magnets, such as lodestones, pieces of naturally magnetic iron ore, to relieve pain in parts of the body. Lodestones have also traditionally been applied in folk medicine, to draw out illnesses of all kinds, especially infections, fevers and disorders of the pancreas and lower glands of the body, to clear headaches and blockages within the circulation, alleviate rheumatism and heal wounds. Small lodestones were set in silver or kept with a silver coin to make vision more acute, and when set or kept with gold, to strengthen and regularise the heart and encourage clear thinking.

This process had a magical as well as a medical basis. Lodestones were regarded until about five hundred years ago as living spirits. A single lodestone was used for healing, being passed anti-clockwise over the problem area or held above the painful spot and then shaken vigorously. The illness was believed to be attracted to the lodestone by a process akin to sympathetic magic, and thus would leave the patient. Afterwards the lodestone would be buried in the earth for a week, then dug up and fed with iron filings and kept in a red bag when not in use. Lodestones were also used in spells to attract love and wealth.

In recent years, scientific research has confirmed the positive benefits of magnetic healing for people, animals and even plants, and it has been discovered that magnets do increase blood circulation when applied to the body, so improving the flow of oxygen to injuries and to sites of pain.

Aromatherapy

Aromatherapy is an ancient art in which pure essential oils are used to encourage the body's and the mind's innate healing energies. Essential oils are highly aromatic, concentrated liquids extracted from various parts of plants, such as flowers, stems, leaves, woods and resins. As well as their therapeutic benefits for the body, essential oils also help the mind, mood and emotions, reducing stress, lifting depression and giving confidence and energy.

Although the therapeutic effects of essential oils have been known for thousands of years, the word *Aromatherapie* was coined in 1928 by a French chemist Henri Maurice Gattefosse, who worked in his family's perfume business. His research into the therapeutic effects of oils began as the result of an accident. An explosion in his laboratory badly burned his hand and he plunged it into the nearest cool liquid, a vat of pure lavender oil. What stimulated his interest in oils was the unusual speed at which his hand recovered with little scarring.

At around the same time in Italy, research was being carried out into the psychological benefits of citrus oils such as bergamot, lemon and orange. During the Second World War another Frenchman, Dr Jean Valnet, used essential oils such as lavender and myrrh in the battlefield when conventional medicines were scarce, and discovered how effective they were in healing wounds and infections.

How Essential Oils Work

Essential oils can enter the body through inhalation or be absorbed through the skin directly into the bloodstream when diluted with carrier oils, using massage, poultices or baths. The sense of smell is a very powerful trigger for the human nervous system. An aroma usually has an immediate effect and over the centuries certain aromas have consistently had a sedative or relaxing effect, or have proved instantly energising. In rituals, an oil burner can combine the Air and Water elements and each oil has its own magical significance.

Colour Healing

Colour therapy, also known as light therapy, chromatherapy or colourology, involves restoring or improving health and well-being by means of adding or removing certain colours from a person's current environment. It has a long history. The Babylonians called the healing power of light the 'medicine of the gods'. Healing colours have also been used for thousands of years in China and in Ayurvedic medicine. The Ancient Egyptians wore amulets of coloured stones: red to treat disease; yellow for happiness and prosperity; and green for fertility.

Subjects bathed in blue light for thirty minutes experienced a drop in blood pressure, while if they were bathed in red light their blood pressure rose. Exposure to blue, often called the healing colour, also decreases perspiration, respiration and brainwave activity, while red increases the metabolic rate. Orange stimulates the pulse, while pink can, in the short term, have a soothing effect, especially upon aggressive people. In the long term the effects of the colours are reversed, so colour therapy should only be related to immediate feelings and situations.

Modern colour therapy takes several forms: the use of coloured lights or sunlight through coloured glass or perspex; wearing certain coloured clothes to enhance or dispel different moods; eating different coloured foods and drinking water seeped in sunlight from coloured containers to introduce healing colour to the body. Eating different coloured fruit or other natural foods also enhances the pranic or natural life energy. Each colour has an antidote or complementary colour which can be used to correct imbalances. Breathing in coloured light, whether visualised or from a natural source, for example a brilliantly coloured flower or fruit, is a way of absorbing missing colours from the aura, and also for repairing tears or holes in the aura that may be causing a loss of energy or a tendency to minor illnesses.

Crystal and Gem Healing

From earliest times, gems and crystals have been crushed into powders and used as ointments, soaked in water which is then used as a restorative drink, placed on painful areas of the body, or carried as amulets. The energies of crystals form a natural focus of healing from the earth and amplification of personal healing powers.

Rose quartz, amethyst and clear crystal quartz seem naturally tuned for healing work, and these three crystals can be used for virtually all forms of relief. For example, amethyst and rose quartz will relieve headaches when dipped in cold water and placed on the temples or the point of pain. Along with jade they also soothe hyperactive children and prevent night terrors.

Crystal quartz is known as the All-Healer in many indigenous cultures. The Celts referred to clear quartz crystals as star stones, because they were believed to be frozen stars that had fallen to earth. A traditional Celtic method of cleansing the body and mind of impurities was to boil nine small quartz crystals found naturally in a stream or on a shore, in what was the equivalent of two litres of pure spring water. The water was allowed to cool and a little drunk in the morning for nine consecutive days.

Crystal quartz, like green malachite, is also effective in relieving toothache if rubbed on gums. Clear crystal spheres were traditionally used to concentrate the rays of the sun upon a diseased or painful area of the body or in the direction of a malfunctioning internal organ. A blue lace agate soaked in water for twelve hours and gargled with water will cure sore throats, while crystal pendulums and crystals of appropriate colours are also effective in energising or unblocking chakra points in the body.

Flower and Tree Essences

Flower essences are extracted from wild flowers and tree blossoms and work on a spiritual level to alleviate negative emotional states, transforming them into a more positive form. The healing properties of flower essences are linked with the life-force of flowers, each flower's unique energies corresponding with a specific human emotion, and are a tangible and readily available concentrated form of pranic light.

The healing power of flowers was known to the Ancient Egyptians and Australian Aborigines, however flower essences were first created by Dr Edward Bach during the 1930s in England. From the original 38 remedies have evolved thousands of flower essences, being produced around the world from native flowers and trees. There is even a range made from Joseph of Arimethea's original sacred thorn tree and sold at Glastonbury.

Flower essences differ from aromatherapy since they do not have a fragrance. What is more, they are normally taken orally (a few drops under the tongue from a dropper bottle) rather than inhaled or applied to the skin, although a few drops are sometimes added to baths. Nor are they herbal remedies, since the healing essence contained in the liquid is an energy pattern rather than a tangible substance with specific medical properties.

Essences are taken either individually or in combinations, usually made up by a practitioner. Flower essences can be used for both a sudden crisis and longer-term healing and growth. They are frequently associated with the healing energies of devas and nature spirits (see p. 154).

Healing Magic

Healing magic is practised by many Wiccans and other Neo-pagan groups or individuals. Healing rituals often involve the use of herbs and may centre around the creation of a poppet or doll to represent a sick person. Cloth poppets – rough, featureless images in green or blue cloth – have been used from early times in the Western folk tradition as a focus for healing. Permission is usually asked of the person to be healed, unless it is a very young child and the spell-caster is the parent. They are also used in animal healing. The poppet is sewn and filled with a selection of healing herbs, for example cinnamon, eucalyptus, lavender, myrrh, peppermint, rose, rosemary and sage, and a ribbon may be tied around the area where there is pain or disease in the actual body. A healing incense stick of frankincense or myrrh is circled anti-clockwise over the poppet to remove all negativity and pain.

Herbal Healing

Folk remedies involving herbs are increasingly entering mainstream medicine, as detrimental side effects of chemical compounds are coming to light. Most recently, the midsummer love herb, St John's wort (*hypericum*), has been used as an anti-depressant without the side effects of some seratonin-based drugs.

Used in a variety of ways, from infusions and teas to sachets and bath solutions, herbal remedies are still handed down through the generations in country areas. With the revival of interest, increasing numbers of modern children are growing up with herbal knowledge and hopefully the tradition will continue.

TRADITIONS, MYTHS & FOLKLORE

INCENSE

Incense is an aromatic substance, obtained from certain resinous trees. It has been used in religious worship and formal magical rituals in cultures as far apart as India and Native North America, both for purification purposes and to carry prayers and petitions to the Godhead, Sky Gods and Goddesses, or the Great Spirit in the Amerindian world. In formal magic, incense represents the elemental substance of Air and it stands in the east of a circle, also being used to consecrate it.

Since the 1960s, the popularity of incense sticks, cones and burners has increased for home use for cleansing negativity, to induce meditative states and also as part of personal rituals for power, love and protection. Incense is now on sale in floral fragrances as well as the more traditional ones.

The Origins of the Use of Incense

In ancient times incense came from two trees, the *Boswellia sacra* of Arabia and the *Boswellia papyrifera* of India. To increase the thickness of the smoke and make the incense fragrant, between four and 13 specified ingredients were ritually added. In the world of the Old Testament, this sacred process was carried out only by chosen families in the community.

Incense was used in religious ceremonies among the Assyrians and Ancient Babylonians, and on Egyptian monumental tablets kings are depicted with incense censers (known as thuribles in the world of magic). God commanded Moses to build an altar of incense on which only the sweetest spices and gums were burned. The daily renewal of these fragrant offerings was carried out by a special branch of the Levitical tribe. In the classical world, incense was burned as an offering to the gods when a

sacrifice was made. In mediaeval times the correct use of incense was central to ceremonial magic, each incense having a magical and astrological meaning. Less fragrant scents were burned to drive and keep away demons.

Incense still forms an important part of ceremonies in the Roman Catholic, Eastern and High Anglican churches.

Incense in Modern Magic

Incense burning differs from that of essential oils, in that the fragrance is transmitted on the smoke and so tends to be more concentrated and pungent than is the case with slower burning oils. It is therefore very effective for spells that require instant impetus and for rituals focused on a specific need.

For the purposes of informal magic, non-combustible incense is made from any plant material, sometimes combined with essential oil. It is burned by smouldering it on charcoal blocks and is known as raw or granular incense. It is very potent because it is endowed with the hopes and desires of the maker. One essential ingredient is a gum resin such as frankincense, dragon's blood or the traditional gum Arabic.

Incense sticks and cones are made from combustible incense and are more difficult to make at home, but are very easy to light and use. Unlike non-combustible incense, the fragrance of the stick does not alter when burned.

Magical and Planetary Associations

Incense	Magic qualities
Allspice, ruled by Mars	Money, strength, action
Bay, ruled by the Sun	Healing, protection
Benzoin, ruled by the Sun	Money, increasing mental powers and concentration
Cedar, ruled by Mercury	Healing, cleansing redundant influences and negative thoughts
Cinnamon, ruled by the Sun	Increases passion, money-bringer, psychic awareness
Cloves, ruled by Jupiter	Love, repelling hostility
Copal, ruled by the Sun	For protection, purification and for cleansing crystals
Dragon's Blood, ruled by Mars	Love, protection and passion
Fern, ruled by Mars	The initiator of change, travel and fertility
Frankincense, ruled by the Sun	Courage, joy, strength and success
Juniper, ruled by the Sun	Protection, cleansing and healing
Lavender, ruled by Mercury	Love and reconciliation
Myrrh, ruled by the Moon	Healing, peace and inner harmony
Rosemary, ruled by the Sun	Love and happy memories
Sage, ruled by Jupiter	Wisdom and enhanced mental powers
Sandalwood, ruled by Jupiter	Spiritual and psychic awareness and healing

Smudging

Smudging is the name of a ritual performed by Native North Americans for the cleansing of energy through the burning of sage, cedar, tobacco and sweet grass. Traditionally, smudging can either be a ceremony in itself or a prelude to other rituals, and is performed by mixing the sweet grass, sage, cedar and tobacco in a bowl, usually an abalone shell, burnjing the ingredients, and then blowing or fanning the smoke over oneself or the person to be healed or cleansed. An eagle feather fan is used as Native Americans believe that the prayers and thoughts contained in the smoke are carried to the Creator on the wings of eagles – birds they believed flew close to the sun.

Smudging removes any negative feelings, depression and anxiety and restores a state of harmony, so that healing will occur naturally as positive energies are absorbed. It can also be a very empowering process as negative energies are replaced with positive ones.

Sage

Sage is a herb of wisdom and when burned offers protection from all forms of harm and negative feelings in the self and others. The negativity rises into the cosmos to be transformed by the Great Spirit or Wakan Tanka in Sioux as healing sunbeams. Because it grows in the desert, sage represents the energies of the Sun and Fire in the south, and the Earth in the north.

Sweet Grass

Sweet grass grows high in the Rocky Mountains, and is known as the grass that never dies. It is also found on marshes and near lakes and so combines the power of Air, the east, and Water, the west. Its power lies in connections with the world of spirit, calling down health and plenty from the benign forces above as it burns.

Cedar

Cedar is a herb of purification, protection and healing and can be used either with the two other substances or as a substitute for sweet grass.

Making and Using a Smudge Stick

- Use six or seven sprigs of the fresh herbs, each about 22cm (9in) long. Hold these tightly together and bind them with cotton thread. Secure the bundle every centimetre and leave the herbs to dry for two or three weeks.

- Light a candle of green or brown for the Earth Mother and hold the smudge stick about 8cm (3in) above the flame until it glows and smoulders, releasing a thin trail of smoke. You can trim the end for use at another time. Alternatively, follow the traditional method of using a bowl or deep shell to contain rolled and dried herbs, lit from the candles.

- Move from the bottom to the top of the body in a clock- or sunwise direction, making an anti-clockwise circle above the crown or centre of the head to remove negative influences.

- Carry out this ritual six times for the six cardinal directions: east, south, west, north, up and down. Feel all unhappiness, anger, fear and pain leave and be replaced by golden healing light. If you have a specific need, see your dreams and wishes spiralling upwards into a single white cloud of smoke to fall as fertilising rain. Use a feather or your hand to waft the smoke all around you or the person to be healed. Another name for this ceremony is 'sweeping medicine'.

- You can sometimes buy ready-make smudge sticks. Alternatively, incense sticks can be substituted. Use two contrasting herbs, sage and cedar, or sage and sweet grass, the banishing substance followed by the attracting herb of positive energies. Sandalwood can be substituted for cedar or sweet grass, and rosemary or thyme for sage. Use three separate cycles:

  1. sage is swept upwards anti-clockwise, followed by an anti-clockwise circle round the crown to banish negativity
  2. cedar is swept upwards clockwise to attract positivity, ending with a clockwise circle around the crown
  3. the cycle of sage and cedar is repeated twice more as above.

LOST WORLDS

The most recent evidence of a Lost World was revealed in 1985 when a Japanese diver discovered a stepped pyramidal structure off the coast of Yonaguni Island which, if man-made, predates the earliest known Japanese civilisation by more than 5,000 years. It is remarkably similar to various pyramidal and temple structures in the Americas, for example the ancient Temple of the Sun near Trujillo in Northern Peru. Such discoveries reawaken the debate as to whether there are advanced civilisations buried beneath the waves or whether people simply need to believe in a lost Golden Age and weave their dreams around evidence some scientists explain away as natural structures.

Atlantis

Never has the human imagination been so fired as with the lost civilisation of Atlantis. Facts are sparse, based mainly on two books, *Timaeus* and *Critias*, written by the Ancient Greek philosopher Plato around 360BC who, especially in the *Critias*, described the lost Atlantis as a paradise on earth.

Plato's Account

Plato spoke of the idyllic island nation that existed more than 1,000 years ago in the middle of the Atlantic Ocean. It was founded by Poseidon, god of the sea, and populated by a powerful race of demi-gods. Atlantis was ruled over jointly by Poseidon's five sets of twin sons, born from his marriage to the mortal Cleito. Atlantis was very wealthy, with splendid buildings, walls studded with precious metals, a huge golden statue of Poseidon in his chariot pulled by winged horses dominating the central hill, flowing fountains, exotic fruits, canals that enabled a second harvest to be reaped each year, and animals of all kinds including elephants. However, because the people became corrupt, Zeus caused a huge tidal wave to submerge Atlantis in a day and a night.

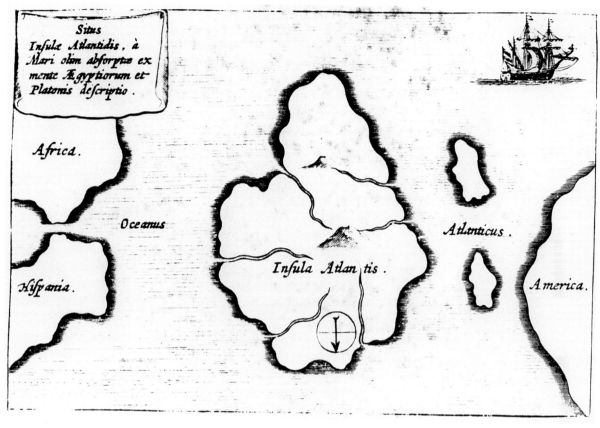

Psychic Accounts of Atlantis

The visionary Edgar Cayce portrayed an Atlantis so advanced in learning that much of modern-day science and technology is only rediscovering what perished beneath the waves thousands of years ago. Cayce spoke of the exodus of many Atlanteans through Egypt and beyond. This offers one explanation for the continuing mystery of the amazing feats of design, such as the Pyramids and Stonehenge, that occurred simultaneously in culturally unconnected lands around the globe and revealed knowledge far beyond that of the contemporary civilisation. He predicted that Atlantis would be found once more in the late 1960s. In 1968–69 two parallel lines of rectangular stones about 2,000 feet long were discovered under twenty feet of water in North Bimini in the Bahamas. Some of the stones were hand-made and a stone head was also found. They became known as the Bimini Road. However, there is debate as to the true age of these findings.

The Russian occultist Helena Blavatsky, one of the founders of Theosophy (see p. 80), claimed the inhabitants of Atlantis were the fourth race on earth, and that they were all natural mediums. Other accounts obtained through channelling or past-life visions claim that extra terrestrials intermarried with the Atlanteans, which might account for the Atlanteans apparently possessing such an advanced civilisation – Cayce talks of crystal power plants generating what seems to be a kind of nuclear energy. The Atlantean exodus as a result of the sudden destruction of their land – a disaster that

Cayce believes triggered the Floods, described in the cultural myths of many societies – might also account for the number of consistent descriptions of golden-haired creator Sky Gods in early myths of different civilisations.

Where is Atlantis?

Plato located Atlantis in the Atlantic Ocean opposite the Pillars of Heracles (the Straits of Gibraltar). In the late 1960s a Greek archaeologist, Angelos Galanopoulos, became convinced that Atlantis was the Minoan island of Thera, which was devastated by a volcanic explosion around 1500BC. The disaster left more than half of Thera underwater. Plato suggested that the story of Atlantis came via Egypt and there had been strong trade links between Egypt and Thera. The date discrepancy was, thought Galanopoulos, caused by a scribe accidentally multiplying all figures by ten, mistaking the Egyptian symbol for 100 – a coiled rope – for the symbol for 1,000 – a lotus flower. The dimensions cited for Atlantis were also, he claimed, disproportionately larger than would be realistic. For example, he cites that the width and depth of the canal, described by Plato as 300 feet wide and 100 feet deep, would more realistically have been 30 feet by 10 feet. Crete itself he identified as the Royal City.

Another possible location for Atlantis is around the Azores, a group of islands set in the Atlantic Ocean about 900 miles (1,500km) west of the coast of Portugal. The islands could, in this theory, be the towering mountain tops described in the accounts of the sunken continent of Atlantis.

The Russian Viatcheslav Koudriavtsev, however, believes that Atlantis was not located in the middle of the Atlantic but on the continental shelf surrounding much of England. The Celtic Shelf, as it is known, currently underwater, was above water during the last Ice age, over 10,000 years ago. In another theory, Brian Slade, the Kent archaeologist and historian, has unearthed evidence that Atlantis may have been located in the Thames Estuary.

Lemuria or Mu

The physical evidence is even more slender for the existence of Lemuria, which is believed to have existed 14,000 years ago and to be the source of much of the wisdom of indigenous peoples, for example the cultures of Native North America and the Australian Aborigines. Lemuria is also sometimes referred to as Mu, or the Motherland (of Mu), the Earth Mother.

It is believed that Lemuria was situated in the southern Pacific, between North America and Asia/Australia. Tamil bark writings in southern India recall the huge area of southern India which used to connect with Australia before it slowly sank into the sea. Some evidence of Lemuria's existence is offered by its name, given by zoologist L.P. Sclater, who noted that lemurs could once be found from Africa to Madagascar, and suggested that a single land mass had connected the two. The last surviving lemurs are now under threat in Madagascar.

Legend has it that the holy people or prophets of the Lemurian culture had foreknowledge of the Flood and began to store information in crystals. These crystals were taken deep within the earth, thus all crystals are said to be a powerful focus of channelled Lemurian wisdom. A year before the Flood, the Wise Ones began going underground and created communities there. The people living beneath the earth were safe from the Flood, and when the waters receded the people emerged once more to impart their wisdom, in lands now separated from each other by water. This emergence from the earth is recorded in the creation myths of a number of indigenous peoples, in which the sacred ancestors or Wise Ones emerged from a hole in the ground. For example, an Australian Aboriginal creation myth recounts: *'The sun, the moon, and the stars slept beneath the earth. All the eternal ancestors slept there, too, until at last they woke themselves out of their own eternity and broke through to the surface.'*

Recently, the oldest known mummy in North America, the Spirit Cave man, was rediscovered on the shelves of the Nevada State Museum. It had originally been found in Nevada in 1940 and had been dated as being about 2,000 years old. However, recent radiocarbon tests placed the mummy around 7,400BC. The mummy was wearing moccasins and its shrouds were of woven marsh plants and seemed to have been created on a loom. This would seem to indicate that, more than 9,000 years ago, people in North America had the ability to make looms and weave on them. Could they have been the descendants of the wise Lemurians?

Playing Card Divination/Cartomancy

Cartomancy refers to all forms of card divination, but has become specifically associated with playing cards. Gaming and divinatory aspects were interwoven almost from the beginning of playing card history, a hand of cards indicating whether a venture or journey might be propitious according to whether the player won the game. But gradually cards were interpreted without their being used in a game and the separation was probably completed once formal card layouts were introduced in the 1790s.

Playing Cards and Magic

Playing cards are often considered unlucky, partly because of their association with Tarot cards (see p. 77), with which, in mediaeval times, they were often interchangeable, but even more so because the evils of gambling are emphasised by various churches and at times by the State. As early as 1423 Bernadine of Sienna preached against the evils of gaming at Bologna and thousands of cards were publicly burned, while in England Edward IV's first parliament in 1462 forbade card playing except during the 12 days of Christmas.

The captains of some fishing vessels will not allow the 'Devil's picture books' on board. If they are used and anything goes wrong, the cards are thrown overboard as a precaution. Miners also consider playing cards a bad omen in a pit, while it is said that thieves will never steal cards for fear of detection and will throw away any packs that are found among stolen goods.

Even more than the Tarot, playing cards have been given set predictive meanings over the centuries. However, the modern simplicity of design makes them a perfect vehicle for the inner eye to cast images upon a basic template of meanings, almost as a form of scrying (see p. 136). Like tea leaves, card divination became less fashionable in the 1960s as the New Age movement saw the introduction of more esoteric and complex forms of self-discovery. Until then they were the domestic equivalent of the Tarot in ordinary homes, for Tarot cards were a rarity outside occult households and even clairvoyants were more likely to read playing cards for clients.

The Origin of Playing Cards

The first cards were probably invented in China. It is said that on the eve of the Chinese New Year 969, the Emperor Mu-tsung played domino cards with his wife, a game that resembled a traditional playing card game. Chinese 'money cards' are even closer to Western playing cards. The Chinese engraved copper and silver with designs and numbers based on the four suits. These were copied on to paper and used for games. Indian cards of a similar time showed the Hindu gods holding sceptres, swords, cups and rings.

The origin of the European playing card is thought to be traced to a region near Mameluke in Egypt. A Mameluke card deck dating around 1400 comprised 52 cards with four suits – swords, polo-sticks, cups and coins. Each suit was numbered 1–10, and there were three court cards in each suit, called *malik* (King), *na'ib malik* (Viceroy or Deputy-King) and *thani na'ib* (Second Under-Deputy). It seems likely that the na'ib court card was the source of the early names of European cards: *naibbe* (Italian) and *naipes* (Spanish).

It has also been suggested that Marco Polo returned from his 13th-century voyages to China with playing cards. The Crusaders are another possible source, as are the gypsies (see p. 248) who came to Europe from India through Egypt, since playing card divination was a popular Romany art. As with the Tarot, the playing cards may have had several different sources.

It is known that playing cards were used at the French court. In 1390, Odette, the mistress of King Charles VI, introduced a pack brought by gypsies and decorated with Eastern potentates. Based on these, Odette designed her own pack, depicting members of the French Court. This gave the name of court cards to the picture cards. A visiting gypsy demonstrated the oracular power of the cards to Odette and the King and correctly foretold future events as well as secrets from the past and present known only to the King and his mistress.

Four hundred years later, Napoleon planned and, he was convinced, won several battles and successfully wooed the empress Josephine using the prophetic power of playing cards.

Playing Card Divination

Traditionally, a special pack is kept for divination and when not in use is wrapped in black silk and placed on a high shelf. This is believed to elevate its messages above worldly concerns. The meanings are not direct parallels with the Major Tarot cards, but in modern interpretations have acquired similar echoes to the Minor Arcana. The Knaves playing card combines the Page and Knight of the Tarot, giving a pack of 52 cards, plus two jokers which are discarded for divination except as place markers for certain layouts.

Rather than having positive and negative aspects within each card as the Tarot does, in traditional interpretation certain playing cards are naturally positive and others negative. For example, the 19th-century astrologer Zadkiel, who wrote several important books on dreams and divination, said that the Ace of Diamonds promises a ring or similar gifts of eternal devotion while the Ace of Spades, the unluckiest card in the pack, warns of quarrels and misfortune. In modern interpretation, each card is seen as symbolising potential opportunities or challenges, and even with the older meanings skilled card readers would use the playing cards as a focus for their own intuitive interpretation.

Mondays and Fridays are considered the best days for card divination. A significator, the card of self, is chosen from the court cards before the readings. In the system advocated by Zadkiel, the significator chosen by a married or emotionally committed questioner is a King or Queen and is matched by the corresponding King or Queen of the spouse. An unattached person selects a King or Queen according to the characteristics sought in a potential partner. The Knave is used by a married questioner of either sex to represent the hidden thoughts or intentions of the partner. A great deal of information is derived from the cards surrounding these key personality cards in a layout. In some systems, the twos, threes, fours, fives and sixes of each suit are discarded for readings, but most modern cartomancers advocate using the full pack.

Many spreads are incredibly complex, involving up to 15 shuffles and redealings until the final cards for divination are selected. This is akin to the yarrow stalk method in the *I Ching* (see p. 25) and stills the conscious mind. But some of the old forms of card divination are very simple and retain the gaming aspect. For example, the ancient love card game Cupid and Hymen is played with three young girls who are in love or seek a lover. It uses all the court cards along with the nines, threes and Aces, which are dealt equally among the players. Three Kings in a hand represent friends who will help the love match; two or three Queens indicate love rivals; Knaves an unworthy lover, but a single Knave a lover who will be true. Threes bring surprises, perhaps an unexpected love match; three Aces denote sorrow; two Kings a child out of wedlock. If a single King is with the Aces, the parents will marry, but if a Queen also appears they will not. The Nine of Hearts brings happiness and is the wish card; the Nine of Diamonds promises a wealthy lover; the Nine of Clubs a new gown; the Nine of Spades predicts the maiden will have a poor lover. A Knave and Queen represent a secret intrigue.

In more general readings, Diamonds refer to travel, business undertakings, letters and gifts; Hearts to love, affection and family ties; Clubs to power, money, fame and talent; Spades to misfortune, loss and betrayal. Two red Tens are a sign of marriage; the Ace of Clubs indicates a letter on the way; the Ten of Clubs a journey by water; the Two of Spades a false friend; the Five of Hearts a present from a lover or admirer; the Four of Hearts a marriage bed; the Four of Spades a sick bed; the Seven of Clubs a prison.

SCRYING

S crying means seeing magical images in a reflective medium, such as a crystal ball, mirror or a natural moving source of inspiration such as fire, water or clouds. The word 'scry' comes from the Anglo-Saxon word 'descry', which means 'to perceive dimly'.

Scrying in shiny surfaces has been practised in almost every culture and time, not only by mystics, clairvoyants and magicians, but by every girl who has gazed into a mirror and performed rituals on the old fire festivals such as May Eve and Halloween, in an attempt to see her lover's face in the glass. Water is considered especially potent for scrying, because its surface constantly varies as the sun, moon or candles cast light on the surface, shadows fall or the wind creates tiny waves. Therefore it can capture a series of fast-changing images that together may give the answer or a magical insight.

Aristotle, the Greek philosopher, explained the scrying process in his *Prophesying by Dreams* in 350BC:

> *... dream presentations are analogous to the forms reflected in water. In the latter case, if the motion in the water be great, the reflection has no resemblance to its original, nor do the forms resemble the real objects. Skilful, indeed, would he be in interpreting such reflections who could rapidly discern, and at a glance comprehend, the scattered and distorted fragments of such forms, so as to perceive that one of them represents a man, or a horse!*

How Scrying Works

A visual system used by children in place of words when they are young gives access to deeper levels of wisdom and power, and is an ability cultivated by adults in creative visualisation. It is this visual imagery that is invoked in scrying and explains why children are adept at seeing pictures in the clouds or fire, as were Druids (see p. 107) who practised cloud and fire divination.

Scrying in Water

Traditionally, hydromancy, or water scrying, was practised by the side of a dark silent pool or lake, the surface of which was used like a crystal ball. Lakes were called Diana's Mirror because, when the full moon was overhead, diviners would scry in the dark water, illuminated, it was believed, by the Moon Goddess's path across the skies. Modern scryers use dark bowls of water or water dyed black with ink and float candles on the surface to create a similar effect.

In Ancient Greece, where wisdom was obtained from the sound of springs bubbling over stones, for example at Zeus's sacred grove at Dodona, a mirror held just below the surface of the water captured rippling impressions. Often too, in the Classical world, young boys divined the future by gazing into bowls of pure water lit by burning torches. They studied the changes in the flickering light and invoked the gods (in modern interpretation their *divus* or god within) to provide a meaning.

In early French tradition, water used for scrying was obtained from a pure spring. Saffron was burned during divination and the divinatory bowl of water surrounded by ash boughs, vervain or periwinkle flowers. Immediately after scrying, the water was poured away on to soil to maintain the connection with the earth.

The 16th-century French physician and astrologer Nostradamus used a bowl of water on a brass tripod to make detailed prophecies for ten centuries ahead. His admirers say he predicted the assassination of Abraham Lincoln and John F. Kennedy, the rise of Hitler and the abdication of Edward VIII using this method.

Among Hindu and Arab peoples ink was traditionally either poured into the palm of their hand and then into a shallow bowl, or sometimes dropped directly on to water as a focus for inspired images. The method is still popular, using a clear glass or wide, deep white bowl and either calligraphy inks or permanent ink cartridges, squeezed directly into the water drop by drop. Alternatively, a brush or dropper can be used to add the inks one or two drops at a time.

Ink scrying is the easiest form to master and the images are interpreted in the same way as tea leaves or dream symbols, but have the advantage of forming slowly in front of the scryer's eyes and so are more evocative than static tea leaves or coffee grounds.

Mirror Scrying

Long before glass was made, polished metal was used for mirrors. The origin of mirror scrying is attributed to the Ancient Egyptians. It is said that Hathor, Goddess of love, music and dancing, was once entrusted with the sacred eye of Ra, the Sun God, through which she could see all things. She also carried a shield that could reflect back all things in their true light. From her shield Hathor

created the first magic mirror. One side was endowed with the power of Ra's eye to see everything, no matter how distant in miles or how far into the future. The other side showed the gazer in his or her true light and only a brave person could look at it without flinching.

However, mirrors of highly polished metal were also consulted in Ancient China to determine what would come to pass. So it may be that mirror scrying is a technique that naturally evolved simultaneously in different cultures from water scrying whose origins are much earlier.

The Greeks used bronze mirrors to see into the future, and in Ancient Rome practitioners called *specularii* were highly regarded as soothsayers. According to myth, Vulcan, God of Fire and Metalworkers and husband of Venus, fashioned a mirror that showed past, present and future. The mirror was given by Cupid to Ulysses' wife Penelope.

Black, shiny mirrors, called witches' mirrors, were popular in mediaeval times, but because of their association with darker practices are now rarely possessed by ordinary scryers.

Interpreting Mirror Images

As with crystal ball reading, the hour before sunset is considered the best time for mirror scrying as the sun's dying rays will reflect in the glass. However, many modern practitioners prefer to scry after dark, using candlelight to create ripples and shadows on the glass. Any mirror can be used, the idea being to throw the normal visual processes slightly out of focus by the contrasts of light and shadow, or sometimes by looking into a slightly convex glass, so that the psychic vision of the inner eye may be evoked.

Pink or orange candles, Hathor's colours, are lit on either side of the mirror and their flickering light helps to evoke psychic images. Rose incense, the incense of Hathor, is also burned to stimulate the psychic senses. The questioner should sit so that his or her image is not seen in the glass. The simplest way to practise mirror scrying is to focus on a question, stare hard into the mirror, close one's eyes, open them and blink rapidly. In that second of intensity and altered vision, the secret is to allow a picture to form from the mind's eye that you can project and magnify it in the mirror, if you do not already see one in the mirror. In time and with practice, the image will appear in the mirror when you blink. You can repeat the process two or three times to build up a number of images that may form a story related to your life. As you extinguish the candles, you may obtain a final image in the momentary after-glow.

An image moving towards the scryer suggests that the event or person will occur or appear very soon; an image moving away suggests that the event or person that occurred is either moving away from the scryer's world, or that a past issue or relationship may still be exerting undue influence on the scryer; images appearing on the left are said to represent actual physical occurrences, while images appearing in the centre or to the right tend to be symbolic. Pictures near the top of the mirror are regarded as especially significant and need prompt attention; those in the corners or at the bottom are less prominent or urgent. The relative size of the images can indicate their importance.

Tasseography or Tea Leaf Reading

The History of Tasseography

In Chinese tradition tea was used as early as 3000BC as one of the elixirs of long life and for divination. It was said to have come from an egg when the Divine Artisan was creating the world. According to Buddhist legend, the first tea leaves were made from the eyelashes of the Holy One, who cut them off to prevent himself from falling asleep while he was meditating. From China, the secrets of tea cultivation and divination spread to India and Sri Lanka, the former Ceylon. From India, the Romany gypsies brought the magical art to Europe.

Tea did not arrive in England until around the middle of the 17th century and was very expensive. It was not until 1885 that tea from India and Ceylon reached England in any quantity, and so even in Victorian times tea was considered a great luxury and kept in a locked wooden box by the lady of the house. Tea leaf reading reached its height of popularity in ordinary households around the time of the First World War, when those left at home were anxious about the well-being of soldiers in the trenches.

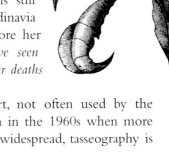

Coffee was introduced into Europe a century before tea and the first London coffee shop was opened to the public in 1652. Because coffee was not as expensive as tea, coffee ground reading was, for a time, more popular and is still favoured over tea leaf reading in Turkey, Greece, Scandinavia and the United States. In Mérimée's story *Carmen*, before her lover Don José kills her, the gypsy tells him: *'I have seen more than once in the coffee grounds that we would meet our deaths together.'*

Tasseography has remained primarily a domestic art, not often used by the professional clairvoyant, and after a period which began in the 1960s when more exotic versions of divination such as the Tarot became widespread, tasseography is again gaining popularity.

Tea Leaf Reading

Tea leaf reading is bound with a number of specific and highly stylised rituals as a way of stilling the conscious mind and allowing the visual imaging processes that form the basis of all scrying to operate. For in spite of the continuing popularity of books with hundreds of set, highly predictive meanings, tasseography is primarily an intuitive art. While working with groups of people I have found that virtually the same formation of leaves will be interpreted in widely divergent ways by individual readers, but that this intuitive interpretation provides the reader with accurate information about the questioner's situation.

Reading From a Full Cup – Traditional Interpretations

- A single tea leaf on the surface of a cup of tea heralds unexpected money coming to the questioner.

- A single leaf on the side of a cup of tea suggests meeting a new friend or romance for the unattached.

- Several floating leaves indicate exciting days ahead, while a clear surface promises rest and relaxation, even an unexpected holiday.

Tea Leaf Reading Rituals

With very traditional readers, even making and drinking the tea is governed by ritual, akin to a Japanese tea ceremony. Sufficient liquid is left in the bottom of the cup so that the leaves are floating. The questioner swirls the remaining tea three times round the cup with the left hand, clockwise for a man and anti-clockwise for a woman. The questioner then places the cup upside down on the saucer to drain it, twisting the cup a further three times, this time anti-clockwise for a man and clockwise for a woman, again using the left hand. The reader then takes the cup and holds it the right way up, with the handle towards him or her. The cup is read from left to right.

Areas of the Cup

The inside the cup is divided into imaginary quarters around the circumference.

The handle quadrant

This represents the questioner and therefore leaves in this area concern him or her, the home and those emotionally close.

The area opposite the handle

This is the realm of strangers, acquaintances, colleagues and matters away from the home, including work and travel.

The quadrant to the left of the handle

Images here represent the past or people moving out of the questioner's life. Any large or very dark images can suggest that there may be unresolved matters from the past that are affecting the current issue, especially if this area is crowded.

The quadrant to the right of the handle

Symbols here are indicative of people and events moving into the questioner's life. If this area is blank it does not mean there is no future, merely that energies are concentrated on present or past endeavours.

When Will Events Occur?

Leaves at the rim of the cup represent events that will occur in the near future, within weeks or even days. Leaves halfway down the cup suggest people or events moving in or out of the questioner's life within a few months, according to the quadrant. The area close to the bottom of the cup is believed to portray the distant future, a year or more away.

Joys or Sorrows

The number of good omens and bad omens, as interpreted by reading specific images, can be counted to weigh up a decision.

- Leaves near the top of the cup promise happiness.

- Tea leaves from the centre upwards indicate a relatively peaceful period.

- The lower half of the cup suggests that there may be some challenges and obstacles to overcome to achieve any goal, but that persistence will pay off.

- The bottom of the cup, traditionally seen as foretelling tears and sorrow, indicates that it may be necessary to compromise to succeed and that setbacks can be turned to advantage with patience.

- A pile of leaves at the side of the cup opposite the handle suggests that to overcome certain obstacles requires the co-operation others, while a pile of leaves close to the handle says that the solution lies in the questioner's hands.

The Alphabet

Letters of the alphabet are traditionally seen either as important people currently in the questioner's life or the name of a significant person entering the questioner's life in the near future. The position of the letter is indicative of the relationship: the closer to the handle, the closer the relationship either emotionally or in terms of the actual meeting place to the home.

Numbers

Numbers represent the number of months that will elapse before an event occurs. The time scale is usually taken from the area of the cup in which the number occurs. For example, a number eight at the top of the cup would indicate perhaps eight days; above the centre eight weeks; just below the centre eight months; at the bottom of the cup eight years. This time scale is applied to the symbol to which it is closest, for example a six next to a boat or plane below the centre of the cup might suggest an unexpected journey overseas in about six months.

The Size of a Symbol

These may vary considerably. The largest symbol is usually the dominant one. If a symbol is large in relation to the others then it may represent, according to the meaning of the symbol, a large success or sum of money or a major problem.

The Clarity of a Symbol

If a symbol is clear and well formed, then the issue is clear-cut or the offer or relationship definite. Mistiness and unfinished outlines suggest that all may not be as clear as it seems. It might also indicate that a problem appears more daunting than it really is because of personal fears.

PART THREE

Magical,
Mystical and
Otherworldly
Beings

ANGELS

Who Are Angels?

Personal angels are sometimes regarded as an externalised form of the individual's higher self, and Archangels as archetypes of spiritual qualities and powers. However, the more traditional view is that angels are separate entities who have never lived on earth, but are of a higher order of existence, some of whom choose to guide a particular person or act as guardian to a city or even a nation. Though angels are often envisaged with huge feathery wings and long flowing robes, such perceptions are influenced by the cultural and religious background of those who study and believe they have seen angelic beings. A typical description was given by Norah, a terminally ill woman whose vision gave her the ability to die without fear:

St Michael came with the faintest of sounds like the softest of sighs. He was so beautiful, about eight foot tall with ash blonde hair, just above his shoulders. He was wearing a full length cream gown, edged at the neck with gold … His feet were bare.

In his hand he held a magnificent sword, enormous and very heavy, yet he raised it as though it was no heavier than a feather. He opened his wings slightly. The feathers were like the softest down and cream, edged with apricot. He closed his wings around me and I knew I was safe.

Angels are traditionally found in the Judaic, Christian, Islamic and Zoroastrian religions. The word 'angel' comes from the Latin '*angelus*', itself stemming from the Greek '*aggelos*', which is a translation of the Hebrew word '*mal'akh*', meaning a messenger. In formal religion, angels are regarded as intermediaries between God or the gods and humankind.

Angels are androgynous, but some, for example St Michael, are associated with male qualities. In Kabbalistic lore and mediaeval angelology, angels are traditionally associated with the powers of the four elements, directions and winds, the seven older planets and the 12 zodiacal constellations, so endowing them with magical as well as religious significance. The angels of the Kabbalah and ceremonial magic come from the Jewish tradition, dating from times when ancient Israel incorporated earlier gods as angels serving the one true God. Indeed, angelic lore flourished in lands where Jewish and Christian religion transformed the former pagan gods of light into angels or saints. Many of the old Sun Gods were absorbed into the person of St Michael, Archangel of the Sun, and churches dedicated to him were built on the sites of former sun temples.

In Islam there are four main angels: Jibril who corresponds with the Archangel

Gabriel and is the angel of revelation; Mikal is like Michael, but is the angel of nature; Izrail mirrors Azrael, the Jewish angel of death; Israfil is the angel who endows the body with its soul and heralds the Last Judgement. In Islam, angels were said to be formed from pure gems.

After the Babylonian exile (597–538BC), Jewish artists and writers influenced by Mesopotamian art gave angels wings, and specific attributes and hierarchies were formalised. The Judaic angels were divided into Seraphim, Kerubim, Thrones, Dominations, Powers, Virtues, Principalities, Archangels and Angels. Mediaeval magicians would seek to summon good angels into divining crystals or stones by invocations that included reciting the names of Archangels, and bind them with incantations until they had revealed the necessary information about future events.

The Archangels

Best known in art and religious writings are the seven Archangels, although the names of these vary widely throughout different traditions. Archangels form a basis for empowering and protective magic in both traditional and modern Western tradition, and are often represented by candles in their colour at the four corners of a room or the four directions in a magic circle.

The most usual rituals invoke the following Archangels.

Michael

Michael is the Archangel of light and the warrior angel. He appeared to Moses as the fire in the burning bush and saved Daniel from the lions' den. As commander of the heavenly hosts, Michael, who is pictured with a sword, drove Satan (Lucifer) and his fallen angels out of the celestial realms and is constantly at war with the great dragon or serpent often identified with Samael, the Angel of Darkness in Jewish sources. As Angel of Judgement, Michael carries a scale weighing the souls of the dead. According to the Koran, the cherubim were created from Michael's tears.

His candle colour is gold.

His crystal is a citrine or pure crystal quartz.

His incense or oil is frankincense or orange.

Gabriel

Gabriel means Strength of God. He or she is said to bestow the gifts of vision, hearing and psychic abilities, as well as the powers of life, procreation and equilibration. Gabriel is most likely to speak through dreams. Sometimes called the Archangel of the Moon, the messenger Archangel and the heavenly awakener, he or she appears many times in the Bible, visiting the Virgin Mary and her cousin Elizabeth, mother of John the Baptist, to tell them that they are to bear sons who will lead mankind to salvation. It was Gabriel who parted the waters of the Red Sea so that the Hebrews could escape from the Pharaoh's soldiers.

Gabriel is usually pictured holding a sceptre or lily.

MAGICAL, MYSTICAL AND OTHERWORLDLY BEINGS

145

To the followers of Islam, Gabriel is the Spirit of Truth who dictated the Koran to Mohammed.

His or her colour is silver.

His or her crystal is the moonstone or fire opal.

His or her incense and oil is jasmine or mimosa.

Raphael

Raphael is a healer and travellers' guide and so is often associated with Mercury. He is the Archangel who offers healing to the planet and to mankind and all creatures on the face of earth, in the skies and waters. He

is also guardian of the young. He is depicted with a pilgrim's stick, a wallet and a fish, showing the way and offering sustenance to all who ask.

His colour is green.

His crystal is jade or aquamarine.

His incense is myrrh or pine.

Uriel/Auriel

Uriel, whose name means Fire of God, is associated with earthquakes, storms and volcanoes, and is the Archangel of Salvation. Auriel means Light of God. He is sometimes linked with the courage of Mars, warned Noah of the impending flood and led Abraham out of Ur. Believed to have given alchemy to mankind, he also imparted the wisdom of the Kabbalah to Hebrew mystics.

His colour is scarlet or orange.

His crystal is carnelian or amber.

His incense is sandalwood or rosemary.

Modern Views of Angels

The most influential writer on angels since biblical traditions is Emanuel Swedenborg, the 18th-century scientist, Christian mystic and visionary, who in his 30 large volumes made more than 7,000 references to angels and angelic life. His views have influenced a great deal of modern angelology, especially regarding contact with personal guardian angels.

Swedenborg believed that angels are not a divinely-created separate race but experienced human existence and now live in the spiritual dimension after physical death. He taught that all people are born to become angels, whatever their religion; if they choose the path of virtue, they can continue on an angelic path after death. He said that every angel remains fully human until eternity but in a more beautiful and perfected form; after death these evolved angels continue to live in communities with homes, gardens, countryside, and places of work. The only difference is that their environment is not fixed by physical or material restrictions but is created by thoughts. A special angelic function is caring for young children who have died as they grow up in heaven, and in helping newly deceased souls. Swedenborg said that at least two guardian angels are constantly with each individual during his or her time on earth, and that a person may become aware of them in times of crisis or choice, or by seeking contact if this is appropriate for the stage of spiritual development of the individual.

The concepts of angelic voices and wings which appeared in paintings were, Swedenborg explained, for those who had hard lives, a way of glimpsing a more perfect form of existence. Thus they might understand that it was possible to escape from the physical limitations of mortality and soar spiritually as well as physically in the next world if one took the angelic path in life.

BLACK MADONNA

Darkness precedes light and she is mother

INSCRIPTION IN THE ALTAR OF THE SALERNO CATHEDRAL IN SALERNO, ITALY.

Black Madonna figures are shrouded in mystery as to their origins and purpose, but all the explanations point to them as the alter ego or shadow side of the Virgin Mary (see p. 336), representing power, wisdom and fecundity and linked with the ancient Earth Mother. In this section I explore some of the complex webs of inter-action surrounding Goddess worship that have become entwined with the Black Virgin, perhaps the most powerful icon of the Divine Feminine.

The official definition of the Black Madonna is an image of the Virgin Mary and her child that either turned black from some natural cause, such as candle smoke or tarnish, a chemical imbalance of the paints, or was naturally black because of the kind of wood or stone used when carved.

However, though this may explain the identity of some of the Black Virgins, the icon has become associated with the symbolic as well as the actual blackness of the power goddesses of the ancient world, from Lilith, Adam's first wife who was cursed for her refusal to submit to him sexually and subsequently coupled with demons, to Kali-Shakti, the Hindu Goddess of Destruction and Transformation who empowered the gods. Many Black Madonnas are in locations previously dedicated to fertility goddesses and with pilgrimage sites related to the Holy Grail quest; they also have strong links with the Gnostic (heretic) religious sects of the 11th and 12th centuries, with the Crusaders who may have brought back dark Madonna-type statues from the Middle East, and with the Moorish occupation of Spain. Many of the Crusaders' Black Madonnas were in fact statuettes of Isis.

Black Madonnas are found all over Europe, with the most famous ones being at Chartres in France, Czestochowa in Poland and Montserrat in

Spain. In France, the statues or paintings are called *Vierge Noires* or Black Virgins. France has more than 300 Black Virgin sites, with over 150 still in existence, though in many cases it is difficult to see them as they may be locked away.

A group of post-Renaissance Black Madonnas whose colouration is more directly related to the racial and ethnic types appropriate to their geographic location also exist, the most famous being Our Lady of Guadalupe in Mexico.

The Black Madonna as Isis – the Pagan Goddess Link

Black Madonnas are most frequently associated with the Egyptian Mother Goddess, depicted with the infant Horus in her lap, the original Mother and Child. During the later centuries of the Roman Empire, Isis, Cybele and Diana of Ephesus, all black goddesses, were universally worshipped in France and the Mediterranean coast from Antibes to Barcelona, a tradition that continued secretly in spite of Christianisation through to the Middle Ages – the Mediterranean region shares many links through the Moorish conquest as well as being geographically close to Africa and the Middle East. Many Black Madonnas still exist in this area.

In the Middle Ages when the majority of these statues were created, perhaps modelled on older statues that had been lost or destroyed, there was still a strong undercurrent of the 'old ways', given impetus by the Crusader Isis images.

Black Madonnas were frequently discovered hidden in trees in France and Spain, and may have been representations of the pagan goddesses who were still worshiped in groves, especially the woodland Goddess of the Hunt Artemis in her black eastern form, known also as Diana of the Wood or the Golden Bough. The Montserrat Black Madonna was discovered among rocks by shepherds in Barcelona.

The Black Madonna as Sophia, Greek Goddess of Wisdom

As mediator between heaven and earth, the Black Madonna represents Sophia, the Gnostic Great Mother, symbol of female wisdom and symbolised by the dove of Aphrodite, and so by transference associated with the dove that represented the Holy Spirit in Christianity. Sophia came to represent God's female soul and source of His power in Gnosticism, in the same way that Kali-Shakti empowered the Hindu gods.

Said by some Gnostic sects to be the Mother of God before He created the world, Sophia was Christianised as a saint, but in Eastern Christianity she was unofficially venerated as a goddess. The concept that she was the Mother of God as well as Christ links the Madonna image with the old son/consort sacrifice myths.

The Black Madonna as the Earth Mother

Black Madonna shrines are usually found in or near caves, wells or mountains, or kept in a crypt or subterranean part of a church or cathedral, usually near a sacred spring or well. Her dark or black skin is said to represent the Earth Mother in her underworld or winter aspect. In this sense she links with the winter aspect of the Corn Goddess Demeter, whose daughter, Persephone, remained in the underworld for six months, thus causing winter on earth. Both these goddesses were linked with ancient mystery religions.

With the beginning of the Christian era, the cult of the Mother Earth was transformed into veneration for the Virgin Mary. The concept of the wise Earth Mother Goddess of the pagans incorporates the ideas of fertility, of sensual, uninhibited woman, very different from the Virgin Mary of the Immaculate Conception. This sensuality was embodied in Christianity in Mary Magdalene, the sacred prostitute who, it was said, became the wife of Christ and mother of his son.

Mary Magdalene and the Black Madonna

It is known that the Merovingians in France worshipped Cybele as Diana of the nine fires, and in 679 Dagobert II, who became Saint Meroginy, established the cult dedicated to *the one which today receives the name of Our Lady and who is our Eternal Isis.*

They incorporated this into the identification of the Black Madonna as Mary Magdalene, and through her the Merovingians claimed to be the rightful Kings of France, with descent from Christ's son by Mary Magdalene, the infant in her arms in the Black Madonna statues. Some legends say she married Christ at the wedding at Cana where he turned water into wine.

According to the folklore and mythology of Provence, Mary Magdalene migrated with her son from the Middle East to Saintes Maries de-la-Mer, a small village on the French Mediterranean. The myth speaks of her coming by boat with a small entourage 13 years after the Crucifixion. She reportedly spent the last 30 years of her life in seclusion at the cave of St Baume in the French Alps. Although the literature in the monastery that is currently at St Baume contains this story, it has never entered mainstream Christian doctrine. In south-eastern France is the highest concentration of Black Madonnas in the world, and many local fêtes are held in honour of the Black Madonna.

The Magical Powers of the Black Madonna

Healing and fertility powers are associated with the Black Madonna and many of the sites are situated on ley lines. The original Black Madonna of Chartres stood in a grotto underneath the mediaeval Cathedral with its own healing well, dating back to time immemorial. The statue was burned during the French revolution in the town square.

But it is the painting of the Black Madonna of Czestochowa, Poland, that is credited with the most magical powers to protect Poland from attack and is revered by Polish people throughout the world. It is a painting of the Madonna and Christ Child which legend states was originally painted by St Luke the Evangelist, on the top of a table built by Jesus. The picture itself has been damaged in battle. In 1430 in the town of Czestochowa, where the painting was kept in a specially created monastery church, Hussites overran the monastery and one of the invaders slashed at the painting twice with his sword, but fell dead to the floor. The sword cuts and an arrow wound in the throat of the Madonna from an earlier attack by invaders can still be seen.

In 1655, Poland was overrun by the forces of the Swedish King Charles X. The monks defended the portrait against a 40-day siege and, it was said, as a result of the Madonna's intervention Poland was able to drive out the invaders. In 1920, the Russian army gathered on the banks of the Vistula river, threatening Warsaw. The image of the Madonna was seen in the clouds over the city and the Russian troops withdrew.

There have been many reports of miraculous healing by those who have come to the portrait seeking help. Interestingly, this is one of the Black Madonnas said to have been created by soot residue from centuries of votive lights and candles burning in front of the painting, thus turning it black.

DEMONS AND DEMONOLOGY

Demons are found in almost all religions and in many Westernised faiths are regarded as the dark side of the angelic hosts; fallen angels who challenged the authority of God. Like Lucifer, formerly Archangel of Light, these dark angels were cast out of heaven to reside in an underworld of fire, darkness and suffering, to which sinners were also condemned. Though defeated, these angels of darkness were considered, mythologically and psychologically, a continuing threat to humankind by offering the fulfilment of earthly desires in return for acknowledging their dark powers. Like angels, demons were attributed hierarchies, names and characteristics. Generally, the more polarised the view of the Godhead as Total Light and Goodness in a religion which demands total adherence to a rigid code of worship, the more potent and fearsome it has depicted its demons.

In contrast, many Eastern religions embody a system of dualism, an ongoing struggle between the powers of darkness and light. For example, one of the main features of Hindu mythology is the constant struggle between the gods and the demons for supremacy. Like the gods, the demons were created by Brahma or Prajapati, Lord of All Creatures, and are said in some accounts to be dispossessed older brothers of the gods fighting for their rightful inheritance. In one conflict, Shiva, one of the three Supreme Beings, was compelled by the demons to give them greater power and strength than the gods. But Shiva tricked them, and his consort, in her dark, destroyer aspect of Kali, went into battle and defeated them.

The Devil, Divination and Psychic Powers

Where magic and spirituality are concerned, even in the modern world the Devil, chief of the Fallen Hosts, remains as an almost superstitious dread in popular consciousness, even for those who profess no formal religion. He is personified in the Judeo-Christian image of the Devil card in the Tarot (see pp. 77) that has undeservedly contributed towards the Tarot's reputation as the Terror Cards.

From the Chaldean, Egyptian and Arabic worlds via the Jewish Kabbalistic magical tradition, came a belief in nine orders of demons. The Medariorum, the second order of demons, was said to be ruled by Python (of the Greek Oracle at Delphi) who deceived through oracles, divination and predictions. It was said that using divinatory powers would put a man under the control of evil spirits, a powerful mechanism of the early and later medi-aeval church designed to keep psychic phenomena out of bounds to the laymen, though many of the mediaeval Popes practised ceremonial magic which harnessed demons as well as angels.

THE DEVIL.

This association between the paranormal and the Devil still unconsciously underpins both official and popular prejudice against psychic development and healing practices. Even miracles were, according to the mediaeval church, the work of the Devil unless manifest by a saint, and the modern church is still very ambivalent about lay miracles and even Marian apparitions.

Witchcraft has also been associated with Satanic worship, and many innocent men and women confessed under torture to consorting with the Devil in the form of a goat during the witch burnings that continued throughout Europe and Scandinavia from mediaeval times for three centuries or more. The vast majority of those who practised witchcraft were not worshipping the Devil, but probably following the nature religions that continued in remote places until Victorian times. The Goat God was a descendant of the Shaminic Horned figure who appeared on cave walls thousands of years ago.

Do We Create Our Own Demons?

Demons may not be either discarnate forces of evil or mere projections of a troubled mind. Rather, like those troublesome spirits summoned through a ouija board, they may be low-level spirit entities, the restless souls of people who did bad deeds in life, now claiming to have demonic powers. They may have fuelled some of the tales of devil worship in mediaeval times by those who practised Necromancy, the summoning up of spirits, and then perceived them in hideous demonic form, an image of evil popularised by the church.

But many people are convinced that the Devil is merely the externalisation of the shadow side we all possess, or, in Jungian terms, that we are afraid to acknowledge and so project into a mythological bad guy. The Vikings had a similar idea with their trickster God Loki, who was necessary to bring about change, and whose evil deeds were the manifestation of the darker side of the nature of the gods and goddesses that gave fulfilment to their secret and less laudable desires.

Buddhists (see p. 229) believe that we create our own demons. They say that in the second state after bodily death, the *Chonyid Bardo*, the deceased spontaneously create encounters with good and evil powers, peaceful and angry deities. Because the demons, like the benign god figures, are only thought forms, if the deceased person could realise that he or she was creating a personal hell it would be possible to escape and enter Nirvana – the state of cosmic bliss.

Political Demons

Historically, it can be argued that the role of demon vs deity was dictated by whoever held the power. Conquering peoples would impose their own deities on the subjugated nation and transform former deities into demons. Christianity and its powerful missionary movements led to the demonisation of many indigenous deities who could not be Christianised as saints, for example, Brigihde the Celtic Triple Goddess merged happily into the 5th century Irish saint Brigit. On the whole, male deities became the demons, not least the Horned Pan and Odin or Woden who can still be seen as Black Peter or Knight Rupert, the black, demonic character who accompanies Good St Nicholas on the eve of his festival in December in Germany and Austria.

Demonology and Angelology

Demonology and angelology were twin and sometimes interchangeable powers used by ceremonial magicians from mediaeval times right up to the 18th century across Europe, whereby demons and angels were harnessed to perform magic. There were various tests, especially when summoning angels in crystals spheres, to ascertain whether they were indeed angels of the higher order, but obviously it was a very borderline activity fraught with hazards. There was a distinction made between sorcerers and those black magicians the Necromancers who summoned demons to work for them and made a pact with the Devil, signed in their own blood, in return for knowledge and power. Most infamous was Faust who became the subject of Marlowe's play the *Tragical History of Dr Faustus* and Goethe's play *Faust*. Faust was born in 1491 and died in 1549, strangled by the Devil, it is said, with so much force that his head was found facing the wrong way.

But most sorcerers used magical rituals and even summoned angelic help to bind the demons to their service. They summoned mainly the fifth order of demons, the Prestigators, whose chief demon was said to be Satan. The Hebrew name Satan signifies an adversary or an accuser.

The sorcerer practised in secret in such locations as dark vaults between midnight and 1 am, either under a bright moon or during a storm. He created a magic circle nine feet in diameter for himself and his assistant and they would remain within a square in a second circle about six inches inside the first until the demon had been summoned and bound, done its work and departed.

Demonic Attack in the Modern World

A minority of adolescent girls or women in their twenties and thirties, perhaps far more than officially admit to such experiences, are plagued by the 21st-century equivalent of the Incubi – sexual demons from the mediaeval world who prey on women.

The following accounts of teenage experiences come from my own casebook. Jill, now a married woman in her thirties, said:

When I was 13 or 14, I started to have a dream about an upside down cross. We weren't a religious family and never went to church. I was horrified to be told by my friends that it was to do with the Devil. Not long after I had an awful vision of the Devil. He had huge horns like a ram and a horrible face. His face was dark and half ram, half human. I think I said a prayer. I felt a physical force. He was trying to crush me. I was absolutely terrified. It lasted 10 or 15 seconds I suppose, but it was like eternity.

Janet, now in her late thirties, told me of a similar experience:

When I was about 16 I woke to find a heaving weight on my chest choking the life from my body. The room was freezing. I could see the dent on the bed this invisible force was making and I was fighting to breathe as it grasped me and pressed my neck till I thought I would suffocate from my veins. At last it went suddenly, leaving me shaking and exhausted. This happened on two occasions. The second time I said the Lord's Prayer and the fiend, as I thought of it, never came back.

My own view is that these experiences originate in the inner conflicts about power and sexuality that can be especially problematic for sensitive women whose families will not talk about such matters. However, I know that some clergymen disagree with me and see these as demonic attacks.

ELEMENTALS, DEVAS AND NATURE SPIRITS

Nature Spirits and Animism

Animism, from the Latin *anima*, meaning breath or soul, is the belief that a soul or spirit exists in every animal, bird, flower, tree, stone, body of water and mountain. Plants and trees are especially sacred, and even today in Iceland people ask permission of tree and land spirits before building a new dwelling. Corn and other grain was traditionally regarded as containing the spirits of fertility, and so many fertility rites were centred around the land – the scattering of the ashes of a ritual fire on the fields was regarded as the first sacrifice of a nature deity. The superstition of touching wood for luck predates even the Druids (see p.107) in its origins.

Nature spirits, which include elementals, the spirits of the four elements, are, like other essences, regarded as having supernatural powers, the crucial difference being that they reside on a different plane of existence from humans and so are invisible except to children and those with evolved clairvoyant powers.

Lilian, a clairvoyant from Berkshire, was ill for several months as a child during the 1940s and used to watch nature spirits:

I got very close to nature and began to be aware of the presences in the countryside around me. I started to use my willpower to bring out the essences of these presences. I found myself looking at the little people in shadowy forms – I was aware even then that other people did not have time to see them.

Among the Native North American peoples (see p. 271), each herb and plant is said to emanate a special aura, either a colour or an unmistakable essence, and healing herbs were sometimes adopted as a power totem. Some Australian Aborigines derive their origins from the original plant beings. In Classical tradition, hamadryads, who lived within a tree, were believed to die when their tree was cut down.

Some of these nature spirits fell in love with Greek and Roman gods and heroes and married or were spurned by them. For example, in Ancient Greece, the youth Narcissus, son of Cephisus, who so admired his own beauty that he gazed constantly at his own image in a pool, was loved by the young nymph Echo who called him in vain. One day, reaching out to embrace his reflection, Narcissus fell into the pool and was drowned. A single narcissus, the white daffodil-like flower, tinged red in the centre for Echo's pierced heart, was found floating on the surface of the water. To this day her voice is said to call her lost love in rocks and hollow places, especially near water.

Neo-paganism has restored the sense of interconnectedness with natural phenomena to the modern Westernised world, and the spirits of nature have once more become recognised as sources of spiritual inspiration.

Devas

Devas, or *adhibautas* in Sanskrit, are higher nature spirits regarded as part of the Angelic Kingdom. They are said to appear human in form though they inhabit the etheric or astral plane and can change size and appearance almost at will.

Devas are credited with the power to explode star clusters, move tides and create perfume in flowers. Some live in forests and maintain the healing, life-giving force that is being damaged by deforestation. They are said to be aware of the thoughts of humans and to serve humanity, not least by channelling messages to those who are sufficiently sensitive to hear them. Though the word 'deva' is of Hindu origin, in the Western world, through the influence of the Theosophists (see p. 80), their presence has become recognised.

The Devas of Findhorn

Findhorn in Morayshire, north-east Scotland, is a wonder of nature, where a beautiful garden grew on barren soil and evolved into a centre of world spirituality. Peter Caddy, an ex-senior officer in the Royal Air Force, his wife Eileen, their three sons and Dorothy, a colleague, created the Findhorn garden in 1962 with the help of devas who instructed Peter on the planting and care of the vegetables and flowers. Before long, vegetables and flowers rich in colour flourished, growing far beyond their usual size.

Earth Guardians

Land Wight, or Landvaetir, is the name given to these guardians of the earth, especially in northern Europe and Iceland where certain fields and hills were sacred to them. Wights also acted as guardians of settlements and villages, travelling along fairy paths at dusk to their watch posts at crossroads, sacred trees and standing stones, thus preventing any harm from entering the settlement until morning.

These spirits were blamed for an earthquake that rocked Cornwall on November 10, 1996. Cassandra Latham, a white witch and the first approved pagan chaplain at Treliske Hospital in Truro, told reporters:

> In Penwith we have seen adverse attention and the desecration of the Merry Maidens [stone circle], the Sancreed Holy Well and the Boscawen-Un stone circle. So the pagan network throughout the country has been holding ceremonies at special sites since Hallowe'en to evoke ancestral earth spirits which act as guardians of the Earth.
>
> But I must admit I was not expecting the earth to move as it did! I found it quite awesome.

MAGICAL, MYSTICAL AND OTHERWORLDLY BEINGS

The Elementals

Elementals are a lower type of nature spirit than the devas and are ruled by specific devas or Archangels who in modern Wicca are called Lords of the Watchtower and protect the four quarters of a magic circle.

Elementals are traditionally associated with magical traditions, because they are said to work with thought forms and the manifestation of magical desires into reality. Elementals were first categorised by the Greek neoplatonists around the 3rd century AD, though they were recognised much earlier as being present in Earth, Air, Fire and Water. Mediaeval magicians and alchemists sought to manipulate their powers to gain mastery over nature. The alchemist/magician Paracelsus in the 16th century gave names to the personified elemental forms: the Gnomes of the Earth who may also be manifest as rock sculptures, the Salamanders or legendary Fire lizards, the Sylphs of the Air, and the Undines of the Water.

Nature Spirits and Healing

In more recent years, nature spirits have been associated with the discovery and creation of flower and tree essences. In the creation of the Findhorn flower essences, different flower devas offered their healing powers and guided the creator to the flowers with the necessary healing qualities to create a comprehensive range. As Marion Leigh, née Stoker, who came from Australia to Findhorn describes:

I had no overall plan to include any particular flowers in the range, so that the flowers found me. The exception to this was the Scottish primrose, a rare plant: the message that came through [from this flower] was so powerful: The gift I bring is peace. Just one drop of my essence has the power to infuse the hearts of the masses, so treat me with great respect and I will manifest peace in God's graceful timing.

The Australian tree essences were developed by Judi Harvey in 1992, but her inspiration began in her childhood. She grew up in a cool, subtropical rainforest in northern New South Wales, a forest used by Aboriginal peoples for at least 4,000 years. Her knowledge was developed while studying at the Flower Essence Centre in Melbourne, but as with all flower and tree essences, the discovery of their powers is frequently a process rooted in spirituality and magic, actively inspired by interaction with the nature spirits. Judi wrote:

Each of the 13 trees appeared to me – each tree had positive and adverse healing properties. Each tree was connected to counsel, a colour and sound tone, I started to receive through my meditations and intuitions. At the New Moon I was to collect new and old leaves, twigs and barks, put them in Australian spring water in a diamond-cut, diamond-shaped crystal bowl and leave it under our avocado tree during the new moon. Then do a hand dance to invoke the appropriate spiritual hierarchy and nature spirits to help co-create and co-manufacture each new essence. At the full moon, I was to collect the new bud, the flower, the seedpod and the seed. This went on for thirteen lunar moon cycles, a complete lunar year.

The Australian Native tree essences work on the mind and spirit, but as a result better health follows as the user is reconnected with the life-force. As Judi comments:

The essences raise our consciousness to the level of the plants, birds, minerals and devas to make us aware of our connection with and interdependence with nature. These essences reconnect us to the universe and especially to the rhythms of the Moon.

As well as a personal tool for holistic healing, these essences are used for planetary- or self-healing and to heal physical imbalances in plants and trees.

FAIRIES

The word 'fairy' or 'faerie' comes from the old French word faes derived from Latin *fata* or fate, and was first used around the 13th or 14th century. Originally it meant a state of enchantment or glamour, the power of illusion.

Fairies *per se* are especially associated with the Celtic tradition of Wales, Ireland, Brittany and Cornwall, and with northern Europe, Scandinavia and Iceland. Their tradition travelled to the US with the colonists and has survived in remote mountainous regions, intermingling with the mythology of indigenous nature spirits.

They are popularly regarded as either tiny gossamer-winged Andrew Lang flower fairies who can stand on a drop of water without rippling the surface, or Enid Blyton's slightly sturdier moralistic or mischievous advisers of wayward or lost children. Yet, according to legends and reported sightings over hundreds of years, they are more ambivalent, able to endow either great good fortune to the favoured few or enchantment, disaster and even death to mortals who have offended them. Fairies reached their height of authenticity in mediaeval times. In France, a full description of fairies was given in the trial of Joan of Arc as part of the evidence of her heresy.

Like witches, fairies were held responsible for the failure of crops or the deaths of animals, and rituals and offerings were made to appease them or protective charms such as iron or rowan wood used to keep them away.

Belief in fairies declined both as a result of the Age of Reason and Darwinism and with increased industrialisation and urbanisation. But in rural areas, where Celtic influence remains strong, the little people never cease to hold sway. Few people in Ireland will build a house on a fairy path, lines which connect ancient hilltop forts.

In the closing decades of the 20th century, as people became increasingly concerned for the natural environment, so the possible existence of nature essences or spirits, personified as fairies, once again fascinated adults as well as children. A

Wiccan tradition known as the Faerie Faith has become increasingly widespread, especially in America.

The Origins of Fairies

An Icelandic legend, perhaps Christianised by missionary monks in the 11th century who saw fairies as part of the pagan world they sought to eradicate, says that Eve was washing her children when God spoke to her. In fear Eve hid the children she had not yet washed. When God asked if all her children were present, Eve said that they were. This angered God who declared: 'As you have hidden your children from my sight, so shall they forever more be hidden from yours.'

Another religious theory says fairies are fallen angels, driven out of heaven with Lucifer but not sufficiently evil to be cast into hell (see Demons, p. 150). A fairy's station in life is determined by where he or she fell to earth: water fairies are those that dropped into the sea or rivers, land fairies on to the ground and house fairies on to roofs.

Others believe that the fairies are earlier gods and spirits of wise pagans, such as Druids (see p. 107), whose power dwindled with the coming of new faiths, especially Christianity. This accords with an old belief that a deity can only be powerful as long as he or she is worshipped, and is certainly the most common origin cited for the *daoine sidhe*, the underground fairy court of Ireland, the inhabitants of which were once the old gods of the *Tuatha de Danann*. The deities of the Old Religion that were not demonised were translated into fairies. The Goddess survived in myth and secret worship as the Good Fairy, the Fairy Godmother or Queen of the Fairies.

Another theory holds that fairies are descendants of the small, dark Neolithic people who retreated to remote areas, especially islands, to escape from Iron Age invaders. In Ireland they were the Feinne, in Scotland the Picts (after whom pixies may have been named), and in Scandinavia the Finns and Lapps.

Professor Howard Lenhoff of the University of California has put forward the theory that the 'little people' owe their origins to Williams syndrome, a hereditary condition that affects one in every 20,000 births. Williams children are known for their unusual faces: they have full cheeks, large eyes, small upturned noses, wide mouths, tiny chins and oval ears. They grow slowly and many remain small. They have difficulties in some areas of learning but are gifted in others, such as music, and have a remarkable empathy with people.

The more frightening aspect of fairies stems from the belief that they are spirits of the restless dead; indeed, throughout Ireland and Britain there are accounts which link fairies to the dead. For example, it is said that the High Fairy King of Ireland, Finvarra, King of the *daoine sidhe*, has as his entourage a vast host of both the recent and ancient dead. This may be linked to the fact that Bronze Age burial mounds have been excavated on sites regarded as fairy forts.

Changelings

Perhaps the most common tale told is about fairies who carry human babies, especially fair-haired infants, to fairyland where they are highly prized. Some substituted changelings were reputedly enchanted with glamour to make them appear human, and so were only identifiable by a sudden alteration in eye or hair colour, or a previously healthy young child becoming ill, weak or even dying. In times of high infant mortality the changeling explanation offered some external scapegoat for parental grief.

Other legends describe the changeling as a wizened, misshapen baby, hairy and with a monstrous head, which is left in the cradle as a substitute for a human child snatched by the fairies or underground elves.

Was the changeling tradition a way of exonerating a family from the stigma of a deformed child in less enlightened times, when poor nutrition and conditions for maternity and post-natal care resulted in many disabled or disfigured children? As late as 1843, the *West Briton* newspaper reported the case of A. J. Trevelyan of Penzance who was charged with ill-treating one of his children. The child was said to have been regularly beaten by the parents and the servants, and from 15 months old had been left to live outside. The parents' defence was that he was not their child but a changeling and the case against them was dismissed.

Fairies were also believed to steal away grown women to act as midwives to fairy women; sometimes they were impregnated and bore the fairy children themselves (a tradition that has sprung up again in modern accounts of alien abductions). This provided an excuse for potential cruelty and wife beating, and in extreme cases even murder. As recently as 1894 in Clonemel in County Tipperary, a young woman called Brigit Cleary was tortured and killed by her husband because he claimed she was a witch changeling.

The Case of the Cottingley Fairies

The only apparently scientific evidence for fairies is the still controversial and unresolved Cottingley affair. In 1917, cousins Frances Griffiths, aged 11, and Elsie Wright, aged 16, claimed to have played with fairies in a glen at Cottingley in Yorkshire, and produced photographs which baffled the experts, including Kodak and Sir Arthur Conan Doyle, the creator of Sherlock Holmes and an ardent spiritualist.

Some 60 years later, the cousins admitted that four of the photographs had been faked; they had made cut-outs of fairies and placed them in the glen. But Frances insisted that they did take one genuine photograph. Elsie maintained that all the photographs were fakes. But along with Frances, she claimed that there actually were fairies in the glen. The reason the children had faked the pictures was to prove to jeering adults that the fairy folk did exist.

GHOSTS OF THE PLACE

Many apparitions are attached to a specific place and may be seen by different people over a number of years or even centuries. For this reason, these phantoms are more amenable to formal investigation and measurement than family ghosts who may appear only once, often without warning. Ghosts that are attached to specific places may seem unaware that they are perceived, and are perhaps like photographic impressions etched on locations by strong emotion at the time of death, a trauma or great happiness. However, some phantoms do interact with observers, suggesting the survival of the essential person, who either chooses or feels unable to leave a specific location that was of significance during earthly life.

What are Ghosts? – a Biochemical Explanation

Gilbert Attard, a French parapsychologist who has studied the geophysical aspects of the paranormal for 20 years, offers a scientific explanation for phantoms:

> At the moment of death everyone gives off a magnetic field intensified by emotion which can penetrate the surrounding matter and modify the biochemical functions of molecules. The result will be to impregnate the matter with the magnetic field of the deceased. This field is also charged with the emotion felt at the time.

This force, says M. Attard, could explain why clocks often stop at the moment of their owner's death. It would also account for feelings of sorrow, fear or peace at certain sites.

Measuring Ghosts

In recent years, technology has enabled ghost investigators to measure the physical effects of the presence of an apparition. However, some say they are unable to perceive the phantom who is affecting the dials and they rely on a clairvoyant to pinpoint the ghost's position and to provide information about its possible identity. Some more psychically-tuned ghost hunters prefer to rely on a pendulum to identify the presence or the path along which he or she walks. Certainly where ghosts are sensed or sighted, high and wildly fluctuating magnetic fields are measured.

Portable infrared thermometers record temperatures at intense cold spots in a building where the ghostly presences are detected, confirming the spontaneous shivering experienced by traditional ghost hunters. These spots are said to be places where there is an in-rush of air from another dimension. Radioactivity is also noted at hauntings.

Howard Wilkinson, a veteran British investigator now retired from the department of psychology at the University of Nottingham, and Alan Gauld of Britain's Society for Psychical Research, have studied records of alleged hauntings since

the mid-1800s. They found a link between ghostly sightings and sunspot cycles that can trigger magnetic storms on earth. This increased electromagnetics would, it is argued by sceptics, cause hallucinations and therefore ghost sightings.

However, believers would say that the entities themselves possess some kind of electromagnetic energy, manifest as the mist or ectoplasmic vapour seen around ghosts. Increased levels of electromagnetic activity during sunspot cycles, or the extra gravitational pull on the earth when the moon and sun are aligned, provide the energy for phantoms who are ever-present to be seen more easily by humans. The drop in temperature is explained in this theory as ghosts drawing the surrounding energy into themselves to fuel their manifestation.

The same interpretation might also account for the number of ghosts who have over hundreds of years been sited around ley lines and old stones circles, the latter where both electromagnetic energy and radiation have been measured as particularly high.

Ghosts of Battlefields

Since battlefields are places of great human suffering and high mortality, many ghostly soldiers and sounds of fighting have been reported. One of the most haunted sites is Culloden Field in Scotland, where the sorrow has, it seems, been etched on the land.

On April 16, 1746, the Hanoverians and the Jacobites supporting Prince Charles Edward Stuart, Bonnie Prince Charlie, met at Culloden on Drummossie Moor. Many were killed, especially the Jacobites who fought valiantly to the end. But English soldiers who died far from home have also been seen, often searching for wounded comrades.

Mark Fraser of *Haunted Scotland* magazine received the following story from a couple who live not far from Inverness. He recounted:

As John and Mary walked over the ground where the battle took place they both heard a lone piper playing a sad lament. Look as they might they could not discover its source. The pipes faded away to make way for the sound of many marching feet and the monotonous tone of a drum beat.

Then the sound of desperate fighting for their homes filled the air. Screams and shouts, the clash of swords and the resounding crack of musket fire all around them. Highland men ran screaming with their battle cries heading towards the organised ranks of redcoats – a tall man in Highland battle dress bellowed out the name 'Jamie' which drowned the sounds of the battle and hung in the air long afterwards. The scene stopped suddenly as though someone had pressed the freeze frame on a video recorder, and there in front of the now motionless battle was the Highlander who turned to look at John and Mary with his grief stricken face. The man stood well over six feet tall.

The tall Jacobite searched the faces of the dead, gently turning them over as he did so. The scene completely vanished and John and Mary were left looking at the bleak landscape.

Afterwards the couple confirmed they had witnessed the same details. John had at least one ancestor – Euan – who had fought and died in the battle.

Ghosts that Interact

The tall highlander at the battle scene seemed aware of John and Mary. I have also encountered cases in which it seems the two dimensions merge and a phantom will speak to the perceiver as though he or she was part of the original scene. Sheila, who lives in Lincolnshire, described:

During the late 1960s, when I was 17, I had just bought a motor scooter and my father was teaching me to ride it. We decided to go to a disused Second World War airfield at Barkston in Lincolnshire, near where we lived.

I rode up a high grass bank. Reaching the top I was surprised to see an old-style small plane, which I have only ever seen in war films. The door opened and two airmen in Second World War caps and greatcoats stepped out. One looked up and noticed me. I realised I must have been staring because he turned to the other man and pointed at me. They seemed surprised that I could see them. They were very young.

One of them shouted at me not to cross the line and told me to go back. I turned round to call my father and when I turned again the men and the plane had disappeared without any sound. I was baffled. It was just as if I had entered another dimension.

It had not dawned on me that they were ghosts because they were so solid and real. Some years later I was listening to the local radio station and a news item mentioned that a number of ghostly sightings had been reported at Barkston Heath.

Why Should Ghosts Return?

One of the strongest motivations for a ghost to return is unfinished business or a sense of injustice. One of the most famous cases is that of the Black Lady who haunted the Bank of England in Threadneedle Street. Sarah Whitehead was the sister of Philip Whitehead who had worked at the Bank as a clerk. In 1811 Philip was hanged for forgery, but Sarah was not told his fate, simply that her brother had gone away and left no forwarding address.

Desperate with worry, Sarah visited the Bank, seeking information of his whereabouts. When she learned his true fate, Sarah went insane. Every day thereafter she wandered up and down Threadneedle Street looking for her brother. Sometimes she entered the Bank, asking where her brother was. She wore mourning clothes, her face hidden behind a thick black veil.

Sarah continued her daily vigil for more than 25 years. She was buried in the graveyard of the old city church of St Christopher-le-Stocks, which later became the garden of the Bank of England.

An ethereal figure shrouded in black was seen regularly after Sarah's death along the stone pathway of the Bank's garden, wandering among the former grave slabs. The phantom has also been sighted on her knees among the graves weeping and scratching at the stones. Staff have also seen the Black Lady wandering down the corridors of the Bank, looking in rooms and approaching people, only to disappear. The majority of reported appearances were during the 1890s.

THE GODDESS

In modern spirituality, the Goddess has reassumed a central role, especially for women. In more formal magical rituals and Wiccan ceremonies, the Goddess, either alone or with her consort, the Horned God, form the focus for empowerments and spells. The revival of the ancient matriarchal tradition that has continued over the centuries, even in Christianity through the veneration of the Virgin Mary, reflects the growing realisation by many seekers after truth that a purely paternalistic Godhead forms an incomplete picture of divinity.

Female earth divinities, even when inferior in the heirarchy of the Sky Father deities, have always provided a personalised face of the Divine for both men and women. In remote villages in India today, the small shrines of local earth and fertility goddesses, who have remained largely unchanged for 5,000 years, are regarded as more potent that the major divinities in their ornate temples. In the section on Fate (see p. 113) I have described the female deities of fate and justice in several cultures who temper the power of even the most powerful Sky God. Jupiter, for example, ruled not alone, but was influenced in his decrees by Juno, his consort, and Minerva, Goddess of Wisdom.

The Earth Mother was, in early Palaeolithic hunter-gatherer societies, worshipped as the giver of all life and fertility and as mother of the animals. In the Shamanic religions in Siberia and Lapland, the Mother of the Herds is still a central icon of power, while shamans among the Inuits in the far north of America and Canada appeal for the release of the fish and whales and for healing to the ancient fertility mother, the Old Woman who lives under the sea. She is given different names throughout the Arctic: Nerivik in Alaska and Arnarquagssag in Greenland. The most common name is Sedna.

The Neolithic period began in approximately 8000BC, as the hunter-gatherer way of life was gradually replaced by agriculture. This was reflected in the evolution of the Mother Goddess as the bringer of fertility to the land as well as to animals and humans and so the great seasonal celebrations of sowing and planting began. In honour of the Mother Goddess, Neolithic homes and burial shrines found in Catal Huyuk, now part of Turkey, had vulva-shaped roof entrances, while images of the Triple Goddess were created on the walls of the shrines, showing the three stages of womanhood: maiden, mother and crone. The Triple Goddess was also associated with the waxing, full and waning phases of the moon – the birth, maturity, death and rebirth of the Great Mother's daughter. Neolithic shrines also contained large goddess statues giving birth to male bull horn figures, early representations of the union of the goddess to her son/consort that gradually replaced the lunar mother/daughter cycle.

The Mother Goddess and her Consort

During the Bronze Age, from about 350BC to 1250BC, the consort/son theme developed. The traditions of Sumeria and Ancient Egypt pervaded the Greek and Roman worlds, whereby the Father God was sacrificed and restored by the Mother Goddess. This is seen in the cycles of Innana and Tammuz in Sumeria, and Isis and Osiris in Egypt where the rebirth was linked with the annual flooding of the Nile. This particular image persisted throughout the Greek and Roman Empires, eventually culminating in the union of Sky Father and Earth Mother, personified as Zeus and Hera, Jupiter and Juno, and the supremacy of the Sky Father who overcame his own father to allow evolution.

But the Mother Goddess concept remained vital for the continuation of both agriculture and the life of the God himself, and during the Roman Empire worship of the Anatolian Cybele, Great Mother of the Gods, became a threat to the supremacy of Jupiter and later even to Christianity. A temple was erected to her honour on the Palatine Hill in Rome in 204BC. Cybele in turn became associated with the Classical Corn Goddess Demeter/Ceres, whose daughter Persephone was doomed to the underworld for part of the year. This accounted for the dearth of crops in the winter, as Demeter searched for her daughter in a return of the mother/daughter annual death/rebirth cycle.

The Scandinavian Frigga, or Frige in the Anglo-Saxon tradition, consort of the Father God Odin, also represented the three stages of womanhood and thereby the cycle of creation, destruction and rebirth. In her maternal aspect she was Goddess of Women, Marriage and Motherhood. Though she had knowledge of the future she would never reveal it.

In her youthful aspect she was Ostara, Goddess of Spring or Oestre as she was known among the Anglo-Saxons, and remembered in the festival of Easter. In Germany the first eggs of spring were offered to her, brightly painted. In her role as Valfreya, the Lady of the Battlefield, Frigg recalled the northern tradition of a mother warrior goddess, a being of magical power who rode the sky, mail-clad, and led the spirits of the slain to a spiritual resting place. She was guardian of a fountain called Quickborn, the waters of rebirth, and would invite devoted husbands and wives after death to her Hall that they might never be parted again. As Hulde, or Mother Holle, she presided over the weather. White clouds were her newly bleached linen hung out to dry. She gave flax to mankind and taught women how to spin. Finally, as the White Lady or Bertha in Germany she cared for the souls of unborn children. As Goddess of Agriculture her little souls helped Bertha to water the plants.

Many cultures have their Bone Goddess, a role assumed by such goddesses as Isis who rearranged the bones of the dead and gave them rebirth. Like Hecate the Greek crone or night hag, the Goddess continued in her role of life-giver, destroyer and restorer, albeit through different persona. Indeed it has been said that the Greek goddesses especially reflect the different faces of womanhood on both a psychological and spiritual level, from flowering of womanhood to the grave.

The Two Faces of the Goddess

One of the most fascinating aspects is the dark and light faces of the Goddess, although in Christianity, as the goddess temples were destroyed, the virgin and pure mother aspect of the goddesses was polarised in the Virgin Mary and the female saints. The dark aspect was emphasised throughout the Dark and Middle Ages by the demonisation of the more powerful and sexually potent former pagan goddesses. For example, the Norse Goddess Freyja, Goddess of Beauty and Fertility, whose chariot was drawn by black cats, was transformed into the witch with her black familiar. Black Madonna figures, linked with Isis in her icon as a mother suckling the infant Horus, were gradually hidden in crypts, locked away or even destroyed. It is the fierce avenger aspect of the Goddess that has over the centuries proved most problematic to the accepted view of the gentle mother stereotype.

Among some indigenous peoples, the two aspects remained integrated. For example, to Australian Aborigines, Mother Eingana is the world-creator and birth mother, maker of all water, land, animals, and kangaroos. The Aborigines believe that this huge snake goddess still lives in the Dreamtime, the eternally present place of the ancestors. But Eingana is also the death mother who holds a sinew of life that is attached to each of her creations; when she lets it go, the person, animal or even plant dies.

The most dramatic unbroken tradition of the two faces of the Goddess comes from the Hindu tradition. Shakti is the female energy or power of Shiva, the Father God. Her name is also used for the wife of any god. She is the Mother Goddess and, like Shiva, creator and destroyer in her different aspects.

Although there are several female goddesses, they form aspects of Shakti and often their identities merge. The light form is polarised as Parvati, the benign and gentle Mother Goddess, consort of the god Shiva and the goddess daughter of the Himalayas. Her name means 'mountain' and she is associated with all mountains. She and Shiva are often pictured as a family in the Himalayas with their sons Ganesha, God of Wisdom and Learning, and the six-headed Skanda, the Warrior God.

Kali, the dark side of the Mother Goddess, came into being when Shiva, whose body was covered by white ashes, taunted Shakti for her dark skin. In fury she carried out rituals until her skin became golden inside. Shakti shed her black outer skin like a snake and it formed the avenging, destroying persona of Kali, her four arms holding weapons and the heads of her victims, and her tongue lolling out, covered in blood. Kali is often pictured dancing on Shiva whose body she trampled on, destroyed and then danced on once more to restore him to life, transforming Shava (Sanskrit for corpse) to Shiva (the living one). Once again this is the idea of the Bone Goddess who transforms through death.

MAGICAL, MYSTICAL AND OTHERWORLDLY BEINGS

VAMPIRES AND WEREWOLVES

This is an area where myth, fiction and historical events merge in the attempts to express a primitive human fear of being eaten alive that lurks behind such fairytales as *Red Riding Hood* by the Brothers Grimm, who also wrote several tales about werewolves. Both vampire and werewolf legends and reports of attacks on humans persisted, especially in Germany and Eastern Europe, from earliest times until the end of the Victorian era.

In recent years both the vampire and the werewolf have acquired cult status, partly linked to their primal blood-letting powers that hark back to the Icelandic beserker warriors who appeared in battle like huge wild animals and fought in a trance state that made them invincible. Both the vampire and the werewolf also have magical shape-shifting abilities that are associated with occult and often malevolent powers. The vampire can, it is said, transform himself into a wolf, bat or, according to the Romans, an owl, and drink the blood of babies. The werewolf in human form had the ability to become a wolf and wreak destruction on herds and neighbours alike. Both have sexual connotations: the vampire would seduce victims with great charms, while the male werewolf would sometimes rape women, including pregnant women and young girls, before tearing apart their flesh and eating their hearts – back to *Red Riding Hood*.

Vampires

Dracula by Bram Stoker, and Irish writer, was published in 1897, providing through the voice of Van Helsing, the vampire hunter, a great deal of legendary vampire lore that has since fuelled a whole vampire industry. Ironically, Van Helsing claims that the original Dracula was a genuine historical character – the 15th century Vlad Tepes (the Impaler), King of Wallachia, which included the current vampire Mecca of Transylvania (now part of Romania). Vlad killed his enemies by impaling them on stakes – it is estimated that he killed 10,000 in this fashion during his lifetime.

Cases of vampires began to filter into Western Europe after Charles VI, Emperor of Austria, drove the Turkish out of Eastern Europe in 1718. The most famous was that in the village of Medvegia near Belgrade in 1732, when five Austrian officers signed a sworn statement about a spate of murders apparently by ghosts who throttled sleeping victims, leaving small livid marks on the necks. These spirits had supposedly been infected by vampires during their lifetime and, according to the officers, their exhumed corpses spurted fresh blood and their skin and nails were freshly grown.

Vampires and Science

The tradition of the sun being fatal to vampires may, according to recent medical research, have its roots in the rare genetic blood condition porphyria, which causes its victims to be extremely sensitive to light, and makes the skin pale and the incisors look bigger than normal. Sufferers may have been blamed for outbreaks of ill luck in villages in more superstitious times and lost their lives for it. Vampires traditionally return to their coffins at dawn, and only in some traditions appear briefly at noon.

In September 1997, Dr Juan Gomez-Alonso, a neurologist at Xeral Hospital in Vigo, put forward the alternative view that rabies was behind the outbreaks of vampirism that allegedly plagued 18th-century Europe. The doctor was inspired while watching a Dracula film. He noted that the classic characteristics of a vampire – frothing at the mouth, bared teeth, an aversion to mirrors and nocturnal habits – were all well-documented symptoms of rabies. Another symptom is hypersexuality. In his paper published in the journal *Neurology*, he says that rabies victims have been known to have intercourse up 30 times a day. Rabies would also explain the deadliness of the vampire's 'kiss', as biting transmits the disease. And the bats and wolves who were said to be vampires in disguise are common carriers of rabies. The doctor makes a convincing case when he points out that early tales of vampires frequently coincided with reports of rabies outbreaks in and around the Balkans, stretching back to a particularly devastating epidemic in dogs, wolves and other animals in Hungary in 1721–1728. Others say that the vast literature on the subject would suggest more occult forces at work.

Vampire Lore

In some legends the vampire becomes a vampire only after death, while in others, children or grandchildren of existing vampires inherit the trait. Other myths tell of people becoming vampires by being bitten, but not killed, by a vampire, or by eating an animal that had been bitten by a vampire.

Immortality is thereby granted to the vampire as long as he (the vampire is more commonly regarded as male because of the Vlad/Dracula association) can feed on the blood of the living, preferably of humans. Vampires usually obtain blood by biting a victim's neck and drinking the blood, in some legends sucking the blood through long, hollow front incisors. Vampires throw no shadow and do not have a reflection in a mirror.

It is said, too, that he can only pass running water at the slack or the flood of the tide. Traditionally, vampires can be repelled with garlic, holy water and the crucifix, a branch of wild rose on his coffin, the coffin containing the vampire within. But total destruction results when a stake of hawthorn is driven through the heart. In some versions the vampire needs to be sleeping for this to work, or sometimes fire, exposure to sunlight or beheading is also considered necessary to be sure the impaled vampire will rise no more.

Werewolves

The most common method of becoming a werewolf involved tying around the body a strip of leather made from wolf skin which still had its hair. A more spontaneous change to lupine appearance was triggered by the full moon. Some legends tell that a person is born a werewolf; in others a person becomes a werewolf by being bitten by a werewolf. Until the early 19th century the most popular explanation was that the person had made a pact with the Devil.

The purpose of becoming a werewolf is said to be the craving for flesh, sometimes human, but more usually it is cattle and sheep that are attacked. The werewolf can be male or female and appears throughout the literature of northern Europe, with Germany being a particularly rich source of werewolf legends. A popular protective device against werewolf attack, documented as being used by the farmers in the Hesse area around 1854, was to throw a knife or a piece of shiny steel over the werewolf who would instantly be transformed into his true human form and stand there completely naked. If successful, the werewolf's pelt burst crosswise at its forehead, and the naked human emerged from this opening.

The most famous werewolf case is perhaps that of Stubbe Peeter in June 1590, '*a most wicked sorcerer, who in the likeness of a wolf committed many murders, continuing this devilish practice for 25 years and killing and devouring men, women and children.*'

Peeter lived near Cologne in what was then High Germany and was said – having confessed rather than be tortured – to have made a pact with the Devil. After his execution, which began with his body being laid on a wheel and the flesh pulled off from the bones with red hot burning pincers, the imprint of a wolf was found on the wheel.

The most recent werewolf sighting was in 1998 at Hahn Airforce Base, Germany, just outside the village of Wittlich, the last town where a werewolf was killed. There is a shrine just out the town where a candle always burns, and legend has it that if the candle ever goes out the werewolf will return.

One night during 1998 the candle went out and security policemen investigating alarms at the base saw a huge wolf-like creature, seven or eight feet tall, jump a 12-foot security fence after taking three huge leaping steps.

PART FOUR

Nature Magic and Mystery

BIRD MAGIC – AUSPICY

Origins of Bird Magic

Birds were regarded as magical in every culture because of their power of flight. They were believed to be messengers of the gods, or even a deity in disguise, and so were regarded as harbingers of success or disaster. For example, an eagle soaring with out-stretched wings is a universal symbol of coming prosperity. Omens were gathered either through the singing, crowing or croaking of birds, or through the pattern and direction of their flight. The cooing of sacred pigeons or doves in the oracular groves dedicated to Zeus at Dodona was used for prophecy. The term 'aruspex' for a prediction comes from the Latin for an observer of birds.

Native North American Feather Magic

Four feathers were used in Amerindian magic, typically an eagle feather in the east for spring, a hawk feather in the south for summer, a raven feather in the west for autumn and an owl feather in the north for winter. In some tribes the owl represented summer and the hawk winter.

The feathers would be placed in the four cardinal directions in sweat lodges, and used to guard those who went on vision quests – private journeys for initiation or enlightenment. They were also used as talismans, carrying within them the qualities of the totem bird, so, for example, eagle and hawk feathers, from birds of prey that were said to fly closest of all to the sun, transferred vision and courage to warriors by a process of contagious magic.

The **eagle** is the Tribal Chief of all birds and soars high in the sky, yet sees everything below. He is said to carry the prayers of the people to Father Sun. He is associated with the mythical Thunder Bird, the rain-bringer whose flashing eyes are the lightning and whose flapping wings bring thunder. His feathers are often found in medicine bundles and worn by warriors during the sun dance.

The **hawk** is called the Messenger of Spirit and his feathers are used in healing ceremonies. Tribes in the south-east used their hawk feathers to bring rain in times of drought. Sometimes, like the eagle, the hawk is associated with the Thunder Bird and the power of the sun. Pueblo Indians refer to red-tailed hawks as red eagles.

The **owl** is called the Night Eagle, being the bird of the night and moon as the eagle rules the day and the sun. To the woodland tribes of south-east America, the Owl is Chief of the Night and a sacred protector of all who must travel or work in darkness.

The **raven** is a teacher of magic, regarded as both the Great Trickster and Creator. He is sometimes called the Big Grandfather, Raven Man, and like the hawk was

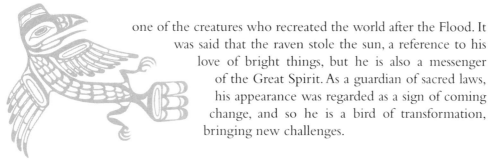

one of the creatures who recreated the world after the Flood. It was said that the raven stole the sun, a reference to his love of bright things, but he is also a messenger of the Great Spirit. As a guardian of sacred laws, his appearance was regarded as a sign of coming change, and so he is a bird of transformation, bringing new challenges.

Bird Divination

Although auspicy, divination by bird flight, was practised in many cultures, it is best documented in Ancient Rome where it was the principal form of augury. The augurs (trained philosophers) would interpret the auspicy, which was seen as a message from Jupiter, and the appointment of officials – even consuls – was under their control, as well as matters of peace and war.

Auspicy took place within a sacred space, called a templum, that was not a building but invisible divisions marked off in the sky or on the ground by an augur. The augur would face the east and mark out with his curved staff the quarters in the sky, so that south was to his right and the north on his left. He waited for a single bird to appear, noting the spot from which it rose, its upwards or downwards course and the point at which it disappeared. But flocks of birds were also used for divination, both by the augurs and by ordinary people.

Interpreting Bird Flight

Dark and light

If there is more than one species of bird, a light or bright-coloured bird indicates immediate action, while darker ones predict a delay. If the question involves options, the arrival or movement of a light-coloured bird would indicate to act, a darker one to wait. Sometimes darker and lighter birds are found among the same flock and observations can be as to which arrive or depart first.

Direction

Birds flying from the right or to the right indicate a smooth passage in any venture and that confident action should be taken. Birds flying to or from the left indicate delays and counsel waiting or remaining silent for a while. Birds flying straight towards the questioner indicate that happier times are coming. Those flying directly away suggest that opportunities are temporarily receding, but old sorrows may also be departing.

Height

The higher the flight, the more favourable the omen. If a bird flies directly upwards, then the venture should achieve swift success with little effort.

If the flight is horizontal or veers up and down with the bird landing and flying off then landing again, there may be initial obstacles that can be overcome with perseverance.

Changing course
If a bird suddenly changes direction, there may be sudden changes of heart, inconstancy or sudden doubts.

Hovering
If a bird hovers directly overhead, it warns of hidden criticism or new friends who may be less than direct.

Bird Song
If a bird sings or utters a cry as it takes flight, it is a good sign to go ahead at once with any matter. A bird who calls as it lands may indicate that caution is needed.

If a dark bird or a bird of prey screams as it circles, unless it is near its nest, there may be unexpected opposition to overcome.

Divination by Selection – Alectromancy

Traditionally, sacred chickens or white cockerels would be released to peck corn in areas or circles drawn on the ground and marked with letters or special signs to designate different options. The areas in which the chickens pecked first indicated the answer. Sometimes a grain of wheat was placed on each letter and magical incantations uttered. Prophetic words might be obtained by combining the letters touched by the birds, or the identity of a thief revealed. This method was used by Roman legions who carried the caged sacred birds on military expeditions.

The Lore of Birds

The kind of bird seen in flight added significance to the divination, especially if a bird was seen at an unusual time or in an unexpected place. What is more, as with Ameridian feather magic, the particular quality associated with a species of bird could be transferred to the practitioner, not only by its feathers but by a small representation, charm or picture of the bird totem. So carrying a stork talisman was believed to help women become pregnant, a dove to bring love and peace, and a crane good health.

Folk Divination – Magpies

Magpies have been used for centuries by country people to predict the future and the ancient sayings have entered the nursery rhyme tradition. One magpie alone is traditionally considered a bad omen, and unless a second follows rapidly you should take off your hat and bow, saying, 'Good morning [or afternoon or evening], Mr Magpie, and how are you today?' This ensures that any news you receive that day will be good.

There are several versions of the children's rhyme referring to the prophetic nature of the magpie:

One for sorrow,
Two for mirth,
Three for a letter,
Four for a birth,
Five for silver,
Six for gold
And seven for a secret never to be told.

Another version says:

One's sorrow,
Two's mirth,
Three's a wedding,
Four's a birth,
Five's a christening,
Six a dearth,
Seven's heaven,
Eight is hell
And nine the Devil's self as well.

In the Far East, the magpie's arrival is welcomed wholeheartedly for the bird is a symbol of happiness and prosperity, and its chattering, according to modern usage, heralds unexpected but very welcome visitors bringing good news.

EARTH MYSTERIES

Earth mysteries is a generic term for the study of earth energies, including megalithic sites of power (see p. 196), dowsing (see p. 26), geomancy (see p. 188) and earth spirits (see p. 154). This section looks at phenomena that seem to suggest that the earth is a living entity, communicating with humankind through crop circles and earth lights.

The earth has been regarded as a living entity since the beginning of human consciousness and is still seen in this way by indigenous peoples such as the Native North Americans and Australian Aborigines. The Gaia Hypothesis, named after Gaea, the Greek Goddess of the Earth, was first proposed by James Lovelock, a British biologist, in the early 1970s. While working for the Jet Propulsion Laboratory of the National Aeronautics and Space Administration in Pasadena, California, Lovelock realised that the earth was a biological self-regulating mechanism. His work in the field of evolutionary biology suggests that all the needs of a species are met by its environment, including healing of body, mind and the psyche. So if people harm the earth, spiritually as well as physically, this damages their own life support system and that of their descendants.

Crop Circles

Crop circles in fields of grain are regarded by some researchers as a direct warning by the earth that humankind should cease pollution, deforestation and destruction. One theory is that this is a deliberate communication by earth entities. However, it may be that energy vortexes from within the earth, spiritual as well as physical, create sacred geometric patterns and ancient magical symbols, images that were first based on natural observable patterns millennia ago. Circles tend to reappear over a period of years on the same site near sacred centres, for example Stonehenge, Avebury and nearby Silbury Hill. These places are known for their high energy vortexes.

Although crop circles are a phenomena associated with more recent decades, legends and woodcut pictures depict their existence as early as 1590. Since the early 1970s, at least 10,000 crop circles have been reported in Australia, Brazil, Canada,

Germany, Hungary, Japan, Romania, the UK and the USA, with the majority appearing in England. The counties of Wiltshire and Hampshire have experienced the largest incidence of crop circles, especially in the vicinity of ancient sites and areas where UFO activity has frequently been reported. This apparent UFO activity sometimes coincides with the time at which the crop circles appear, leading to a suggesting that in the case of simple formations, circles may be created by UFOs landing. More complex formations are interpreted by the UFO theory as warnings from evolved extra-terrestrials that humans should treasure the earth before it is too late.

Crop formations continue to increase in complexity and number. For example, a crop circle appeared on June 17, 1996 in Alton Barnes, Wiltshire, that was almost the equivalent of two football fields in length. It was made up of spiralling spheres, which were said to resemble a DNA double helix. Another circle appeared overnight at Etchilhampton, Wiltshire, on July 29, 1996 that was almost a mile (1.6km) in length. Certainly the crop circles seem to contain great physical potency. Even sceptics who stand in or near them suffer dizziness and disorientation and may even be hurled to the ground by an unseen force.

Investigating Crop Circles

Though some crop circles, especially in England and New Zealand, have been acknowledged either as hoaxes or as human attempts to convey environmental messages in a dramatic form, the majority are inexplicable in material terms, appearing in a relatively short time and with no sign of human intervention.

In June 1996, a 90 ft (27 m) long formation with 151 circles appeared in a field close to Stonehenge in what seemed to be the space of less than half an hour. This was verified by a pilot who flew over the field during the late afternoon when the crops were growing normally, but on returning half an hour later saw the completed design. There are also at least fifty verified cases in the UK of people witnessing the circles forming spontaneously.

The original explanation, put forward in 1980 by Dr Terence Meaden, a Bristol physicist and editor of the *Journal of Meterology*, was that crop circles were caused by a fair-weather stationary whirlwind that momentarily circled over an area of the field, and that this phenomenon occurred mainly during summer. However, that would not account for more complex designs or those that had spiritual significance.

Some researchers have measured radioactivity in the vicinity of circles and discovered cellular changes in the affected crops. Dr W.C. Levengood of the Pinelandia Biophysical Laboratory in Grass Lakes, Michigan, compared plants taken from a crop circle with identical ones in the same field. He also tested the ability of seeds taken from a crop circle to germinate compared with control plants. He discovered significant differences and concluded that the plants from the circle appeared to have been exposed to transient high temperatures. This would be consistent with either the Gaia, vortex or UFO theories.

Experiments in Wiltshire by Dr Steven Greer, an American who has researched earth lights in Florida (see below), have attempted to contact the entities he believes create the circles. In July 1992, it was claimed that during a week-long vigil at Woodburgh Hill, near Alton Barnes, Wiltshire, Dr Greer and his group used sophisticated communication equipment to try to contact the extra-terrestrials and had a close range encounter with a huge UFO craft and also witnessed a number of floating lights. This work has been developed by other investigators who created crop messages and in one case received a reply of crop squiggles in an adjacent field. While this may all seem like *X-Files* fiction and an area rife with accusations of hoax, it may be that it is possible to contact this power, whether it is some form of consciousness within the earth or beyond it, and so explain the crop circle phenomena.

Earth Lights

Earth lights are glowing, changing circles that may either hover or whirl through the skies. They measure only a few centimetres across, although the largest are several metres in diameter. In the daytime they are perceived as metallic or black circles. Some UFO sightings may be explained as the incidence of large earth lights.

Origins of Earth Lights

Earth lights are an ancient phenomenon and are accepted as quite normal by indigenous peoples such as the Native North Americans who interpret them as manifestations of the Earth Mother.

In northern European folklore, the Will o' the Wisp or Friar's lanthorn was regarded as a malevolent fairy who guarded lost treasures. Will o' the Wisps are said to elude all who attempt to follow them and lure many lost travellers to their end on marshes and bogs. According to scientists, this flame-like phosphorescence floating over marshy ground is due to the spontaneous combustion of decaying vegetable matter, but Will o' the Wisps have been known to respond to travellers, beckoning or calling them. It is the interaction between earth lights and people that makes them especially remarkable.

Earth lights also hover over ancient stones, especially on the old festivals. At Avebury Rings they have been perceived, in accounts spanning centuries, as small luminous figures dancing around the stones just above the ground.

Research into Earth Lights

In the 1960s, the Ufologist John Keel and French researcher Ferdinand Lagarde identified a connection between earth lights and areas of geological faulting and magnetic irregularities. In the USA, Michael Persinger, a neuroscientist and geologist at Laurentian University, Canada, and Gyslaine Lafrenière discovered a correlation between reports of UFO activity and earthquake epicentres. Persinger regarded UFOs as 'eletromagnetic phenomena arising from the tremendous energy associated with the constantly rising and falling stress in the earth's crust, whether or not full-blown earthquakes occurred', that was particularly intense in areas of instability, caused by such factors as fault lines, mineral deposits and mountains and so on.

In 1986, a further study by Michael Persinger and the US geologist John Derr involved charting the phenomenon of earth light sightings that had been reported in a sample period of 13 years in the Yakima Indian Reservation, Washington State. Native North Americans had seen the lights since they first settled in the area many years before. In recent times, fire wardens had regularly described very large orange light balls floating above rocks, and smaller balls of light that seemed to bounce along the ridges. The lights were most commonly observed where the fault cut across the reservation. Reports intensified during the seven months immediately before the biggest earthquake that occurred during the period under investigation.

However, investigations centring on Hessdalen, a valley 70 miles (112km) south-east of Trondheim in Norway, cast doubt on a purely geological explanation. White and yellow spheres and also bullet- and inverted fir tree-shaped lights were first seen in the area in November 1981. This phenomenon continued and in the summer of 1983, after hundreds of reports of earth lights from locals, Project Hessdalen was instigated by Norwegian and Swedish UFO groups. The area was continuously monitored for just over a month, beginning on January 21, 1984. During this period, photographs of the lights were obtained and subsequent research continued intermittently. However, these lights actually seemed to read the thoughts of the investigators and responded to them.

If, as it seems, earth lights do possess some form of consciousness, then they may, like crop circles, demonstrate the living essence of Gaia – or alternatively of an extra-terrestrial force.

FESTIVALS OF LIGHT

Festivals of Light form a religious focus in many cultures on the darkest days of the year. Their roots may be found in the ancient sympathetic magical tradition of attracting light and new life back to the world at the coldest part of the year. In modern magic, invocations for personal illumination are carried out by covens and individuals at times of spiritual and emotional as well as seasonal darkness, and fires, candles and torches are used in these rituals to mirror the energies of the more formal festivals.

Christmas/Yule

Light was the focus of the annual midwinter solstice around December 21, from which the modern Christmas derives. These magical solstice ceremonies to celebrate the rebirth of the sun and later the Sun Gods, and in Christianity the nativity of the Son of God, date from Palaeolithic times and are found in many cultures, especially those in the northern hemisphere such as Scandinavia that have long, cold winters.

The Advent Candle

Light marks every stage of the Christmas celebration, beginning with the Advent candle and ending with the Twelfth Night fires and candles to mark the last day of the

festivities and to bring protection to cattle and the following year's corn. In Scandinavian homes, a circle of four Advent candles that are lit one at a time on each of the four Sundays of Advent, is still an important feature of the pre-Christmas period. In Sweden, too, from Advent on every window in the home is illuminated with electric branch candelabras to dispel the darkness.

A single Advent candle that traditionally has 24 marks on it is once again becoming popular in the UK, with a section of the candle lit at dusk and burned for each of the days of Advent.

The Feast of St Lucy, December 13

A Swedish celebration, the Festival of St Lucy on December 13 commemorates the Christian Saint Lucia or Lucy, who in legend went down into the catacombs to take food for the Christians who were hiding from persecution. She wore a wreath of candles so both her hands were free.

The festival, like the midwinter solstice a few days later, symbolises the return of light to the world. It is shrouded in mystery as to how the Sicilian Christian St

179

Lucy, Patroness of Blindness, has become intermingled with the traditions of an earlier Northern Pagan Goddess of the Returning Light.

In Denmark, Lucy's Eve is a night when young women practise divination, seeking the identity of their future husbands. In Sweden, a girl is chosen by the community as St Lucy, dressed in white with a wreath of candles round her head. She is accompanied by her maidens, Tallia, carrying St Lucy buns and blue-clad Star Boys, bearing stars on poles and lanterns. The custom is also practised in parts of the USA.

The Christmas Eve Candle

A Christmas Eve candle is traditionally left burning throughout the night of Christmas Eve, surrounded by nuts, fruits, spices, a small piece of coal or wood, silver coins and a small ear of corn saved from the previous harvest, as a magical gesture to ensure there will be sufficient light, warmth and food throughout the winter. Like the golden candle that is frequently lit on Solstice Eve instead of the traditional bonfire, this custom is a direct descendant of the ancient magical solstice fire which gave strength to the dying sun.

During the mediaeval period, and up until the Industrial Revolution, any stranger who called at a house on Christmas Eve having seen the light would be made welcome, in memory of Mary finding no room at the inn. In Ireland, Brittany and among American families who have Celtic connections, the Christmas Eve custom of leaving a lighted candle in the window to light the Virgin Mary on her way still survives. Food and drink is left in the kitchen, in case she is hungry or thirsty.

Twelfth Night

This is a magical but frightening period when Odin and the Wild Hunt rode across the skies on the Eve of Twelfth Night, or Epiphany Eve, in England and parts of Europe. Twelfth Night fires were lit on the highest point of a sown wheat field – twelve fires in a circle with a larger one in the centre. In Ireland, twelve lighted candles were placed in a sieve of oats with a larger one burning in the centre. In both instances they represented Jesus and the Apostles. In an older custom the central fire was said to represent old Meg, a witch, associated with the Celtic *Callieach*, or Hag of Winter, who was burned as a corn sacrifice.

Candlemas

Candlemas Day, at the beginning of February in the Christian calendar, coincides with the anniversary of the Purification of the Virgin Mary 40 days after the birth of Jesus, also the occasion when the infant Christ was taken to the Temple and hailed as the light of the world.

On Candlemas Day, all the church candles to be used for the coming liturgical year were blessed at High Mass. Blessed candles were also distributed to the congregation, and the festival, like many others, was grafted on to the Celtic pre-

Christian Festival of Light, Imbolc, which was held for three days from sunset on January 31 to sunset on February 2. In the glorious mix of folklore and religion, the Christian Candlemas candles were preserved at home because they were believed to have healing powers, and if rekindled to act as a charm against thunder, lightning and earthquakes.

One of the Celtic names for the pagan festival was Brigantia, after Brighid, the Celtic Triple Goddess, here in her maiden aspect replacing the old Hag of Winter's rule. She was Christianised as St Brigit of Kildare, Saint of Candlemas, at whose shrine a perpetual flame was kept burning. Blazing torches were carried clockwise around the still frozen fields at Brigantia and sacred fires lit on hilltops to attract the new sun.

Easter Candles: the Paschal Candle

In the early Christian tradition, Easter, itself a relic of the old spring equinox, was a celebration of the Resurrection of the Light. Candles in churches were extinguished on Easter Eve and the Paschal candle was lit from the new *nyd* fire which was kindled outside the church using an oaken spindle from nine different kinds of wood. This custom is being revived in parts of the USA.

In pagan times, the effigy of a Judas Man – a straw man – was burned on this fire as a sacrifice for a good harvest. Charred sticks were taken from the fire and placed on newly kindled home fires or kept through the year as protection against thunderstorms. St Cyril of Jerusalem described the profusion of light on Easter Eve as being as bright as day, and Constantine the Great made the Easter Eve celebrations even more dazzling by placing lights not only in basilicas, but in streets and squares. Homes were also illuminated with candles in every window to welcome the rebirth of the longer days and the risen Christ.

The Paschal candle makers of mediaeval times vied with one another over the splendour and size of the Paschal candle. In 1517, the Salisbury Cathedral candle was 36ft (11m) in height, and in 1558, 3cwt (152kg) of wax was used for the Paschal candle of Westminster Abbey.

Chanukkah or Hanukkah, the Hebrew Festival of Light

The Talmud, the body of Jewish Oral Law, decrees that starting on the 25th of Kislev, which falls during November/December on the conventional calendar, eight days of Chanukkah, or Hanukkah, the Jewish Festival of Light, are observed. The extra-biblical holiday, Hanukkah, commemorates the Jews' victory in 165BC over the Hellenist Syrians. After their victory, the Hasmoneans, or Maccabees, cleansed and rededicated Jerusalem's Holy Temple and celebrated the first Hanukkah – the Hebrew term for dedication – in memory of their victory.

In memory of the miracle of the Holy Temple menorah that burned for eight nights on a single cruse of oil, all that had not been defiled, a special menorah called a Chanukiah, or Hanukkiya, was created and this is the origin of this special candelabrum used at the festival today. It is usually a nine-branch candelabrum whose candles are lit by a *shamash*, or servant candle, which then takes its own place at the centre of the menorah. On the eve of Chanukkah, the *shamash* candle is lit first and is used to light the first Chanukiah candle One candle is added each night until all eight candles are present and alight. The Chanukiah is usually placed near a window or a door so its light can be seen by passersby on the street. As the candles are lit and the blessings given, family and guests gather together and the candles continue to shine until they burn themselves out.

Divali, Deepawali or Diwali

Divali, also celebrated in the Sikh tradition, is the autumnal Hindu Festival of Light. Rows of *diyas* (clay lamps), oil lamps and candles illuminate every home and building. Even on the waterways tiny boats of leaves or coconut shells carry lights and there are magnificent firework displays to illuminate the skies. Divali is celebrated 20 days after Dussehra, on the 13th day of the dark fortnight of the month of Asvin in October/November.

This festive occasion also marks the beginning of the Hindu New Year. Perhaps the most significant deity worshipped during this period is Lakshmi, consort of Vishnu, the Goddess of Wealth and Good Fortune. Lights and candles are placed in windows so that Lakshmi will look in and endow the family with prosperity, and *rangolis*, or coloured patterns, are painted on floors and walls to attract her benevolence.

FIRE MAGIC

The Origins of Fire Magic

From earliest times fire came from the sky in the form of lightning or thunderbolts. Such portents were regarded as the gods, expressing their anger with mankind. In every culture the discovery of fire transformed life: men and women could cook their food, while fire kept them warm, protected them from fierce beasts and allowed them to shape metals. It was hard to believe that the gods would give such a precious gift willingly, and many myths tell how heroes stole the fire.

In Greek mythology, Prometheus, a Titan, stole the fire from Hephaestus, God of Fire and Metals, because Zeus had denied its use for mortals. Zeus punished Prometheus by chaining him to Mount Caucasus, where an eagle ate his liver each day until he was rescued by Heracles. Birds are also seen as the bringers of fire. For example, in the Caroline Islands east of the Philippines, mortals received fire from the gods through the bird Mwi, which brought it to earth in its bill and hid it inside trees. The fire was released when people rubbed two sticks together.

Fire gods began as sun gods, but gradually the role of fire was assigned to a specific Fire God, sometimes linked with the smelting of metals, as with the Greek

Hephaestus. In India, the great Fire God was Agni, who ruled not only over the fires of lightning and heaven, but the sacred fires on earth, carrying sacrifices from man to the gods on the dark canopy of smoke. Sacrifice to the fire deity was the first act of morning devotion as the sun rose.

In Ancient Persia, fire was regarded as the earthly manifestation of Divine power. The ceremonial 'keeping of the flame' formed a central role in Zoroastrian religion. A priest is called *athravan*, belonging to the fire, in Zoroastrian holy writings.

From Classical times was derived the custom of a sacred fire that was kept perpetually burning and from which, on ceremonial occasions, all other fires were lit (as with the Olympic flame and those burning on the graves of unknown warriors who fell in battle). The vestal virgins kept burning a sacred flame, dedicated to Vesta, that was said to embody the heart of the Roman Empire and so was never allowed to be extinguished.

Fire Festivals

Fire has been central to festivals throughout the world, especially on the major solar festivals such as the summer and midwinter solstices. It represents the power of the sun and life and was used to persuade the sun to continue to shine at times when early man feared its power was declining. Yule logs were burned on the midwinter solstice, around December 21, and at the summer solstice, on or close to June 21 when the sun reached its height, fields were circled with blazing torches. The Oak, King of the Waxing Year, was sacrificed on the ceremonial pyre. The summer solstice fires were in Christian times transferred to St John's or Midsummer Eve, the evening of June 23. In Portugal, young people wishing for love and health would leap over the Midsummer Eve fires after drinking from seven springs of water.

At other seasonal festivals, especially in the Celtic and Teutonic traditions, fires were linked with the fertility of the land and ashes from ceremonial blazes were scattered on the fields to make them fertile.

Beltane, which extended from sunset on April 30 for three days and celebrated the beginning of the Celtic summer, was also linked with human fertility. Young men would leap over the fires with the girls with whom they had spent the night looking for the first may (hawthorn) blossoms to decorate the houses. Women who wished to become pregnant would also jump over or run between the twin fires; as a result it was said, they would have a babe by the next Beltane fires. A Beltane cake was baked, divided into portions and placed in a bag. The person who picked out the piece marked with a charred cross was the *carline*, the mock sacrifice (and in ancient times, the real fire sacrifice).

It may be that all fire festivals originally involved animal or human sacrifice and all sacrificial fires were considered potent for divination. The direction in which

NATURE MAGIC AND MYSTERY

the smoke blew, the intensity of heat and even how far the festival fires could be seen (they were often lit on hilltops) would indicate the extent to which their magical powers might extend. In South Africa too, around April, the Matabeles would light huge fires to the windward of their gardens so that the smoke would ripen them.

The May fires, like the Hallowe'en fires that celebrated the beginning of the Celtic New Year, were considered protective against the supernatural creatures associated with transition times of the year when the dimensions parted. Germans call the May festival *Walpurgisnacht*, the night of the witches, after Walpurgs, the pagan Goddess of the Springtime Sacred Marriage. Hilltop fires were built to drive the witches off and stop them gaining new powers to ruin the coming harvest.

Pyromancy

Pyromancy is the art of divination by fire. Because of its volatile and unpredictable nature, fire was seen as a perfect medium for interpreting omens, especially on the old festivals, and was seen as auguring for communities as well as individuals. In the Western tradition of fire divination, the future was considered promising if a fire burned vigorously and the fuel was quickly consumed. It was also considered a good omen if a fire was clear, the flames transparent rather than dark red or yellow, and the fire crackled. A fire that burned silently, was difficult to light, blown about by the wind or slow to consume the offerings placed on it, indicated that the coming days and events were not so propitious.

Ordinary people, as well as seers, divined the success or otherwise of future plans by observing the flames of torches or by throwing powdered pitch on to fires. If the pitch caught and flamed quickly the outcome of any action would be favourable. The flame of a torch augured well if it formed a point, but was less promising of success if it was divided. However, if it did divide, three points were considered best of all. Sickness or financial difficulties were, it was said, foretold by the bending of a flame.

In popular tradition, another form of fire divination involved interpreting pictures in the embers of a fire, a family pastime that has been revived with the advent of the barbecue.

Tibetan Fire Divination

This begins with the invocation of the fire deity and is practised by observing the nature of the flames in a divinatory fire, while concentrating on a specific question. The omens differ slightly from those of the Western tradition:

- A bright, long-lasting gold- and orange-coloured flame without smoke or crackling that either burns to the right or upwards in a single point offers a positive affirmation to the question that prompted the divination.

- A white gentle flame indicates that any past omissions or sins are now expiated.

- A yellow flame promises power and wealth; a red flame success; and clear, smokeless blue good health and fertility.

- Illness or misfortune is foretold if the fire blazes fiercely with dark smoky flames.

FLOWER FESTIVALS

Flowers form an integral part of major Buddhist, Hindu, Chinese and Japanese celebrations, and the dates of the festivals coincide with the blossoming of flowers and trees, especially the cherry blossom in Japan. In Ancient Greece, the Sacred Marriage of Zeus to Hera was celebrated in January, as new life began to bud. Hera, as well as being the chief Mother and Fertility Goddess, guardian of marriage and childbirth, was also Goddess of Flowers. Her statues were decked with lilies, which became part of the bridal bouquet or headdress throughout Western Europe and the Mediterranean.

The festival of Flora, Roman Goddess of Flowers, lasted from April 26 to May 3. Japan celebrates its main flower festival on April 8, the birthday of Buddha. Children carry flowers in procession, offering them at tiny temples. Hydrangea and other floral teas are consumed and homes are decked with flowers. This festival is rooted in traditional ancestor worship. In earlier times, family members would go to the hills in spring to bring back the first wild flowers for the family shrine as a sign of regeneration.

Flower Myths and Legends

In Classical mythology, many flowers were said to have divine origins, emanating either from the blood of slain deities or nymphs, or from the tears of spurned lovers. For example, the Ancient Greek legend relates that the water nymph Clytie was so sad that her love for Helios, the Greek Sun God, was not returned that she sat on the ground day and night, watching his fiery chariot pass across the sky as the sun rose, reached his height and descended into the ocean. So long did she watch that her limbs became rooted in the earth and she was transformed into a sunflower, symbol of constancy. Her gaze is forever fixed sunwards as she climbs towards her love.

A single flower can acquire a mythology from a variety of sources. The lily of the valley was said to have been created by Eve's tears as she was expelled from the Garden of Eden. Yet, according to Irish tradition, lilies of the valley form ladders that

NATURE MAGIC AND MYSTERY

fairies climb to reach the reeds from which they plait their cradles. In addition, it is said that St Leonard was wounded while fighting a dragon and tiny lilies grew on the spot where his blood fell. Another legend says that the first lily of the valley loved a nightingale, but because she was so shy, she hid in the long grass to listen to his song. The nightingale became lonely and at last said he would no longer sing, unless the lily of the valley bloomed every May for all to see. Now when the moonlight shines upon the delicate white bells, the nightingale sings his sweetest and the returning song of her tiny bells can be heard in the stillness.

The Language of Flowers

The language of flowers was used by the Ancient Egyptians, the Chinese, Indians and Ancient Greeks. During the time of Elizabeth I in England, flower meanings appeared in verse and Shakespearean plays: gilliflowers as symbols of gentleness, cowslips of wise counsel, pansies for thoughts, the flowering rosemary for remembrance and marigolds for married love.

It was formalised as a system of communication, especially between lovers, in the early 18th century. Lady Mary Wortley Montagu was living in Turkey at this time with her ambassador husband and discovered the hidden meanings that could be concealed in a bouquet of flowers.

Bouquets containing floral messages were a safe and secret way of sending loving thoughts, a promise or offer, warning or instruction, even across language barriers. White flowers indicate innocence or secrecy, red flowers love or passion, and yellow flowers warnings or jealousy. Spring flowers talk of new hopes, summer blooms of high passion or fulfilled love, while autumn blooms speak of waning or gentler affections. A full-petalled flower represents an intense emotion, while a small flower can indicate uncertainty. A tall flower talks of lofty ambitions or spiritual desires, while a flower close to the ground or folded shows affection, friendship or uncertainty. The following are examples of a system that incorporates hundreds of flowers in its different versions.

Anemones I hope to see you very soon.

Apple Blossom You are both beautiful and worthy of respect.

Azalea Be careful we are not seen together.

Bee-orchid Forgive me. You misunderstood my words.

Bluebell I will be faithful to you.

Buttercup All I own I will share with you.

Campion Meet me at dusk.

Carnation (pink) Thank you for your token/message. It was welcome.

Carnation (red) I must see you very soon. Your absence is too painful to bear.

Carnation (yellow) You have proved unworthy of my affection.

Chrysanthemum (brown)   Let us still be friends, even if love has faded.

Chrysanthemum (red)   I love and desire you.

Chrysanthemum (yellow)   My heart belongs to another.

Chrysanthemum (white)   I will never lie to you.

Harebell   I hope you may change your mind.

Hibiscus   Your gentle nature is matched only by your beauty.

Hollyhock   May our love bear fruit.

Hyacinth   I regret our separation.

Hydrangeas   Why have you changed your mind?

Jasmine (Europe)   I desire you night and day.

Jasmine (US)   We may be parted, but we are together in my dreams.

Passion Flower   We are twin souls.

Peony   Forgive me for my insensitivity.

Rose (pink)   I am afraid to show my feelings.

Rose (red)   I love you with all my heart.

Rose (white)   Our love must remain a secret.

Rose (wild)   I love you from afar.

Snapdragon   Rejection. You mean nothing to me now.

Star of Bethlehem   Can we forget the harsh words we spoke?

Violet   I will not betray your trust.

Wallflower   I will love you in sad times as well as happy ones.

Ylang-ylang   I am intoxicated with joy.

NATURE MAGIC AND MYSTERY

Giving Flowers in Person

The way a flower is given can also convey a wealth of meaning. A single rose on a plain stem offered flower uppermost showed positive hopes and intentions. A rosebud surrounded by thorns and leaves, offered upright, conveyed uncertainty that the love was returned. If the recipient inverted the rosebud and handed it back, he or she was equally uncertain but not entirely rejecting the overture. If, however, the recipient removed the thorns and returned the rosebud upright, he or she was saying that there was true feeling. However, if the leaves were removed, there was no hope of the love progressing.

NATURE MAGIC AND MYSTERY

Secret Trysts

'Meet me' or 'do not meet me' was conveyed either by an iris (inverted for do not meet me) or by a green fern (meeting). The first fern given is either upright or inverted according to whether the meeting will or will not take place. The rest of the ferns are upright and the total (including the first) should be counted to give the day. One fern means today, two means tomorrow, and so on through the days of the week. A small many-headed flower was used for the hours of the day to indicate the meeting time.

Flower Divination and Rituals

- The earliest form of flower divination has survived as a children's game. Lovers would pluck the petals of a daisy, flower of Venus, chanting, 'He/she loves me, he/she loves me not'. The flower is said to be a talisman for all who are pure of heart and loyal in love. Mediaeval knights wore daisies when they went into battle as a sign that they rode in the name of a lady whom they loved. A daisy root, it is said, can bring back an absent lover if placed under a pillow at night.

- The carnation is used for divination in parts of the Far East. A cluster of three carnations on a single stem is placed in the hair of a young person and left there until the flowers begin to wilt. If the top flower dies first, it is said that the later years of the wearer's life will be the hardest. If the middle flower dies first, the middle years will be more difficult. If the bottom flower dies first, then the earlier years will be more problematic. If the flowers remain fresh for a long time, life will be happy.

- In Eastern Europe, it was believed that if a person took the soil from beneath a lover or potential lover's shoe print and put it in a pot with marigold seeds, the love would bloom with the flowers and last throughout many winters and summers.

GEOMANCY

Geomancy is usually associated with earth energies, but is also the name given to a form of divination using the Earth element. Just as skilled hunters could read the tracks of animals, so the geomancers tried to read the future from patterns made on the ground from throwing down handfuls of pebbles, nuts or seeds.

The Origins of Divinatory Geomancy

The art originated in Africa but spread from Arabia to Europe where a new system sprang up. The original marks on the ground became a system of 16 geometrical shapes, each with its own name and meaning. According to Arabian tradition, the prophet Idris was taught the art by the Angel Gabriel. The Jewish prophet Daniel is regarded as another early source of inspiration. Geomancy is also associated with India. Its popularity over the millennia, and the fact that there seem to be several parallel sources for its origin, owes much to the fact that once the system has been memorised it is very portable.

It was recorded that during the siege of Syracuse, Archimedes, the mathematician who lived from 278–212BC, created designs of figures in the sand to predict the outcome of the battle using some form of geomantic practice, possibly with Ancient Egyptian roots.

In the Middle Ages geomancy was developed into a complex art by many practitioners. Cornelius Agrippa, the Renaissance adept, wrote about it in his books on occult philosophy and associated geomantic figures with astrology. In his *Purgatorio*, Dante refers to: 'the hours when Day's heat can no longer temper the cold of the Moon, when the geomancers see their Fortuna Major rise in the East before Dawn.'

Although geomantic consultations were sought by both royal and religious patrons, it was officially outlawed because of its alleged associations with black magic and witchcraft. Despite the condemnation of the Church, students of the occult continued to practise geomancy in secret and to refine the methods. An African version, Ifa, from the oracular tradition of the Yoruba people in south-west Nigeria, spread to America. In Europe during the 19th century, geomancy was developed as part of Napoleon's Book of Fate, although it has no connection with the Emperor Napoleon. Geomantic practices were also adopted by the members of the Order of the Golden Dawn during the early years of the 20th century.

Below are the 16 basic shapes that underpin the system. I have used the Latin names as these are the most common in Western geomancy.

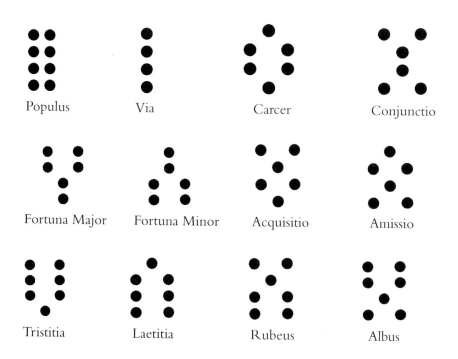

Populus   Via   Carcer   Conjunctio

Fortuna Major   Fortuna Minor   Acquisitio   Amissio

Tristitia   Laetitia   Rubeus   Albus

Puella   Puer   Caput Draconis   Cauda Draconis

NATURE MAGIC AND MYSTERY

The Geomantic Grid

For divinatory purposes the figures are made up in a grid, traditionally drawn with a stick in sand or earth. A stone, marked with one dot on one side and two dots on the other, is tossed to create the appropriate figure/s. Modern practitioners sometimes draw the grid on paper and toss a coin, heads for odd and tails for even numbers.

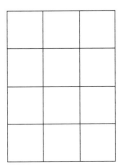

The geomantic grid

Making Geomantic Figures

- Four odd or even numbers make up the shape that answers the question. The actual number does not matter, only whether it is odd or even. Four separate throws make up each geomantic figure.

- An odd number is represented in geomancy by a single dot which is always recorded on the central column of the grid, beginning at the top of the grid. An even number is represented as two dots, recorded as one dot in each of the outside columns.

- For example, throw one was an even number.

- Throw two was an odd number.

- The third throw was another odd number and another single dot.

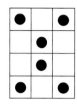

- The last throw was an even number giving two dots for the outside columns and the figure of Carcer.

Traditional Meanings for the 16 Figures

Populus is Latin for people. Its meanings include an assembly, union, society generally, a workplace, or social gatherings. It is a neutral symbol, but can be good or bad depending on circumstances, just as a group of people can be a friendly society or a mob. Matters of the law and justice also fall within this context.

Via is Latin for road. Its meanings include physical travel and the journey through life, a sense of direction, the end of a journey, or perhaps a solution to a problem. It is a neutral symbol but when joined to other signs can suggest a danger of being side-tracked.

Carcer is Latin for prison. Its meanings include confinement, delays, frustrations and limitations, whether in family, personal or financial matters. It is a rather negative symbol, but it can represent the need to seek freedom from the limitations imposed by self as well as circumstance.

Conjunctio is Latin for union. Its associated meanings are connection, togetherness and contracts. It usually has a positive meaning and is linked with partnerships of all kinds, personal as well as business. It is also the symbol used for legal matters and contracts, often where these will have a strong personal effect; it favours compromise.

Fortuna Major is Latin for the Greater Fortune. It is an extremely good symbol to cast, especially in questions concerning career or major life decisions. Its meanings include good luck, fortune, success, victory, property and status.

Fortuna Minor is Latin for the Lesser Fortune, and is the figure of Fortuna Major reversed. It is not as immediately promising as Fortuna Major, but assures positive assistance from others, protection from harm and the granting of reasonable favours. As a sun symbol, it represents the utilisation of hidden talents and cautious progress.

Acquisitio is Latin for gain. Its meanings include profitable business dealings, gifts and the acquisition of new talents or qualifications. This is usually a

NATURE MAGIC AND MYSTERY

positive symbol whether in financial or property matters, in concerns over health and in questions of love. The gains may not be tangible nor immediate, but are always worthwhile.

Amissio is Latin for loss and the symbol can mean loss of personal property through carelessness, loss of health or loss of confidence, unless care is taken to avoid exhaustion, quarrels and unreasonable demands.

Tristitia is Latin for sadness, and symbolises personal regrets and guilt, family feuds, worries over money or relations, especially elderly ones, restlessness, free-floating anxieties and lingering resentments.

Laetitia is Latin for joy. This heralds delight, gladness, optimism, confidence, beauty, grace and good health. It favours any celebration such as birth or marriage, holidays, family matters and all love relationships and friendships, both new and established.

Rubeus is Latin for red and can indicate danger, fiery passions and tempers, over-indulgence of all kinds, obsessions and impatience. It can be a negative symbol, but as justifiable anger or the impetus to right injustice, the energy can be very positive in initiating change and clearing stagnation.

Albus is Latin for white. This indicates illumination, wisdom and harmony, and augurs all new beginnings, new relationships and ventures, openness in approach, and babies and children. It is a symbol of healing, both physical, mental and spiritual, of reconciling old quarrels and replacing doubts with enthusiasm.

Puella is Latin for girl. Traditionally it symbolises a girl, daughter, young wife, purity, innocent joy and the blossoming of potential, especially in sexuality, friendship and romance. This can be a good figure to make in the early stages of a relationship or venture, but it can be deceptive.

Puer is Latin for boy and indicates the youthful follies of rashness, inconsiderate-ness, lack of care about the consequences of actions, and aggressiveness if thwarted. On the plus side, there are times when youthful energy and single-mindedness can overcome stagnation.

Caput Draconis is Latin for the Head of the Dragon. This positive symbol indicates a place of entry, perhaps to higher realms of consciousness, and a good beginning to a major project or life change. The Dragon is a symbol of power and strength, of courage and determination, and promises success if the questioner does not waver.

Cauda Draconis is Latin for the Tail of the Dragon, the reverse of the Head of the Dragon. Its meaning can be negative – an indication of troubled times not ahead, but which are or have been clouding the life of the questioner or someone close. More positively, this figure may indicate an exit from the lower realms or a possible way out of disaster if the questioner does not lose courage but keeps going.

A Full Geomantic Reading

To resolve complex matters, four figures are obtained by divination and arranged in horizontal rows. The first row is called the Mothers, who are combined mathematically to form the four Daughters. They give rise to the four Nephews who in turn create the two Witnesses. Finally, the Judge, made from the Witnesses, gives the outcome of the reading.

LEY LINES

By the 19th century, the term geomancy (see p. 188) was applied to Chinese feng shui (see p. 238), a method which sites tombs, houses and other buildings where earth and sky energies are harmonious in order to ensure the well-being of those within. The concept reached the West during the early 20th century with the discovery of what were called ley energies, psychic lines of power running through the earth.

Ley Lines

There is often a distinction made between energy leys and true ley lines, although the definition of the latter also contains many variations. Energy leys are said to be 6–8ft (2–3m) wide beams of yang, or male, sky power that coincide with alignments of ancient sacred buildings precisely because our ancestors were drawn instinctively to places of great natural power on which to construct sacred structures. For example, the Benedictines in the Middle Ages had great knowledge of these spiritual energies, and their mediaeval abbeys invariably have a ley running through them.

True ley lines are defined by the most stringent assessment as having at least five aligned pre-Reformation sacred sites within a relatively short distance, not much more than 10 miles (16km), measured as straight to the standard of an H pencil line on a 1.25,000 scale map. These sites can include tumuli and single menhirs or standing stones. They may be visible on the ground for all or part of the length by the remnants of an ancient straight traders' track.

History of Ley Hunting

On June 30, 1921, Alfred Watkins, a Herefordshire miller, naturalist and photographer, was studying a map. His attention was drawn to a straight line that passed over hill tops through a number of ancient sites. Suddenly, he described seeing the whole pattern as though he were experiencing it:

… a fairy chain stretched from mountain peak to mountain peak, as far as the eye could reach, and paid out until it reached a mound, circular earthwork, or clump of trees, planted on these high points, and in low points in the valley other mounds ringed around with water to be seen from a distance. Then great standing stones brought to mark the way at intervals …

From the insight, Watkins developed the theory that the straight tracks, or ley lines as he called them, were once prehistoric trading routes. In 1925, *The Old Straight Track*, his best-known book, was published. In 1936, the first psychic associations with these tracks were made when Dion Fortune published her novel *The Goat-Foot God*, hypothesising that ley lines were energy lines linking prehistoric sites.

Over the years ley lines came to be regarded as channels of cosmic energy, similar to ch'i, and dowsing rods were used to trace them. With the increased interest in extra-terrestrial activity during the 1960s and the observation that UFO activity seems focused around known leys and sites of earth power, a theory arose that leys might act as landing markers for extra-terrestrial craft.

Sites of Power

The fact that ley lines link what were once sacred sites and temples has led to research into the nature of earth energies concentrated within the sacred sites themselves, that were invoked for the fertility of people, animals and land in dance, song and ritual at ancient seasonal festivals. Stonehenge and Avebury Rings are just two megalithic sites that stand at the hub of a wheel of intersecting leys.

These power centres are believed by some geomancers and dowsers to be places where natural cosmic energy enters the earth through ley channels at a point where there are underground water domes – where water rises vertically from deep within the earth. The yang of the Sky Father power therefore joined the yin of the Earth Mother that was manifest as the water flowing from her womb to form an epicentre of energy. For at these special sites, the universal Sacred Marriage was constantly being re-enacted, and so many early rites involved sex within or close to the stones to transmit the powerful earth energies to the participants.

Negative Earth Energies

Though our ancestors built their temples and abbeys on ley lines, few people actually built houses on them because the power was so overwhelming, especially at points where leys cross. In Ireland today few would erect a building on a fairy path, the track stretching between ancient hill forts.

Another cause of negative earth energies is when the natural flow of energy becomes blocked, either physically or spiritually, by pollution or negative events on a piece of land. This may sour the energy. The downstream line of this blocked energy is popularly called a black stream and may be actual water in the form of an underground vein. Major construction works such as building a motorway, or existing or former mine workings, can also sour the energy. In addition, electrical disturbances from transformers and house circuits are sometimes implicated. Dwellings or workplaces built on black streams may seem dark and damp even on a summer's day and may create a hostile working environment where there are frequent absences for minor and stress-related illnesses.

One explanation attributes negative forces to Hartmann and Curry energy fields. These are named after their discoverers and are thought to divide the earth into square lattices. Where two Curry lines or two Hartmann lines cross, strong energies occur. Where a Curry and a Hartmann cross coincide the effect is doubled. Curry and Hartmann lines vary in location according to the time of day and the phase of the moon.

Some expert dowsers such as the UK's Dr Arthur Bailey who created the Bailey Flower Remedies, believe that the influence of geopathic stress can be felt about 10ft (3m) either side of a ley line or underground stream. Trouble can be expected, especially where these energies cross.

Leys Around the World

There are identified leys throughout Europe, Scandinavia, India and the United States. For example, the Cree Indian trails invariably followed straight tracks, while in Chaco Canyon, New Mexico, long straight tracks were laid down by the Anasazi peoples.

In Ancient Egypt cairns were set up on hilltops as markers for the caravan trails. The Sun Temple built in the middle of the city of Cuzco, Central Peru, has 41 lines radiating into the surrounding countryside. Along them lie shrines, temples, graves, sacred hills, bridges and even battlefields.

The most famous ley is perhaps the St Michael or Sun line that centres on Mont St Michel on the borders of Normandy and Brittany. Studies of the geography of Mont St Michel reveal a ley that travels from Mount Carmel through Delos (sacred to the Sun God Apollo), Corfu, the Monte Gargano in Italy, the Sacra di San Michele in Piedmont (a famous Benedictine monastery 330ft (1,000m) high), Mont St Michel itself, St Michael's Mount in Cornwall and the Skellig Michael, an islet off the southwest coast of Ireland.

The aisle of the French cathedral is aligned with Mount Dol in the south-west and Avranches in the north-east. Mount Dol had a temple dedicated to the Sun God Mithras which was destroyed on the orders of Samson, a monk from across the English Channel in AD548 who founded the diocese of Dol. A church dedicated to St Michael was set up in place of the temple.

There is also a geographical correlation between Mont St Michel and other standing stones in the region. Three menhirs and a passage grave to the south-west are exactly in line and form a system stretching over 19 miles (30km). The line begins at the grave of Tresse, la Maison-es-Feins and continues through the standing stones Pierre du Domaine at Plerguer, le Champ-Dolent at Dol, La Roche Longue at St

Marcan, to finish at Mont St Michel itself. There is a rich collection of folklore concerning the megaliths and Mont St Michel.

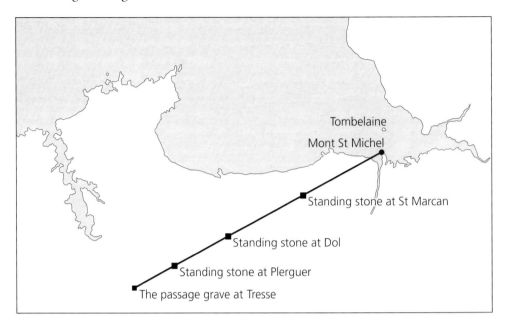

The significant feature of the St Michael line in England is that there are so many churches along it dedicated to the saints who replaced the pagan Sun Gods, St Michael, St George (Og is the Gaelic Sun God), and St Mary who replaced the female principle. Sixty churches or more including Ogbourne St George run via Glastonbury and Avebury to Hopton in East Anglia. All these holy places are linked by the visible line of sunrise at the beginning of May. If a beacon fire were lit on each high point, the sun would be seen to rise behind it when viewed from the next place on the line.

MEGALITHS

M egaliths, or mighty stones, have astronomical as well as spiritual significance. Many have survived as a focus for the fusion of celestial and earth power for more than 4,000 years, though others were eradicated with the coming of Christianity and the new style of stone used for building churches and secular edifices.

From early in the fifth millennium BC, as Neolithic agriculture began to replace the predominant hunter-gatherer way of life, stone structures were created as permanent sites of worship throughout Western Europe and parts of Scandinavia, including the Canary Islands, Spain, Portugal, Brittany, Ireland, Britain as far north as the Scottish isles, and Sweden. They were built on places of power and frequently aligned with each other along the great ley lines that spanned Europe.

History of the Megaliths

The oldest, and also the largest, megaliths in the world are at Carnac in Brittany. More than 3,000 stones are arranged as avenues, mounds, cromlechs (a chamber of stones consisting of either a small circle or a single one) and dolmens (a horizontal stone supported by several vertical stones, thought to have been used as a tomb).

Originally there were thought to be more than 11,000 stones around Carnac. The earliest dated mound-covered cromlech at Kercado in Brittany was built in about 4800BC, thus pre-dating the Pyramids. Stone circles were built from about 3000BC and similarities between them would suggest a common origin and purpose.

Who Created the Megaliths?

Radiocarbon dating has recently demonstrated that the Western European megaliths considerably pre-date what were believed to be their Mediterranean prototypes. What is hard to explain is not only the advanced astronomical and mathematical knowledge used in their creation, but the sheer logistics of creating the megaliths with relatively simple tools, especially when stones were brought great distances overland to the sites. One theory is that Atlanteans who survived the submerging of their land were the instigators, a theory strengthened by the fact that many circles were created close to the Atlantic coastline.

The Magic of the Megaliths

It is not known when magical and healing properties were first associated with megaliths. In 1410, the Bishop of Hereford prohibited worship of the stone and well at Turnastone in Herefordshire, but his edict and similar ones throughout the Middle Ages had little effect. At Stonehenge, water with which the stones were washed was used for healing baths for a variety of ailments, as well as for fertility and power. Two of the Rollright Stones in Oxfordshire also have a long healing tradition, one for headaches and the other for arthritic/muscular problems, and are still believed to be active.

Single standing stones or menhirs, with holes in the centre, are said to represent the power of the Earth Goddess and are acknowledged as potent sources of healing. One of the most famous Mother stones is Men-an-Tol near Madron in Cornwall. As late as the 18th century, cures were reported when those with back and limb pains crawled through the hole. Children were reported to be healed of rickets by being passed through the hole nine times moonwise or anti-clockwise. It is popularly known as the Crick stone because of its ability to cure cricks or stiffness in the neck.

Fertility is not surprisingly another attribute associated with both Mother stones and stone circles, since through circle dances around and love-making within a stone circle on the solar and lunar festivals, the fertility of people and land were ritually intertwined. One of the most famous fertility rings is the Rollright, supposedly the petrified forms of an invading king and his knights who were turned to stone in Celtic times by the legendary hag of Rollright. At midnight, a woman who wanted to

NATURE MAGIC AND MYSTERY

become pregnant would go to the stones alone and press herself against the King Stone so closely that her breasts and thighs were chilled. Within nine months she would bear a strong son. At Avebury Rings in Wiltshire, on May Eve young girls would slide down the stones and afterwards make a love wish, sitting on the large stone called The Devil's Chair.

Magic and fairies are also associated with standing stones and stone circles. Photographs from different sources have identified lights emanating from menhirs which are said to be doorways to other worlds. People have heard music coming from them and seen presences through openings in the stone. Crop circles and earth lights are also common around stone circles.

Standing stones are believed to have the power to move on New Year's Eve and Day. The Rollright Stones are said to drink, move and eat at midnight on New Year, while in Scotland the Stone of Quoyboyne walks to the nearby Loch of Boardhouse. It is said that if mortals watch the moving stones, they will be spirited away forever by the fairies.

Megalithic Power and the Dragon Project

Geiger counters and ultrasonic detectors have recorded abnormal patterns of pulsations within stone circles that do vary with the seasons. The Dragon Project Trust, centred on the Rollright Stones in Oxfordshire, has detected ultrasonic rays as well as radiation and magnetic energies coming from these stones. There is a radioactive hot spot just behind the tallest stone.

The pattern of the recorded energies varies in accordance with the cycles of the moon as well as the seasons. Such research into earth energies may be a way forward for other investigations, combining the skills of archaeology and physics with dowsing and psychometry, detecting the history of a site by holding objects found there.

Stonehenge

Stonehenge is probably the best-known stone circle or megalith in the world, located on the Salisbury Plain in Wiltshire. Investigations over the past 100 years have revealed that Stonehenge was built in several stages from 2800–1800BC. It is oriented to mark the sunrise and moonrise at the summer and winter solstices. The Heel Stone, or Helios Stone after the Greek Sun God, is known as the Sun Stone, for the sun rises over this at the summer solstice. At sunset on the summer solstice the Heel Stone casts a shadow on the Altar Stone, thus marking the beginning of the dying of the year. Modern Druids (see p. 107) still welcome the summer solstice at Stonehenge as their Mecca. For though Stonehenge was in existence long before the original Druids worshipped there, there may be connections with earlier megalithic priests /astronomers /sacred geometrists who transmitted their wisdom to the Druidic order who have carried it into the modern world.

Newgrange, Eire

One of the most remarkable prehistoric monuments is at Newgrange in County Meath, Eire, once called *Grian Uaigh*, or Cave of the Sun. Created near the end of the fourth millennium BC, Newgrange consists of a mound containing a passage to a burial chamber and surrounded by almost a complete circle of twelve giant stones. Close to Tara, the sacred hill and former palace of the *Tuatha de Danaan*, the Celtic hero gods and later home of the high kings of Ireland, there are symbols inscribed on these circle stones recording movements of the sun, moon and planets, that reveal highly accurate ancient astronomical calculations.

Newgrange is aligned to the midwinter sunrise so that the beam of the rising sun falls directly into the main chamber. Knowth and Dowth, known as its sister sites, make up the main spokes of the wheel of the year. Knowth is aligned to the vernal and autumnal equinoxes, while Dowth is aligned to the summer solstice sunrise, thus giving an accurate reckoning of the four sun-markers of the year. The midwinter sunset also illuminates one of the chambers at Dowth, thus making it a monument to the return of the light. The twelve stones surrounding Newgrange point to the solsticial and equinoctial sunrises and sunsets, and also align to Knowth and Dowth.

MOON MAGIC

The Lunar Path

The moon – feminine, mysterious, intuitive, nurturing – represents deep, unconscious widom, divergent thinking, in alchemy Queen Luna or silver to King Sol or gold. Lunar wisdom resides in the right side of the brain, the hidden potential of the human mind and psyche that is manifest in such powers as telepathy, prophecy and the ability to perceive other dimensions. Robert Graves described in his book *The White Goddess*, a name by which the moon is known, the archetypal lunar knowledge that extends back to the dawn of human consciousness, that was the inspiration of poetry and music and that holds the most profound secrets buried in myth and hidden symbolism.

Early Beliefs about the Moon

Because the cycles of the moon mirror the female menstrual cycle, the moon has been linked to motherhood throughout history. Women who wanted to become pregnant would traditionally sleep under the rays of the moon, from waxing to full, to ensure conception. In indigenous cultures women would withdraw to the Moon Lodge at the Dark of the Moon, which coincided with their menstruation, to rest

NATURE MAGIC AND MYSTERY

and contemplate, while the men and older women cared for the home and children.

The moon was recognised as having three main phases: waxing, full and waning. These echoed human existence: birth, maturity and death. Consequently, the Moon Goddess has been represented as the Maiden, Mother and Crone or Wise Woman in many cultures. A trinity of huge carved lunar stone goddesses was found in a cave at the Abri du Roc aux Sorciers at Angles-sur-l'Anglin, dating from the time between 13,000 and 11,000BC.

Once the hunter-gatherer way of life gave way to agriculture, the Moon Goddess's fertility became identified with the fecundity of the earth. When it was realised that the tides rose and fell with the moon, the concept was applied to agriculture. In planting and reaping, the waxing moon was said to increase all growth and ripening while the waning moon decreased the speed of growth and richness of fruit.

The Moon and Rebirth

Because the moon disappears from the sky for three days at the end of every cycle and is reborn again as a visible crescent, it became associated with rebirth. Plutarch, the Ancient Greek philosopher, described the moon as a resting place for souls following death. The soul and psyche returned to the moon where the soul was able to retain memories and dreams of its former life. The mind was absorbed by the sun and reborn as a new mind, travelling once more to the moon where the waiting soul rejoined the regenerated mind and adopted a new earthly body.

The Hindus also believe that unenlightened souls return to the moon to await rebirth, while those who have attained freedom from the Wheel of Reincarnation take the path to the sun.

According to popular legend too, every evening the moon gathers unfulfilled wishes, discarded hopes, unwanted memories and disappointments, and takes them into herself to be restored as the morning dew.

The Man or Woman in the Moon

Even before moon deities were given names, legends grew up about the man or woman who lived in the moon whose features could be seen at certain times of the month. One myth makes Judas the man in the moon, while a German version has both a man and woman on the moon: the woman is banished to the lunar wilderness for churning butter on the Sabbath, and the man for casting brambles and thorns across the path of worthy folk walking to church.

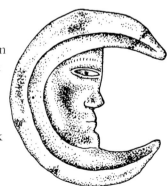

The Hare in the Moon

The hare in the moon stories probably began in India where the man in the moon is said to be Chandra, Hindu God of the Moon. He is depicted carrying a hare or *sasa*. In India, the moon is called *sasin*, or *sasanka*, which in Sanskrit means 'having the marks of the hare'.

NATURE MAGIC AND MYSTERY

The Toad in the Moon

According to Chinese myth, a three-legged toad lives in the moon, its legs representing the three main phases. At lunar eclipses, the toad swallows the moon and great noise is made with drums, cymbals and fireworks to drive it off.

The Lunar Calendar

The earliest calendars were based on the lunar cycle, and moon time is still used in the modern world in both pagan and religious rituals. In the Christian church, Easter is calculated as the first Sunday following the first full moon after the spring equinox (around March 21). Now, calendar makers mark the new moon as the time when it is dark, but early astrologers took it as the time that the first cresent appeared (this is the time for magic).

The Lunar Phases

The cycle from new moon to new moon lasts 29.5 days. It rises around 52 minutes later each day, although this can vary and be as little as 13 minutes depending on the time of year. It takes just over 27 days for the moon to complete its orbit round the earth. For this reason, phases can vary in length by a day or so each month. Magically, too, there is an overlap in energies, so that for example full moon energies are evident in the two days either side of the full moon, though obviously the day of the full moon is the most potent in the lunar cycle.

New Moon / Crescent Moon

For wishes of all kinds, new beginnings, candle magic, money magic and the safety of travellers, especially sailors.

At the new moon the sun and moon rise and set together. Since the sun and the moon are on the same side of the earth, they are in conjunction and in the same astrological sign, resulting in a surge of combined directed energy to give impetus to any new action. The waxing crescent does not appear on the day of the new moon, but three and a half days later in the evening sky, and this is traditionally when wish magic occurs. Traditionally, on the new moon, children whose fathers were fishermen or sailors would bow to the moon three times and chant:

I see the Moon
The Moon sees me
Guard the sailors
on the sea.

Turning silver over three times on a crescent/new moon and bowing to the ancient Egyptian Trinity Osiris, Isis (the Moon Mother) and Horus, the infant Solar God, is perhaps the oldest money spell in the world.

LEFT: A wooden church roof boss depicting the Green Man.

BELOW: Detail from a 1st century Celtic cauldron showing the stag god Cerunnos surrounded by animals.

BELOW: Photograph of a 14-pointed star crop circle near Devizes, UK.

LEFT: A carved standing stone from County Fermanagh, Northern Ireland.

BELOW: The Ring of Brodgar, Orkney, Scotland, built c. 5000 BC.

LEFT: Sigurd's Stone from Sweden. This shows a carving of the Norse hero Sigurd surrounded by runic script.

BELOW: Stonehenge, Wiltshire.

The Waxing Moon

For all forms of attracting magic, especially for good fortune and career; also for healing energies, visualisation work and astral projection.

The waxing moon period begins two or three days after the new moon and lasts for almost two weeks. By halfway through this phase, the sun and moon are square to each other, which astrologically indicates a challenging aspect. The moon is visible during the daytime for much of the waxing cycle, and so can also be used for daytime or prolonged rituals. The waxing moon is associated with the Greek Artemis or the Roman Diana, Goddesses of the Hunt.

The Full Moon

For love, passion, marriage, fertility, abundance and sex magic.

The day of the full moon sees it rising at sunset as the moon and sun are on opposite sides of the earth and in opposite astrological signs. This therefore is a time of instability but also a catalyst for a surge of power. When women menstruated by the moon cycles, this was the time of conception. Witches' *esbats*, or meetings, are held on the full moon. In addition, because the solar and lunar energies are pulling in opposite directions, there are more reported traffic accidents, more suicides and a greater incidence of emotional crises than at other times of the month. The full moon is represented by the Greek Selene and Diana, especially in the Wiccan tradition.

The Waning Moon

For banishing magic, psychometry, divination and past life work.

Beginning at the full moon, the moon rises an hour later ever night: by the half-waning phase, sets at noon and is visible every morning. During the waning half-moon crescent, the sun and the moon again form a square to each other. This is the time for reaping what was begun in the waxing moon or at least completing the first stage, and healing involving removing pain or anxiety. As the visible moon grows smaller, so do the energies flow towards the state of stillness and letting go of what is redundant. The waning moon is ruled by the Crone Hecate, Goddess of Night.

The Dark of the Moon

No magic is practised.

The dark of the moon occurs on the last three days of the new moon, before it is visible in the sky. It is a time for resting, for developing the inner world of dreams and waking visions, a time of dreaming, power and quiet, for letting worries take care of themselves. It is in a sense the most spiritual phase and as the cycle begins again as the dark of the moon gives way to the new moon, new energies emerge once more and there is rebirth of hope and new beginnings.

SACRED WATERS

Myths from many lands tell of a World Tree, the axis supporting the heavens, the earth and the underworld; at the foot or beneath the roots was found a Well of Knowledge, guarded by the Three Fates under various guises, or by a female who was the Goddess of the Earth and Underworlds (see Runes (p. 62) and Fate (p. 113)).

In Celtic tradition, the Well of Wisdom, called Connla's Well in Tipperary, stands at the centre of the Otherworld or the Land of Eternal Youth, and all other sacred wells and springs throughout the world are believed to be tributaries. On the tree hanging over the water were nine nuts of poetic art. The nuts would periodically fall into the water and were eaten by salmon, Celtic fish of knowledge and mystic inspiration, who sent the husks floating down the five streams that flow from the well, so endowing other sacred waters with an ever-flowing source of wisdom. At St Cybi's Holy Well in Llanybi Caernarfon, Wales, when the sacred eel was removed, pilgrims believed that the well had lost its healing powers.

The Origins of Sacred Water

The Zuni people of the south-eastern United States believe that the first humans, the daylight people, came through a spring from the world below, and that all springs are linked by giant underground networks to the ocean, like the roots of a giant tree.

The Maya regarded wells as sacred to the Rain God, Chac. The two most famous sacred cenotes are both in Chichen Itza, sacred city of the Mayans and Toltecs in Central America that was abandoned by the Maya around AD900 and rebuilt by the Toltecs a century later. A cenote is a natural well formed by the collapse of subterranean limestone caverns. A particular red algae turned the well, known as the Well of Sacrifice, the colour of blood.

Because water is vital for life, it has become associated with healing through the washing away of sins and disease and is used in baptismal and initiation rites throughout the world. Many Christian churches were erected near pagan sacred wells, and the early Celtic church used these for baptism, before Roman Christianity decreed that a baptismal font should be placed inside the building. A number of old churches contain a crypt or grotto that contains a subterranean spring. At Chartres Cathedral in France, for example, the old well behind the Cathedral was probably used by the Druids.

Divination and Sacred Water

Some of the wells and springs were also used for divinatory purposes. Researchers have noted that people become drowsy and spontaneously fall asleep at holy wells, which has partly been associated with the mildly radioactive properties found at many of the sites, a reaction which encourages divination and other world visions. At St Gwenfaen's Well in Rhoscolyn, Anglesey, the well was said to tell the future according to the way the bubbles rose after two white stones were cast into the water.

Even during Victorian times country girls would visit holy wells to dream of a future husband. One such divinatory well was the Fairy's Pin Well in Selby, Yorkshire, so named after the custom of dropping bent pins, made of gold or silver if the suppliant was wealthy, as offerings. At some of these wells, the finger of the supplicant was pricked with the pin before casting it into the well, a throwback to ancient sacrificial wells. Goddess wells that were not Christianised became known as faery wells, especially those with strong Celtic connections. The girl drank from the well, asking the faery of the well to bring her a dream of the man she would marry.

Even Christian wells were used for magic. On November 25, the feast day of St Catherine, the 4th-century patron saint of young women, young spinsters would pray to her for a husband. In the grounds of the churchyard of the ruined abbey at Cerne Abbas in Dorset is a sacred well above which the chapel of St Catherine formerly stood. Here young girls would turn round three times clockwise and ask St Catherine for a husband, making the sign of the cross on their foreheads. Those who wished to get pregnant would then go up to the Cerne Giant to make love.

Well Guardians

Wells and springs were regarded as the places from which living water spontaneously emerged from the ground – entrances to the womb of the Mother Goddess. This connection is shown by the sheela-na-gig carvings close to holy wells in Ireland and parts of England and Wales that were formerly pagan fertility wells. These stone carvings of the archetypal female fertility figure in the process of giving birth date back thousands of years.

From pagan times, healing well water was also associated with the breast milk of the Earth Mother. At the well of St Illtyd near Swansea, Wales, for example, in legend the well flowed with milk not water around the time of the old summer solstice.

Because the sacred wells in the UK held such a central role in religious practices, the early Roman Church transformed them into Christian shrines during the 7th–9th centuries, complete with a Christian legend to account for their origin that gradually became grafted onto the former goddess connection.

Where the Christian association was female, for example the numerous Bride wells named after the 6th-century Brigit of Kildare (the Welsh St Bride), herself formerly Brighid or Brigid, the Celtic Triple Goddess, there are often reported sightings of a ghostly white lady. Those dedicated to Anu, the Celtic Mother Goddess, were transferred to the protective powers of St Anne, mother of Mary, and so associated with fertility and all matters connected with children.

Fertility Wells

Because of their association with the womb of the Mother Goddess, many of the ancient wells were visited by barren women who, in age-old ceremonies, would walk sunwise around a pool or well three times, washing their abdomens in the healing waters, while the keeper of the well, a female who in some places cared for the well into the 19th century, chanted *eolas*, ancient magical songs, over the women's womb and breasts. Although we do not understand in rational terms how these healing miracles came about, it may be that the power of these ancient sites has been amplified by the prayers and offering of pilgrims over thousands of years.

Obtaining a Cure – Well Rituals

Virtually all of the healing wells had specific rituals which had to be performed in order to activate the power of the water. The power of ritual is scarcely understood but it may be that at natural seasonal change points certain times do have particularly powerful energies. May Day and Midsummer (June 24, but in earlier times the summer solstice or longest day itself) were traditionally potent times for visiting wells for healing, and the dates of ancient fertility festival transitions in the Celtic year when the gates between dimensions parted. Christianised wells were officially considered most potent on the guardian saint's day or on Easter Sunday or Whit Sunday, but the earlier Celtic festivals continued to hold sway, especially when asking for a child to be conceived.

The best time of day for healing was just before sunrise and the ritual would often be completed before dawn. A well was usually approached from the east or rising sun and the suppliant would walk round it sunwise, or *deosil*, a required number of times, generally three for the Trinity and Triple Goddess, or nine, an ancient mystical number of perfection.

The Giving of Offerings as Part of the Healing Process

Offerings were invariably left for the spirit of the well or spring. The origin of modern wishing wells lies in the Roman practice of casting coins into the waters to pay for healing. Many treasures have been discovered at the bottom of wells used in Celtic and Roman Britain and some of these offerings date back to the Bronze Age or even earlier. At Coventina's well in Carrowbaugh, Northumberland, for example, more than 14,000 coins, bronze figurines, jewellery, glass, pottery, and a human skull, symbol of power and wisdom in Celtic times, were discovered in the shaft.

Well dressing ceremonies still take place in Derbyshire, Wales, Cornwall and parts of Ireland.

SALT MAGIC

S alt rituals are among the oldest forms of magic and are used not only for psychic protection but in money-making and healing rituals. Salt has always been central to religious and magical practices because it was the one absolutely pure substance. It was regarded as precious because it was the main preservative of food through the long winter months for early settlers around the globe. The Westernised name comes from Salus, Roman Goddess of Health, whom the Greeks called Hygeia.

The Greeks and Romans mixed salt with their sacrificial cakes and threw salt on sacrificial fires. Salt was also used in ceremonies of sacrifice by the Jews. In later Christian belief, salt and water were considered potent in restoring health to the body and in the exorcism of evil spirits.

The preservative quality of salt endowed it with religious symbolism of purity and incorruptibility. Salt was traditionally placed in coffins as protection against the Devil. In lands populated by the Celts, a plate containing a pinch of salt and a pinch of earth was laid upon the breast of the newly deceased to indicate the mortal corruptible body and the immortal, incorruptible soul.

Salt was also used with Holy Water to ward off evil and increase physical strength as well as powers of fertility; it is still used in the preparation of Holy Water. Mediaeval alchemists regarded salt as one of the three major essences that made up life, along with mercury (quicksilver) and sulphur.

When brewing mash for animals, a handful of salt was sprinkled on top to keep witches from poisoning the food. Salt also formed an early antiseptic. In honour of Salus, nursemaids would put a pinch of salt into the mouth of newborn infants, and salt was also put into the first pail of milk from a cow who had just calved.

In Ancient Rome, Salus rings dedicated to the Goddess Salus were worn as a talisman against ill health and sudden disease. The ring was engraved with a five-pointed star surrounded by a coiled serpent swallowing its own tail, the ouroboros, a symbol of healing and regeneration.

In formal magic, salt traditionally represents the Earth element and so has a powerful earthing or grounding energy. Ancient rituals blessed salt in the name of the prevalent deity.

The Sea and Salt

Salt for use in magic has traditionally been extracted from the sea. Three-quarters of the world is composed of saline oceans, and salt is also a vital component of the human structure. Salt regulates the tides and the internal flow in and out around our body cells.

All seafaring nations have their legends of how the sea became salt. An intriguing but lesser-known Viking legend explains that Frodi, King of Denmark, was given a magical mill that would grind anything he wished. So great were the magical grind-stones that even his mightiest warriors could not turn them. He therefore bought two giantesses, Menia and Frenia, as slaves, and they ground wealth, peace and prosperity for him. The land prospered, peace reigned, the gold overflowed and so the gift had served its purpose. Yet Frodi would not let the exhausted giantesses rest and in anger they ground an enemy army of Vikings who landed and killed the Danes.

The Viking chief proved an equally cruel master and made the giantesses grind salt on board his ship without rest, as salt was a very valuable cargo that could be exchanged for treasures on their travels. At last Frigga, the Mother Goddess, took pity on the weary women and avenged the chief's cruelty. The weight of salt was so great that it sank the ship and all were drowned. From that time on the sea has been salt and so the gift was shared throughout mankind.

The following rituals are based on the idea that by returning to the sea her own (i.e. salt), the sea would return sailors safely to land.

- Scattering fishermen with salt provides protection and a good catch at sea.

- Women left at home by their seagoing husbands would go to rocks by the sea edge and pour salt into the cracks as a tribute.

- Sailors' and fishermen's wives would fill a bottle with sea water when the boat departed, and just before their return would tip the salt water back into the sea chanting: *I return what is yours, Return now what is mine.*

Protective Salt Rituals

Spilled salt would be cast over the left shoulder into the 'eye of the Devil' or evil spirits who were believed from Roman times onwards to lurk on the left or 'sinister' side, and this is a practice that has continued in modern society. The ritual of spilling salt came from the idea that accidentally tipping such a sacred substance would invite retribution. In Leonardo da Vinci's painting 'The Last Supper', the upturned salt cellar reflects the belief that such an action represented a breaking of trust and friendship.

Salt was also traditionally scattered around thresholds and in protective circles around children and other vulnerable individuals against evil influences. It is still used to protect homes, both those in which magic is practised, and in remote country places where folk customs survive. Traditionally, salt is dissolved in water that has been placed in a clear glass container in sun and waxing moonlight for 24 hours. The mixture is then sprinkled in the four corners of every room and around the boundaries of the house/apartment and garden if there is one.

Salt carried in a tiny drawstring bag can offer protection while travelling or when facing a potential confrontation.

Salt and Money Rituals

Because salt was so highly prized in Ancient Rome, soldiers of the Emperor were sometimes paid in salt, hence the expression 'worth his salt'. Salt was traded for treasures and the Celts would barter their salt for rich artefacts for their burial mounds.

Salt, therefore, became associated with material prosperity and so has formed a focus for spells for money and necessary material possessions. Salt rituals for prosperity are carried out on the crescent moon.

- A cone of sea salt is created and surrounded with a circle of golden coloured coins.

- Gold candles are lit outside the ring of coins at the four compass points.

- By visualisation the salt is transformed symbolically into a mound of golden coins.

- When the candles have burned away, the salt cone is transferred to a clear crystal container and kept uncovered on a window ledge for the intervening days and nights until the morning of the day of the full moon.

- At dawn, the salt is dissolved in pure water and tipped into flowing water to allow the money-making potential to increase as it flows towards the ocean, its natural source and home.

SEASONAL MAGIC

Seasonal magic and rituals celebrating the passing of the year formed a focus for both folk magic and more formal religious ceremonies long before records were kept. They were practised by hunter-gatherer peoples to invoke the powers of the earth and sea deities at the time of the annual coming of the herds or shoals.

Once the hunter-gatherer way of life had been replaced in more temperate regions by the farmers of the Neolithic period, the ritual year became inextricably linked with sowing and reaping and with the fertility of land, animals and people.

The Solar Tides and Seasons

The four solar tides and seasons of the year are marked by the equinoxes and solstices. Seasonal influences are especially powerful for major life changes, long-term plans or gains that may take many months to reach fruition. They are also associated with the Four Winds which form major divisions on Native North American medicine wheels.

Spring Its direction is east and its colour yellow. This is the quadrant of the element Air, which offers the impetus for change and growth.

Summer Its direction is south and its colour is red. This is the quadrant of Fire which promises dynamic results, inspiration and success for any venture when the sun is at its height.

Autumn Its direction is west and its colour blue. This is the quadrant of Water and augurs well for rituals of reconciliation and harmony both within the self and with others.

Winter The direction is north and its colour green. The quadrant of Earth promises rest, regeneration, wisdom and psychic awareness.

The Eightfold Year

The Eightfold Wheel is an ancient magical and spiritual division of the year that may date back to the first agricultural societies, though it was formalised by the Celts. However, some historians believe that before the eightfold division that existed among the Germanic peoples as well as the Celts, there was an earlier threefold division that celebrated the beginning of winter, the midwinter and the midsummer. The Wheel of the Year co-exists with the wider seasonal divisions of the year, incorporating the four Solar Festivals that fall on the solstices and the equinoxes, the astronomical marker points of the ebbs and flows of cosmic energies. Between each of these is one of the four Great Fire Festivals that are major rites in the Wiccan and Neo-pagan calendars, as they were to the Celts. These are especially associated with

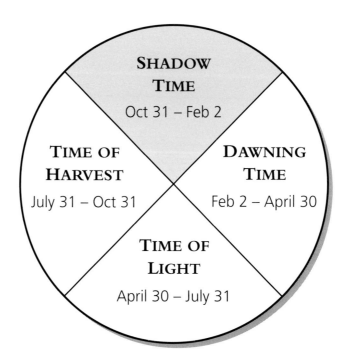

the energies of the earth, so completing the Sacred Marriage of Earth and Sky within the Wheel. In the southern hemisphere some people reverse the magical associations so that midwinter will fall in mid-June rather than December.

The transition point of the Celtic day was at sunset, so the time when two periods met was very magical. Each of the major festivals ran for three days from sunset to sunset. As shown in the illustration on p. 210, in magical terms the energies for each three-month period are regarded as dating from the more mystical Fire Festivals, rather than the seasonal divisions. The Wheel of the Year began at Samhain, on the evening of October 31, the Celtic New Year, but I have described it as beginning with the first stirrings of life after the winter.

The Festivals

IMBOLC – *from Sunset on January 31 to February 2*

Imbolc, the Return of Light, is a Fire Festival, Christianised as Candlemas on February 2. It was the time when the Celtic Triple Goddess Brighid first appeared in her maiden aspect and mated with the young God of Light born at the midwinter solstice. The festival was also called Oimelc (the feast of the first ewe's milk after winter) or Brigantia. Sacred fires were lit on hilltops to welcome and encourage the growing light and warmth. In the USA even today, Groundhog Day (February 2) recalls the ancient weather prophesies made to foretell whether it would be a good or hard spring.

On Bride's Eve, January 31, a Bride's bed made from a sheaf of corn, sometimes with corn preserved from the last corn cut down at the first harvest at Lammas (at the end of July), would be decorated with ribbons to represent the Earth Goddess. It would also be adorned with any early spring flowers. The bed was made in front of the fire and the inhabitants would shout: '*Bride, come in, your bed is ready.*' The symbolic Bride maiden would leave her cows and a cauldron at the door, bringing in peace, fertility and plenty. From this comes the term 'bride' for a woman who is about to be married.

Milk and honey were poured over the Bride bed by the women of the household. The menfolk were summoned and, having paid either a coin, a flower posy or a kiss, would enter the circle of firelight and ask for help with their craft or agriculture and make a wish on the Bride bed.

Brighid crosses were woven from straw or wheat to hang around the house for protection, a custom that continued in Christian times in honour of St Bride whose festival fell at the beginning of February.

The festival of Imbolc is a time to carry out spells for new love, fertility, and for any projects that start in a small way, using a circle of candles and a container of fresh milk as a focus.

The incenses and herbs of Imbolc include angelica, basil, benzoin, celandine, heather and myrrh. White, cream and pink or any pale colour are the candle colours associated with innocence and gentleness, the qualities of this time.

THE VERNAL OR SPRING EQUINOX OR OSTARA TIME – *for Three Days from Sunset Around March 21, According to the Calendar*

The vernal equinox marks the transition point between the dark and light halves of the year. At the spring equinox, the sun rises due east and sets due west, giving exactly twelve hours of daylight.

The first eggs of spring were painted and offered on the shrine of the Anglo-Saxon Goddess Eostre, or the Norse Ostara to whom the hare was sacred (this is the origin of the Easter rabbit). Before the days of intensive farming, the festival of Eostre, after whom Easter itself and oestrogen are named, was the time when hens began to lay eggs after the winter.

It is also the occasion on which, in the old Celtic tradition, the God of Light overcame his twin brother the God of Darkness, so marking the coming of days that were longer than night.

It is the time during which Brighid, or in some traditions the Mother Goddess, conceived a child, to be born at the next winter solstice. This links with the Christian Annunciation of the Blessed Virgin Mary, the day on which the Angel Gabriel told Mary she was to conceive a son.

At the spring equinox, bonfires were lit and the corn dolly of the previous harvest (or in Christian times a Judas figure) was burned on the Easter fires. The ashes were scattered on the field for fertility. It is said that if you wake at dawn on Easter Sunday, you will see the sun dance in the water and the angels playing.

The spring equinox is potent for rituals of the rebirth of joy, energy and above all new beginnings, whether for a new career, a new stage in life or a sudden determination to follow a particular path.

Special flowers and herbs of the spring equinox are celandine, cinquefoil, crocus, daffodil, honeysuckle, primroses, sage, tansy, thyme and violets. Yellow and green candles represent optimism and clear focus, the energies of this time.

BELTANE – *from Sunset on April 30 to Sunset on May 2*

Beltane, or Beltain, is named after the Irish *Bealtaine* meaning 'Bel-fire', the fire of the Celtic God of Light, known as Bel, Beli or Belinus. This is the second most important festival in the witches' year and the second most important Fire Festival of the Celts.

Also known as May Eve, May Day, and Walpurgis Night, Beltane occurs at the beginning of May. It celebrates the coming of the ancient summer and the flowering of life. The Goddess manifests as the May Queen and Flora, Goddess of Flowers, whose festival was celebrated in Ancient Rome in early May, the final appearance of the Maiden aspect of the Goddess and the time of her marriage to Jack O'Green who is associated with the Horned God. In very early times, if there had been a bad harvest the previous year, the sacrifice of a willing male virgin was made to the fire, but by

Druidic times the huge wicker man they burned was probably filled with animals. By early Christian times a mock male sacrifice was burned, chosen by selecting a piece of carlin cake that was marked with a charred cross from a bag of similar pieces of the cake.

Sundown on May Eve was the signal for Druids to kindle the great Bel-fires from nine different kinds of wood by turning an oaken spindle in an oaken socket on top of the nearest beacon hill. By mediaeval times, every village had Beltane fires which were attributed with both fertility and healing powers; in remote areas of lands where the Celts have settled they are still lit.

Young couples, sometimes naked, leapt over the twin Beltane fires, ran between them or danced clockwise. Cattle released from the barns after the long winter were driven between two fires to cleanse them of disease and ensure their fertility and rich milk yield for the coming months.

The Maypole, which symbolised the ancient cosmic tree and the phallus of the Sky Father, formed the focus of fertility dances whose origins have been lost in the mists of time. Red, blue, green, yellow and white ribbons, representing the union of earth and sky, winter and summer, water and fire were entwined.

But the chief feature of the festival was the custom that dates back to the first farming communities and finds echoes worldwide of young couples going into the woods and fields to make love and bring back the first may or hawthorn blossoms to decorate homes and barns. May Day is the only time of year, according to tradition, that hawthorn may be brought indoors.

Beltane is therefore a potent festival for fertility magic of all kinds, whether conceiving a child, the flourishing of a financial or business venture, an improvement in health or an increase in energy as the light and warmth move into summer.

The incenses and herbs of Beltane include almond, angelica, ash, cowslip, frankincense, hawthorn, lilac, marigold, and roses for love. Beltane candle colours are red and silver for passion and secret dreams.

THE SUMMER SOLSTICE – *for Three Days from Sunset on Around June 21, According to the Calendar*

The summer solstice marks the high solar point of the year, the longest day, and is the zenith of the light and of solar magical energies. The summer solstice has been celebrated in cultures as far apart as Russia and Native North America, where sun dances were an assertion of power and courage. It was a time associated with the Great Rite, the sacred coupling of the mature Sun God and Earth Goddess.

Just as the midwinter solstice became Christmas with the spread of Christianity, so was the summer solstice linked with the feast of John the Baptist on June 24. In mediaeval times, on the day of St John the Baptist, fire or sun wheels were rolled down hillsides and bonfires were lit on the highest points to mark the highest position of the sun, as they had been ignited for thousands of years.

The golden herb of midsummer and symbol of the summer solstice, St John's Wort, if picked at midnight on the Eve of St John, or on the actual Solstice Eve, offers fertility and powers to attract a lover if carried or placed under a pillow.

The summer solstice is still one of the chief festivals of the Druids who keep watch through Solstice Eve and continue their celebrations until noon of the Solstice Day.

The summer solstice is the time for rituals for success, power and health.

The herbs and incenses of the summer solstice include chamomile, elder, fennel, lavender, St John's Wort and verbena. Candle colours are gold or orange for joy and confidence.

LUGHNASSAH – *from Sunset on July 31 to August 2*

This is The Feast of Lugh or Lug, Celtic God of Light, the first Harvest Festival to give thanks to the earth for her bounty.

It was considered unlucky to cut down the last sheaf of corn as this was thought to represent the corn sacrifice, in Celtic times Lugh himself, who was willingly offering his own life so that the cycle of life, death and rebirth, planting, growth and harvesting might continue. Harvesters would all hurl their sickles at the last sheaf so no one knew who had killed the Corn God. This last sheaf was made into a corn dolly, symbol of the Earth Mother, and decorated with the scarlet ribbons of Cerridwen, the Celtic Mother Goddess, in the Welsh tradition or Frigga the Mother Goddess of the Vikings. It would be hung over the hearth throughout winter.

The Christianised version, Lammas, which means Loaf-Mass, was the mediaeval Christian name for the day on which loaves of bread were baked from the first grain harvest and placed on the altar to symbolise the first fruits. As Lammas was a time for feasting and meeting for distant members of the tribe, it was a natural occasion for arranging marriages and for settling disputes and claims.

Lammas rituals therefore focus on justice, rights, partnerships, both personal and legal, promotion and career advancement and the regularising of personal finances.

The herbs and incenses of Lammas are cedarwood, cinnamon, fenugreek, ginger and heather, myrtle and sunflowers. The candle colours of Lammas are purple for justice and dark yellow and orange for the coming of autumn.

THE AUTUMN EQUINOX – *for Three Days from Sunset on Around September 23, According to the Calendar*

The autumn equinox was traditionally celebrated as the second 'Wild or Green Harvest', a time of celebration for the fruits and vegetables of the earth and the Earth Mother. The harvest supper pre-dates Christianity. On the day when equal night and day heralded winter, the feast formed a sympathetic magical gesture to ensure that there would be enough food during the winter, by displaying and consuming the finest of the harvest. In the story of the year, the God of Light is defeated by his twin and alter-ego, the God of Darkness.

Michaelmas, the day of St Michael, the Archangel of the Sun, was celebrated on September 29 with a feast centred around a goose. St Michael was patron saint of high places and replaced the pagan sun deities. Druids climb to the top of hills to bid farewell to the summer and the God of Animals, the ancient Horned God, retreats and assumes his aspect as God of Winter and the Underworld.

The autumn equinox is potent for rituals that focus on the completion of any unfinished tasks, the ending of quarrels and the setting down of unresolved anger; also for family matters.

The herbs and incenses of the autumn equinox include ferns, geranium, myrrh, pine and Solomon's Seal. Autumn equinox candle colours are blue for the autumn rain, and green for the Earth Mother and the wild harvest, to reflect the merging of disparate aspects of life and balanced thinking.

SAMHAIN – *from Sunset on October 31 until Sunset on November 2*

Samhain, meaning summer's end, known in the modern world as Hallowe'en, is the beginning of the Celtic year and a time for welcoming home family ghosts. It incorporates the Christian Days of the Dead – All Souls Day and All Saints' Day. This is the major date in the witches' calendar and the most important Fire Festival of ancient times.

It was the time when the cattle were brought from the hills for the winter and either put in byres or slaughtered for meat, having been driven through twin fires to purify them. These fires also served to drive away bad spirits who were believed to lurk at the transition of the year, as well as lighting the way home for both living and deceased family members.

It was believed that bad witches and malevolent fairies were especially powerful at this transition of the year but could be kept away by *bon* (good) fires or a Jack o'Lantern or candle in a pumpkin or turnip, placed in windows to frighten off evil spirits. In parts of the UK, Bonfire Night on November 5 has replaced the Hallowe'en fires that still burn brightly on this night in Ireland and parts of northern Europe. As a transition time, All Hallows Eve, or Hallowe'en, is considered the best time for love divination.

Samhain rituals are potent for protection, overcoming fears, for laying old ghosts, psychological as well as psychic, and for marking the natural transition between one stage of life and the next.

Herbs and incenses of samhain include cypress, dittany, ferns, nutmeg, sage and pine. Samhain candle colours are black, navy blue or deep purple for letting go of fear, and orange for the joy of immortality that is promised at this time.

THE MIDWINTER SOLSTICE – *for Three Days from Sunset from Around December 21, According to the Calendar*

The midwinter solstice marks the longest night and shortest day, and pre-dates organised religion. Because early humans saw the sun at its lowest point and the vegetation dead or dying, they feared that light and life would never return. So they lit great bonfires from yule logs and hung torches from trees to give strength to the sun. They also decorated homes with evergreens to persuade the bare trees to grow again after the winter.

The present Christmas festival is a glorious amalgamation of many ancient festivals that centred around the midwinter solstice, Norse, Celtic, Mithraic, Greek and Roman as well as Christian celebrations. The common theme is that the sun itself, the Sun God or Son of God, is reborn at the darkest hour of the year and life begins again.

The feasting of Christmas, like the Harvest Festival, formed a magical gesture to ensure there would be food again in the spring and good harvests the following year, through eating abundantly at a time of dearth.

Midwinter rituals are potent for prosperity as well as abundance in many less material ways.

The herbs and incenses of midwinter include bay, cedar, feverfew, holly, juniper, pine and rosemary. For midwinter solstice candle colours use white, scarlet, brilliant green and gold.

TREE WISDOM

Sacred trees were found in all cultures, although the species varied according to the land in which they grew. Early Japanese texts refer to holy sakaki trees growing on the Mountain of Heaven; Buddhists talk of the Tree of Knowledge; the Persians of the Tree of Immortality; while in the Old Testament the Hebrews' Tree of Knowledge of Good and Evil became the tree whose fruit lost man his immortality. In Hindu mythology, Vishnu, the preserver God, was born in the shade of the sacred banyan tree which became known as the Tree of Knowledge. The Chinese described the Trees of Life as peach and the date palm. The fig tree was also worshipped as the Tree of Knowledge in Middle Eastern cultures, while in Norse tradition, Yggdrasil, the world tree, was seen as a great ash, a prop to the sky, its topmost branches hung with stars, its axis the link between the worlds of heaven, earth and the underworld. In Ancient Egypt, both the cedar and sycamore were the holy trees of Osiris.

To the Celts, trees were especially magical. Their seven sacred trees were birch, willow, holly, hazel, oak, apple and alder; in more recent times these have been linked with the days of the week, beginning with the birch as Sunday.

Creation Trees

The Norse Father God Odin and his brothers fashioned the first man, Askr, from an ash tree and his wife Embla from an elm. In the Classical world, Zeus created the bronze race of men from the trunks of ash trees, and the Ancient Greeks believed that the ash was an image of the clouds. Ash nymphs were regarded as cloud goddesses.

From early times, there have been sacred groves for worship and divination. Oak groves, sacred to Zeus, were found at oracular sites such as Dodona, where the priestesses used the rustling of the leaves for divination. The Druids used oak or apple groves for their ceremonies and for divination.

The Druidic Tree Staves

The Celtic Tree Alphabet, a device by which the Druids transmitted secret wisdom through the times of persecution after the Roman conquest, was a magical and divinatory tool. Twenty original symbols, each representing a tree, later increased to 25, comprising the main letters of the Tree Alphabet, were etched on staves of wood; the staves were cast for prophecy beneath an ancient oak at sunset, the beginning of the new Celtic day. They were later called the Ogham Staves after Ogma, Warrior God, deity of wisdom and champion of the gods at the Battle of Moytura. Ogham staves were also associated with colours, birds, animals and kings, and so served as transmitters of many forms of Celtic lore.

Tree Magic

Even in the modern world, relics of tree magic can be seen in the custom of hanging evergreen boughs at Christmas to persuade the spring to return and the leafless trees to emulate their green sisters. On May Day, decorated maypoles form the centre of traditional earth magic dances in Europe, a custom practised in earlier times by Romans and Celts. Below I have listed some of the magical associations from different traditions, along with the Ogham name and stave symbol.

ALDER: *Fearn*

The alder is the tree of fire, known as the tree of Bran the Blessed, eldest son of Llyr, the Oak Father. Bran was a mighty giant who, in Celtic tradition, ordered his own beheading as he lay mortally wounded. His severed head is said to be under the White Mount or Tower Hill in London, as protection so that his beloved land will never be invaded. Whistles made of this wood were traditionally used to summon and control the four winds, so offering security and control against seemingly uncontainable elements.

ASH: *Nuinn*

The ash became the tree of seafaring throughout the northern hemisphere, being associated with Poseidon-type deities of the sea. Ash staves were used to keep away snakes and to cure diseases of farm animals. As recently as the 19th century in Killura, Ireland, a descendant of the original sacred ash of Creevna was used as a charm against drowning. After the potato famine in Ireland, emigrants to the USA carried the tree away with them to protect them in the new land.

BIRCH: *Beith*

The birch is sacred to Venus. In northern climes the birch symbolises the rebirth of spring and is sacred to the Mother Goddess. It was the first tree to grow after the Ice Age retreated. A relic of this early goddess worship is found in Russia, where in remote parts at Whitsun a birch is dressed in female clothing to represent the coming of the summer.

ELDER: *Ruis*

The elder is also dedicated to Venus and is associated with seeing other dimensions. It is said that if you wear a crown of elder twigs on May Eve (April 30), you will be able to see magical creatures and ghosts. Native North American Indians call the elder the tree of music. Elder trees were one of the guises assumed by witches.

HAWTHORN: *Huathe*

The hawthorn is the tree of Mars and also Thor and other Teutonic thunder gods. It is believed to act as a shield against physical and psychic harm. In pre-Christian times it was planted around sacred boundaries. The hawthorn, whitethorn or may tree has an unjustifiable association with ill luck, because of the belief that it is a bad omen to bring hawthorn blossoms indoors except on May morning.

Hawthorn twigs gathered on Ascension Day are believed to have exceptional powers for healing.

NATURE MAGIC AND MYSTERY

HAZEL: *Coll*

Druids used the hazel rod as a symbol of authority and wise judgement. Viking courts were surrounded by hazel staves to mark their limits. In Wales, it is said that a hazel cap woven from its twigs can be used to make wishes come true. Hazel nuts are also considered a symbol of fertility and old women in parts of the south-west of England and Western Europe would traditionally present brides with a bag of hazel nuts or even pelt them with the nuts. Hazel rods were also taken by Irish settlers to the USA to keep away snakes.

HOLLY: *Tinne*

The Holly King rules the Waning year from midsummer to the midwinter solstice, and each year according to Welsh legend the Oak and Holly King fought for supremacy on May 1. The original holly tree of the Celts was probably the twin brother of the common oak tree, the evergreen scarlet oak or holm oak or holly oak.

Holly was sacred to the Celtic God Taranis, a Thunder God/Giant who carried a club made of holly – the Green Knight referred to in the old Irish legend of Sir Gawain and the Green Knight. Holly is sometimes used as a symbol of Christ.

OAK: *Duir*

The oak was King of the Waxing Year from the midwinter solstice, around December 21, to the longest day, which falls about June 21. The midsummer fire was always oak and the ceremonial need fire, lit at the great festivals, was kindled in an oak log, thus symbolically fuelling the power of the sun. Duir means the door and its roots are believed to extend as far underground as its branches, so embracing the three realms of the underworld, earth and heaven. The space between two oaks was said to be the doorway to unseen realms where fairies lived and gave access to other dimensions.

ROWAN: *Luis*

This tree, sacred to the moon, is known as mountain ash, quickbeam or the Tree of Life. It is the tree most used against lightning and the power of all psychic harm. Berries on rowan healed the wounded and, in Irish myth, were said to add a year to a man's life. In ancient Ireland, the Druids of opposing forces would kindle a fire of rowan and say an incantation over it to summon spirits to take part in the battle and protect them.

YEW: *Ido*

The yew is known as the death tree in all European countries. As an evergreen it stands in graveyards as a symbol of immortality for a yew can live for 2,000 years or more, and when it decays a new trunk forms inside the old. Its branches grow downwards to form new but interconnected stems. In the old Irish tale, *Naoise and Deidre*, stakes of yew were driven through the dead bodies of the hero and heroine so that they would remain apart. However, the stakes grew and joined at the top over Armagh Cathedral.

PART FIVE

Wisdom from Other Cultures, Other Lands

AFRICAN MAGIC AND DIVINATION

Traditional and Modern Religion in Africa

In tribal Africa, each person is born into a tribe and remains a member of it even after death; the ancestors still play an important part in everyday life. Each tribal group has its own religion, although where there are similarities of language, there are considerable overlaps in myth.

Although most modern Africans now embrace either Christianity or Islam, magical and divinatory practices are still prevalent in both rural and urban areas, co-existing with the more formal religions. Assessments of the number of witch doctors, or *sangomas*, practising in South Africa alone range from 300,000 to a million. Acting as community doctors, psychologists and spiritual advisers, they are held in high regard. In Zimbabwe they are known as *n'gangas*.

Sangomas and prophets, the latter Christianised magic men or women, act as intermediaries between humankind and the ancestors or the Holy Spirit. The majority claim to derive their power from both sources.

The High God

Almost all African peoples believed in a supreme god who created the universe and all within it; this belief pre-dated the infiltration of the Christian or Islamic religions. This deity was personalised in their individual mythologies, usually as a bi-sexual or non-sexual being, father and mother of all creatures and creator of every plant and animal on earth, with a number of demi-gods serving beneath him.

Among the Zulu peoples, *Unkulunkulu*, The Ancient One, created people and cattle from reeds. He taught the Zulu how to hunt, make fire and grow food. He is said to be within everything that he created.

Yemoja, *Yemayah* or *Ymoja* of the Yoruba, the great feminine power who appears in many tribal cultures, gave birth to all the waters of the earth and is mother of many of the Yoruba gods, being depicted with huge breasts. Though she is life-giving and a symbol of motherhood, she is also destructive and called the Great Witch.

The Ghosts of the Ancestors

The ancestors, according to legend, live beneath the earth, as they did in life, carrying on their daily tasks and living in huts. Countless myths tell of people who visited the underworld, often by following an animal into its hole.

Before an earthly journey or undertaking, a man would seek advice from his father's spirit by consulting a diviner. One method involved taking a handful of flour and dropping it slowly and carefully on the ground. If it formed a cone, the signs were promising. The cone was then covered with a pot and left overnight. If the cone had remained intact by morning, the man would go on his journey full of optimism. However, if the cone had collapsed, a postponement was advised.

Magic in African Society

External malice, it is believed, emanated from a living enemy who either attacked by witchcraft or paid a sorcerer (male) or bad witch (female) to provide a curse or a potion to cause illness or misfortune. The potion or curse amulet would be hidden near the victim's house. Nail or hair clippings of the victim might be used or the sorcerer might chew herbs and spit them out in the direction of the victim's home, calling the name of the victim. Although there is a strong belief in bad witchcraft, or *mangu*, anger, jealousy, envy, hatred and negative feelings in the victim are believed to open the way for evil to gain entry.

Some tribes say that a witch's spirit leaves the body during sleep and so the witch might be unaware of her evildoing, but most believe she is deliberately malevolent, aided by her familiars who might be a hyena, an owl, bat or the feared *impundulu*, a lightning bird who brought disaster to crops, illnesses to the chest when he sucked the blood of victims, and even death to animals and people.

The *sangoma*/prophet will help the victim to locate the curse in order to neutralise it, and traditional practitioners will turn the curse back on the conspirator. However, it might also be discovered through divination that the perpetrator of the negative forces was not a contemporary. For it is said that a person who neglected traditional prescribed sacrifices or committed an offence against the social and moral code of the ancestors might be punished by the ancestral spirits by illness or misfortune, or in an extreme case be possessed by the angry ancestral spirit. Wrongdoing by other close family members might also have brought down the wrath of the ancestors, especially if the whole family was suffering misfortune.

The offender and his/her family would then be instructed to perform rituals to propitiate the ancestors, for example sacrificing a goat, sheep or chicken, singing, dancing, sprinkling or drinking holy water, lighting candles or fires.

Casting the Bones

The origins of this form of magic are unknown, since it existed before written records. In 1607 the Portuguese Missionary Joano dos Santos witnessed the divinatory 'throwing of the bones' in Mozambique. It is a powerful method used by *sangomas* to discover the source of misfortune and illness. But diviners are also consulted on matters such as the thriving of cattle and crops and the successful outcome of disputes.

The names of the bones in many areas resemble those of ancestor gods. The Shona tribes of Zimbabwe call their individually carved symbolic divining bones, Hakata. The Hakata and other divining bones are also used less formally as a domestic oracle.

Traditional Bone Divination

Each diviner makes a personal set of divination bones during his or her apprenticeship and asks the ancestors to make the bones powerful. They are the *sangoma's* most sacred possession.

There are two main forms of bone divination. One version has four bones to represent the senior male member of a family, a senior female, a junior male and a junior female. These are usually made of ivory, wood, bone or cattle horn. Each bone is decorated on one side to represent the positive aspect, and the other left plain for negative results. The bones are cast on earth that is swept clean or on a special divination mat and each 'fall', as it is called, has a specific name and a verse known as a praise poem connected with it. Thus there are 16 possible combinations. The diviner considers the problem or question posed and applies the meaning accordingly. Whether a throw is good or bad can depend on the issue to which it refers, and the diviner interprets the meaning in relation to the current problem or decision to be made.

Male/Female

The male/female divide is reflected in the natural world. For example, the earth is female and the sky male. The left side is generally associated with women and the right with men, dark is female and light male. These concepts are also seen in other cultures thousands of miles away, for example, China.

Senior/Junior

The senior/junior precedence system is at the heart of the family and of wider social groups in the village, and in more modern times in work or social hierarchies in the cities. The bone pieces are related to family position, at root father, followed by mother, son and daughter. These basic positions can be adapted according to the question asked or the sphere under consideration. The senior father bone can, for example, also stand for paternal ancestors, the grandfather, the father's brother, the chief, or simply an older man.

Casting the Astragali or Knuckle Bones

This is a more extensive divination system, using anything up to 50 or 60 knuckle-bones. These bones come from different animals, with a male and female bone for each creature. The set also includes pieces of tortoiseshell, representing secrets, shells and stones, found at sites of religious importance.

Again, each bone has a positive/negative side. The astragali are read both according to the clusters of the bones and which side faces upwards. The content of the astragalus set also varies according to the specific totem (power animal and bird groups) of the tribe. These tribal animals are reflected prominently in the sets. A typical South African set would include four flat pieces of ivory, two male and two female.

The four ivory pieces are studied first. These give insights into the general issue. These in turn are related to the position of other key bones, for example the knucklebone of the steenbuck, which in many sets represents the chief or principal character under question. Another key bone might be that of the antbear which represents the ancestors and indicates both from its position and its positive or negative aspect whether a venture is likely to succeed. It also indicates the possible well-being and health of the questioner.

The influence of important or respected people may be indicated by sheep bones, while goat bones tend to refer to the actions of ordinary people. A small and large hyena bone could be used to denote witchcraft or sorcery, and the positive or negative aspect reveals how these powers were implicated. Cattle or leopard bones or teeth would indicate wealth, and sea shells the time scale. The larger the shell cast, the more distant the event would lie in the future; the closeness of the shell to the relevant bone would indicate the immediacy of change.

Although each bone has a fixed meaning, the interpretation of the cast or fall varies according to the kind of problem under consideration. For example, when the four senior male bones fall in a positive position, it might indicate a lot of activity, which in a stable family situation might suggest unrest but would be a good indicator of rain during a drought.

AUSTRALIAN ABORIGINAL SPIRITUALITY

… animals made of dots which were swimming around the room, started coming so close and touching me right next to my face. They were so inquisitive of me. All the dots seemed to be able to change into another animal species. Out of the curtains appeared a huge Aboriginal man and behind him women and children. On the other wall which was dark brick were all the animals again, only this time much smaller, the size of cats.

These areas were once the home areas of the Aboriginal tribes – they were amazed I knew about the Dreaming as many have only heard of it themselves and not experienced it.

Pauline, a Scotswoman living in Queensland, Australia, on her experience
of Aboriginal spiritual realms

The Roots of Magic

The Aborigines have lived in Australia for at least 40,000 years. It has been said that Australia was the Aborigines' garden. The magic of the Aborigines has been shaped by the size, geological and historical stability and emptiness of Australia. Before European settlers arrived 200 years ago, probably no more than 300,000 Aborigines inhabited Australia's 2,967,909 square miles (7,686,855 square km), nine-tenths of which is flat. Originally, the Aborigines lived mainly in coastal areas, in unique unbroken isolation and in harmony with nature, but they were forced inland to the semi-arid or desert interior lands when European settlements were established.

To the Aborigines, magic was indivisible from this natural world and life was a continuing ritual. Their tradition is oral, carried through myth and depicted on cave walls and in natural rock formations. The rock engravings especially illustrate the Aboriginal belief in the Dreamtime, when their hero gods made human beings from plants, animals and natural features; these source species became totem or guardian spirits.

The Story of the Dreamtime

In Aboriginal lore, the Dreamtime is not separate from the material world but co-exists to be accessed in sleep and meditation as a source of inspiration and wisdom, direct from the first hero creator gods. It is the archetype of dreams themselves and in waking is experienced by Australian Aborigines through contact with the sacred earth of which they are a part. Central to Aboriginal spirituality is this interconnectedness of all life, such that if a tree is cut down the man or woman shares its pain.

Each Aborigine believed he or she came from the Dreaming to take human form. Because of this, the Aboriginal lifestyle was bound to specific regions where tribal ancestors had established sacred places during the Dreamtime. Members of each group believed that the spirits of infants existed in that territory until they were incarnated, and after death would return to the same territory. In the Aboriginal world in the Dreamtime there is no real distinction between earth, sky, person, sky hero, ancestor and Aborigine today.

The land is regarded as a living entity. Uluru (Ayers Rock), the vast mass of red rock in the Northern Territory, is called the navel of the earth. The Aborigines talk of *djang*, supernatural earth wisdom. Myths account for the formation of sacred sites, such as Uluru, which are still recalled in story and song, and in the telling connection is made, like switching on a light, with the ever-present energy.

For this reason, the loss of access to their spiritual centres was for Aborigines the hardest blow when they were relocated. In a recent interview published in the *Neo-pagan Times*, Robert Bropho, custodian of the values of Nyoongar at the Swan Valley Nyoongar Community, said:

There are a lot of spiritual things that Aboriginal people can do. They can still track on hard ground, soft ground, over rocks and that type of thing still exists further up in the outer areas of each country town. And it's there forever. It's not going to go away. Most of the old people, they are the real story tellers and the young people are learning. We hope that it will still be around for a long time yet to come.

Natural Phenomena and Ritual

Natural phenomena such as storms are not only portrayed in a mythological way but hold in each individual storm and in their seasonal renewal the continuing link between the world of spirit and the natural world, confirming the eternal presence of the time of Dreaming.

For example, before the rainy season the Lightning Brothers, Jagbagjula and Jabarringa, of Wardaman spirit lore, are said to fight over a wife. Their struggles bring lightning and the rain which is vital for the world's renewal. These sky heroes form the focus of great ceremonial rituals prior to the end of each dry season.

The Aborigines calculate time in sleeps and fix their festivals by the moon. Most ceremonies are linked with the passage of human, animal and plant life, the fertility of the earth, birth, initiation, marriage and death. Initiation at puberty is one of the most central ceremonies and the initiates recreate the journeys of the ancient heroes.

One of the most famous rites is the annual sacred sex ceremonies of Kunapipi, the Earth Mother, and the Rainbow Snake in northern Australia. The Rainbow Snake, Jarapiri, was the manifest form of the formless First Cause or All-Father. Jarapiri came, according to different myths, from the sea or underground and gave form to the land. He still slumbers in sacred waterholes, under waterfalls or in caves and manifests himself in the ritual through the dance, ceremony and love-making of the individual Aboriginal male. Kunapipi, the Earth Mother, is represented in the rite by the female Aborigine and together male and female re-enact the sacred marriage with the earth to ensure fertility of land and people.

Kunapipi is the symbol of the reproductive qualities of the earth, the eternal replenisher of human, animal and plant. Sometimes she appears as two sisters or as her own two daughters. The Waugeluk sisters emerged at the time of Dreaming from the sea with their mother, Kunapipi. They then travelled north, carrying with them knowledge of ritual and fertility. They were eaten by the Rainbow Snake and henceforward he spoke with their voice. They represent therefore the inner voice of instinct and intuition that often gets swallowed up by logic.

Song Lines – Psi-Tracks

It is believed that the song lines of the Australian Aborigines can guide them across thousands of miles by linking a traveller into the song or legend of a natural landmark such as a rock painting. These invisible psychic trails are called psi-tracks and are strengthened each time the song is recalled. In 1987, the Swede Göte Andersson gave this phenomenon its name and defined the force as an energy field created by visualisation that extends between a person and the object on which he or she is concentrating.

Once a new person sings the words associated with the sacred place, the track is reactivated, and so over thousands of years Aborigines were able to cross Australia using only the intricate designs on shields as their aide-memoire.

Totems

Totemism is the most important element in the man–nature relationship. Because all members of a tribe are said to be descendants of a particular kind of plant, animal, bird or fish, totemic ceremonies were held at the time of the year when the totem species bore fruit or gave birth to its young. These secret rituals were believed to ensure the continuity of the totem species through the individual. The secrets of these rites and the myths of the Dreamtime were passed on by the tribal elders to the younger generations at totem initiation rites. Although a totem is usually an animal or plant, it can also be a natural phenomenon such as water, the sun, cloud or wind.

Clever Men or Mekigars – Australian Aboriginal Shamanism

Many Aboriginal tribes subscribed to the belief in a supreme Sky Father called Ungud or Balame, a formless invisible all-embracing power that is manifest in every plant, rock, animal and human.

Becoming a *mekigar*, *karadji* or clever man involves complex and prolonged initiation rites whereby the initiate meets the All-Father or Supreme Sky God by flying to the place of Dreaming, and the initiate may undergo a ritual death in which his internal organs are replaced. Crystal quartz used in the creation of a *mekigar* is especially sacred and is seen as frozen light, the embodiment of the Living Spirit. The throne of the All-Father is said to be made of crystal quartz.

Ungud or Balame uses the magical power of song to sing a piece of quartz crystal into the initiate's head, giving him x-ray vision. Balame removes a sacred fire from his own body and sings it into the initiate's body. Finally, he sings into the initiate a thick sinew cord that enables the newly created *mekigar* to ascend to the Dreaming at will.

It is said that only 'clever men' can ascend the aerial ladder to the spirit world, although all men can on their initiation into their totem learn the sacred language that enables them to conduct a dialogue with the Dreaming, especially during sleep.

Buddhism

What is Buddhism?

Buddhism is the name of a religious philosophy based on the teachings of Siddhartha Gautama, the original Buddha. The term Buddha is not a personal name, but a title given to a person who has become an Enlightened One. It is derived from the Sanskrit root word *budh*, meaning to wake up or to regain consciousness.

Unlike other religious paths, in Buddhism there is no division between divinity and humanity, with each person responsible for his or her own destiny rather than a Supreme Being. So by following Buddhist teachings, it is possible for an individual to reach enlightenment and become a Buddha or *bodhisattva*, who, like the original Buddha, delays his or her final stage of evolution in order to teach the Truth to those who are less spiritually evolved. This potential for spiritual progression, plus the emphasis on peace, doing no harm to any living creature, and selflessness, have made Buddhist philosophy increasingly popular with those seeking spiritual fulfilment in the Western world. Buddhism has more than 300 million followers worldwide.

Buddhism began in India in the 6th and 5th centuries BC, dividing from the Hindu religion, though among Hindus Gautama Buddha is revered as an *avatar* or manifest form of the God Vishnu. As well as his belief that there was no Supreme God, Gautama's beliefs also differed from Hindu doctrine in his denial of the existence of a permanent separate immortal soul or *atman*, as in Hinduism. This doctrine is referred to in Buddhist literature as selflessness or *anatman*. Because he believed that all phenomena lack substantial entities and are characterised by emptiness or *shunyata*, only by overcoming the illusion of a permanent soul or sense of self could there be escape from the Wheel of Rebirth and Karma or the accumulation of desires and actions that bind a person to earthly life. The ultimate aim is to attain eternal peace or Nirvana, which literally means the snuffing out of a candle, in this case the elimination of the separate self.

The Historical Buddha

Siddhartha Gautama was born in northern India in the 6th century BC. His father, Suddhodana, was the ruler of the kingdom. Although he lived in comfort, Siddhartha was troubled by what he regarded as the four inescapable problems of the human condition: birth into a world filled with sorrow; disease and illness; old age; and finally death. At the age of 29, leaving his own infant son Rahula, Siddhartha became a

WISDOM FROM OTHER CULTURES, OTHER LANDS

wandering ascetic, living a life of abject poverty. But deprivation offered no greater insight than his former way of life.

Enlightenment came during his night-long meditation under a Bodhi tree, in Gaya near modern Bihar. He realised that everything in the world was impermanent (*anitya*) and illusory. Even wealth, fame or relationships were sources of suffering (*duhkha*). By dawn he had attained full awareness, understanding that even the existence of a Supreme Controlling Godhead and separate human souls were illusions. Thereafter, for 50 years until his death, Buddha travelled barefoot throughout north-western India, teaching to all regardless of caste, and as his number of disciples grew, they formed the Sangha, a community of monks and nuns and spread the Message.

The Development of Buddhism

Shortly after his death, 500 of his closest disciples, *arhats*, who had transcended all attachment to material desires, met to consolidate the teachings of the Buddha, each recounting what had been spoken. Others would then either confirm the accuracy of the memory or correct minor details. Henceforward, the council declared that no new teachings would be accepted as the word of the Buddha or *buddha-vachana*.

However, new doctrines inevitably appeared, resulting in a split into two schools, the original *Theravada* or *Hinayana*, or Lesser Vehicle, and *Mahayana*, or Greater Vehicle, which emerged during the 1st century AD. *Theravada* means the teachings of the elders.

The aim of *Theravada* or *Hinayana* was a personal path through which a follower might become an *arhat*, who had overcome all ties to the material world and so would merge into Nirvana. *Mahayana* Buddhism emphasised the path of service to others whereby a person would deliberately delay the personal attainment of Nirvana and instead become a *bodhisattva* in order to help others to find the path of fulfilment. This Buddha himself had done. The *Hinayana* School of Buddhism spread from India throughout south-east Asia, especially in Sri Lanka, Thailand, Burma, Cambodia and Laos. The later form of Buddhism became more prevalent in central and east Asia, in Tibet, Mongolia, Korea, Japan, Vietnam and China.

Many forms of Buddhism are now practised throughout the world, but all adhere to the basic principles of attaining Nirvana and the need to become detached from earthly desires to attain this state, although the nature of Nirvana does vary in the different schools.

Buddhist Beliefs

Buddha's teachings are contained in the Four Noble Truths.

The Four Noble Truths

1 The Noble Truth of Suffering
Not only does the very fact of being alive involve suffering, from birth or rebirth, through disease, ageing processes and death, but even in the midst of joy there can be

sorrow through associating with people and situations that one finds difficult or enforced separation from people and places that are loved, as well as the failure to obtain one's desires. Nothing is the same even a moment later and lack or loss of what is seen as permanence also causes sorrow, for stability is a basic human need.

2 The Noble Truth of the Arising of Suffering

Sensual cravings (e.g. the ear for pleasant sounds, the eye for beautiful forms), cravings for life itself and for prosperity and the trappings of wealth, are said to accompany humankind from cradle to grave, accentuated by the need for instant gratification and joy, as well as the urge to attain power and recognition in the world's eyes. In these unremitting desires lies the source of human suffering and discontent.

3 The Noble Truth of the Cessation of Suffering

Suffering can be ended only by the complete cessation of attachment, which detaches the self from desire and cravings for wordly attainments and for permanence, and finally detachment from the self. This is called the Way of Emptiness.

4 The Noble Truth of the Path Leading to the Cessation of Suffering

This is called the Middle Path because it avoids the two extremes of sensual pleasure and self-denial, both of which cause extreme reactions of pleasure or pain. The Eightfold Path, which was practised by the Buddha himself, offers the way to escape from the cycles of rebirth and sorrow and attain Nirvana. The Noble Eightfold Path involves:

Right Knowledge or Understanding

This is an intellectual grasp of Dharma, the true nature of things, i.e. the Four Noble Truths and the Law of Karma. It is also called Right View, which means the right way to view and understand the world. Wrong understanding occurs when expectations are imposed on events and people as hopes and fears about the way things might or might not be. Right Understanding occurs when the Seeker can view life objectively.

Right Thought or Intention

This proceeds from Right View, for if expectations, hopes and fears can be abandoned, there is no need to be manipulative. The way to achieve this is by eliminating ambition, revenge, desire, hatred, greed, lust and violence, and so create inner purity.

Right Speech

This involves speaking the truth that comes from the heart. All lies, malicious words, blame and gossip are thus replaced by kind, compassionate, wise and considered words.

Right Action of Discipline

This is the avoidance of causing pain to or the destruction of any living being, plant, seed or flower, of not taking what has not been offered, of renouncing frivolity, passion and excesses of the body.

Right Livelihood

This means avoiding jobs that exploit or damage the self or others, avoiding self-seeking and above all performing every task no matter how mundane or lowly as well as possible.

Right Effort

This refers to gentle non-aggressive effort towards goodness, not subjugating the shadow side or driving it out with a struggle by punishing, or denying the body its basic needs, but actively cultivating positive thought and through meditative practices achieving mental stillness, wherein resides a natural state of goodness. Thus new negativity cannot enter.

Right Attentiveness

This involves precision and clarity. It is a state of awareness that is above instinctive and subconscious actions. It is attained by becoming and remaining aware of every detail, of speech, action, work, attitudes to others and their effects on the world now and in the future, of moving towards true unity with all things.

Right Concentration

Right Concentration, or Absorption, is the total and complete absorption in the present that alone gives freedom from past and future. Meditation is a good way of attaining this. It is the threshold of Nirvana.

Chanting and Meditation

Meditation is one of the most important methods in Buddhist life for attaining a higher level of awareness. The ultimate goal of meditation is to become an awakened being who is completely freed of the wheel of becoming, and so cannot accumulate any more Karma.

There are two basic kinds of Buddhist meditation. *Saamatha* involves concentrating the mind upon a single focus, whether breath control, a mantra, a candle flame, a flower or a conundrum or spiritual puzzle, and gradually leads through the eight stages of full absorption into the higher energy field. The first stage causes bodily awareness to cease, while the highest reaches the state where there is neither perception nor non-perception.

The second kind, *Vipassaba*, the path of mindfulness or awareness, at its highest enables the meditator to lose attachment to the world and with this all negativity.

In Zen Buddhism, a form that came to Japan from China, words are regarded as only the surface of expression, and it is important to get beyond words to the true meaning, using meditation whether on a beautiful garden or a single phrase or sentence called a *koon*, which may be a riddle such as: what is the sound made by one hand clapping. Some Buddhists meditate for months or years on the same *koon*.

Buddhists also chant phrases, verses or passages from Buddhist scriptures as a way of focusing and stilling the mind. In some Far Eastern schools, chanting is the most important path to Nirvana, as sacred sound enables the initiate to rise beyond the trappings of the world. The repetition of *Om*, the sound which, it is said, brought the universe into being, is central to Buddhist chants, and in meditation helps to create the spiritual light and power that can remove disharmony. Buddhists also use beads to assist the recitation of long chants.

CELTIC SPIRITUALITY

Spirituality in the Western world has been greatly influenced by Celtic wisdom. Many magical practices focus on Celtic deities and mythology, for example the Wiccan and Neo-pagan festivals that follow the Celtic Wheel of the Year, and in the continued use of sacred waters and trees in modern healing and empowerment rituals.

Who Were the Celts?

Though there is a root Celtic culture and language, there is not a single Celtic race. Recent evidence suggests that in the UK signs of the Celtic culture appeared from the second millennium BC, and that though the Druids (see p. 107) were not responsible for building Stonehenge, nevertheless the priestly culture that inspired the megaliths (see p. 196) was already in existence in Western Europe. It is known that the Celts preserved and developed existing nature shrines, sacred wells and stone circles, and the Celtic coligny calendar continued to combine lunar and solar cycles that were already recorded in the astronomical correspondences of the stone circles built from about 2600BC, especially in Western Europe and Scandinavia.

So the Celtic invasion was in fact a two-way cultural absorption that took place over centuries rather than decades. The most accurate accounts of the Celts – apart from the more biased references by hostile Classical chroniclers such as Julius Caesar – come from Native Celtic mythology. The remains of an oral tradition, preserved over the centuries by Celtic bards and minstrels, were recorded by Christian monks from the 8th to 13th centuries, and were also collected as folklore in areas where Celtic descendants remained from the 17th century onwards.

In Ireland, the four chief myth cycles are the Ulster Cycle, the Fionn Cycle, the Invasion Races, and the Cycle of King, and in Wales the myths are contained in *The Mabinogion*. Because Celtic culture was preserved in Ireland until almost AD500, this has proved the richest source for Celtic mythology.

As a living tradition, some Celtic poems, stories and prayers continued to be created and transmitted orally in an unbroken line, even after they were written down. During the 20th century some previously unwritten material was recorded, notably the *Carmina Gadelica*, a collection of folk prayers from the Hebrides of

Scotland. These later Celtic jewels have been instrumental in the revival of Celtic spirituality interest, especially in the UK and USA over the past three and a half decades.

With the advent of Christianity, the pure religion and the mythology of the Celts was diluted into Celtic Christianity, and the deities, ancient sites and wells were given new Christian identities – and sometimes new histories. Nevertheless, in charismatic figures such as St Bride and St Patrick and the legends that grew up around these early saints, the vitality of the Celts survived. One example is a poem said to have been written by St Brigit:

> I would like to have the men of Heaven
> In my own house
> With vats of good cheer laid out for them.
> I would like to have the three Marys,
> Their fame is so great.
> I would like people from every corner of Heaven.
> I would like them to be cheerful in their drinking,
> I would like to have Jesus too here amongst them
> I would like a great lake of beer for the King of Kings,
> I would like to be watching Heaven's family, drinking it through all eternity.

The Celtic Cosmology

The Celts did not have a hierarchy of divinities in the sense of a coherent pantheon dwelling in a remote place, separate from their people. Indeed, the *Tuatha de Danaan*, the Irish deities were said to reside on the Hill of Tara, not far from the Newgrange megaliths. In addition, the human and the Otherworld formed a unity in which the human and divine regularly interacted. Nor did the Celts worship their deities through statues in human form, but as crude representations of these figures, though their jewellery and artefacts revealed their skills in art.

What is more, humans could be reborn divine, whether through courageous deeds, the will of the deities or by magical means. The Celtic Otherworld is therefore a realm that can be entered during life, on spiritual quests by heroes, is the source of the earthly Well of Wisdom, of which all other sacred wells and waters are tributaries. It has many entrances from the physical world, either across water or through doorways in places of natural beauty, for example the top of Glastonbury Tor in Somerset.

The Celtic Otherworld

The Otherworld is sometimes pictured in Celtic mythology as the Isle of the Blest, a concept found in many cultures, including the Chinese, as mist-shrouded paradises located in the remote west. One of the best descriptions of the Celtic Otherworld is in the Welsh poem 'Preiddeu Annwfn' which calls this paradise island Annwfn. Here, the hero bard Taliesin, son of Cerridwen, Welsh Goddess of Inspiration, went in search of the Holy Grail. There are three regions, the first the land of the Silent Dead in which the Lost Ones were contained within a glass fort known as Caer Wydyr and also referred to as Nennius.

The second realm is Caer Feddwidd, the Fort of Carousa, ruled by Arianrhod, the Goddess of Time, Karma and Destiny. Here a mystical fountain of wine offered eternal health and youth for those who chose to spend their immortality in the afterlife.

The third realm, the most divine, has become known as Avalon, the sacred Isle of Arthur, where only the most spiritual or those who sacrificed a great deal for the benefit of others could enter. King Arthur was its most famous inhabitant.

The Isle of Arran, an alternative Isle of the Blest, is the seat of the Cauldron of Plenty, which many scholars believe was the inspiration for the Holy Grail. This Cauldron, known also as the Undry, is one of the original four Celtic treasures, corresponding to the suit of Cups in the Tarot (see p. 77). It provided an endless supply of nourishment, had great healing powers and could restore the dead to life, either to their former existence or a new life form. Like the Well of Wisdom, the Cauldron was also accessed by magical means or through spiritual quests by the living.

The Celtic Deities

Celtic religion had many female deities who, as women in Celtic society, occupied warlike and destructive/transformative roles. Because each tribe or clan used its own names for the deities, more than 300 different Celtic god/goddess forms have been recorded. The following are those that have retained significance in modern Celtic spirituality or whose myths have reflected universal magical themes that have influenced modern ritual. The major deities represent different manifestations of aspects or stages of the divine masculine and feminine principles.

Arianrhod

This Welsh Goddess whose name means Silver Wheel is associated with the constellation of the *Corona Borealis*, the Crown of the North. Her original consort was Nwyvre, the sky. She was worshipped during the full moon and, like Cerridwen, was regarded as a Goddess of Inspiration and the Bards.

Brighid

The Irish Goddess Brighid is daughter of the Dagda and an important member of the *Tuatha de Danaan*. She took on the role of Dana who was an archetypal goddess form rather than an actual goddess.

Brighid's name means High One, and she is sometimes seen as three sisters, daughters of the god Dagda, the Divine Father, or as the three generations – maiden, mother and crone Triple Goddess. Patron of smiths, healers and poets, Brighid was also an important fertility goddess, and in the early spring softened the earth with her white wand and so awoke the spring at the festival of Imbolc at the beginning of February and restored fertility to land and people.

With Christianisation, as St Brigit of Kildare she was in legend, though not in chronology, said to be the midwife of Christ and known in Ireland as Mary of the Gaels. As the Virgin Mary replaced the Mother Goddess sacred sites, so were wayside shrines and wells once dedicated to Brighid, transferred in virtually the same form to the protection of St Brigit who herself had different saint names but the same form throughout the British Isles.

Callieach, the Old or Veiled One

Her origins are so ancient that she may be an archetypal Bone Goddess. Also called Gyre Carlin, or the Grey Hag of Winter, she was in Ireland, Scotland and Wales known as the Dark Wise Woman, who with her cauldron healed the archetypal hero and so endowed him with the necessary wisdom and knowledge to complete his task.

The Morrigan is a form of the Callieach with whom Dagda, the Father God, mated on November 1, the first day of the Celtic winter and the Celtic New Year. Callieach is associated with death and life and prophesied the ultimate doom of the world because of humankind's own folly:

> I shall not long see the world I love
> But Summer without flowers,
> Cattle without milk,
> Seas where no fish flash.

Sometimes the Triple Goddess, the maiden, mother and crone are described as Brighid, Danu and Callieach or the waxing, full and waning moons.

Cernunnos

Cernunnos was a generic term meaning Horned One for the various Horned Gods of the Celtic tradition. His origin dates back to the shamanic figures portrayed on cave walls, the earliest being the one found on the cave walls of *Les Trois Frères* in the French Pyrenees that dates from about 14,000BC. Cernunnos was Lord of winter, the hunt, animals, death, male fertility and the underworld, and was sometimes portrayed as a Triple or Trefoil God, an image assimilated by St Patrick with his emblematic shamrock. Other forms of the Horned God include Herne the Hunter, the Greek Pan, God of the Woodlands, and Dionysus, Greek God of Vegetation and the Vine, whose ecstatic mystery cult involved ritual dismemberment and resurrection.

Cernunnos's importance is in his continuing presence as the Horned God, the male principle in witchcraft through the ages, in modern Wiccan and other Neo-pagan faiths.

Cerridwen

Cerridwen, as Welsh Mother Goddess of Inspiration, is associated with the Cauldron of Knowledge and Inspiration (and so the younger form of the Veiled One).

After the boy Gwion was left to tend her Cauldron of Knowledge and unwittingly absorbed some of the brew intended for her own son, he escaped from Cerridwen by turning into a hare, a fish, a bird and a grain of wheat. However, Cerridwen matched every shape with a predatory one – a greyhound, an otter, a hawk and a red hen who finally swallows the grain – thus conceiving Gwion as her own child.

She gave birth to him and placed him in a leather bag, before casting him into the water – Celtic Moses – on May Eve, the beginning of the Celtic summer. He was found by a form of Merlin and raised as Taliesin. This shapeshifting cycle has inspired many folk songs and stories and is a central theme of transformation in modern ritual.

Dagda, the Good Father

In the Celtic tradition, Dagda was also called Eochaid Ollathair (Father of All) and Ruadh Rofessa (the Red One of Knowledge). He was the first King of the *Tuatha de Danaan*, the Irish gods, for it was said: 'it was he who performed miracles and saw to the weather and the harvest'.

He was not Father of all the gods, nor did he have the importance of Danu, the mother. Nevertheless, he was Lord of life and death and the primary Fertility God. With his huge club, he made the bones of his people's enemies 'fall like hail beneath the horses'. With one end of the club he could kill nine men with a single blow and with the other could instantly restore them to life.

His great cauldron was handed on to his daughter Brighid (in the Welsh tradition it passed to Cerridwen). In some legends, Dagda is associated with Balor, the Sun deity of the Formoiri, enemies of the gods, who was slain by the young Solar God Lugh at the Battle of Moytura, thus representing the ascent of the new sun. The death of the old order as a necessary requirement for the new is a central motif in spirituality and is also seen, for example, in the battle of Ragnarok that destroyed Odin and the Aesir in Norse mythology.

Danu

Danu, or Don in the British tradition, was the Earth Goddess, the great Mother of the Gods. She stands at the head of the tribe, superior to the male chief deity. She is not seen as the physical mother of all the gods but some kind of early creatrix, and so does not appear in myths in a personalised form.

Lugh or Lug, the Young God

Lugh, or Lug, was a hero who through courage and persistence became deified as the supreme Sun God of the Irish and of the Euro-Celts, and patron of Arts and Crafts and new leader of the *Tuatha de Danaan*. Lugh the shining one gives his name to Lughnassadh, the Celtic Festival of the First Harvest, when having replaced the Dagda as supreme king, he himself became a willing sacrifice in order to bring fertility to the land. This evolution of the earlier enforced sacrifice is an important motif in spirituality and magic, especially fertility magic, and is expressed in many cultures. This sacrifice was re-enacted annually at the First Harvest in the cutting down of the last sheaf of corn, and later in the Christian tradition of placing a loaf made from the sheaf on the altar at Lammas, the Christianised Lughnassadh.

The Morrigan

The Morrigan is another Irish Triple Goddess of renewal, death and fate, and is the Goddess of Battle, urging on warriors and afterwards appearing as carrion over battlefields, scavenging the bodies of the slain. She is also associated with sexuality and fertility, and her coupling with the Dagda marks the end of the Celtic campaigning season, the onset of winter and the germination of the land in readiness for the following spring. The Morrigan, like Brighid, is associated with sheela-na-gig, the Celtic hag-like fertility figures in the process of giving birth, and in the continuing cycle of conception, birth, death and rebirth that was reflected in the existence of the deities, humankind and the land in the Wheel of the Year.

FENG SHUI

What is Feng Shui?

Feng shui means wind and water, which before the age of high technology were the most powerful forces – *feng*, the power of the sky and *shui*, the waters of the earth.

It is believed that both natural and artificial features enhance or block the flow of the life-force, ch'i, and that by the manipulation, addition or removal of internal and external features in the home, garden, workplace and even public buildings, health, relationships, fertility, career, learning, prosperity and pleasure can be enhanced.

Feng shui dates back 5,000 years to China, and there are two formal systems: the Form School and the Compass School. The former involves learning the traditional principles of harmony with the environment, and the second the more precise measurement of the house or workplace under question. However, the folk system of feng shui has co-existed alongside the more formal methods, and the much popular Westernised feng shui derives partly from this folk tradition.

What is Ch'i?

Known as the Dragon's Breath, positive ch'i or qi is the invisible life-force, the flow of positive energy through everything: people, animals, nature and also homes and workplaces. The regulated flow of ch'i promotes growth, health and vitality. When this positive energy becomes blocked, problems can occur, whether physical or a general feeling of malaise or 'dis-ease'. Certain homes and workplaces seem dark and unfriendly, and those who live or work there may lack energy and direction. If, however, ch'i flows too fast or intensely, it may lead to anger, hyperactivity and an inability to relax, and may carry away prosperity and well-being.

Negative Ch'i

Good ch'i does not flow in straight lines, but circulates gently within and around a building to avoid 'stale air'. In contrast, adverse or bad ch'i, or sha, does travel in a straight line, accumulating in what are called poisoned arrows that can be created by the sharp corners and diagonals formed by adjoining buildings or badly positioned furniture. Negative energy or sha ch'i is sometimes called tiger energy.

Ch'i also comes from four directions as the diagram below shows (in the Chinese tradition, south is at the top of maps and pictures rather than the bottom).

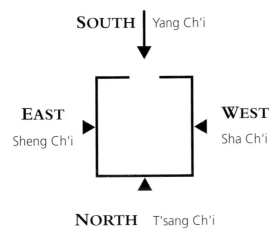

- Sheng ch'i, the ch'i of growth, comes from the east, bringing creative energy and health so this is one to nourish and encourage.

- Yang ch'i, the nourishing power, comes from the south, bringing worldly success, prosperity and fortune. It should be encouraged to flow freely, though not too fast or there will be exhaustion.

- T'sang ch'i comes from the north and needs to flow slowly and gently, bringing harmony and tranquillity, the ch'i of quiet sleep.

- Sha ch'i, disruptive ch'i, comes from the west. It is not to be obliterated for there must be change, but if you have a west-facing front door to home or workplace, the force may be too powerful and you will need a wind chime or deflecting mirror to keep out the full blast.

Origins of Feng Shui

The ancient term for feng shui is *hum yue*, the heavenly and earthly paths. Originally the principles of feng shui were transmitted from master to pupil, orally and through poetry, paintings and drawings. It was not until the Han Dynasty (206BC–AD220) that the wisdom was written down, and even now much remains hidden, especially from the Western world.

Perhaps the most famous text from the Han Dynasty was the *Book of Rites* by Kuo

Po, who applied the principles of feng shui to the siting of graves, especially those of the Great Emperors. The beautiful surroundings of ancient Imperial tombs attests to the harmony attained by these early feng shui masters.

The writings of Yuen Kuen Chok who lived during the Tang Dynasty (AD618–906), formed the basis of modern feng shui, and he preserved many of the older texts that were in danger of being destroyed. However, it was not until the Sung Dynasty (AD960–1279) that the scholar Wang Chi applied feng shui formally to house building.

The Form School of Feng Shui

The Form or Shape method, the more intuitive of the formal Schools, involves visually assessing and identifying rather than measuring the form and nature of the landscape, and the site and the specific location of the building, according to traditional principles set down by the early feng shui geomancers. This information acts as a basis for advising on appropriate settings for work and domestic premises and for advising modifications both internally and externally to buildings. The founder was the Imperial feng shui master Yang Yun Sung of the Kwangsi province, China, around the period AD840–888, and the method was inspired by the dramatic nature of the landscape.

It incorporates consideration of the flow of ch'i and sha ch'i, and also the correct or incorrect positioning of the four symbolic animals who represent the four main directions of any building or room and may be transmitting their energies to inappropriate areas. These findings may lead to modification in structure or internal changes to direct the energies appropriately. The Form method also considers the ideal and actual balance of yin and yang, the negative and positive forces of which all life is believed to be composed.

Finally, the five Chinese elements: Wood, Fire, Metal, Water and Earth are studied. These are represented in different building types and so are suitable for different purposes. For example, metal buildings traditionally have a domed, curved structure, rooms or arches. These are especially suitable for commercial purposes and so even a small business may benefit from the addition of a room or entrance arch. The Form method has adapted itself to popular use in the West, and many books and magazines combine this with the folk method of feng shui for everything from improving health to the ideal office layout.

The Compass School of Feng Shui

It was the nature of the land of the originators that influenced the creation of the more formal Compass School of feng shui that relies on precise measurements and elaborate calculations. For this reason it has remained the province of the expert feng shui geomancer of *xiansheng*, and is generally only practised in modified form by ordinary people. In the 10th century AD, Chinese scholars living on the plains in northern China created the Compass School, using the Chinese geomancer's compass, the *lo pan*, which identified the alignments of a land where there were not the dramatic contrasts of mountain and valley that inspired the Form School.

The *lo pan* is used to determine the flow of ch'i and is especially good for assessing the correct functioning of the internal areas of a home or workplace.

The five elements are possessed in different proportions by different people and so influence the right settings for work and home for individuals. Generally it is the predominant element of the main wage earner in a home or executive in a firm that would determine the overall ideal arrangement, but it can be adapted to suit the needs of the occupants of different units or rooms within the larger structure.

First, personal data, for example the time and date of birth, is calculated by referring to the *Mun Lin Lak*, the Ten Thousand Years Calendar, and then both external and internal features of the building are assessed using the *lo pan*. Finally, a professional feng shui geomancer will consult the *Tong-Shu*, an ancient Chinese almanac, to determine the best time to make recommended changes to the feng shui of the home or workplace.

One of the most important areas of the lo pan is *Pa' Kua*, or *Bau-Gua* (see p. 245), based on the later sequence of the eight basic trigrams that represent the eight basic natural forces, used in I Ching (see p. 251), each representing an area of the home and particular qualities. The *Bau-Gua* is used separately in more popular tradition and in recent years has appeared in many feng shui books as a method by which individuals can determine the best arrangements for their living and work premises.

In ancient China, astrologers used the compass while facing the equator, i.e. in a southerly direction, and this practice has continued.

For the best results, the Form method is used first to assess the general location and predominant flow of ch'i and sha ch'i, and then the Compass method is applied to assess the correct positioning of areas and find out how to modify an existing home or office plan that may be incompatible with the occupants' needs.

Feng Shui in Action

The Importance of the Five Elements

The core of feng shui, as with other ancient Chinese systems of looking at the world, including the Chinese horoscope, revolves around the interaction of the five elements: Water, Wood, Fire, Earth and Metal. According to Chinese tradition, the five elements affect every aspect of life and their balance is central to personal health and well-being.

The Productive Cycle of the Elements

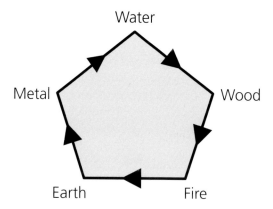

There is said to be a natural creative order of the five elements which, if followed, leads to harmony, prosperity, health and happiness. This sequence is illustrated above.

Wood fuels *Fire* which burns into ashes to form *Earth*.

Earth is the source of *Metal* from which it is extracted.

Metal can be melted, so producing *Water*.

Water nourishes plants and trees, so producing *Wood*.

When this cycle flows harmoniously within our lives we are well, content and creative. It is therefore known as the productive cycle.

The Destructive Cycle of the Elements

There is also a destructive order in which:

Water extinguishes *Fire*.

Fire melts *Metal*.

Metal breaks *Wood*.

Wood as the roots of plants or trees or the wooden spades and ploughs used by ancient farmers splits open the *Earth*.

Earth absorbs *Water*.

Although the destructive cycle is a necessary part of the life cycle, it is not recommended for healthy or harmonious living and you should use a neutralising element if it affects any areas of your home.

The Relationship Between the Elements

Knowing how each element relates to the others is useful in understanding how to strengthen a particular element in the home or workplace. An element can also

WISDOM FROM OTHER CULTURES, OTHER LANDS

become exhausted by helping another element; if, for example, there is metal shelving in an area where Earth should predominate, the Earth is weakened because its energies are being drained by the Metal which it is helping.

Earth helps *Metal*, is helped by *Fire*, hinders *Water* and is hindered by *Wood*.

Fire helps *Earth*, is helped by *Wood*, hinders *Metal*, is hindered by *Water*.

Water helps *Wood*, is helped by *Metal*, hinders *Fire*, is hindered by *Earth*.

Metal helps *Water*, is helped by *Earth*, hinders *Wood*, is hindered by *Fire*.

Wood helps *Fire*, is helped by *Water*, hinders *Earth*, is hindered by *Metal*.

The directional correspondences of the five elements are:

SOUTH: *Fire*

EAST: *Wood*   **CENTRE:** *Earth*   **WEST:** *Metal*

NORTH: *Water*

The Four Symbolic Animal Spirits

The elemental energies of the four cardinal points of the compass are symbolised by four creatures.

The Red Phoenix in the south represents summer, the realm of fame and fortune, and the qualities of light, optimism and joy.

The Black Tortoise or Turtle in the north represents winter, the realm of the family and the qualities of being sombre, mysterious and relaxed.

The Green or Azure Dragon in the east represents spring, the realm of health and protection and the qualities of kindness, wisdom and culture, new beginnings and growth.

The White Tiger of the west represents autumn and the realm of unpredictability, which can be exciting if the balance is right but can lead to a boring existence if the tiger is too weak, or to danger if he is too powerful. His qualities are anger, strength and sudden movement.

In any building the dragon and tiger must be balanced, so that the tiger does not bring disruption.

These terms are also used to refer to the sides of a house. The side with the front door is called the Phoenix side, regardless of the direction the door faces; the back is the Tortoise; the Dragon is on the left when looking out through the front door; the Tiger is on the right. If the front door faces south, then the Phoenix of the building and the Phoenix direction are said to be in alignment.

Harmonising the Animals

The creatures of the four directions or quarters should work in harmony. The house pictured here, nestling amid the mountains and facing a stream is, according to feng shui, ideally placed for the following reasons:

The Tortoise, or back of the house, should form a protective barrier. It is best not to have a watercourse – a canal or river – behind the house. Water is unpredictable and so a screen of trees can help if the house does back on to anything that is not solid. A hill or mountain, as pictured, is ideal as shelter.

The Phoenix, or front of the house, needs an open space at the front of the site or house, gently sloping down, but not too steeply or the Phoenix will fall off. A small pool or a meandering stream is good here. Ideally, the front of the house should not be too close to another building or its view is being blocked and the bird needs room to fly. In the illustration, the house faces a stream.

The Dragon should be higher than the **Tiger**, with hills or a higher building on the left as you look through the front door, as this represents a raised Dragon and on the right a lower Tiger.

But few people live in an ideal location or can afford to move. There are, however, many improvements inside and outside the home that can neutralise any negative elements. Any high Tiger or Phoenix buildings can be flattened by capturing their reflection in a bowl of water or using small concave and convex mirrors in south- and west-facing windows, reflected outwards to turn the images upside down.

The Five Elements and the Home

Some of the following associations are obvious, but all are connected with the energy of the element rather than its actual form, for example computers are Water because the information flows through them.

WISDOM FROM OTHER CULTURES, OTHER LANDS

WATER	EARTH	WOOD	FIRE	METAL
Bathroom	Plants	Plants	Warm colours	Metallic objects including chrome, stainless steel, decorative bronze, chrome, silver, etc.
Computers	Apartment blocks	Bedrooms	Heating	Arches/curves
Irregular shapes	Bricks	Children's rooms	Kitchen	Knives/scissors
Water features	Ceramic/clay objects, pottery of all kinds	Dining room	Stove	Swords
Fabrics in blue, grey, black leather and blue	Basements	Trees	Leather	Workshops
Paintings of water, e.g. sea scenes	Garage/car port	Vegetables	Hearth	Jewellery
Fish tanks	Low extensions	Furniture	Lights	Money/money-making area
Laundry, washing machines, dishwashers	Storeroom	Food	Candles	Hardware of all kinds
Musical instruments	Anything square	Columns	Pointed objects	Dome-shapes
Glass	Pottery	Wood	Plastics	Circles
Anything black	Yellow fabrics or paint	Anything green	Anything red	White

The *Pa'kua, Pah kwa* or *Bau-Gua*

For home use, some people use the *Bau-Gua*, which forms part of the more elaborate Chinese compass, to assess the correct positioning of rooms and furniture at home and work. The *Pa'kua* is more usually known as *Bau-Gua* or 'the eight trigrams', hence its octagonal shape. There are two kinds of *Bau-Gua*. The first is based on what is called the Early Heaven Sequence of the Eight Trigrams, based on the eight forces that are central to the I Ching and other forms of Chinese philosophy: Heaven, Earth, Wind, Thunder, Water, Fire, Mountain and Lake.

It is used as an amulet and is illustrated below. It is not an indoor device as it is said to be too powerful and is usually reflective with a mirror in the middle.

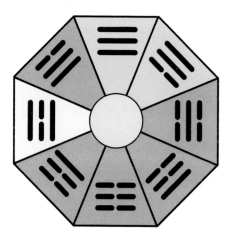

The reflective *Pa'kua* is placed on gates and above the main door to drive away negativity and avert misfortune. It always reflects outwards.

But it is the Later Heaven Sequence of these forces that is used for feng shui assessment.

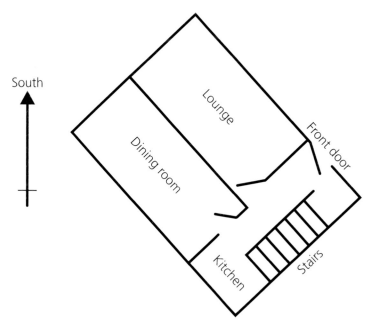

The easiest way of working out how best to use your home is to draw up a floor plan of your house or workplace, using an ordinary compass to find south, and orientating the plan. In the diagram above the house is facing south-west.

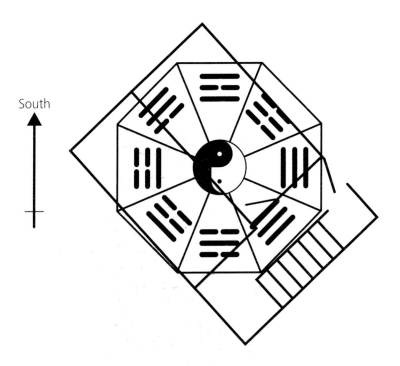

South

Next, copy the *Bau-Gua* and, lining it up with the south, overlay it on the plan. This will show you how the house breaks up into different sections. The centre, which in the traditional Chinese style of architecture was usually a courtyard, is neutral.

DIRECTION	TRIGRAM/DIRECTION NAME	TRIGRAM SYMBOL	SIGNIFICANCE
South	*Li* (Fire), *Wang Ts'ai*		Prosperity and fame
South-west	*K'un* (Earth), *An Lu*		Peace and happiness
West	*Tui* (Lake), *Chang Yin*		Pleasure and indulgence
North-west	*Ch'ien* (Heaven), *Chin Ts'ai*		New beginnings, improvement in situation
North	*K'an* (Water), *Chin Yiin*		Relationships
North-east	*Ken* (Mountain), *T-ien Ch'ai*		Children and family
East	*Chen* (Thunder), *Fa Chan*		Health, wisdom and experience
South-east	*Sun* (Wind/wood), *Huan Lo*		Wealth and money

The above references are the forces rather than the actual five elements.

GYPSY MAGIC

Who Are the Gypsies?

'Gypsy' is a corruption of the word Egyptian, as these nomadic tribes folk were once believed to come from that country. Only in the last century were their origins traced to India through the many Sanskrit-based words in their language. They were also called Gitanos in Spain, and Bohemians in France, but they style themselves Romanies, the Lords of the Earth.

It is uncertain when the Romanies began to leave India. Some authorities say their migration began as early as the 5th century; others date the beginning of the exodus as the 9th century. Certainly a major Romany migration took place in the 11th century and the gypsies travelled across Iran into Asia Minor and the Byzantine empire, moving into Europe by way of Greece during the early 14th century.

By the 16th century, Romanies had spread across Europe, often earning a living by fortune-telling using astrology and palmistry. They avoided intermarriage with outsiders whom they called *gajos* or *gorgios* and lived and worked in extended family groups called *cumpanias*. But what really separates them from other people is their determination to live and die under the stars. Gypsies are often referred to as God's stars, one race that extends across the earth.

Because of the Romany refusal to fit in with conventional society, they were often targets for persecution. The first gypsies arrived in North America when they were deported from England (the first official mention of their residence is in 1695 in Virginia), and hundreds more were deported to Louisiana by Napoleon. This may have been intended as a punishment, but as the author Martin Cruz Smith put it in *A Gypsy in Amber*, sending gypsies to such a wide-open continent was like 'sentencing birds to the sky'.

Legends of the Gypsies

Many legends centre around the wandering life of the gypsy, mingling pagan and Christian traditions (some researchers have noted how the gypsies would adopt the religion of whatever country they were in). One story tells that gypsies were doomed to roam the earth without shelter because they turned away Joseph, Mary and Jesus when the Holy Family was fleeing to Egypt. Another says they are doomed to wander because a gypsy smith (the old Romany name Petulengro means blacksmith) forged the nails for Christ's cross. As a result, the entire race was doomed to wander the earth forever.

However, a Romany counter-legend relates that a young gypsy boy saw the nails beneath the cross and was so moved by the agony of Jesus that he stole one and would have taken them all had he not been seen by a centurion and had to flee for his life. Because of his kindness, gypsies were granted the right to steal small items without blame. Again according to Romany legend, after the Crucifixion, Mary, Mother of Christ, was comforted by a mother frog. Mary blessed the frog for her compassion and said that wherever a frog was found, the water would always be pure enough for humans. For this reason the frog, though not the toad, is considered lucky by gypsies, especially if it hops on to the steps of a caravan as this indicates that fresh water is easily accessible.

Gypsy Rites and Festivals

Mary Magdalene, the Gypsies' Madonna

On May 24 and 25 the Gypsy Festival of the Black Madonna is held at Saintes Maries de la Mer. Gypsies from all over the world gather here at this time to celebrate Sara, Queen of a French gypsy tribe, who is the patron saint of the gypsies and is reputed to have been a member of the group that travelled with Mary Magdalene across the Mediterranean to France. In another legend, Sara rescued Mary Magdalene from the sea by casting her mantle on the waters after the boat began to sink. Intriguingly, she is called Sara-la-Kali, a link perhaps with the original Romany treks from India.

Sara is not recognised as a saint by the Catholic church but she is buried in the crypt where Romanies keep watch on the two special nights in May and dress her statue with flowers. Afterwards the statue is touched with garments and artefacts of sick family members in the belief that this will heal them. Decorated effigies of Sara are carried through the streets on raised carts to the sea where they are immersed in water to bring fertility to the people.

Suggested links with the Romany Saint Sara and Mary Magdalene would place the migration of the gypsies during the 1st century, much earlier than commonly accepted, but as with many such myths, the truth may be a symbolic rather than an actual connection.

The Festival of Snakes

Among Eastern European gypsies, March 15 is the Feast of the Snake, a half-pagan, half-Christian ritual which regards snakes as a symbol of the Devil and of treachery. Therefore, killing a snake on this festival (or on the Ides of March when Brutus killed Julius Caesar) ensures good fortune for the rest of the year.

During Easter, a snake or lizard carcass is bound with red and white wool to represent blood and death and taken around the encampment, defiled, abused and finally cast into running water. Running water was the lifeblood of the Romanies, and while fire could easily be kindled, finding an available source of clean water was the first consideration at any stopping place.

Green Man Rituals

Both in southern and Eastern Europe, the spring festival centred around the Green Man or Green George. He was the spirit of plants, trees and vegetables, fruit and vegetation, the male spring deity, consort of the Earth Mother and an early forerunner of both Robin Hood and St George. A Gypsy clad in greenery would play Green George and represent the rebirth of spring after the death of winter.

In some gypsy communities, on St George's Day, April 23, or sometimes Easter

Monday, a young willow or birch tree was cut down and dressed with flowers and ribbons. Accompanied by Green George, it was taken to a river and cast in as a substitute for Green George to appease the water spirits. The legend of the stolen nails from Christ's cross is recalled in the Easter Green Man ceremonies; a boy dressed as the Green Man takes three nails that have been immersed in water for three days and knocks them into a willow tree, pulls them out and throws them into running water.

Omens

As would be expected of people living in the open air, their omens were linked with the natural world. Falling stars were believed to herald a birth or the coming of money. Some animals and birds were also heralds of good fortune. A wagtail seen near the end of a journey would indicate a fortunate spot to camp. White horses, especially seen looking over a gate, were also omens of good luck. A ring from plaited horse hair pulled from the tail of a wild stallion was considered especially fortunate.

The weasel, however, represented bad fortune. If a betrothed girl met a weasel she would hurry to running water to wash away the taint so that her future marriage would be happy. A *vardo* (caravan) would change direction if a weasel crossed its path. However, weasels could not be killed or misfortune would befall the entire *cumpania*. The weasel's cry when angry and afraid was called the Devil's sneeze.

It was believed that when a tree, or *rook* as it was called in Romany, was felled, woodsmen gypsies had to cover their ears so the cries of the tree were not heard. *Rookomengro*, or squirrel trees, were not felled as the squirrel is a lucky animal.

Fortune-telling

Fortune-telling is known as *dukkerin* or *dukkering* by the Romanies. Palmistry (see p. 49) is a very common form of divination, although gypsies who developed strong intuitive powers would often study a person's face rather than the hands.

Gypsy fortune-telling with a crystal ball was popular at fairs or race meetings where an elaborate booth could be set up. The family crystal was kept carefully in a dark cloth and was handed down from generation to generation. It was believed to tell the future only when used by members of the blood line. Tea-leaf reading (see p. 139) may also have come via the gypsies from the east.

Much gypsy magic was rooted in the rich knowledge of herbalism passed down from mother to daughter. Gypsy cures were often very effective. For many years the *drabarni*, the herb or wise women of the clan, called from door to door and dispensed herbal cures to *gorgios*.

THE I CHING AND CHINESE WISDOM

The I Ching, or Book of Changes, is more than a system of divination. It is also the earliest and most profound classic of Chinese ancient literature that represents one of the first efforts of civilised humankind to understand his or her place in the world, and the course and meaning of his or her life.

Although there are many versions of the I Ching, Chinese scholars differ quite widely in the way they translate the ancient images and judgements into modern language. One problem is that written Ancient Chinese is a pictorial form of communication and so translations into Westernised languages can stifle the natural flow of meaning. In contrast, Chinese paintings, a series of splashes of paint to the analytical eye, are to child and sage alike a mountain, lake or river. And yet no one sees a Chinese picture in precisely the same way.

Another problem of using the I Ching and other profound books such as the Tao Te Ching, whose earliest version was produced around 168BC and attributed to the Taoist sage Lao Tsu, is that the words and concepts are so complex that the struggle for intellectual understanding can take precedence over the symbolism that imparts wisdom intuitively, much as Tarot cards (see p. 77) or runes (see p. 62) do. The most successful interpreters of the I Ching meditate on the images and commentaries rather than trying to analyse the meaning. Therefore, although Oriental business executives consult the I Ching regularly before making decisions, it is a form of divination that lacks popular appeal in the Western world, being perhaps unfairly associated with intellectualism and the need for deep philosophical knowledge to approach it.

Change – the Essence of the I Ching and Chinese Philosophy

The I Ching has been described as a map and guidebook to life's change points. The basis of its philosophy is that nothing is static. The Chinese believe that any quality or state reaches an extreme and tips over into the opposite, from joy to sorrow, love to hate, darkness to light, peace to war and back again.

While some events cannot be changed, people can influence their destiny by their reactions – whether to wait or act, stay or go, use emotion or logic. There must be endings or there can be no beginnings, loss so that there can be an appreciation of gain. So the future written in the I Ching is not fixed but depends on recognising the opportunities and pitfalls highlighted by the chosen hexagram – the eight lined unit of meaning that underpins I Ching divination – and then using the wisdom to determine for oneself the direction of the nature of any change.

Neither the I Ching nor Chinese philosophy generally rests upon the fundamental belief that evil can or should be eradicated. Instead it maintains that evil is as much a part of existence as is good. This dualism that runs through Oriental thought can prove problematic for the Western mind, which is culturally programmed to regard the Devil as a force to be overcome.

WISDOM FROM OTHER CULTURES, OTHER LANDS

The I Ching is usually associated with Confucius, the sage who lived during the 6th century BC and instituted moral and also political forms of organisation that identified the superior or the ideal man in terms of a wise leader or a honest administrator – just but compassionate and benignly paternalistic. In the Confucian system each person occupied his or her rightful place, deferring to those greater in age or experience and seeking not personal advantage or advancement but the general good. Advancement would, Confucius believed, come as a result of right thought and conduct that brought responsibility as well as reward.

There are fierce debates as to whether Confucius himself wrote many of the judgements or explanations of the hexagram meanings and the commentaries, or whether they were added by his followers, for great emperors and philosophers are said to have lived hundreds of years – a metaphor that means wise thoughts and sayings are universal and timeless.

Chinese philosophy and culture has changed remarkably little over thousands of years, and Taoism and ancestor worship are at least as powerful and older in essence than Confucianism. The I Ching embraces not only Confucianism, with its emphasis on correct moral conduct, but the more fluid concepts of Tao, the Way, and ch'i, the life-force that flows through all things.

Taoist belief is that humankind is not separate from nature and the universe, but a part of it. Life, natural forces, people, even food is made up of yang, the original sun concept of light, power, masculinity, assertiveness, logic and action. Yang is depicted as a straight line: ▬▬▬▬

Yang is balanced by yin, the original moon concept of darkness, receptivity, femininity, intuition, acceptance and inaction. It is depicted as a broken line: ▬▬ ▬▬

The ancient meaning of yin was the 'shaded north side' of a hill, while yang meant the 'sunny south side' of a hill. Yang controls heaven and all things positive, active, light, masculine, unyielding, moving and living. Yin controls the earth and all negative, passive, dark, soft, still and non-living entities.

External changes are attributed to the waxing and waning of the relative qualities of yang and yin. Any particular situation at a given point in time contains a specific balance of these qualities and it is this that is reflected in the 64 hexagrams that are formed in the divinatory process in response to an individual question. The changing lines in each hexagram, also determined by divination, indicate the waxing or waning quality of the hexagram. When a total state of yang is reached, it changes to a yin and this accounts for the constant flux in nature and human affairs.

Some say the judgements reflect the Confucian belief in right action, and the images the Tao, and though this is a simplistic view of a complex system, the philosophies do blend to give a total world view in the I Ching.

The Origins of the I Ching

The original inspiration for the I Ching came from the shell of the tortoise. Legends abound throughout the Eastern world of giant tortoises holding up the world, and the Islands of the Blest, the earthly equivalent of paradise where immortality was assured to those who resided there.

For divination purposes the shell of the tortoise was heated until it cracked and the cracks were interpreted. This is still commemorated in the Chinese character for divination:

 This figure is composed of two words: ▭ = interpret and ┝ = crack.

I Ching divination in its purest form dates back about 5,000 years to the time of the ruler Fu Hsi. This monarch was said to have first found the eight trigrams, the building blocks of the 64 hexagrams (two trigrams or three lines of yang and yin, put together) on the shell of a tortoise. Fu Hsi, believed to be descended from the P'au Ku, Divine Artisan, who created the mountains and earth, is credited with teaching laws, introducing fishing nets and building the first permanent dwellings.

It is thought that the I Ching was first recorded in about 1700BC, when it still retained a very simple form and was probably still centred around the basic trigrams and their natural images. The meanings continued to evolve, but the actual recorded I Ching was used mostly for predicting natural events until Lord Wen paired the trigrams to create hexagrams around 1122BC. Lord Wen was said to have been an exceedingly wise and benevolent ruler in the Chou principality in what is now the Shensi province of China. His ways were in sharp contrast to those of the last king of the Shang Dynasty, Choe, who held the land in a grip of terror and squandered its wealth. There was a rebellion against him and although Lord Wen played no part in it he was thrown into prison. During his time there he was inspired by a vision to write the hexagrams on the wall of his cell. His son, the Duke of Chou, wrote commentaries and added the concept of moving or changing lines. So Confucius was a comparative newcomer when he or his followers added yet more interpretations over five centuries later.

I Ching and Divination

The divinatory method for the I Ching involves casting coins, yarrow stalks or stones to create two trigrams, sets of three lines of yang and yin that represent different natural forces and together form one of the 64 hexagrams. The trigrams are created in a vertical column with the bottom line first, and the trigram that is cast last forms the upper part of the hexagram. This hexagram provides insight into a question or decision to be made that prompted the divination.

The Trigrams

The trigrams are the building blocks of the I Ching's divinatory system. According to Chinese philosophy, everything in the universe is made up of either yang or yin or a mixture of these two forces. In the same way, the trigrams are constructed of different formations of yang and yin.

There are eight basic trigrams which naturally form pairs. For example, *Ch'ien*, Heaven or Sky, pairs with *K'un*, Earth, as the nuclear or source trigrams formed from the limitless Tao. *Ch'ien*, the great Father and *K'un*, the Great Mother, were regarded in Chinese mythology as the creators of P'au Ku, the Divine Artisan.

FIRST PAIRING

Chi'en, Heaven or Sky and *K'un*, Earth, are the trigrams of the source of life.

Chi'en, Heaven/Sky

This is the trigram of pure power and energy, of personal identity, assertiveness, directed power and success. As an indicator of action it advises aiming high, developing potential and being confident and single-minded. Its key word is: achievement.

ATTRIBUTES: strength, focused energy, creativity, logic, courage. **Animal**: horse, tiger, lion. **Body**: head, mind, skull. **Family**: father. **Function**: sage, military commander, philosopher, elderly men. **Associated images**: outer garments, cold and ice. **Direction**: north-west. **Season**: the approach of winter. **Colour**: white or gold. **Plants**: chrysanthemum, herbs. **Trees**: fruit trees.

K'un, Earth

This is the trigram of pure receptivity, of considering the needs and feelings of others, of relying on intuition, unconscious wisdom and waiting rather than acting. Its key word is: acceptance.

ATTRIBUTES: docility, receptivity, intuition, nurturing, patience. **Animal**: ox, cow, mare, ant. **Body**: stomach, abdomen, womb, the unconscious mind. **Family**: mother. **Function**: wise woman, old women, ordinary people, especially in crowds. **Associated images**: a seamless cloak that envelops all things without question, an old cart that carries everything. **Direction**: south-west. **Season**: the approach of autumn. **Colour**: black or dark brown. **Plants**: potatoes, all bulbs. **Trees**: tree trunks of all kinds.

SECOND PAIRING

Li, Fire, and *Ka'an,* Water or the Abyss, are the trigrams of diffused energy.

Li, Fire

This is the trigram of illumination and of clinging to whatever fuels it, whether the Fire of the Great Solstices where the Emperor made offerings, or the ritual fires that cleansed what was imperfect or no longer needed. Its key word is: inspiration.

ATTRIBUTES: clarity, illumination, cleansing, communication, inspiration, clinging. **Animal**: pheasant, sacred turtle, goldfish. **Body**: eye, the blood, speech, heart. **Family**: middle daughter. **Function**: artists, young women, generous people, craftsmen. **Associated images**: the sun, lightning, objects with holes, such as shells and armour. **Direction**: south. **Season**: summer. **Colour**: orange. **Plants**: tomatoes, red and yellow peppers. **Trees**: dry trees, hollows.

K'an, Water/the Abyss

This is the trigram of fluidity, of going with the flow, risking uncertainty and danger and tuning into emotions. Its key word is: feeling.

ATTRIBUTES: desire, emotion, instinct, fearlessness, danger, hardship. **Animal**: pig, rat, wild boar, bat. **Body**: ear and kidneys. **Family**: second son. **Function**: young men, the sick, trouble-makers, fishermen. **Associated images**: wells, moon, the deep, rain and rivers, floods. **Direction**: north. **Season**: winter. **Colour**: blue. **Plants**: reeds, water lilies and lotuses. **Trees**: willow, alder.

THIRD PAIRING

Chen, Thunder and *Sun*, Wind/Wood, are the trigrams of movement.

Chen, Thunder

This is the trigram of natural renewal, with the thunder coming out of the earth at the beginning of summer, scattering the seeds of new life. The sudden dramatic thunderstorm, which Chinese mythology claimed was dragons fighting, can be both creative in bringing refreshing rain and destructive. Its key word is: regeneration.

ATTRIBUTES: arousal, renewal, surprise, spontaneity, initiative, male sexuality and fertility. **Animal**: dragon, eagle, swallow. **Body**: voice, foot. **Family**: eldest son. **Function**: men up to middle age, princes, inventors, musicians. **Associated images**: thunderstorms, hurricanes and volcanoes. **Direction**: east. **Season**: spring. **Colour**: yellow. **Plants**: all blossoming flowers. **Trees**: evergreens, blossom trees and bamboo.

Sun, Wind/Wood

This is the trigram of gentle but persistent change, the slow but enduring growth of the tree. It is associated with incense-giving trees and the peach tree as these were believed to be life-giving manifestations of the Mother Goddess. Its key word is: persistence.

ATTRIBUTES: gentle but determined penetration, adaptability, flexibility, endurance, justice. **Animal**: cockerel, snake, tiger. **Body**: thigh, legs, lungs, the nervous system. **Family**: eldest daughter. **Function**: women up to middle age, teachers, travellers and people engaged in business. **Associated images**: the tree, fragrances, clouds, ropes and webs. **Direction**: south-east. **Season**: the approach of summer. **Colour**: green. **Plants**: grass and poppies, lilies. **Trees**: all tall and high trees.

FOURTH PAIRING
Ken, Mountain and *Tui*, Lake/Marsh are the trigrams of stillness.

Ken, Mountain
 This is the trigram of waiting, solitude and a desire to rise above material and daily concerns. Ascending to the Jade mountain was one way, according to Chinese mythology, whereby immortality might be reached. Its key word is: vision.

ATTRIBUTES: stillness, withdrawal, silence, meditation, spiritual aspiration. **Animal**: dog, bull, leopard, mouse. **Body**: hand, back. **Family**: youngest son. **Function**: boys under 16, prisoners, the faithful and sincere, priests and monks. **Associated images**: door opening, narrow path, walls, watchmen and watchtowers. **Direction**: north-east. **Season**: the approach of spring. **Colour**: purple. **Plants**: all mountain plants. **Trees**: nut trees, gnarled trees.

Tui, Lake/Marsh
 This is the trigram of the inner world, of psychic insight, dreams and reconciliation. Its key word is: secrecy.

ATTRIBUTES: pleasure, joy, inner tranquillity, healing and magic. **Animal**: sheep, birds, deer. **Body**: mouth, lips which smile. **Family**: youngest daughter. **Function**: women under 16 and daughters, concubines and sorceresses. **Associated images**: valleys, mist, the harvest, low-lying land. **Direction**: west. **Season**: autumn. **Colour**: red. **Plants**: magnolias, gardenias, all lake plants and spices. **Trees**: trees bleached with salt.

Selecting the Right Hexagram

All the divinatory methods, especially the complex yarrow stalks, rely on calming the conscious mind by repetitive action to allow unconscious wisdom to emerge. As with all divinatory methods, the hexagram selected seems to be a psychokinetic process whereby the mind influences the fall of the coins or stones.

To Create a Trigram or Hexagram Using Coins
Three coins are tossed and the type of yang or yin is determined by adding up the value of the visible faces of the coins. The appropriate lines are then drawn in a vertical column to create the trigram or hexagram. Assign the value of two for a yin and three for a yang.

Finally for each of the six lines in the hexagram a modified or additional meaning is given if the line is designated by the divination process as a moving line, i.e. one in the process of rapidly changing. A moving line is one that is soon to change into its polarity. So that a moving yang would become a yin and vice versa. In divination a moving or changing yin is written as ▬X▬ which will become a yang. A moving yang is written as ▬O▬ . This will become a yin. The more moving lines the more immediate or profound will be the coming change. A moving yin is 6, a yang is 7. A yin line is 8 and a moving yang is 9. Together this information suggests a correct and balanced response to the current situation.

Interpreting the Hexagrams

There are two methods of interpreting the I Ching hexagrams. The first involves consulting one of the translations of the I Ching. In these, each hexagram is linked to a series of responses, expressed in symbolic form; first there is given a Judgement or general assessment of the hexagram meaning, either advising right action or warning of hazards, expressed in terms of the Confucian social and political world. Next is the Image, evoked by the combination of the natural forces represented by the two separate trigrams or three line formations that make up the individual hexagram. Finally, for each of the six lines in the hexagram a modified or additional meaning is given if the line is designated by the divination process as a moving line, i.e. one in the process of rapidly changing. The more moving lines the more immediate or profound will be the coming change. Together this information suggests a correct and balanced response to the current situations. The hexagram is first read as basic yang and yin meanings. A second hexagram is created by substituting a yin for a moving yang and a yang for a moving yin. The new hexagram indicates what lies over the horizon as a result of acting on hexagram 1.

The second method of interpretation is purely intuitive, involving the visualisation of the natural forces symbolised by the two separate trigrams, and allowing a picture to form of the combination of the two forces that holds the key to the question asked. This visual imagery is one that lies behind many natural forms of divination.

HINDUISM

What is Hinduism?

Hinduism is the main faith in India, and there are about 750 million Hindus living worldwide. Hindus refer to their religion as *sanatama dharma*, or the eternal truth. It is a philosophy and way of life and for many Hindus there is no division between religious and secular life. Indeed, much worship takes place at home rather than in formal religious gatherings. The rules for good, or *dharmic*, living laid down in the ancient Vedic scriptures that entered northern India during the second millennium BC with the Aryan conquerors, have provided many of the basic beliefs of the Hindu religion. However, an earlier indigenous religion in the Indus Valley that worshipped the Mother Goddess has also contributed to the Hinduism of today, ensuring the continued importance of mother goddess icons in localised worship, especially in remote areas. Some of these local goddesses have remained unchanged for more than 5,000 years and preside over the fertility of a small area, its people, animals and crops. Fertility stones from the earlier religion have been transformed into the phallic pillar stones, or *lingams*, used as representations of Shiva.

Hinduism has been very influential on Western mystical and magical traditions, for example in the concepts of Karma, chakras (see p. 17) and belief in reincarnation that were introduced to the West by the theosophists (see p. 80). Since the mid-1960s, the gentle faith and meditative practices of Hinduism have offered an antidote to materialism, although unlike Buddhism, relatively few people outside the Asian culture have converted to Hinduism. However, Transcendental Meditation, the continuing fascination with the teachings of various Gurus, Buddhism itself, plus the fact that Sai Baba was born and still lives in India, are all offshoots of Hindu influence that have permeated Western consciousness.

Brahman

Brahman means world spirit or supreme principle. Brahman is said to be present in every living creature and every living creature is also a part of Brahman. The aim of the Hindu life is to work towards returning to Brahman, so being absorbed back into the universal spirit. The state of *moksha* or release from the cycles of rebirth is attained when the individual soul is reunited with the World Soul.

In order to attain this state, the soul, or *atman*, the fundamental unchanging essence in each person, must progress towards increasingly purer states through hundreds or even thousands of rebirths. The Karmic cycle is the chain of lives during which the individual *atman* works through and sheds all negativity, for example hatred, revenge, jealousy, pettiness, anger, over-attachment to material possessions, fame or success, or even excess love of another person. Once the *atman* is purified, it no longer needs the Karmic cycle.

Hindu is monotheistic, not polytheistic, and the supreme Godhead is worshipped in many forms, to incorporate both creator and destroyer aspects and the female principle, each of which exists complete in itself as a personification of Brahman. Worship of the Divinity in many forms is unique to Hinduism, but Hindus also meditate on the formless aspect of God.

The Trimurti

Trimurti means 'having three forms'. In the trinity, the deities Brahma the Creator, Vishnu the Preserver, and Shiva the Destroyer/Transformer, form the *trimurti* of Gods that forms the basis of modern Hinduism. Vishnu the Preserver and Shiva the Destroyer are polarities, and Brahma the Creator provides the balance between them. In modern times, many Hindus worship either Shiva or Vishnu as Supreme God.

Each God has a female counterpart and consort: Vishnu and Lakshmi, Goddess of Prosperity, Beauty and Good Fortune, whose festival is Divali, the Feast of Lights, when she restores light to the darkest days. Shiva's consort is Parvati, the Divine and Gentle Mother, and Brahma's consort, Savarati, is Goddess of Learning and Music.

meditation, draws from all three traditions. I have used the Jewish and source name to represent this more popular form.

The Tree of Life

Central to this wisdom is the Tree of Life, a diagram of the 10 spheres and 22 pathways, the latter originally associated with the 22 Hebrew letters, that attempts to demonstrate the interconnectedness of all life and experience. For in the Kaballah, the world is not created by a paternalistic immanent maker, but by a light or ray emanating or flowing from the Godhead which divides and becomes the *sephiroth*, the splendid lights or shining sapphires that are aspects of the Divine, contained in all life forms, including the Divinity.

The Tree pictures this Divine Force flowing down into the material world from sphere to sphere in what is called the 'lightning flash' through different levels. The lowest *sephira*, Malkuth, the Kingdom, represents the material world. The highest, Kether, the Crown, is the source of the unmanifest, as yet formless divinity. Between these are *sephiroth* representing other powers and qualities, such as intelligence, beauty, justice and harmony, the higher ones in archetypal form.

The Origins and Development of the Kabbalah

There are two versions of the origin of the Kabbalah. It may be that the mythical one contains the essential truth that the tradition goes back to the very first sacred writings of the Jews and was suppressed by early orthodoxy and so transmitted secretly.

The Mother/Father Deity, so called because Chockmah and Binah (the Great Father and Mother), spheres two and three respectively on the Tree, are part of the undifferentiated Godhead, taught Kabbalistic wisdom to the angels. After the Fall, angels taught it to Adam and Eve so that humans might find their way back to Paradise.

But few of their descendants were interested in this quest and so the Father /Mother Creator gave the secret to Abraham, who not only transmitted the sacred wisdom down through the generations to Joseph, but wrote down the lore in the *Sepher Yetzirah*, the first great work on the Kabbalah, which he hid in a cave. But Joseph died before he was able to pass on the Kabbalistic knowledge and the book was not found. The next recipient who was deemed worthy was Moses who received the formal Law and enshrined this as the first five books of the Old Testament that included the Ten Commandments. At the same time, Moses was given the Kabbalah, but because this was secret wisdom he concealed it through codes and symbolism in the official religious writings.

Ever since, Kabbalistic scholars have attempted to obtain this hidden knowledge through complex codes that could be interpreted through *gematria*, Hebrew numerology, whereby each letter is assigned significance and words of the same number value can be linked with other words of the same value. It is said that Moses' secret knowledge was passed orally through the Hidden Masters, a secret Hebrew order, and that after many years they rediscovered Abraham's writings.

The factual version reveals the existence of two books, *Sepher Yetzirah*, the Book of Formation, and *Zohar*, the Book of Splendour, that formed the basis of all Kabbalistic wisdom. The actual date of their original form is not known, but it is speculated that both reflect a more ancient oral tradition. The *Sepher Yetzirah* was written sometime between the 2nd and 6th centuries AD.

Zohar may have been written by Rabbi Simon Ben Jochai, and hidden in a cave because of the persecution of the Romans, and a version of this, or maybe the original *Zohar*, was published in the early 14th century by the Spanish Rabbi Moses de Leon. This brought the tradition to a greater number of people.

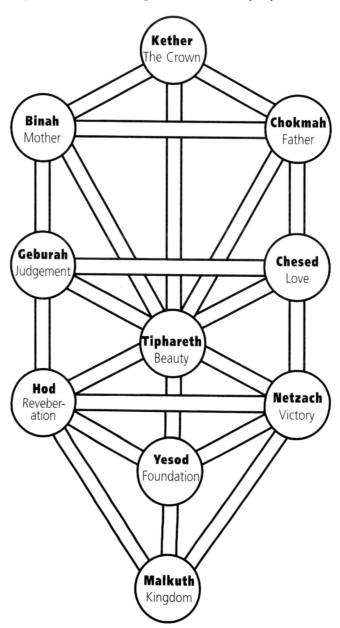

During the Middle Ages the Kabbalah was regarded by Orthodox Judaism as dangerous to the preservation of religious order and so was confined to intellectual study and then only by experienced Rabbis. However, the present Jewish Kabbalistic tradition was heralded in the middle of the 18th century, under the term Hasidism in Eastern Europe, meaning the devout ones.

The Western impetus really began in the middle of the 19th century with the founding of the Western mystery tradition that brought together a number of esoteric doctrines. Around 1856, Eliphas Levi noticed the correspondence between the 22 Tarot trumps and the 22 letters of the Hebrew alphabet and became convinced as he studied the ancient lore, especially the *Sepher Yetzirah*, that with the loss of the Sovereign Priesthood and the destruction of the Temple in Israel, secret wisdom was concealed by Kabbalists in the symbolism of Tarot cards.

The Golden Dawn tradition established by Westcott and Mathers in England saw the Kaballah as central to esoteric wisdom in the West, and during the 20th century, Dion Fortune and Aleister Crowley helped to popularise the Kaballah both as a mystical and magical tool.

The Four Worlds of the Kabbalah

There are several ways of dividing the Tree of Life to explore different aspects. However, all the spheres and realms are interconnected and it is sometimes said that each sphere as well as each realm contains its own Tree of Life. The Tree is divided into four realms. These are based on three main triangles or trinities of spheres, plus a single final *sephira*, Malkuth. The first, the Supernal triangle, represents the Realm of Spirit in Kether, Unity or the Crown, Chokmah and Binah. Kether contains Chokmah, the Great Father, Wisdom, akin to the Word in Genesis, the initiator of creation. Kether also includes Binah, Understanding, the Great Mother or Sea who is the womb of creation.

The second inverse triangle represents the Realm of the Soul and comprises Chesed, Divine Love and Mercy, Geburah, Divine Will and Severity, and Tiphareth, the central sphere of Divine Beauty and Harmony. Like all subsequent middle spheres moving downwards through the Tree, Tiphareth reconciles the opposing qualities of the other two spheres.

The final inverse triangle, the Realm of Personality, is comprised of Netzach, Victory or Feelings, Hod, Thought or Intellect, with the central Yesod the Subconscious or Foundation.

Yesod is the moon and gateway to and from the lower Material Manifestation, as Tiphareth is the sun and gateway to and from the Higher Realms. The final Realm of the Body is centred on Malkuth, Foundation and The Material World, the earth in its physical form and the human body.

Another division, the most traditional representation, creates four worlds or levels of energy. The first world, Atziluth, comprises Kether and Chokmah. This is the World of Creation, with Chokmah as the active phallic Divine will from which creation emanates.

The Second World, Briah, contains Binah alone, the receptive principle in creation.

Because all spheres contain male and female energies, there is no correlation between male and creative/positive energies and female and receptive/negative forces on the Tree.

As a result of the coming together of the first two worlds, the third, Yetzirah, the Formative World, comes into being. This comprises all the remaining spheres except for Malkuth. Here the archetypes find expression through the lower spheres as creative/stability and destructive/change processes that give form to the final fourth world, Assiah, as Malkuth, the physical manifestation of the planet and individual physical forms.

Daath – the Hidden Sphere

Daath, the unnumbered sphere, appears between the Supernal triangle, the top three spheres and the rest of the Tree. This Veil or Abyss was said to have been placed between the Creator and created, the ideal and actual, potential and manifest, so that humans might become aware of their separateness from the creative process and seek to reconnect with the Divinity whose Divine Spark they carried.

Daath is also regarded as the gateway to the reverse side of the Tree, inhabited by demons, or *qlipoth*, who are regarded in more modern tradition as shadow aspects of the self. Because the Kabbalistic principle of creation embraces everything, it recognises that darkness and evil also come from the Unmanifest First Principle and so must be incorporated into life and transformed into positive energy, rather than repressed or projected on to others or separate demonic forms.

The Divine Feminine in the Kabbalah

The reconciliation and restoration of Paradise is not confined to humanity. The Godhead, it is believed, was separated from his female self by the creation of the Orthodox Patriarchal view, but can be reconciled with his lost bride Shekinah, the female deity power who is manifest in Malkuth.

Both the *Zohar* and *Sepher Yetzirah* talk of the essential female counterpart of God. Through sexual union the human male and female are believed to be re-enacting the sacred union, first in the union of Chokmah and Binah, and also Elohim, the personified Godhead, with Shekinah.

The Kabbalah in Action

The Tree of Life was said by the occultist Dion Fortune to be a 'glyph of the Soul and the Universe'. Each *sephira* or sphere and the interconnecting pathways, with their myriad correspondences, can be used both formally and for personal spiritual development, through study of the mystical texts, through *gematria*, Hebrew numerology, and as a focus for meditation, magical ritual and invocation or even divination. The Kabbalah can also be used for personal empowerment in the everyday world. For example, if a seeker needed to temporarily increase speed and accuracy of thought, perhaps for an examination or important project, he or she would focus on the sphere of Hod (splendour and intellectual clarity) and the paths by which it might be attained. Associations with the sphere of Hod would be evoked, for example the

RIGHT: A wall painting from the Hemis Monastery in Ladakh showing the six stages of reincarnation.

BELOW: A sculpture of the Buddha reclining from Polonnaruwa, Sri Lanka.

LEFT: A 19th century Indian
textile showing a mandala.

RIGHT: A brush painting
from the Sung Dynasty
(AD960–1279) showing
Lohan, a student of Buddha.

LEFT: A Mayan censer in the form of a priest wearing ear and nose plugs.

BELOW: Aboriginal bark painting showing the path taken by the soul on its journey to the other world.

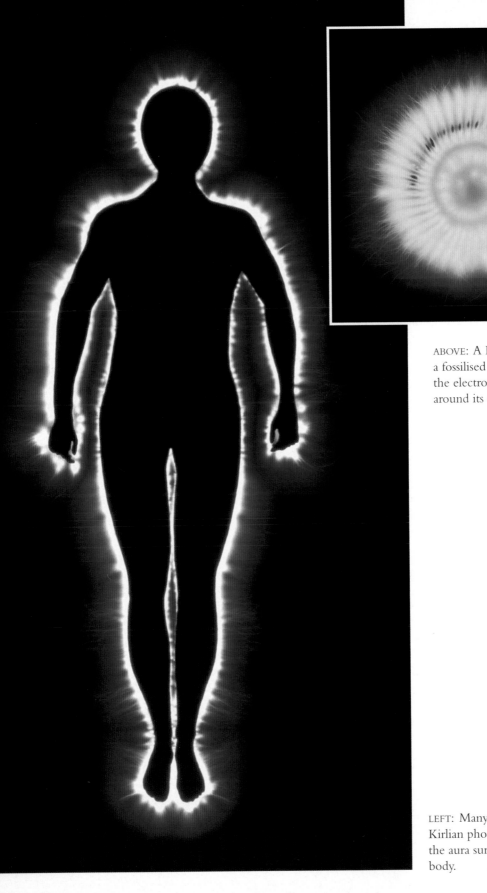

ABOVE: A Kirlian photograph of
a fossilised ammonite showing
the electromagnetic discharge
around its edges.

LEFT: Many people believe
Kirlian photography can reveal
the aura surrounding the human
body.

colour orange, the deity Mercury, the messenger God, the animal the jackal, the demonic animal the cock to dissipate buried doubts and fears, and the herb fennel or marjoram, thereby enhancing the desired power. Its keywords could form a mantra, perhaps spoken into an orange candle flame.

The pathways of the Tree run in two directions – downwards following the Lightning Flash from sphere to sphere from the undifferentiated Godhead to man, and from man spiralling upwards towards the Godhead. This is the path travelled by the unborn soul as he or she is incarnated, and then in reverse order in dying. However, by magic, meditation and divination it can be possible to connect with the higher realms beyond Tiphareth during life – and this is the focus of Kabbalistic exploration.

THE FIRST LEVEL of the Tree is known as the Realm of the Supernals, the first three spheres that together form the Godhead.

Kether: UNITY: *Number One*

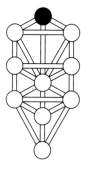

This is the prima mobile, the great creator, the Godhead who is beyond all form or tangible existence. Kether lies on the middle pillar of the Tree of Life. In the beginning, from Kether emanated the left and right poles, topped by Chokmah, (sphere two) and Binah (sphere three), the creative and receptive principles. Many cultures refer to an original creative or undifferentiated life-force from which all life, good and evil, emanated.

Kether can be regarded as ultimate union with the universe. It is symbolised in mystical tradition by the heavenly Androgyne (male and female united in one), and represents a state of mystical transcendence and union with the Supreme.

It corresponds with the crown chakra at the top of the head and can be visualised as a beam of light coming from the cosmos and returning to it.

Its planetary attribution is Pluto; its gem is the diamond; its tree is almond; its flower is the almond blossom; its colour is pure white.

Its key words are: unity, union, pure consciousness, the manifestation, beginning, source.

Its virtue or positive aspect is actualisation or attainment and its negative aspect is dissipation or non-achievement.

Chokmah: WISDOM: *Number Two*

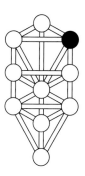

The second emanation on the Tree of Life is linked with the Great Father, the giver of the spark of life, the progenitor and ultimate phallic symbol, and so is the realm of the perfect qualities of initiating life, the wisdom of ages. This is the Logos or Word in Genesis that was in the beginning was 'with God and of God', the Divine Will and Purpose.

Its chakra or psychic energy that it shares with Binah, the Great Mother, is the brow or third eye.

Its planetary attribution is Neptune/the zodiac; its gem is the star ruby; its tree is beech; its flower is amaranth/mistletoe; its colour is silver-grey, a combination of the white of Kether and the black of Binah.

Its key words are: pure creative energy, life-force, the wellspring, light, innovation and initiation based on wisdom and strength.

Its virtue or positive aspect is an outpouring of energy and its negative aspect is destructiveness.

Binah: UNDERSTANDING: *Number Three*

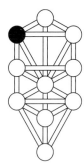

The third emanation is identified with the Great Mother in all her forms. She is the Womb of new life, the Great Water, the life-bearer, vehicle for and transformer of the creative spark of Chokmah into practical form within time and space. Binah represents understanding and unconditional love and fertility.

Chokmah and Binah are not polarities but the two aspects of Kether.

Its planetary attribution is Saturn; its gem is the star sapphire/pearl; its tree is alder; its flower is the lotus/lily; its colour is black.

Key words include: acceptance, limitation, form, constraint, incarnation, fate, time, space, natural law, the womb and gestation, enclosure, fertility, mother, weaving and spinning, death (return to the womb).

The positive aspect is abundance and its negative aspect is secretiveness.

THE SECOND LEVEL of the Tree also contains three *sephiroth* and begins in the world where archetypes are manifest in action and experience. They mirror the higher realms to some extent. This is known as the Realm of the Soul and is separated from the Supernal by the Abyss which contains the sphere without number, Daath.

Chesed: MERCY: *Number Four*

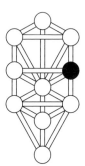

The fourth emanation is identified with the ruler (but not Creator) of the manifest universe, and represents peace, stability, love, awareness and mercy. It is the ruler who commands by example and love, not fear and coercion, and relies on natural justice.

Chesed, Geburah, Judgement and Tiphareth correspond to the heart chakra.

Its planetary attribution is Jupiter; its gem is amethyst; its tree is birch; its flower is olive/poppy; its colour is blue.

Its key words include: vision, wise authority, leading by example, justice, inspiration, patience, persuasion, spiritual love and vision, altruism and forgiveness.

Its virtue is humility and its vice self-righteousness.

Geburah: JUDGEMENT: *Number Five*

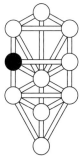

The fifth emanation on the Tree of Life and the alter ego of Chesed represents Severity and Justice. The destructive forces of the sphere of Geburah are intended to have a purging, cleansing effect on the universe.

Geburah represents the Warrior God aspect of the wise ruler who applies discipline and precision in governing the cosmos and removes unwanted or unnecessary elements after their usefulness has passed.

Its planetary attribution is Mars; its gem is ruby; its flower is the nettle; its tree is holly; its colour is red.

Its key words include: justice, retribution (revenge taken not in the heat of anger but calculated redress of what is necessary), severity, necessary destruction, loyalty and persistence.

Its virtue is courage and its vice is cruelty.

Tiphareth: BEAUTY: *Number Six*

This sphere on the central pillar of the Tree links and harmonises Mercy (Chesed) and Judgement (Geburah), higher on the Tree. It is said to be the sphere of the self, poised between the world of the spirit and the material world, just as Binah is the greater Self. Here can be contacted one's personal guardian angel or evolved self.

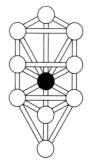

Its planetary attribution is the sun; its gem is topaz; its flower is gorse/vine; its tree is the ash; its colour is yellow.

The key words include: harmony, reconciliation, peace-making, self-awareness, balance, wholeness, clear identity.

Its virtue is integrity and its vice is over-concern with outward appearance.

THE THIRD LEVEL of the Tree of Life is that of the Realm of the Personality. This extends towards the roots of the Tree. It has three *sephiroth* within its control and links the material world below it with the human personality which aspires upwards through the realms of soul and spirit to the material world.

Netzach: FEELINGS: *Number Seven*

The seventh emanation on the Tree of Life, Netzach, is regarded as the sphere of artistic creativity, subjectivity, and higher feelings flowing outwards, rather than emotions that are elicited by responses to the external world. It is sometimes called the hidden intelligence, the lamp that illumines from within.

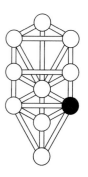

Inspiration is the fount of this sphere, whether in using artistic expression or speaking from the heart.

Netzach and Hod correspond to the solar plexus chakra.

Its planetary association is Venus; its gem is the emerald; its flower is the rose; its tree is the apple; its colour is green.

The key words include: altruism, unselfishness, pleasure, sensual beauty, love, excitement, desire, affection and sympathy.

Its virtue is empathy and its vice excess of emotion and lust.

Hod: INTELLECT: *Number Eight*

Hod represents the mind, logic, order, rational thought and structure. Hod is careful planning, assessing of what is known and deductions made within certain parameters. It is known as the perfect intelligence and its illumination comes from learning and application.

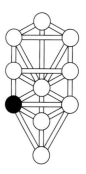

Its planetary attribution is Mercury; its gem is the opal; its flower is the tulip; its tree is hazel; its colour is orange.

Its key words are: glory, splendour, abstraction, communication, clear conceptualisation, logic and rule-keeping.

Its virtue is truthfulness and its vice dishonesty and pedantry.

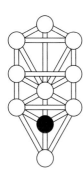

Yesod: INSTINCTS: *Number Nine*

The ninth emanation is sometimes known as the 'animal soul', the seat of instincts, especially sexual and procreative ones. Yesod is the sphere of physical fertility whether in actual deeds or in the act of ejaculation, pregnancy and birth. It is also the source of physical desires. Above all it is the realm of the subconscious, the source of dreams and is associated with the astral plane, with the occult and divination.

Yesod corresponds to the sacral or genital chakra.

Its planetary attribution is the moon; its gem is quartz; its flower is jasmine/mandrake; its tree is the willow; its colour is purple.

The key words include: perception, healing of the mind and spirit, imagination, images reflected from the psyche, the unconscious, instincts, life cycles as mirrored by the moon and tides, and secrets.

Its virtue is focused imagination and its vice self-gratification.

THE FOURTH LEVEL of the Tree is the Realm of the Material World and contains a single sphere. From the totally unmanifest in Kether, the power becomes completely manifest in Malkuth.

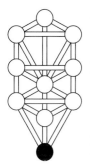

Malkuth: THE MATERIAL WORLD: *Number Ten*

The tenth emanation is associated with the earth itself, the plane of physical reality, and its connections with the underworld and mortality. Sometimes it is called the lower unconscious mind where humanity links with the earth.

Malkuth represents the kinship with all life, animal, plant and stone as well as human. It is the roots of the Tree of Life and ultimately, as earthly vehicle for divine creation, is a part of the Godhead, the manifest Kingdom, the reality principle. The purpose of the Kabbalistic journey that begins here is not to transcend the human form, but to reconnect it with the original unmanifest Godhead Kether by crossing the Abyss. It is also the home of Shekinah, the Divine Feminine, said to be the lost bride of Elohim, the personified Godhead.

It corresponds to the root chakra at the base of the spine.

Its planetary attribution is the Earth, one of the four elements; its gem is rock crystal; its flower is the lily; its tree is the oak, a sky god tree that is a symbol of wisdom; its colour is brown.

Its key words include: reality, healing of the body, physical matter, the natural world, practicality, solidity, death and incarnation and return to the Earth.

Its virtue is connectedness with all life and its vice materialism or inertia.

Daath

There is an invisible *sephira* below Chokmah and Binah, sometimes called Daath or Knowledge of the Shadow, that corresponds with the shadow or hidden side of life and death/transformation and gives access to the reverse side of the Tree where dwells Choronzon, the great demon who absorbs false knowledge and so cleanses the individual of it.

It is represented by the throat chakra.

Its planetary attribution is Uranus and the asteroids; it has no associated gem; its flower is the cuckoopint; it has no sacred tree; its colour is grey.

Its key words include: mystery, abyss, hole, tunnel, gateway, doorway, black hole, vortex.

NATIVE NORTH AMERICAN TRADITION

Native North American spirituality is as varied as the continent it spans – thousands of square miles of high rocky mountains, dense forests, arid deserts and fertile plains peopled by those who were once hunters, farmers and warriors. There are still, in Canada and North America, about 500 separate American Indian nations. Many were moved to reservations, often in arid land, hundreds, sometimes a thousand miles away, for example Cherokee men, women and children who were taken from gold-rich Georgia to Oklahoma, many forced to walk, during the autumn and harsh winter of 1838–39, on a journey known as The Trail of Tears. Along this trail it was said a white rose bloomed for each mother's tear shed, with a gold centre for the gold taken from the Cherokee lands, and seven leaves on each stem representing the seven Cherokee clans that made the journey. Yet the individual tribes have still retained their unique customs and in recent years there has been a great revival in their spiritual traditions, not only within each tribe, but increasingly among non-indigenous peoples, recognising a life path, or beauty way as the American Indians call it, that at its best acknowledges the sanctity of all creation.

Central to the Native North American tradition is the belief that all life stems from a Great Invisible Creator and this life-force is imbued equally in minerals, plants, animals and humankind. The earthly forms of things are said to reflect their perfect form in the spirit world. Black Elk, the Oglala Sioux medicine man, gives the example of the spotted eagle: 'His feathers are the rays of the sun and when the feathers are worn, represents and is the real presence, Wakan-Tanka, the Great Spirit.'

Myths of Creation

There are as many creation myths as there are nations; most tell how the world was ruled by the all-powerful and invisible Great Spirit and that Mother Earth was the source of all life. Their ceremonies honoured the marriage between Earth and Sky and the birth of Life. Great gods such as the Sun, the Moon, Wind and Fire were intermediaries between the Great Unknowable Spirit and mankind. The Earth is sometimes personified as Mother Turtle who carries the entire weight of the world on her back, and many Native Americans referred to America as Turtle Island.

A Wichita creation myth describes how the 'first woman lay on her back naked in the sun and slowly sank into the earth as her nipples turned dark as if suckling a child until her entire body was absorbed, after which the earth became fruitful'.

White Buffalo Calf Woman – the Promise of a New World

The myth that gives most hope to modern generations is that of White Buffalo Calf Woman or Wophe, who is the sacred Creator Woman of the Lakotas and other tribes of the Plains. Legend says she fell from a meteor and gave to the Lakota people the Buffalo Calf Pipe which is still the most sacred religious object of the Lakota today.

The Woman instructed the men in how to smoke the pipe, so that it might be used for prayer offerings to her and for bringing peace to divided nations. She also taught sacred ceremonies for restoring balance and healing to both earth and people. After her final visit, she left the camp, walking to the west. When she reached the outskirts, she rolled over on the ground and was transformed into a buffalo, changing colour several times. Finally, she changed into a white buffalo calf, rarest of the species, promising that when she would be seen again she would restore harmony to a troubled world. The people followed her teachings, the corn grew, the seasons continued to flow in succession and they were hungry no more, as buffalo became plentiful.

By the end of the 19th century there were less than 200 buffalo left, where only years earlier it was estimated there had been several million.

In the summer of 1994, a white buffalo calf was born in Jamesville, Wisconsin. As the prophecy had told, the white buffalo has changed colour since birth, going from white to black to red to yellow and back to white. Since each colour represents one of the four main directions, the buffalo is seen by many Native Americans as a symbol of the rebirth of hope. One Native visionary interpreted the birth of the white buffalo calf as signifying that the human race will be united, in spite of differences in creed and colour, and join together in peace.

The Sacred Circle

The circle lies at the heart of Amerindian spirituality. In 1930, Black Elk, who had been a child at the massacre of Wounded Knee, explained:

> In the old days when we were a strong and happy people, all our power came from the sacred hoop of the nation and so long as the hoop was unbroken, the people flourished. The flowering tree was the living centre of the hoop and the circle of the four quarters nourished it. The East gave peace and light, the South gave warmth, in the West thunder beings gave rain and the North with its cold and mighty wind gave strength and endurance. Everything the Power of the World does, is done in a circle … The Wind, in its greatest power whirls. Birds make their nests in circles, for theirs is the same religion as ours. The sun comes forth and goes down again in a circle … Even the seasons form a great circle in their changing and always come back again to where they were. The life of man is a circle from childhood to childhood and so it is in everything where power moves.

Native American Ceremonies

Ritual and sacred dance have from time immemorial formed a central facet of Native American life. To the beat of the drum which represented the pulse of the universe, braves danced around either a totem pole, symbol of the world axis, representing in its carvings all the power animals of the tribe, or around a sacred fire. These dances marked the great agricultural festivals of the year and also those special to the area. For example, the buffalo dance of the Mandans, a Dakota Tribe, marking the annual return of the buffalo herds, was held when the willow was in full leaf.

The Sun Dance

From early times the sun dance was performed annually in the summer, usually on the solstice or in July, to prevent the sun losing its power and to connect and replenish the powers of the earth and sky.

The great sun dance was the predominant tribal ceremony of Great Plains Indians, danced around a central pole representing the axis of the universe; warriors drove cherry wood skewers connected to the central pole into their chests, to symbolise their connection to all things. The sun dance was forbidden in the latter part of the 19th century, partly because it involved such injury to the young warriors who ripped their flesh as they danced. They would dance for four days and nights without ceasing and their blood was an offering to restore the earth.

In the 1930s, the sun dance was revived among the Crow Indians and became popular among other tribes. In the new form of the ritual, the sun dance chief offers the prayers from the sacred pipe to the four compass points and the earth and sky each day. These sun dance prayer ceremonies are held on every full moon and healing takes place at the end, often using power amulets, feathers from eagles or otter skins from tribal medicine bundles, some of which are sacred to the sun dances.

The annual sun dance is also still performed. Although the dancers are no longer physically attached to the tree, they fast and dance non-stop for two or more days. If a dancer falls, it is no longer seen as a disgrace, heralding disaster for the whole tribe; rather the visions that occur in this exhausted state are regarded as prophetic. On the second day healing takes place for all who need it, and those who dance may be endowed with healing or prophetic powers.

The Ghost Dance

The ghost dance, a ceremony for the regeneration of the earth and the restoration of the earth's caretakers, became very popular during the late 19th century, when devastation to the buffalo and the battles to take possession of the Amerindian tribal homelands were at their height. While performing the ghost dance, it was believed that dancers could visit relatives who had left their bodies, and as so many Native Americans had lost friends and relatives, this aspect of the ceremony was particularly healing. Although the ghost dances were intended to be a peaceful ceremony of unification and regeneration of the wounded land and peoples, soldiers gunned down ghost dancers at Wounded Knee in 1890. Even women and children were shot in the back as they were trying to escape and the massacre is often regarded as taking the heart from the Native American peoples.

The Medicine Wheel

At the heart of Amerindian spirituality lies the Medicine Wheel that is both a physical and psychic entity. Medicine equals energy, the vital life-force in nature, in mankind and in the Great Spirit. A person's medicine is that power generated by his or her own talents and strengths, used in a positive way to achieve the right path in life.

There are almost 500 different versions of the Medicine Wheel in North America alone. The wheels link the celestial, human and natural cycles. Some were 90ft (27m) in diameter but research suggests that some were much smaller and placed around ceremonial tipis, or even individual tipis, to be used not only by the shaman but by anyone seeking a spiritual path. The original Medicine Wheel was made of stones and could be created wherever a tribe camped. Around the wheel are totem animals representing each birth month and season. The totems vary according to each tribe's mythology. At its simplest, it is a circle divided by a cross to create four directions – north, east, south and west.

However, there are more intricate versions involving the tribe's totem animals.

The most famous, the Big Horn Medicine Wheel near Sheridan in Wyoming, dates back perhaps 200 or 300 years, is about 90ft (27m) in diameter and made of stones. Its primary alignments are to the summer solstice, dawn and sunset points, with secondary ones at the rising of various stars. The Moose Mountain Medicine Wheel in Saskatchewan, Canada, is at least 1,000 years older and also aligned to the solstice.

PART SIX

Psychic Powers and Strange Phenomena

ANIMALS AND PSYCHIC POWERS

Dogs have more acute physical hearing and sense of smell than humans, but it would seem that their instinctive powers are also finely tuned to stimuli from non-physical sources. Because animals are not aware of their own thought processes, as humans are, it may be that their sixth sense is not blocked by the conscious mind.

There have been experiments in the laboratory to test animal *Psi*, but animals are even less amenable to formal testing by ethical means than children. In such experiments as those in 1942 in Kharkov in Russia, puppies were given mild electric shocks. At the precise moment they were being hurt, their absent mother became distressed. I hope that such experiments would not be carried out anywhere today, for there is plenty of evidence in the field for animal ESP, especially where mother and young are concerned. Unfortunately, the majority of these experiences are dismissed as anecdotal, because they occur spontaneously and not under control situations.

Telepathy

Dr Rupert Sheldrake, a UK biologist and parapsychologist, has extensively and successfully researched animal *Psi* using clinical rather than experimental evidence. He carried out random household surveys of dog owners and discovered that 46 per cent of dog owners in England and 45 per cent in California claimed that their animal anticipates the return of a member of the household by waiting for him or her at a door, window, driveway, or bus stop. In both surveys, most of the dogs that anticipated the return of a family member did so less than five minutes before the person arrived home. However, 16 per cent of the dog owners interviewed in England and 19 per cent in California said that the dogs reacted more than 10 minutes before the human arrival.

Explanations that the animal picks up cues from others in the home or that it learns the routine do not apply in cases where the owner does not have a set routine and where members of the family are unaware of the precise time of the return home. In these cases it would seem some form of sixth sense is operating.

I have encountered similar cases. Pauline, now in her fifties, told me that when she lived in Liverpool as a child, the family cat and dog would go into the hall about five minutes before her father came home and sit by the door expectantly. Her father worked as a steward on the ships that went to Ireland and it was never known in advance what time his shifts would end or how many days he would be away, as rotas would be changed at the last minute and the family had no telephone. However, he always brought titbits home for the animals and they 'knew' he was coming.

Premonitions

Animals also sometimes seem to be able to anticipate danger, even when there are no physical indications. In *The Magical Child*, J.C. Pearce reports a naturalist specialising in the study of foxes who described his long-term study of a particular fox family located near a creek in a ravine. One sunny afternoon the naturalist noticed the vixen doing something he had never seen a fox do. The mother suddenly left her burrow and cubs, went up the hillside some 30 yards (27m) and began busily digging another burrow. She then carried each of the cubs up the hill to the new den. Several hours later the reason became clear. Although the weather remained beautiful, a flash flood caused by a cloudburst many miles upstream suddenly filled the ravine. Had the family remained in place they would have drowned. It was the sudden apparently inexplicable change of the vixen's activity, a sign that marks many human premonitions of danger, that suggests the act indicated foreknowledge of the disaster.

Animal Premonitions and Health

One of the most exciting developments in the animal/human health field has been the discovery that dogs can anticipate epileptic fits in their owners up to 30 minutes before a seizure occurs. Research being carried out by Support Dogs in the UK, a Sheffield-based charity organisation, follows the discovery that some dogs seem able to detect subtle changes in their epileptic owners that even sophisticated medical equipment misses. The charity is now training certain dogs to alert owners with whom they have a close bond to imminent epileptic seizures.

Scientists have no explanation for the ability of the dogs, although Dr Stephen Brown, chairman of the British Epilepsy Association suggested, 'Dogs have incredible senses, and perhaps their noses can detect something like changes in the level of pheromones.'

Healing Powers

Throughout the ancient world, animals were believed to possess healing and magical properties. In Egypt, animal amulets were placed on the bodies of the dead to protect them against the hazards of life in the next world and were also used by living people to keep away sickness. Many of these were the mummified form of various creatures. The amulet of the crab offered its owner protection against fevers, the fish from gout, a shrew from boils, a claw of a gazelle from ulcers, and a scorpion safety from snake and insect bites. The scarab that symbolised new life was placed on the heart of the dead. It was also dried, powdered, mixed with water and swallowed to counter infertility.

A hawk's head or claw was sewn into children's clothes by Inuit Indians to give the infants the hunting ability of the hawk – and the power to survive in a society that largely relied on hunting. In India, an amulet to endow the wearer with oratory and wisdom was made from the tongues of three birds – a parrot, a lark and a crow – while elephant's hair was believed to promote long life. In Peru, tapir's claws are worn to avert sickness.

The healing potential of animals, especially pets, is immense because of their open unconditional love, loyalty and willingness to give. Recent research suggests that pet owners are healthier than non-pet owners, visit doctors less frequently, have fewer colds and headaches, lower heart rates and lower cholesterol levels. It has been shown that the simple action of petting a dog can reduce blood pressure, and it is said that having a pet reduces an owner's chance of having a heart attack, just as much as a low-salt diet or cutting down on alcohol.

The Human Dolphin Therapy Centre at the Seaquarium in Miami uses 40-minute swimming sessions with trained dolphins as well as intensive conventional therapies to treat children with mental problems. The centre claims a 97 per cent improvement rate. In one case a brain damaged child spoke for the first time as a result of the therapy.

Power Animals

The Native North Americans, the Australian Aborigines, many African tribes and tribes of the frozen North have traditionally associated themselves with power animals that symbolise certain qualities and strengths that are integrated into their personalities; for example, the beaver with adaptability, the deer with fleetness of foot and thought, the eagle with nobility and vision, and the hawk with focus and courage.

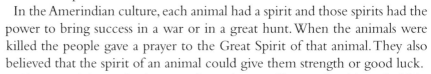

Animals were often chosen as totems because they displayed the skills essential for survival. Many myths tell of Native American braves meeting the chief of an animal clan who would impart his wisdom; or, a boy of 13 or 14, on his initiation quest into the wilderness, encountering a creature who would give him his adult name, for example Running Deer. Girls would similarly encounter a power creature.

In the Amerindian culture, each animal had a spirit and those spirits had the power to bring success in a war or in a great hunt. When the animals were killed the people gave a prayer to the Great Spirit of that animal. They also believed that the spirit of an animal could give them strength or good luck.

Sioux participants in the annual sun dance still wear the skins of rabbits on their arms and legs, because the rabbit represents humility. They do this because they say 'he is quiet and soft, as we must be when we go to the centre of the world'. Another sun dance creature, the eagle, is associated with healing power as well as success, 'for prosperity and wealth follow the eagle, who may bestow the gift of curing'.

AUTOMATIC WRITING

Automatic writing is traditionally regarded as a tool of mediumship, whereby, it is believed, information is channelled from a spirit, whether that of a deceased close relation or someone who needs to communicate to the living information about the manner of his or her death or unfinished business. Automatic writing for this purpose was practised mainly by mediums, the nature of the handwriting sometimes confirming for the sitter the identity of the deceased relation who was communicating via the medium's hand. It lost its popularity after the Second World

War, but enjoyed a revival during the 1970s, this time as a personal art for the purpose of receiving angelic communication and channelling from Wise Masters, evolved discarnate beings from other dimensions.

Automatic Writing – Communication from Another Dimension

I was sent the following account by a sailor who served in the Second World War. William, who lives in Lancashire, told me:

I was training with the Royal Navy. Our instructor, a Chief Petty Officer Telegraphist, was also a Spiritualist medium.

On one occasion our instructor spoke to us of a submarine, newly built and lost with almost all hands on board while on trials off the coast of England. He went into great detail about the accident, which he told us had not been published. Only details of the rescue operation at the time from outside the submarine had for security reasons been released.

Chief produced a couple of letters in different handwriting, one of which was written by a crew member of the ill-fated submarine, blaming himself for the tragedy. The letter spoke of special gauge cocks and visual gauge glasses that when opened would indicate that the outer door was fully closed enabling the inner door to open. This it stated should never be undertaken without rodding through these open cocks and glass gauges, since a blockage could give an incorrect reading. This the letter went on to say had not been done, taking an empty test glass at face value which led to the disaster.

The gauges had in fact been blocked with seaweed, the writer maintained, and on releasing the inner door, it had been burst open by a wall of water. The letter stated the operator panicked, rushing through adjoining compartments, failing to secure these water-tight doors, before a petty officer answering the rating's cries had managed to secure one opening. The rest flooded pulling the submarine down at this end by the sheer weight of water, denying an escape route and causing gassing problems from wetted batteries.

The Chief Petty Officer explained that the letters had been written from a dead submariner through him (by automatic writing).

Many years later, when a civilian, I was walking home from work. I called as usual to collect a newspaper from the railway station. There I found the official account of the submarine disaster. This information had come to light only when the ship was raised and refitted. Naturally there were similarities to the account in the letter, but one thing caught my eye. The official version was that the blockage was ship's paint, not seaweed. The writer if indeed it was a tormented soul, could be forgiven that mistake. He certainly would not have expected a brand new sub to have a blob of paint giving a false reading. Seaweed would be a natural assumption on his part.

The original letters had also given an account of the deaths of two attempting escapees, also the statement that these deaths had prevented the use of that escape route for reasons which were also given in the dead seaman's letter all of which were now proved true.

The authenticity of the letters was not only in the correct details but the motivation of the submariner who had died believing he had caused the tragedy. Time and time again it has been discovered that the dead do not automatically gain full knowledge of earthly affairs and ghosts can be prevented from resting by guilt or the belief that they caused a disaster.

Another case of apparent automatic writing was prolific communication from Patience Worth, transmitted in 1913 through Pearl Curran, a housewife from St Louis in the USA. Patience Worth wrote that she was an Englishwoman from a poor country family in Dorset. Born in 1649, she said she had been killed by Native American Indians not long after she emigrated to the USA. Communicating at first through the ouija board, Patience dictated more and more through automatic writing, eventually leading Pearl to produce 2,500 poems, plays, short stories and six full-length novels, set in different historical periods. She wrote a total of four million words in five years, all apparently dictated by Patience.

Almost 90 per cent of old English was used in some of the stories, a far greater proportion according to academics than in any literature produced since the 13th century. Patience also wrote about periods after she had lived, giving facts which were authenticated but beyond the knowledge of Pearl herself. Explanations include the possibility that, as Pearl herself believed, the spirit of Patience was actually communicating through her, that Patience was an amalgam of Pearl's own past lives, or that Patience was the personification of knowledge that Pearl was unconsciously transmitting via automatic writing from a collective human memory bank. Cryptomnesia, absorbing unusual facts without recalling them consciously, would seem unlikely in view of the sheer volume of knowledge imparted, especially of old English.

Other Explanations for Automatic Writing

The 19th-century US philosopher and psychologist William James was remarkably modern in his view that automatic writing was a way of obtaining information that was buried deep in the subconscious, and it became a valuable form of therapy both for adults and children.

Others considered it a telepathic process whereby information could be transferred between living minds. William E. Stead, the crusading journalist and spiritualist who died on the *Titanic*, at first considered automatic writing a means of communication by the deceased. When he first attempted it, he found the nature of the communication mirrored the views expressed by a deceased friend who had been a journalist and did not reflect his own beliefs at all. However, Stead also found that he could write letters in the hands of various living friends, conveying any news they wished to tell him, facts he could only have obtained by telepathic means.

One example was a letter he wrote in the handwriting of a female friend who was travelling home on a Sunday evening from London after they had spent a weekend together. In the letter which Stead wrote on the Monday morning without any communication passing between them, he described how on his friend's homeward journey she had been distressed on the train by the unwanted attentions of a male passenger. Stead described how she had hit her attacker with an umbrella before he left the train at Guildford, although Stead mistakenly wrote that the umbrella used was hers, not the molester's.

How Does Automatic Writing Differ from Ordinary Writing?

- People who engage in automatic writing may experience a tingling sensation in the arms or writing hand immediately before a message is received.

- Automatic writing tends to be faster than conscious handwriting and generally very prolific, thousands of words being produced in a short time with seemingly little awareness on the part of the receiver who seems in a light trance state.

- Words may be joined together and perhaps spelled unusually. The actual letters tend to be larger than the receiver's ordinary writing and be formed in a different way. Some automatic writers find that they produce the most wonderful copperplate writing, but only during the process of the automatic transmission.

- Automatic writing can also be in mirror script, written left to right, or even diagonally from the bottom to the top of the page.

- The communication may be in verse or contain complicated biblical quotations, foreign languages that are not spoken by the receiver, or even Latin.

Automatic Writing and Divination

One of the great values of automatic writing as a form of divination to answer a specific question, is the same as the way in which one might open a profound book, apparently at random, and use the words for symbolic guidance. Like many forms of divination, such as casting the runes or selecting Tarot cards (see p. 77), it may rely on unconscious muscular movements of the hand guided by psychokinesis (the power to make objects move by mind power) to convey through the written word information not accessible to the conscious mind of the automatic writer. Such information given by this method may be symbolic rather than actual.

Danger of Practising Automatic Writing

For some people, automatic writing can allow an aspect of their own personality to emerge and so help to strengthen the writer psychologically and spiritually by expressing ideas that might have been suppressed or not acknowledged.

However, because the messages, whether psychic or psychological, may involve an intimate connection, they can create a secondary personality that can merge with or dominate the writer's own, especially if the writer is feeling insecure or is easily influenced. The danger occurs when this intrudes upon the everyday world or the recipient assumes the role of the apparent transmitter in everyday life. A truly benign higher source would not intrude on daily consciousness.

CLAIRVOYANCE

What is Clairvoyance?

Clairvoyance is sometimes referred to as sixth sense or second sight, and literally means clear seeing. It is defined as the ability to look beyond the normal world and describe people and events far away, perhaps in the future or in other dimensions, for it also incorporates the ability to see ghosts. It is said that clairvoyant abilities reside in the Third Eye, biologically associated with the pineal gland located in the back of the brain almost in the centre of the head, that is believed to have shrunk during human evolution. Early humans were hypothesised to have breathed through this gland rather than the nose and mouth, which thus operated as a constant doorway to the world. This, it was said, connected people to the energies around them rather than isolating them within their skulls. The Third Eye is also the name given to the brow chakra, a psychic energy centre that is linked with all forms of spiritual and psychic functioning. Most researchers, however, are convinced that clairvoyance is purely a psychic skill, based on the ability of the mind to travel mentally backwards and forwards in time and to see at a distance of even hundreds of miles, a related ability called remote viewing.

Children are naturally clairvoyant, but lose this ability once the rational mind develops. From my own research, I have discovered that many young children see a

mother or father's thoughts as actual images, and it is only when verbal and logical processes become important in a child's functioning that clairvoyant abilities correspondingly diminish. Creative visualisation is a technique practised both in modern magic and in positive thinking, whereby a person visualises a desired result into becoming actuality. Mothers seem to regain clairvoyant powers on giving birth, especially concerning their children, and can on occasions foresee dangers miles away. Other people may regain this ability after trauma in their lives, but some retain it undiminished and develop the power through mediumship. It is possible to reawaken clairvoyant abilities by practising scrying techniques (see p. 136), for example tea-leaf reading or dropping coloured oils in water and interpreting the pictures.

Throughout the ages, certain people have manifested this ability through prophecy (see p. 307). In fact, one of the earliest recorded experiments in parapsychology was carried out to test clairvoyance. In 550BC, Croesus, King of Lydia, wanted to discover which of seven oracles in the known world possessed the greatest prophetic ability. He sent messengers to ask each of the oracles simultaneously what he was doing at a certain hour. To make the test as difficult as possible, Croesus selected an activity that could not be deduced logically. He chopped up a tortoise and boiled it with lamb in a brass cauldron. The Oracle of Delphi was the only one to accurately report, not only the vision, but the smell of the tortoise and lamb cooking in a brass-lidded cauldron (clairsentience).

Clairvoyance is an ability often associated with people of Celtic origin. The Scots are said to possess the Sight, while the Irish people are famed for their clairvoyant powers, not least in seeing the fairy folk or the Little People, as they are called in Ireland.

Scientific Evidence for Clairvoyance

On March 30, 1999, it was reported that researchers at Harvard University had been investigating the human ability to respond to an object that was travelling literally too fast for the eye to have time to transmit its image to the brain. Tennis players and cricketers, for example, routinely react to balls travelling at up to 100mph (160kph), when technically their brains should not be able to register the objects before they have passed out of range.

Professor Markus Meister and his colleagues at the Harvard University Department of Molecular and Cellular Biology discovered that the human eye contains cells known as ganglions that can calculate the future position of a moving object. These ganglions transmit a message to the brain thousandths of a second before the detected object actually arrives in the field of vision.

They also suggest that successful cricket and tennis players may possess a slightly greater ability to see into the future than the average person. While this does not explain clairvoyance in terms of viewing past scenes, known as retrocognition, or events occurring simultaneously miles away, remote viewing, the experiments do demonstrate that the human mind does possess capacities only just coming within the sphere of scientific investigation.

Remote Viewing

This is a technique whereby a viewer can detect an unknown object, person or scene in another place, beyond the range of the physical eye, whether this is in another room, another building or a hundred miles away. Some people can not only see, but hear sounds or detect fragrances connected with the scene or person, and even the emotions of their targets. Indeed, it is this ability to pick up strong emotion that is so crucial in cases where a mother detects a child's distress, when he or she is in another room or location.

In America during the 1970s, a great deal of research was carried out into remote viewing abilities. The term 'remote viewing' was first used by Russell Targ and Harold Puthoff. After hundreds of experiments over 10 years at Stanford Research Institute International in California, they concluded that remote viewing is a psychic power that many people experience spontaneously. The researchers found that even subjects with little previous psychic experience could quite easily be taught to accurately describe buildings, geographic features, people and activities, in distant locations. People were also taught to see and describe the contents of opaque containers.

There is no way of knowing whether remote viewing involves actual etheric or astral travel, or whether the mind can project itself to see over great distances and across dimensions. Certainly some subjects in these experiments found they were most successful in utilising what they described as a form of astral projection. When asked to look into a sealed room or at a distant place, they felt that their spirits actually left their bodies and travelled to the scenes which they later accurately described.

MATERNAL INTUITION

Maternal intuition is the most common and easily understood of all psychic phenomena. Yet it is also one of the least researched aspects, relying almost entirely on anecdotal evidence, although examples of the psychic bond between mother and child are frequently verified by independent witnesses. At its most dramatic, maternal instinct has in thousands of cases saved a child's life.

One of the most remarkable cases I have come across is that of Annette who was enjoying a rare evening at the cinema with her husband. Their baby daughter was safe at home with a friend but, she said, 'We had not been in the cinema for more than a few minutes when a terrible uneasiness came over me. I could distinctly smell burning.'

Her husband could smell nothing and there was no one smoking near them. Annette tried to calm her fears but the smell of smoke and sensation of dread became overpowering. 'Eventually I told my husband I was leaving. He followed me reluctantly, muttering something derogatory about women.'

As the bus took them the six miles to their village in Surrey, she prayed for it to go faster. 'At last we were sprinting down the lane leading to the cottage. The smell of burning was now very definite to me though my husband still could not smell anything. We reached the door. Dense smoke poured out and a chair burst into flames. I rushed through to the bedroom and got the baby out while my husband dragged out the unconscious babysitter. She had fallen asleep and dropped her lighted cigarette into the chair which had been smouldering.'

This incident happened in 1936.

Such examples are inexplicable in scientific terms. This 'power' seems to operate as an automatic radar from a mother to her infant that enables her to detect unvoiced distress or unseen danger to her child, whether they are together or miles apart. The maternal automatic radar is strongest before an infant has a sense of his or her own danger and the ability to take effective action.

Is Maternal Intuition Paranormal or Normal?

The sixth sense communication of danger from the mother's protective psyche in which she envelops her young child is superior to the conventional, albeit evolved, five established sensory organs. A mother in a completely different room from her baby may detect the child's silent distress even when others in the same room as the infant notice nothing. This destroys the common argument that it is a change in the baby's sounds or even breathing pattern that alerts the mother to danger.

Carolyn, a mother of five children who lives in Salt Lake City, Utah, did trust her instincts and so saved her child:

I felt an especially close bond with my second daughter Sarah. I remember one evening when she was about eight months old. I was in the kitchen and she and her sister were in the living room with my husband. Suddenly I saw a blinding flash and heard the words in my head, 'The baby is choking.' I rushed to the living room where my husband was reading and my older daughter was playing. The baby was lying in the corner on her stomach apparently quite happy. I flipped her over and saw that Sarah was silently choking on a balloon. My husband and daughter were not aware of the emergency.

Carl Jones in his book, *From Parent to Child the Psychic Link*, comments: 'We call ESP paranormal because no sensory channel has yet been discovered which mediates the information. However, ESP may be a natural and normal part of the parent/child relationship. Perhaps all parents and offspring share a lifelong ESP connection, a link that knows no geographical barrier. And if so, perhaps the paranormal is not paranormal after all.'

Is it Coincidence?

One common feature of these crisis situations is that the mother acts in an unusual and seemingly irrational way that is only later understood. Such experiences happen once or twice usually in a mother's lifetime, and stand out years later as having an entirely different quality and intensity.

Routine Spontaneous Links

Many people can identify with the phenomenon of telephoning their mother on impulse, to find that her number is engaged because she is phoning her son or daughter at precisely that moment, even though it is not a regular time or day to call. These everyday links are so common as to pass largely unremarked, but on examination are quite startling. It may be that this link can be traced back to the pre-technological forms of communication still experienced by those now rare, remote tribes who have not come into contact with the modern world, whereby they can contact one another by mind power.

Enid from Berkshire, England, is in her fifties. Her son David, a sailor, is in his thirties. Enid always knows when David is going to telephone, although during his long periods at sea he cannot often get a shore line from one week to the next. She will suddenly say to her husband: 'We can't go out. David is going to ring.' Five minutes later, David phones from the Falklands or Fiji.

Is the Bond Genetic?

The mother/child bond is not one that can be entirely explained in terms of biological links. Anecdotal but powerful evidence has suggested that adoptive mothers have the same maternal instincts as a birth mother, and these can begin even before the child is born.

Linda, who lives in Oklahoma in the USA, described a vivid dream she experienced when she was hoping to adopt a baby, although she had not been allocated a child:

> It was so real I could almost touch the woman, a blonde, fair-skinned woman. I watched the baby being delivered, a dark-skinned, dark-haired boy. The moment was incredibly moving and I was convinced I was witnessing an actual birth. Then I was in my bedroom, wide awake. I noted down the date and the time.
>
> I told Dick, my husband about the dream and we discussed what it might mean. When we were given Ivan, our adoptive child, he was indeed the child whose face I had seen so clearly that night. The date and time of his birth exactly coincided with my dream. I knew that I had witnessed his birth for a reason, to confirm the rightness of the adoption.
>
> Sadly, Ivan's mother died and I was sent some photographs from her family for Ivan. She was the fair-skinned, blonde-haired woman in my dream.

Conventional wisdom lacks the tools to explain this phenomenon. We can only speculate about why Linda's dream was so uncannily accurate. Did she somehow telepathically tune into her prospective adoptive son, as one might suddenly come across a distant and unfamiliar radio station? Or was the source of the dream the boy itself, who, as a child in the womb does with a birth mother, was reaching out to his new mother?

The Mother as Seer

Even more remarkable is the way that the mothering instinct can apparently break the time barrier and foretell danger to her child. The mothers concerned usually have no special psychic abilities and this moment of crisis is the only occasion on which their prophecies are accurate. The mother will suddenly act in an unusual or seemingly illogical way to avert a potential disaster that could not have been foreseen on a conscious level. Michelle, who lives in Liverpool, England, told me:

> I always left Demi in her pram if she was asleep at one end of the nursery classroom while I went down the other end to hear my daughter Samantha and her classmates sing or act rhymes. However, when we went to the St Andrew's Day concert in November 1995, for the first time I lifted Demi out of the pram and took her with me, although she was in a deep sleep. It was as if someone was tapping me on the shoulder, telling me to lift Demi out of the pram and hold her in my arms.
>
> Moments later the ceiling at the end of the classroom where the pram was standing started to crack and a huge chunk of masonry crashed down on to the pram.

MEDIUMSHIP

What is Mediumship?

Mediumship is the process by which a sensitive person, a medium or channel, is used by spirits to communicate with the living. During physical mediumship, mediums also act as a channel for spirit-initiated kinetic activities, for example those that cause furniture to move, or messages to be tapped out on a table or spelled on a planchette or letter board without apparent human intervention. This physical mediumship is very different from spontaneous poltergeist activity (see p. 301), since the medium is trained to deliberately provide a channel for controlled paranormal activity. What is more, the communication is two-way, with the sitter asking a question and the spirit replying in a tangible way. Many mediums do operate within the Spiritualist Movement, but a number also practise privately.

How Does Mediumship Operate?

The spirit world is said to function at a higher vibrational level than that of the earth plane, and mediums are therefore people who are sufficiently spiritually evolved and experienced in spirit contact to raise their own vibrational levels in order to communicate with their own spirit guides and with the deceased relations and friends of those who consult them.

Though mediumship is conventionally divided into two manifestations of the same power, mental and physical mediumship, and most mediums prefer to work primarily in one mode, there can be an overlap in the abilities. For example, mental mediums may occasionally give teaching channelled directly from their spirit guides and speak with the Guide's voice or adopt the Guide's script in automatic writing. Most modern mediums tend to be mental mediums.

Mental Mediumship

This involves a medium relating information through thought transference, and therefore it usually takes place while the medium is conscious. He or she may talk to a spirit guide who acts as an intermediary, or communicate directly with the spirits of deceased loved ones. The messages from the spirit world are transmitted in words, generally using the medium's own voice, and the medium can simultaneously communicate with the living person seeking the contact. The deceased person will offer idiosyncratic or personal information so that the recipient or sitter can identify the spirit who is making contact.

The mental medium may see the spirit through clairvoyance or hear him or her through clairaudience, but the sitter, unless clairvoyant, will not.

Physical Mediumship

Physical mediumship involves the manipulation and transformation of physical systems and energies. This form of communication comes via a spirit operator, often a spirit guide, and the results can be seen and heard by the sitter as well as the medium. However, spirit operators are also communicators and may use the medium's face and body to superimpose either the form of the spirit guide or a deceased family member in order to deliver a message or manifest as a separate ectoplasmic or etheric entity. This form of mediumship is most usually associated with trance states.

Famous Mediums

The constant pressure to offer mediumship on demand has on occasions created a situation in which it is difficult for a medium to say to an audience or investigator that he or she can get nothing from the spirit world and that the spirits are unwilling or unable to communicate in a meaningful way on this specific occasion. One wise medium told me that spirit communication is like a very poor phone connection.

In the case of the late medium Doris Stokes, many who witnessed her work, especially in the early days, would agree what a gifted and spiritual person she was. But as an ordinary woman, Doris was thrust into a media circus and sometimes those around her may have been less than scrupulous in the need to provide a good show; towards the end of her life Doris herself felt pressurised to deliver messages of comfort to the thousands who had paid to see her.

But the truly great mediums came from the mid- to late-19th and early 20th centuries on both sides of the Atlantic, and demonstrated amazing physical manifestations: spirits playing invisible or actual instruments that were lifted into the air by invisible hands, tables tilting and lifting, perfumes filling the air, heavenly choirs, the sudden appearance of flowers or gifts from discarnate but visible hands, luminous changing forms dancing in the air, sparks and floating balls of light, and mediums levitating before a crowded gathering. These feats have never been explained or replicated in recent years.

It may be that, as was foretold by Andrew Jackson Davis, the American seer and a Father of Spiritualism, the Spiritualist Movement was initially established by remarkable demonstrations of mediumship, just as other religions began with wondrous acts.

Daniel Dunglas Home

Daniel Dunglas Home was a flamboyant 19th-century medium who worked throughout America and Europe for more than 25 years, except for a short period when he believed the spirits removed this mediumistic power to punish him for becoming too proud. He performed astonishing feats in broad daylight that have never been explained in rational terms, in which heavy articles of furniture floated up to the ceiling. Home himself would regularly rise effortlessly to the ceiling, and on one occasion even floated out of a third floor window and in another. He angered the poet Robert Browning when a spirit hand placed a garland of flowers on his wife Elizabeth's brow.

Florence Cooke

One of the most noted materialisation mediums was Florence Cooke, who was studied for a long period by Sir William Crookes, the chemist, who declared she was entirely genuine. Her spirit guide, Katie

King, had promised to speak through Florence for three years, and through Katie, Florence became the first English medium to exhibit full materialisation of a spirit form in a good light. The first attempt at self-materialisation was made by Katie King in April 1872. A face, similar to a death-mask, was seen between the curtains of the cabinet. Gradually the degree of manifestation increased so much that Katie King was able to walk from the cabinet and allowed herself to be recorded with flash photography.

Only once when Florence Cook was under the control of a new spirit guide, Marie, on January 9, 1880, during a materialisation, was she caught cheating.

It may be that the rigorous measurement of mediums, which included tying them up, dipping their hands in dye, and even monitoring them with rudimentary equipment to record any movement, actually diminished their natural powers through the anxiety caused. The standards demanded, especially of physical mediums, to perform wonders on every occasion, led to the discrediting of good mediums on occasions on which they failed, and so to the decline in this art.

Gladys Osborne Leonard

On December 18, 1906, when Mrs Leonard was a young woman, she woke at 2am and saw 'a large, circular patch of light. In this light I saw my mother quite distinctly. Her face looked several years younger than I had seen it a few hours before.'

Her mother died at that moment. So began Mrs Leonard's adult awakening to mediumship. Though Mrs Leonard was, primarily, a mental medium, she functioned through trance and it was Feda, her Hindu Spirit Control, who gave messages from the spirits.

As a medium, Mrs Leonard was continuously investigated for more than 50 years by scientists such as the physicist Sir Oliver Lodge. On September 25, 1915, Lady Lodge visited Mrs Leonard anonymously. The Lodges' late son Raymond, who had recently been killed during the First World War, sent a message through Mrs Leonard: 'Tell Father I have met some friends of his,' and mentioned specifically that he had seen the late Frederick Myers, Founder of the Society for Psychical Research, a close friend of Sir Oliver.

Another medium, Alfred Vout Peters, told Sir Oliver two days later about a photograph of a group of officers with Raymond among them, and on November 25, 1915, a stranger, Mrs Cheves, wrote to Sir Oliver and Lady Lodge saying that she had in her possession a photograph of the officers of the South Lancashire Regiment of which Raymond was second lieutenant. On December 3, 1915, Raymond described himself to Sir Oliver through Mrs Leonard as sitting on the ground with a fellow officer's hand on his shoulder at the time the photograph was taken. During the mediumistic sitting, many other details of the photograph were described, all of which proved accurate when the Lodges subsequently received the print.

Helen Duncan

Helen Duncan, a skilled medium, became a British war security risk in 1941, precisely because she was so gifted. Her crime was that during a seance she contacted the spirit of a dead sailor. The Navy had kept secret the fact that the deceased sailor's ship, the HMS *Barham*, had been sunk some days earlier. Helen continued to give comfort to relatives anxious for news of their sons' or husbands' fate, information that had been withheld by officials.

The Government authorities were terrified she might accurately discern the date of the D-Day Normandy landings. Police raided a seance held by Helen on January 19, 1944, arrested her, and after a seven-day trial she was found guilty of being a witch and sentenced to nine months in prison. Once freed, Helen Duncan returned to her work, but died in 1956, five weeks after another police raid. Her imprisonment shocked many people outside the Spiritualist Movement and eventually led to the Fraudulent Mediums Act of 1951, replacing the Witchcraft Act of 1735.

Examples of Mediumship

I have recorded many examples of mediumship in my case files, some of which I have personally witnessed. However, to avoid any suggestion that a medium may be operating telepathically, the following example is one that was based on information unknown to the sitter. Wayne, who lives in Leicestershire, England, wrote to me about his experiences:

> *About 20 years ago, my wife Jenny and I used to attend the local Spiritualist Church in Kettering. Jenny was an adopted child and longed to know about her real parents. One evening, Jenny was given a message by a medium that there was a lady in Spirit who was watching over her whose name was Peggy. The medium told Jenny that the lady was showing her the tip of her ring finger on her left hand and said that it was missing. Peggy had passed over quite recently from an internal complaint. Jenny could not identify Peggy.*
>
> *About twelve months later, new laws were passed and Jenny obtained her birth certificate. From it we discovered that Jenny had been born to an unmarried mother named Peggy.*
>
> *The door (of Peggy's former house) was opened by a woman who was Jenny's aunt and had been hoping she might call. Peggy had died three years before from cancer of the liver. Peggy had worked in a shoe factory, and several years earlier, a ring on her finger had become trapped in the machine she was operating and had cut off the tip of the ring finger of her left hand to the first joint.*

MIRACLES

What is a Miracle?

Collins Concise Dictionary of the English Language defines a miracle as: a marvellous event attributed to a supernatural cause; any amazing or wonderful event and a marvellous example of something e.g. a miracle cure.

Miracles have occurred in all times and places to people of many faiths and those who have none at the time of the miracle. The crucial aspect from my own research seems to be that a miracle is a life-changing event for those who experience or witness it. What is more, like a stone cast into a pond, a miracle can confirm for those who hear of it that there is a Divine force in the universe who can and does intervene in the lives of men and women, thereby transcending the natural and logical course of events. Though miracles are by their nature endowed with mystical or religious significance, nevertheless they are manifest in physical terms during normal states of consciousness, and are perceived through normal sensory channels, often by a number of people simultaneously, thus for a short time uniting the Divine and spiritual planes.

Traditional Religious Faiths and Miracles

Both Judaism and Christianity recognise the concept of miracles, and they have formed the cornerstones of faith, for example the Exodus of the Jews from Egypt, the parting of the Red Sea and the Resurrection of Christ in Christianity.

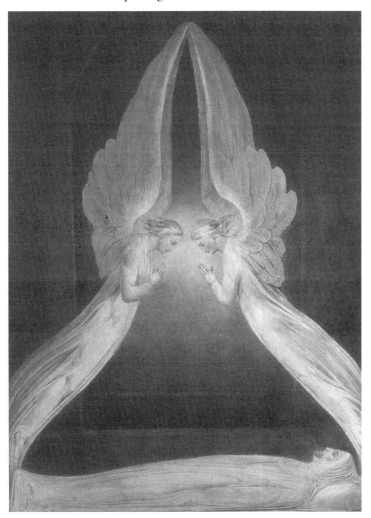

The 'gift of miracles' is mentioned by St Paul in his First Epistle to the Corinthians as special and extraordinary powers endowed by God to only a chosen few, for example saints, primarily for the spiritual good of others rather than of the recipient. Christ, it is believed by the Catholic church, was the only person who could perform miracles when he wished. Thereafter the power to perform miracles was a transient gift that was sometimes manifest through contact with the relics of the saints or visits to sacred shrines, and served as a confirmation of faith.

The Hindu Milk Miracle

The greatest simultaneous universal event in modern times is probably the milk miracle that was witnessed on Thursday September 21, 1995, by people all over the world. Milk is the sacred fluid in the Hindu religion, much as holy water is regarded in Christianity. The ritual offering of milk, fruit, sweets and money to the gods is an established practice in the Hindu faith, and milk is poured over Shiva and Ganesha, his son, during festivals.

The milk miracle was foretold in the Punjab. Pandit Chaman Prakash, Head of the Khampur Shiv Mandir Temple in Chandigargh, was approached by a young woman before sunrise on Thursday September 21. She told him that her sister had dreamed that Ganesha would come to earth to drink milk at 4am. The priest reluctantly opened the Temple, and at 4am the statue accepted milk from a spoon.

News spread throughout India and to Hindu communities all around the world. In India, during Thursday morning, many of the statues of Ganesha were reported to be drinking milk. Within hours, millions of Hindus worldwide flocked to their nearest temple where statues of Ganesha were also witnessed accepting milk. By Thursday evening the phenomena was reported in Calcutta, Madras, Singapore, Hong Kong,

Indonesia, Bangladesh, Nepal, Dubai, Kenya, Germany, Bangkok, Brisbane, Toronto, New York and New Jersey City and throughout the UK. Other idols, Shiva, Krishna and Brahma were also accepting milk.

In the UK, 10,000 people visited the Vishwa Hindu Temple in Southall, West London, where the white marble statue of Nandi, Shiva's sacred mount, was also said to be accepting milk. A few hundred metres away in the home of Asha and Anil, a Hindu couple who came to England from Uganda, a small clay statue also began to drink milk. Before long devotees crowded the small suburban living room, waiting patiently to offer the small painted statue of Ganesha teaspoons of milk.

Asha explained to me: 'My statue is made of clay but when I felt inside it was completely dry and no milk had seeped through. This continued for about a week and then the statue would accept no more.'

From India, confirmation came by Friday afternoon that Ganesha and the other deities had ceased drinking.

The phenomenon was regarded by Hindus as a sign that the problems of the world would be overcome through faith. The fundamentalist World Hindu Council declared the milk-drinking a manifestation of Divine Blessing.

Scientists have put forward many theories to explain away the milk miracle, such as capillary action and natural absorption by marble. But the fact that the statues did not before and have not since accepted milk suggests that this is not the entire story. What is more, where statues were tiny or made of solid metal, as many were, there seems no adequate explanation for the absorption of such relatively large amounts of liquid.

A Modern Muslim Miracle

Mohammed himself did not perform miracles, telling his followers that since all things were made by Allah, they were in themselves signs of his goodness and power. Therefore, small signs of Divinity in the everyday world assumed great religious significance as confirmations of faith and blessing among ordinary Muslims.

One example of this was demonstrated in March 1996 in a terraced home in Bolton, Lancashire. Salim, a local mill worker, opened his house to pilgrims from all over Britain who came to view an open aubergine, fruit of the egg plant, which spelled out in its dark seeds the message in Arabic script: *Ya Allah, Allah exists*, or in another translation, *Oh Allah*.

Salim's wife Ruksana, told reporters:

I had bought three aubergines from the local shop and the same night I had a dream telling me that one of the aubergines was holy. When I opened it, I would find Allah.

When I got up, I discovered my dream was true. As I cut one of the aubergines, the seeds spelled out the name of our God. Although I have always been religious, now I believe with all my heart.

After Ruksana discovered the message, Salim ran to tell the local priest who confirmed it as a sign that Allah was with the people. People from all faiths came and were welcomed by Salim and his wife.

Personal Miracles in the Modern World

My own research has concentrated mainly on the miracles experienced by ordinary men and women whose lives were changed or whose faith was increased by what they regarded as Divine Intervention. The miracles I have described were witnessed independently by a number of people.

Pauline, a nurse living in Australia, described an experience she had in New Zealand:

I was sitting in a Healing Circle that I regularly attended. I half-closed my eyes. The next thing I knew Jesus was standing in front of me in an area of pure light. Jesus had his hands open and his palms uplifted. I asked Him for healing for my father-in-law in Northern Ireland. For some reason I had been worried about my father-in-law for about twelve hours. I did not know that he had been admitted to hospital [for a heart operation] until I went home after the meeting. The brilliant light faded and I found myself falling through blackness, with flashes of colour.

The vision of Jesus had occurred at 8.15pm. In New Zealand we were twelve hours ahead of Northern Ireland. The operation that afternoon had gone wrong. My father-in-law was unconscious and had a very high temperature. My mother-in-law had been warned that he would die and there was no hope. At exactly the moment I had the vision of Jesus, I later discovered, my father-in-law had suddenly woken up with no temperature whatsoever, to the amazement of the staff in intensive care.

The Rosary Miracle

Miraculous signs have been reported over the centuries at sites of religious significance, especially those associated with apparitions of the Virgin Mary.

Des, who lives in Bristol, England, visited Medjugorje in February 1991 with his wife Charmaine. He told me:

My rosary was very special to me as it had been given to me in 1979 by my mother when I still lived in Ireland. It was made up of brown wooden beads, linked by steel-coloured small chains.

We went to Mass on our first day in Medjugorje and during the service I took my rosary from my pocket and saw a thread of gold running through it. I turned to Charmaine and showed her and her eyes filled with joy. Then the transformation stopped, but the links that had changed colour remained a brassy gold.

The strange thing was that not all the links had changed colour, but those that had formed a definite pattern. The four sets of chains running from the cross to the centre were now gold and at 10 regular intervals along the rosary the links had also changed to gold – it was the fourteenth day of the month.

I was suddenly confronted by evidence of another reality. Before that I had hoped that God was true. Now I was shocked to discover that He was indeed true and that I, an ordinary man, had received personal Grace from our Lady.

NEAR-DEATH EXPERIENCES

What is a Near-Death Experience?

The term 'near-death experience' was coined in 1975 by Dr Raymond Moody, Jr, to describe the clinical death experiences of the people in his book, *Life After Life*. The majority of these experiences occur when a person momentarily dies during an operation or accident, or is close to death due to illness. However, remarkably similar experiences can occur at times of emotional and spiritual intensity, for example women who are giving birth, even when no drugs are used to alleviate pain and the woman's life is not in danger. Saints and religious mystics have reported related phenomena, for example during deep prayer states or meditation, and others can occasionally reach such heights during altered states of consciousness. There is obviously an overlap between this and the far more widespread out-of-body state, but near-death experiences (NDEs) are far more prolonged and cannot be deliberately induced.

Because true near-death experiences do occur spontaneously and mainly under crisis, they cannot be replicated in the laboratory and so evidence lies in collecting the testimonies of those who have experienced them and deducing patterns from these. The organisation International Association for Near-Death Studies (IANDS), was founded in 1978 to study the phenomena and its impact upon human consciousness. Though the crisis NDE has a physical trigger, the experience is intensely spiritual.

The near-death experience is reported by religious and non-religious people alike, regardless of their culture, race or education, and is remarkably consistent in its characteristics. NDEs have been reported over the centuries and it has been suggested that these originally contributed, at least partly, to religious concepts of life after death.

A third or more of people who have suffered a brush with death or similar crisis may, during the period of unconsciousness, report something akin to a near-death experience. Gallup Polls and other surveys have estimated 13 million adult NDEs in the USA alone. With children, the figure is significantly higher; Dr Melvin Morse, the main researcher into this field, has estimated that about 70 per cent of children who die momentarily in an accident or operation or are on the point of death in a serious illness, have a near-death experience. The adult near-death experience includes some of the following sensations:

- A sense that the self has moved beyond the body, usually by floating. The person looks down on his or her own inert body. The person is later able to describe this scene in detail, including words spoken, and even objects on shelves that could not be seen from the bed, disproving the theory that the unconscious mind was filtering information.

- Travelling through a dark space or tunnel towards a point of light, sometimes accompanied by rushing wind. This can occasionally be frightening, especially if the journey seems to be downwards.

- Reaching a place filled with golden or white light, usually resulting in a sensation of bliss. There may be beautiful gardens or cotton wool clouds.

- Meeting deceased relations, recognised from life or verified as relations after the experience by old photographs. Women giving birth, like children, may see living relatives as well who act as intermediaries between the two worlds.

- There may also be encounters with sacred beings of light, or icons such as angels from one's own or other religious traditions. Alternatively, an authoritative voice may be heard.

- A life review may occur either while travelling down the tunnel or on encountering the divine being/s. There may also be a sense of understanding the mysteries of the universe, insight that is lost after the experience.

- At this point either the relative or angelic being will instruct the experiencer to return to life, or there may be a dialogue as a result of which the decision is reached to return, perhaps because there is a child to care for back on earth or unfinished work. The decision to return is followed almost immediately by the sensation of returning to the body, sometimes quite dramatically accompanied by an awareness of physical pain as well as sorrow at leaving the other world.

While such experiences are usually immensely enriching, offering reassurances that there is life after death and often changing a person's whole life view – one woman took a theology degree after her NDE – for a few it may be terrifying. Counselling may be needed in such cases, especially where the person who experienced the NDE was not believed by doctors or relations.

Children's Near-Death Experiences

Young children have pictorial, vivid experiences, in some instances almost shamanistic. He or she may initially briefly see living relatives and then deceased relatives who may have died before the child was born, a deceased pet, angels or a god figure from the child's religion, as well as lights, tunnels and gardens. They may also be immersed in a comforting darkness akin to the womb. Ten-year-old Megan whose case I studied described a near-death experience near Christmas in which she was following Father Christmas who was rising into the light.

Six-year-old Jacques, who was pronounced dead after a fall in India, spoke of:

… walking along a rough-hewn tunnel with walls that looked as if the rocks were of copper and gold lit by firebrands on the walls. I came to a round chamber, and seated on a marble seat of very beautiful design was this enormous figure of a man in a white robe with long,

flowing white hair and a beard. With a lovely smile, he pushed me back with the words, 'Not now, not now'.

Impartial Evidence for Near-Death Experiences

I have come across several cases when at the time a person was visiting another realm as part of the process of an NDE, a relative who did not know that the person was dying has witnessed him or her in an out-of-body state, or even shared the vision. Adam, an engineer from Bristol, England, described to me:

My father was in hospital for a minor operation, but he had a bad reaction and at 3.10am he blacked out. His heart temporarily stopped and he momentarily clinically died. I knew nothing of this but at 3.10am I woke up suddenly with an incredible feeling of lightness.

I was half-way out of my body when I felt my father slipping away. I was willing him to pull and to fight and was pulling with him. After about 20 minutes I went back to sleep.

When I visited my father early the next day, I told him of my night-time experience and he spoke to the nurse who showed me the record of the time my father had died. He told me that as he was dying he knew I still needed his help and so he had pulled himself back.

Experiences from children are especially valuable as evidence, since they would know nothing of the classic characteristics of the NDE. Fourteen-year-old Ben's experience is remarkable because he is autistic and he described himself during an operation, 'being a ghost'.

Ben's mother explained:

Ben communicates through a mixture of speech and sign language. I asked Ben what he meant and he said that when he was asleep during the operation, he was looking down from the ceiling and saw himself lying on the table as the doctors operated on him. He said the doctors were wearing masks and green gowns and he was lying with his eyes closed.

He described going through the wall to a place like a big cloud. There he saw Sai Baba who welcomed him and materialised vibhuti [sacred healing ash] which he then sprinkled over the site of Ben's operation. Then Ben described his grandmother's dog who had been put to sleep 18 months previously. Ben said the dog was now 'new' and was jumping up so excitedly at Baba.

Ben also saw the 'taxi lady'. She had been the escort for the school taxi and had died very suddenly just before Christmas last year. She hugged him and told him to be a good boy. Then he mentioned another lady with eye glasses who turned out to be his great Auntie Annie who had died two years earlier.

Ben saw the doctor tapping him on the arm, telling him to wake up. He went quickly back into his body and woke up. Ben does not usually display any emotions but as he was telling me about his experience, he kept wiping tears from his eyes.

OUT-OF-BODY EXPERIENCES

It is estimated that more than a third of people in the Western world have had at least one out-of-body experience. In the rest of the world these are a more common occurrence. In tribes as far apart as Greenland and New Guinea the soul is said to travel astrally during sleep to live in a special dream world, and these experiences are remembered on waking.

The Australian Aboriginal nocturnal walkabout, not only by *mekigars*, or magic men, but ordinary people, is as real to them as daytime physical journeying. As contact with the material Westernised world increases, some Aborigines, like other indigenous peoples similarly affected, seem to be losing direct, easy access to this natural ability.

Buddhists believe that adepts can visit the world of Brahma in a mind-made body, complete with all its limbs. Shamans, magic men who enter into states of altered consciousness (see p. 74), are able to induce trance states whereby they travel astrally to obtain herds or shoals of fish for their people to hunt or to recover a lost soul. Winged shamans with bird heads to suggest flight practices are recorded in Palaeolithic cave paintings.

Etheric Projection and Astral Travel

Eileen Campbell and J.H. Brennan, in *The Dictionary of Mind, Body and Spirit*, distinguish between etheric projection, 'stepping out of the body to function like a ghost' and true astral projection, which is 'closer to visionary experience and is believed to be experienced nightly by everyone during dreams'.

The majority of out-of-body experiences involve etheric body travel, but there are many overlaps between the two states. Etheric journeyings involve feeling the self rising above our body and seeing it sleeping or resting below. This can occur in times of illness, stress, relaxation, or is sometimes triggered by a sudden noise.

Though out-of-body experiences are usually spontaneous, with practice it is possible to control the floating sensation, and even to evoke an astral journey, the state in which we dream or daydream of flying or floating and

noteworthy is that the phenomena occurred sporadically, as with observed poltergeist activity. While electromagnetic pollution is not the entire answer and would not explain cases that were reported hundreds of years ago, it may be that the closeness of power cables to a home, as in one example, may increase the potency of psychokinetic activity. Indeed, the advent of mobile phones and their masts may correlate with future increased poltergeist activity.

The Australian Guyra Poltergeist

On April 8, 1921, banging on the walls and a shower of stones broke the windows of a small cottage just outside Guyra near Sydney, belonging to the Bowen family. The continuing attacks with stones as large as walnuts were centred around 12-year-old Minnie Bowen. Alarmed by local panic, the State Government sent a team of detectives from Sydney who maintained a constant surveillance as the banging shook the cottage to its foundations and was audible to observers a hundred yards away.

Ben Davey of Uralla, a student of Spiritualism and Theosophy, discovered that May, a daughter of Mrs Bowen's by a former marriage, had died about three months earlier. Minnie admitted that May had communicated with her. This admission led to a short pause in poltergeist activity, but after its resumption Minnie was sent to her grandmother's house in Glen Innes, 37 miles (60km) away. The poltergeist activity followed the child and eventually she returned home. Gradually, as is quite common, the activity diminished and eventually ceased.

The Enfield Poltergeist

Poltergeist activity began in late August of 1977 at the home of Peggy Harper, a divorcee in her mid-forties with four children. The paranormal researcher, Maurice Grosse, plus a reporter from the Daily Mirror initially investigated. Grosse was subsequently joined by the psychic author Guy Lyon Playfair for a study of the case that continued for two years. As the incidents – and media interest – escalated, interference occurred with electrical systems in the house, camera flashes were drained of power, BBC Radio reporters discovered that their tapes had been erased and metal inside recording devices was warped.

Incidents included loud rapping sounds on walls and floors, furniture apparently moving of its own volition and being thrown downstairs by an invisible power. Toys, Lego bricks and marbles would fly across the room, the marbles and bricks becoming hot in the process. There were outbreaks of fires which were spontaneously extinguished. Activity centred around 11-year-old Janet who began to speak in a harsh rough voice, identified at one time as 'Bill', who claimed to have died in the house, a fact that was later verified but not known to the family at the times of the possession.

Grosse discovered that the poltergeist source of energy interacted with him and would rap out answers to simple questions. Janet was taken to Maudsley Hospital in South London, specialists in neurological disorders, but during the six weeks she was there, no physical or mental abnormalities were discovered. However, while Janet was in hospital, the poltergeist activity stopped.

Subsequent investigation suggested that initially the poltergeist effects were genuine but that the children, Janet and her 13-year-old sister Rose, may have resorted to trickery to satisfy the media, and also because the attention had become central to their lives. The girls may have been unwilling to let the activity peter out, as it inevitably does in poltergeist cases. Certainly in the case of Grosse, the practical and emotional help given to the family may have relieved the trauma that triggered the original attack.

PRECOGNITION OR PREMONITIONS

Precognition or foreknowledge can be manifest as prophecies about general or global future events. But for every prophet such as Nostradamus are a thousand ordinary men, women and children who may have previously displayed no unusual psychic powers, yet are suddenly aware of impending danger to a family member or friend. This forewarning may occur in a dream, be heard as a disembodied voice, or be experienced as a feeling of dread about a particular person or a specific future event; it is a fear that is qualitatively different and far more intense and focused than free-floating anxiety. Children and mothers are especially adept at displaying spontaneous precognitive powers, in the former case perhaps because natural intuitive abilities are not limited by logic and learning. Maternal concern for a child's well-being seems to call into existence a strong radar of protection that does alert mothers to a child's imminent danger or distress, whether an infant or adult (see p. 284).

This spontaneous predictive ability is very different from trying to tell the future through divinatory or mediumistic means, and over the past 10 years I have collected hundreds of cases of premonitions that in a high proportion of incidents have been authenticated by a third party, usually a friend or relation to whom the premonition was voiced. However, as with other psychic abilities, these spontaneous, emotionally driven examples cannot be replicated in the laboratory. Examples in the field suggest even more remarkable, spontaneous precognitive abilities among the general public than formal testing would ever indicate.

Premonitions in Dreams

David, a Birmingham vicar and radio presenter, described to me:

I had a dream in which a car came out of a field and smashed into our family car. I told my wife, but I was not worried as I was not anticipating any travel that day.

However, unexpectedly I was asked to make a journey and we set off in the car. I came to a spot and recognised it from my dream. I told my wife this was the place the accident had occurred, but she reassured me that there was not even any other traffic.

At that moment a car did come hurtling out of the field. I swerved into the ditch and the family was saved. I believe this was because I was alerted.

David was fairly certain his dream referred to an event that would happen quickly and trusted his forewarning. Premonitions are variously attributed to an outside source, God, a deceased relation, a guardian angel, or to the deep inner intuitive abilities that allow us access to information beyond the conscious sphere. Although patterns can be derived from case studies and precognitive abilities demonstrated experimentally, the explanation for the power remains elusive.

It may be that premonitions occur more easily during dreams because that is the time the conscious barriers of the mind are at their lowest, thereby allowing information from a normally inaccessible source to surface. Often it is the intensity and seeming reality of the dream that lingers the next day that separates it from general nightmares that may express fears as symbolic disasters. From a survival point of view, premonitions are valuable in allowing people to change their actions or be alerted to danger, whether seemingly entirely unpredictable as David's was, or perhaps a result of a cue that the subconscious mind has noted, such as a flat tyre or loose wire. Early humans may have relied on this ability to protect them from predators while hunting or gathering.

Though the majority of premonitions do centre on the personal sphere, some people link into a national disaster, and this differs from prophecy in that the premonition usually occurs shortly before the predicted event. Those few who regularly predict disasters are closer to modern-day prophets. But there can be a terrible dilemma, especially if the details are not specific. James told me that when he was thirteen 'I had a dream about a big boat that left the harbour then went half-way out and then crashed and was lying on its side. In the morning, I told my mum and she said, "Don't worry". I wondered if I ought to phone the police, but I thought they would think it was a stunt or I was a crank. Then two days later there was the Zeebrugge disaster.'

One Theory for Precognition

Dr Chet B. Snow, in his book *Dreams of the Future*, writes:

Our use of past, present and future is – relative – due in part to the dual hemispheres of our brains, we have two fundamentally different ways of consciously expressing what our minds know, including future predictions. Thus we either develop right brain imaginational and prophetic systems to tell us what tomorrow will bring or we set up rational left brain ways of collecting, organising and comparing as much past and present sensory information as possible and try to predict from correlations among the data. Today we call the first kind predicting and the second forecasting.

Experiments to Test Premonitory Powers

In experiments carried out by the late Helen Wambach, a hypnotherapist, Snow reports that she discovered that at least half the lightly hypnotised subjects in her workshops could pick up thoughts and feelings telepathically, and between 50 and 60 per cent consistently received answers and impressions before they heard the questions.

Professor Dean Radin, a parapsychologist at the university of Nevada, carried out tests on premonitions of impending bad news in 1997. He studied the so-called orienting response, the physiological changes triggered when we are exposed to something we find emotionally disturbing – typically our heart rate drops, we start to perspire and our pupils dilate. Less noticeable but more easily measured are a fall in both the electrical resistance of the skin and volume of blood passing through the fingers. Radin reasoned that if people could sense when they were about to have an emotional shock, it might be possible to detect these physiological changes a few moments before the trigger occurred.

He collected scores of images of emotionally shocking scenes, such as close-ups of mutilated bodies, and mixed them randomly among a much larger number of innocuous scenes of cheerful people and pleasant landscapes. He then wired up subjects to see if their physiological responses changed significantly just before they were shown a shocking image, but remained flat for the innocuous ones, which he considered would be evidence of the existence of a sixth sense.

Sitting in front of a computer screen in Radin's laboratory, each subject pressed a button to start the experiment. The computer would choose an image at random then wait five seconds before displaying it on the screen which remained blank until then. The image was displayed for three seconds before the screen went blank again. The procedure was repeated 40 times and the subjects' skin resistance, heart rate and blood volume were constantly measured.

Radin discovered that, as expected, the emotional images provoked major changes in the physiological response of the subject. However, he also found that similar changes also appeared three seconds before the emotional images were shown while the screen remained blank. When the next picture was a soothing landscape the subjects did not respond, supporting the hypothesis that subjects could sense the content of the next picture several seconds before it was shown.

Joyous Premonitions

Although premonitions are usually associated with disasters, there can be ones that bring hope. Maura who lives in Mexico City wrote to me saying:

I had lost two babies which had left me in a terrible depression. I was in bed and (my second son) Omar, then four years old, stood by my side talking and playing. Suddenly he said very seriously, 'When my brother is twelve years old and I am seven years old, you will get pregnant again and this time we will have a baby.'

Before this happened I lost another baby [three babies in a row] and also lost all hope of having another child. My husband and I decided that we would not try again. In January 1990 I got pregnant again when my son Rodrigo was twelve and Omar seven. This time my baby was born. He is four months old now. During this pregnancy I had started to bleed as in the previous ones. So I told my sons not to get excited about the baby and to be prepared to not have him.

Omar looked at me straight in the eyes and said loud, clear and sure: 'This baby will be born.' It happened as he foretold.

PROPHECY

Prophecy refers to precognition about global events by a seer who is chosen to convey warnings or messages of importance to humankind. Prophecies tend to be far-reaching, sometimes referring to events hundreds or even thousands of years in the future, as in the case of the Mayan prophecies.

This Divine knowledge, believed to be emanating from God, or in earlier times the deities of the prevalent culture, may be manifest either as words, writing or signs, known as omens, through visions, dreams, as discarnate voices or in an ecstatic state, known in mystical terminology as rapture. The Sibyls, or prophetesses, of the Classical world would sometimes chew laurel or bay leaves and inhale other herbal substances with hallucinogenic properties, such as incense or the fumes that were naturally emitted from the rocks in oracular caves.

Prophecy is regarded, according to some modern interpretations, as wisdom from within the prophet, drawn from the collective mind or tribal voice of humankind, to which the prophet connects in a higher state of consciousness. Even where disaster is foretold, as with the apocalyptic prophecies of all cultures, the wisdom offers a chance of redemption through a change of attitude or action by a state, a leader or humankind in general.

Prophecies can also herald the ending of difficult times. This was manifest in the prophetic visions of the 19th-century Native North American visionary, the Oglala Sioux shaman Black Elk, who in old age foretold that the sacred hoop or circle of life would be restored and all nations would shelter under the great flowering tree in the centre of the circle, through the wider dissemination of the Native North American philosophy, and that this was the new purpose of the dispossessed indigenous peoples of North America.

Who Are the Prophets?

Prophets are intermediaries who may be set apart from ordinary people and everyday life, perhaps adopting celibacy, isolation, following special diets and cleansing rituals, as well as developing themselves spiritually through prayer, rites and meditation, in order to be a pure vessel for higher communication. Though the great Old Testament prophets such as Isaiah or Samuel are the archetypes of prophetic wisdom, almost anyone can be the recipient of profound and global prophecies. Samuel himself prophesied as a child, and the Marian prophecies at Fatima in 1917 were given to three peasant children, eight-year-old Lucia Santos and her two cousins, Francisco and Jacinta Marto, who were tending the sheep.

Many of the early prophetesses were female, following an oracular tradition that began in sacred caverns, inspired by worship of the Mother Goddess.

The Oracle at Delphi

The most famous oracular site in the Ancient world was at Delphi in Greece, whose name comes from *delphys*, meaning the womb. The Mother Goddess in her form of Delphyne as Goddess of the Earth's Womb or Creation was worshipped here with her son/consort Python, the Great Lightning serpent whom, it is said, descended into the womb to fertilise the Mother Goddess. In this sense, Python pre-dated all other gods and was later called the Dark Sun, Apollo's alter ego.

According to legend, thousands of years ago Kouretas, a shepherd, told villagers that his goats acted strangely whenever they grazed near a particular opening in the earth. His neighbours were curious and entered the cavern, went into a trance and began to speak prophetically. As a result of many similar experiences that in a few instances ended tragically, a priestess was appointed to the shrine and was later adopted as the Sibyl.

The Ancient Greeks rededicated the shrine to Apollo. The Oracle at Delphi, consulted by kings and leaders throughout the civilised world, was destroyed by the Christian emperor Arcadius in AD398. The prophetic responses were frequently enigmatic, so that an unwise seeker might interpret the words as affirmation of personal ambitions without considering their deeper implications.

The Cumaean Sibyl

The Apollonian Sibyl who lived by the spring at Cumae, was the chief oracle of Ancient Rome. According to history, the Cumaean Sibyl originally offered Tarquinius Superbus (534–510BC) nine books of oracular utterances written in Greek hexameters. Tarquinius refused, but discovered on subsequent visits by her to his palace that she was gradually destroying the books. When the Sibyl offered the remaining three books for the same price as the original nine, he agreed and the Sibylline Prophecies were carefully guarded and consulted in times of earthquake or potential diaster. After fire destroyed the books, prophecies were collected by envoys from several oracles to serve the same purpose.

The early Cumaean Sibyl would write her prophecies on oak leaves and lay them at the edge of her cave, from which they were blown by the wind, thus requiring the petitioner to piece together the mysteries of the revelations – again part of the process of the need to interpret and not just follow prophecy blindly. The Cumaean Sibyl foretold the birth of Christ, and was in myth said to have led the Trojan exile Aeneas to the Underworld where his dead father Anchises told him he would found the Roman race which would produce many great heroes.

Cumae was destroyed by soldiers from a Saracen fleet in AD915.

Mother Shipton

Mother Shipton in a sense followed the same female oracular tradition, being born in 1488 in a cave at Knaresborough near Leeds in Britain. From the first, she displayed prophetic gifts predicting major historical events, such as the defeat of the Spanish Armada in 1588 and the Great Fire of London in 1666, as well as modern technology.

Carriages without horses shall go.
And accidents fill the world with woe.
Around the world thoughts shall fly
In the twinkling of an eye.
Under water men shall walk,
Shall ride, shall sleep, shall talk;
In the air men shall be seen
In white, in black, and in green.
Iron in the water shall float
As easy as a wooden boat.

Nostradamus

However, it is Nostradamus whose prophecies have attracted the most veneration over the centuries. Nostradamus was an astrologer who was born in 1503. He published 942 prophecies in all, beginning with the first volume of the *Centuries* in 1555. He wrote ten in all and each century contains 100 prophecies, except one which only has 42. Each prophecy is a quatrain or a four-line poem. They were written mainly in French, interspersed with phrases of Italian, Greek and Latin. Nostradamus said that he deliberately made the quatrains obscure, using symbols, metaphors and changing proper names by adding or removing letters, because he feared accusations of witchcraft.

He is credited with successfully foretelling the rise and fall of Napoleon, the Second World War and the fall of the Berlin Wall. Some also say that Nostradamus predicted the end of the world at the end of the 20th century, but as the date has passed the original prophecy has been reinterpreted as warning of both natural and human-induced disasters in 1999, of which there were many.

His most famous prophecy concerns Adolf Hitler and one translation reads:

Beasts ferocious from hunger will swim across rivers:
The greater part of the region will be against the Hister,
The great one will cause it to be dragged in an iron cage,
When the German child will observe nothing.

In spite of other interpretations, such as that of Robert Graves who links Hister with the name of a river Ister, now the Danube, and the prophecy with the 16th-century Charles I of Spain, the references to Hitler and the Second World War would seem quite clear.

Edgar Cayce

Edgar Cayce, who was born in 1877, was considered one of the most remarkable US psychic healers of the 20th century. He cured many a number of serious as well as minor illnesses and diseases, and while in a trance state displayed detailed knowledge of medicine and of drugs that were not yet on the market or had fallen into disuse, though he had no formal training.

Called the sleeping prophet, Cayce would, during his trances, make prophecies not related to the purpose of the reading. He predicted the First and Second World Wars, the independence of India and the 1929 stock market crash. He also predicted, 15 years before the event, the creation of the State of Israel. Six months before the 1929 financial disaster, in a trance he warned people to sell everything they owned. In October 1935, Cayce spoke of the coming holocaust in Europe. His most disturbing predictions, however, concern vast geographical upheavals which by the year 1998 he claimed would result in the destruction of New York, the disappearance of most of Japan, and a cataclysmic change in northern Europe. Though the last have not come true, there have been vast upheavals in the world's geological features, partly due to global warming.

PSYCHIC CHILDREN

Mighty prophet, seer blest, on whom those truths do rest
Which we are toiling all our lives to find.

That is how William Wordsworth, the Romantic poet, described young children in his poem 'Ode on the Intimations of Immortality', a view diametrically opposed to those of the American behavioural psychologists such as John Watson, and the 17th-century rationalist John Locke, who believed the child is a *tabula rasa*, a blank slate to be written on by educators.

From my own research into this area over 11 years, I have discovered that many children do display seemingly inexplicable psychic powers without being aware of them. These are not generally of the overtly spectacular spoon-bending or levitation genre, though quite tiny children do routinely describe classic out-of-body experiences without having any knowledge of the subject, floating downstairs being the most common sensation (see Out-of-Body Experiences, p. 298). But toddlers effortlessly and frequently mind hop, reading other people's minds, most frequently the mother's (see Maternal Intuition, p. 284), make predictions that come true and see ghosts that are later independently verified.

Testing these abilities is problematic, since few of the incidents are replicable under test conditions, and the only witness is the mother who is not regarded in conventional research as an independent witness. For this reason, quite remarkable examples of psychic ability go unrecorded and are not taken seriously by the majority of scientists. Tests tend to be confined to card guessing or to fairly trivial tasks involving guessing the colour of sweets in packets. Cases abound of children caught cheating under test conditions, either through boredom or to please the tester when spontaneous powers disappear in the laboratory.

One of the most inexplicable cases, and one that inspired my own research in this field, was when my young son Jack told me one morning at breakfast that his father had fallen off his motorbike, but was all right; at that moment, or as near as we can ascertain, my husband John's motorbike was skidding on a patch of oil 40 miles (64km) away on the M4 motorway in west London. John did fall off, but, as Jack told me, he was relatively unscathed. Coincidence? The timing was so precise and the remark so out of context that it would seem unlikely to be chance. In addition, thousands of other case studies I have collected from parents, especially mothers whose testimony I rate highly, have confirmed that such incidents are not uncommon.

Children have traditionally been regarded as having second sight. Until the mid-19th century, young boys would travel around Europe interpreting the crystal ball for their frequently fraudulent masters. In Ancient Greece, virgin boys were used for 'scrying' – divining the future by gazing into bowls of pure water lit by burning torches (see p.136). They studied the changes in the water and invoked the gods or demons, whom it was believed would provide a meaning, but which most probably came from the child's unconscious mind, uncluttered by rational processes.

Telepathy in young children is the most common psychic experience reported. During the 1960s, Dr Ernesto Spinelli was unique in carrying out successful tests with children as young as three, that seemed to show that small children had considerable telepathic powers. He found that three year olds did best of all, and the apparent ability declined from then on until, at the age of eight, the results were like those of most adults, the same as chance guessing. Dr Spinelli thinks that telepathic powers come from the same source as ordinary thought, but that in the young child this ability has not been suppressed by learning. Telepathic powers are a kind of externalised thinking that disappears once the child learns to do his thinking inside his head.

He told me in response to my own findings that most examples of routine telepathy occurred when the child was relaxed or travelling:

My own feelings are that this is linked with the limitations of self-consciousness that are typically imposed, but which become more blurred when one is in a relaxed, meditative or altered state. Since young children are only just beginning to have a clearly defined sense and restrictive sense of self, it is possible that their superior ability at telepathic tasks is a reflection of their open self-consciousness. Telepathy only strikes us as odd or unusual because we have a sense of self-consciousness, a notion that our thoughts are ours and ours alone.

The same concept would explain how children are able to make predictions and see ghosts, simply because to them such phenomena are not unusual, or in Words-worthian terms they can pass easily between dimensions.

Imaginary friends are a common feature of childhood. Surveys have shown that about a fifth of young children seem to have permanent invisible companions. Among gifted children the proportion rises steeply. The US psychologist Lewis Terman found that of 554 gifted children aged between five and 13, 72 per cent of girls had permanent invisible companions and 37 per cent of boys. From my own research, a proportion of these seem to be more than imaginary, and Spiritualists believe that children have spirit guides, perhaps children who had died young.

Jan is now a mother of three children and lives in Berkshire, but she still remembers and believes in the reality of her childhood invisible friend, a girl named Jellot: 'She wore clothes that weren't like mine, old-fashioned, and her brown dress used to come below her knee.' Jan still insists that Jellot's hand felt warm to her and could be held like anyone else's. Some evidence came in a later incident that demonstrated that Jellot was perhaps a discarnate being and not a product of Jan's imagination.

One day I was sitting with Mum in our small front room (we shared a house with an old man), listening to Listen with Mother on the radio. I was about four. There was a knock at the door and I went to answer it. She hadn't heard the knock. I turned the big handle. Jellot was standing there.

'Oh, hello, Jellot,' I said. 'Yes, I'll tell Mum.'

'Mum, why has Aunty Bea died?'

Aunty Bea was the old lady who lived across the road.

Mum told me not to be silly, but a neighbour came over in the afternoon to say that Aunty Bea had died in the night and they (the police) had found the body.

How could Jan have known that Aunty Bea was dead unless she was told by her invisible friend?

Equally remarkable are the number of children who see deceased grandmothers or great-grandmothers whom they perhaps never knew and yet will describe down to the last detail, including the voice and special phrases or details from many years before, perhaps when the children's parents were young or which again are verified by older surviving family members. These grandmothers seem to act as guardian angels to their grandchildren (see Angels, p. 144). In the case of Sadie who lives in Yorkshire, her son formed a bond with a great-grandma, Jayne, who had seen him only once as an infant shortly before she died. Sadie explained:

After my husband Glen's grandmother's death we continued to visit his father regularly. One Sunday when Lewis was four, Lewis was playing on the living room floor at Glen's grandfather's house.

'Where's that lady gone?' he asked suddenly. 'There was a lady with dark hair sitting there.'

He was staring at the chair where Glen's grandmother always sat. When we got home, we asked him about the lady.

'She had dark curly hair, big glasses and a mark on her neck,' he told us.

Jayne had worn big glasses, had dark curly hair and had a dark mole that was very noticeable on her neck.

'She had her hands out like this,' said Lewis, putting out his hands in the way his great-grandmother had cradled him as an infant. Lewis had never seen a photograph of Jayne. Those that existed were in family albums he had never been shown.

But even a photograph would not have revealed the mole because it was on the back of her neck.

A rational explanation for the reappearance of grandparents could be that the child is confusing a memory with reality. In Lewis's case, he had never known his great-grandmother. What is more, a child will describe an old lady or man who comes into their bedroom, usually immediately after the family have moved into a new house. Enquiries from neighbours invariably confirm the child's description as the former occupant of the property who died there or had lived there for many years before dying in hospital.

Though psychic abilities may become dormant during the school years, adolescence causes a resurgence of these powers as again the barriers of self are lowered and the teenager comes to question the world around him or her. But while for a young child a prophecy is something of which he or she may be totally unaware and it is the mother who later realises the significance of a child's words, for adolescents to predict a disaster may be very distressing. Berenice who lives in Wiltshire and is now in her seventies, told me that when her father James was 12, he was walking past a wall that workmen were erecting when he heard a voice say: 'By tomorrow they will all be dead.'

The boy did not know what to do and said nothing. The next day the wall collapsed and all the workmen were killed. James felt responsible for their death, although of course even if he had spoken out he would not have been believed, especially in Victorian times. But the guilt lingered for many years and James shut his mind entirely to any intuitive faculties he possessed.

Things have not improved significantly, certainly in the UK, for though sex, drugs and alcohol are openly discussed in schools with quite young children, the para-

PSYCHIC POWERS AND STRANGE PHENOMENA

normal is all too often a taboo subject. Few teachers are trained to deal with a child who claims to have seen a ghost, especially of a dead sibling. Particularly in lower socio-economic groups in the UK, I have come across several mothers who have been investigated by social workers for suspected abuse, or whose young children have been referred to psychiatrists because they claim to have been visited in their bedrooms by a dead grandparent or strangely dressed old man or woman. Official statistics would suggest that 10 per cent of children have paranormal experiences. I would estimate it closer to two-thirds, certainly in the pre-school age group. Teenage magazines tend to focus on more bizarre and sensational aspects of the paranormal which may leave young people feeling very alone or afraid of demonic possession and evil spirits, or tempted to experiment with ouija boards at a time when their natural psychic abilities have re-emerged.

PSYCHOKINESIS

What is Psychokinesis?

Psychokinesis is the creation of movement in physical objects by the exercise of psychic or mental powers, which may be manifest as either a conscious or more usually as a spontaneous and unconscious ability. Telekinesis, described as the movement of objects by scientifically inexplicable means, for example by psychic power, is a virtually interchangeable term.

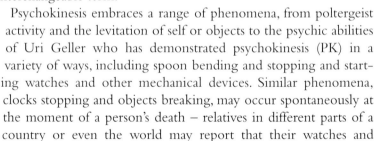

Psychokinesis embraces a range of phenomena, from poltergeist activity and the levitation of self or objects to the psychic abilities of Uri Geller who has demonstrated psychokinesis (PK) in a variety of ways, including spoon bending and stopping and starting watches and other mechanical devices. Similar phenomena, clocks stopping and objects breaking, may occur spontaneously at the moment of a person's death – relatives in different parts of a country or even the world may report that their watches and clocks stopped at the moment of a parent or grandparent's death, a time that is later verified by hospital records. The power is also implicated in absent healing, magic spells and curses, the sudden appearance and disappearance of objects, the luminosity of objects, weather spells to create rain, wind or sunshine, even the teleportation of a person or object from one destination to another, a power demonstrated by many religious figures including Sai Baba.

Mind or Spirit Power?

One theory is that psychokinesis is not a power of the mind at all, but of the spirits operating through the human mind. Evidence for this is suggested by the fact that physical mediums, when in trance, have caused heavy tables to lift (see p. 287). In poltergeist activity (see p. 301), large objects have apparently travelled through walls and furniture has been thrown that subsequently could not be lifted by a strong adult. In contrast, in experiments only very small objects have been deliberately moved by mind power. But it may be that under circumstances of a trance and in situations where the emotions of family members, especially adolescent girls, seem to be triggering poltergeist activity, the mind may have great powers that are only manifest at times of deep emotion or detachment from the body. This is demonstrated when a mother displays almost superhuman strength in lifting heavy objects, even a car or lorry, off her injured child.

In some Far Eastern philosophies, for example the Hindu tantric tradition, it is believed that by meditation on the chakras or psychic energy centres (see p. 17), *siddhas*, or supernormal powers, including levitation, could be attained by dedicated yogis. Even in cases of apparent spirit possession, where the possessed person has been lifted, seemingly by invisible hands, it may be that a troubled mind is implicated and that exorcism or sprinkling with holy water takes away the powerful inner negativity that is causing the phenomenon.

The History of Psychokinesis

The term 'psychokinesis' is derived from the Greek words *psyche* meaning breath, life, or soul, and *kinein* meaning to move. The power has been manifest throughout history by saints, mystics and magicians. For example, in the Acts of the Apostles 16, v19 onwards, it is described how St Paul and Silas, who were in prison in Ephesus, prayed and at midnight their chains were broken and the prison doors opened. Druids meanwhile were adept at cloud dissolving (see p. 107).

Since the 1930s, psychokinesis has been investigated extensively in both America and Russia. Previously, PK had been investigated only in the field at demonstrations of physical mediumship. The American parapsychologist J.B. Rhine began research into this field in 1934, working initially with a gambler who claimed that he could influence the fall of the dice. Early experimental data showed results far beyond the probabilities of chance.

During the late 1960s, the American physicist Helmut Schmidt created an electronic coin flipper that removed any possibility of cheating by subjects, one of the main criticisms of earlier experiments. Using this, some subjects successfully influenced by thought whether coins fell as heads or tails. From this invention were developed computerised random event generators and these have produced significant results in the field of psychokinesis.

In 1968, Nina Kulagina, a Russian housewife, demonstrated for Western investigators her psychokinetic powers to move and levitate objects, which included the ability to affect by thought the rate of the heartbeat of a frog, which had been removed from the animal (but was still attached to its body). Eventually she stopped the heart. This perhaps morally dubious experiment demonstrated the effect of negative thoughts on others and perhaps the potential power of curses.

The Geller Effect – Demonstrations of Psychokinesis

Since the 1960s, Uri Geller has conducted numerous experiments on television in which audiences at home have reported that broken watches and appliances suddenly started to work again, while their cutlery bent as they watched Geller perform. The fact that Geller has not replicated these experiments under laboratory conditions may indicate that while scientific methods can measure relatively minor, although remarkable, effects such as psychokinetic coin flipping, many demonstrable effects can only be observed in the field. Indeed, formal measurement may actually block the powers it seeks to investigate. However, success did come when Ingo Swann, a New York artist, demonstrated experimentally that he could change the temperature of an object close to him by one degree.

The healing of plants and animals and the damaging of plants by negative thoughts have also been demonstrated experimentally, and the latter may offer an explanation for ancient fertility rituals, where couples made love in the fields on May Eve and other festivals to make the crops grow.

By hooking plants up to electronic equipment, researchers discovered that plants respond intensely to the thoughts of people in their environment. The death or threat of death to living cells, whether human, plant or animal, caused intense electromagnetic reactions in plants that were not personally threatened. One plant energy researcher, Marcel Vogel, experimented with children and plants, instructing the children to move their hands backwards and forwards gently over the leaves. Eventually, the plants began to sway with the movement of the child's hand, although there was no physical contact between the child and the plant and no breeze.

Levitation

Levitation is a phenomenon of psychokinesis in which objects, people and animals are lifted into the air without any visible physical means and float or fly about. Levitation has been associated with physical mediumship (see p. 287), shamanism (see p. 74) and mystical states (see p. 40).

Numerous incidents of levitation have been recorded throughout history. The most famous and best recorded example of spontaneous levitation was demonstrated over a period of 35 years by the Italian monk Joseph of Copertino, who lived during the first part of the 17th century. His power seemed linked with moments of joy. The first recorded incident of his levitation was in his own church of St Gregory of Armenia. As in all similar experiences, Brother Joseph uttered a cry and flew vertically upwards, with arms outstretched to the cross on the high altar. The nuns who were present were afraid he might burn himself on the candles, but before long he floated down again and danced and sang as he chanted the name of the Virgin along the aisles.

On another occasion he levitated when overcome by emotion at meeting the Pope. Joseph's levitations continued regularly until he died at the age of 60.

Other attested levitators include the mystic Saint Teresa of Avila, and the physical medium Daniel Dunglas Home, who once floated out of a third floor window.

PSYCHOMETRY

Psychometry has been described as the etheric or soul's eye, and is the ability to detect information about people, places and events, past or present, by holding an artefact connected with that person or place. The term is derived from the Greek words *psyche*, meaning soul and *metron*, measure.

Spontaneous psychometric ability is common among ordinary people as well as recognised psychics.

Theories of and Research into Psychometry

Though psychometry has been practised throughout history, the power was first fully investigated and identified in 1842 by an American scientist, J. Rhodes Buchanan. He believed that all thoughts, actions and events were permanently impressed upon the ether or spirit level of existence, and that these impressions were absorbed by artefacts and especially by trees and stones. This history could be accessed by touching an object or stones and trees at an ancient site, thereby releasing emotions as well as actual information from the past.

Another related explanation saw psychometry in terms of animism, whereby even inanimate objects possess a life-force and memory of their own that enables them to receive and transmit impressions. In this way the emotions and thoughts of the owner of an artefact or building would be transmitted to the artefact, and years or even centuries later the object would transmit these impressions to any receptive person who touched it.

During the 1930s, Stefan Ossowski, a Polish chemical engineer and skilled psychometrist, took part in many experiments. Some of the information he obtained by touch was not verified for years after the experiments, thus excluding the possibility that the experimenter was unconsciously relaying information telepathically. In one case, Ossowski identified a bow and arrow as being about 15,000 years old and owned by the Magdalenian people, a fact that even experts at the time of the experiment were unaware.

Canadian archaeologist J. Norman Edison worked with psychic George McMullen who claimed to see cinema images when he held artefacts. He believed he was assisted by Beings of Light. In the late 1970s McMullen went to Egypt and gave psychometric help to locate a buried city, Cleopatra's palace and Mark Antony's burial chamber.

Cryptoscopy

This form of psychometry involves reading the contents of sealed envelopes by touch, though in practice it is difficult to distinguish this from pure clairvoyance. Indeed, many skilled clairvoyants and mediums will ask for an object belonging to a deceased person with which to make contact at a sitting.

In a series of tests, Buchanan gave Charles Inman, one of his students, some letters from his personal correspondence. Two of the letters were from a surgeon called J.B. Flint and a doctor Charles Caldwell who had founded a medical college in Louisville. Inman detected such animosity between the two medical men emanating from the letters that he had to put the correspondence down. He could feel that Caldwell had the power to crush Flint. In fact, Caldwell had Flint removed from his Chair of Surgery shortly after the experiment.

Psychometry of the Place

This is the easiest form of psychometry for a beginner. Here it is the history of an object or its place of origin that is the prime focus. If an article has remained in the same family for generations, it can retain a whole family history. Objects from sites of antiquity, in Buchanan's view, could even hold the secrets of lost civilisations.

The strongest impressions from place psychometry come from dramatic or violent events – such as murders or battles – or from long periods of unbroken tranquillity, for example an abbey where monks may have lived over a period of hundreds of years in the same pattern so that their individual life spans merged into one.

Jenny Bright, a professional medium and skilled psychometrist, described how her mediumistic powers manifest themselves through psychometry:

I am always very at home in abbeys and churches and have a oneness with them. In Rivaux Abbey in Yorkshire I was instantly at home. As I went inside, I heard and sensed the voice of an old monk: 'You will like this place. Put your hands on here.'

As I placed my hands on the old stones, as if on a smoky-black transparency or negative, I saw how the Abbey used to be, the old library full of mediaeval manuscripts. I could make out the building housing the information centre in its old form – I walked round the old buildings, now sometimes just part of a wall, and saw the life inside them through the misty greyness, the monks working, silently praying or eating their simple food in silence in the old refectory. I could see without a plan how everything was and when I read the notices and guidebook it was all where I had pictured it.

Clairsentience, sensing an atmosphere, is closely akin to psychometry, as is clairaudience, hearing voices from the past or from spirits. These are frequently part of a psychometric experience, being triggered by touch. Retrocognitive clairvoyance (see p. 282), where figures or scenes from the past are seen either externally or in the mind's vision, can also be stimulated by a psychometric experience. Indeed, for many people it is through psychometry that other psychic abilities develop.

Object Psychometry

This is an extension of place psychometry in which a specific artefact belonging to a person or family is held to reveal the history of the owners, past and present. Because it is a single object it can be harder to trust instincts as the object is out of context, but this can be helpful in preventing a psychometrist from using logical processes to deduce a likely history. Many beginners find it easier to close their eyes or have the object placed in an open container and feel the inner artefact rather than see the outer forms. For example, one of my students Pauline felt what seemed to be a china figure, but was overwhelmed by impressions of a cold metal container, crowds of people, noise and confusion. The item was a figurine of a Dresden shepherdess that had been taken as a talisman by a soldier on the D-Day landing – the container was the inside of the landing craft.

Predictive Personal Psychometry

This forms a potent alternative to more conventional divinatory methods, such as Tarot (see p. 77) or runes (see p. 62), and especially where issues are complex offers insight into the links between past events and future action in the life of an individual. A personal item is used, one worn or carried frequently, for example a ring, watch, necklace or a key ring, belonging to the person seeking the reading. The item need not be particularly old, but if it has sentimental value this will increase the emotional energy that enhances psychic transmission. The past, especially childhood, is usually seen first, then the present and future concerns of a person.

In all forms of predictive psychometry, first the owner holds the item while focusing on the area under question in the reading, and the object is then held at the same time by the owner and psychometrist to allow the flow of psychic vibrations. Finally, the psychometrist continues to run fingertips and palms over the artefact while talking to maintain tactile contact. Frequently the item becomes warm as the psychic energies build up. It is the object itself that serves as the mediumistic channel for the psychometrist's intuitive powers, and so this is a particularly good psychic art for those who do not trust their innate clairvoyant powers.

Initially impressions will be of the questioner's childhood, then more recent past, and so a timeline is formed that will, if allowed to flow uninterrupted, reveal potential paths just over the horizon, transferred from the questioner's auric radar to the object.

Flower Psychometry

Flowers are traditionally a good focus for personal predictive psychometry as they form a living transmitter between questioner and reader and readily absorb psychic impressions. It is most effective when the questioner has picked the flower or chosen it, because the species has some special significance – flower evenings are very common at Spiritualist churches.

REGRESSION/PAST LIFE RECALL

A significant number of children seem able to recall automatically glimpses of past lives before they reach the age of seven. Fewer adults spontaneously receive images of past worlds. Theosophists (see p. 80) believe that there is a collective psychic memory bank of all human experience from all times and places called the Akashic records. These records contain information of individual lives, past and present, and can be accessed in an altered state of consciousness, whether a trance or through meditation or dreams. The seer Edgar Cayce, who gave many past life readings while in trance, believed that he acquired his own extensive medical knowledge from a former life as a healer and apothecary in Grecian Troy.

The concept of past life recall was first expressed in Eastern mysticism. Patanjali, the early 5th-century author of the *Yoga Sutras*, stated that past life memories are retained in the subconscious mind, to be retrieved through yoga mediation.

Beginning in the mid-1950s, fascination with exploring past lives through hypnotic regression grew steadily in the Western world and is now recognised as a valid healing therapy for phobias and obsessions that seem to have no obvious root cause in the present world. Through regression, missing pieces seem to fall into place, and in many cases the phobia improves or disappears.

Alternative Explanations for Past Life Recall

Some psychologists and psychotherapists suggest that past life recall is a channel through which our secondary or inner personalities develop through creative

interplay with a therapist. Others argue that what is experienced during regression is a symbolic representation of an area of life that is problematic or underdeveloped. Those, in both the East and West, who believe in reincarnation but do not think that the soul retains conscious identity between incarnations, feel that what is retrieved as past life recall is an archetypal life form from the Great Tribal Memory or Jung's Collective Unconscious that has a message for the person being regressed.

Paranormal explanations include retrocognition, clairvoyance into the past that may be experienced in an ancient place or when practising psychometry, or even rarely spirit possession, when a past life seems to dominate the present identity.

Cryptomnesia

The unconscious recall of knowledge learned through normal channels but subsequently forgotten is the most usual explanation for non-authentic cases of past worlds. Carl Jung believed that cryptomnesia was a necessary mental process by the subconscious to avoid mental overload of the conscious mind.

During the 1960s, Reima Kampman, a Finnish psychiatrist, hypnotised secondary school children in Finland, and some who recalled past lives were in subsequent regressions able to identify books or films that triggered false memories of the earlier world. However, one girl recalled in great detail a life in mediaeval England and could sing in mediaeval English the Cuckoo song or '*Sumer is I Cumen In*'. One possible explanation was that the library in the Finnish town had a manuscript of the song and that this had at one time been displayed. There was the possibility that the girl may have unconsciously memorised it photographically, but nevertheless her knowledge of the period and place of her past life was remarkable. Sometimes a rational explanation can, as in this case, disregard the most likely explanation – that the girl in question had lived before.

Bridey Murphy

One of the most famous cases of past life recall that led to more general interest in past lives was that of Bridey Murphy. In 1952, Morey Bernstein hypnotised Virginia Tighe, a Colorado housewife. During the regression Virginia spoke in great detail in an Irish dialect of her life as Bridey Murphy, who lived between 1798 and 1864 in Cork, Ireland. In subsequent sessions, she sang Irish songs and told Irish stories.

However, one newspaper claimed that an Irish woman called Bridey Corkell had lived in the house across the street from where Virginia Tighe grew up. What was not reported was that the newspaper carrying the apparent exposé was one that had failed to get serial rights of the book Bernstein had written, and that the son of Mrs Corkell was editor of the Sunday version of the same paper. Virginia had not met the Irish woman until she was eighteen and had never been in love with her son, as was claimed.

Twin Souls

In my own research, I have come across cases of couples who, before meeting, had separate regressions in which their lives were entwined. While it could be argued that similar regressions might lead two people to feel that they were destined to be together in this lifetime, the regressions may be unknown to the other party at the time of meeting. This was the case with Jenny who lives in Nottinghamshire, who had a past life regression in which she was a nurse in London during the Second World War and recalled how she and her fiancé, a pilot in the RAF, used to walk in Regent's Park in London together. He was killed and Jenny herself in later regressions discovered that she had also died when a bomb exploded on her house, six weeks after her fiancé's crash.

Jenny and David met through a series of coincidences and a chain of unconnected people who seemed to be drawing them together. They experienced instant recognition and six weeks after meeting they moved in together. David had experienced a similar regression and had previously been told by a medium about his life as a pilot.

Jenny Cockell

Jenny Cockell was born in Northamptonshire in 1953, and since childhood had constant dream-memories of another life that through hypnosis she identified as that of Mary Sutton, an Irish woman who died more than 20 years before Jenny's own birth, leaving eight young children.

Jenny relates that, as a child, she frequently woke sobbing with memories of Mary's death and felt fear for the children she regularly dreamed she had left behind. At this time, Jenny did not know Mary's last name, but would sketch maps of Mary's Irish village that when she found the place fitted her childhood scribblings. Memories of Mary became even clearer when as an adult Jenny was hypnotised for the first time in 1988. Under hypnosis, she finally identified herself as Mary.

Jenny subsequently advertised, sent letters and studied maps to find the place she had seen so many times and the former life which evoked such strong emotions. At last Jenny discovered a village called Malahide near Dublin in which she was able to locate the now ruined cottage in which Mary Sutton had lived during the 1920s with her eight young children until her premature death. Jenny had recalled under hypnosis the name O'Neill in connection with Mary, and she later discovered this was the name of a wealthy family for whom Mary had worked. Jenny visited the village, made contact with some of her children from the earlier life, and felt that at last she had resolved the unfinished business from the past – and had come home.

Xenoglossy and Xenography

Xenoglossy is the ability to speak a foreign or ancient language that has not been learned, an ability which has been a feature of a significant number of past life recollections. While Xenoglossy is sometimes attributed to telepathy between a hypnotist and a subject, the hypnotist in many of these cases has no knowledge of the language spoken, which may be an obscure or defunct dialect that is only recognised by linguistic experts from a tape recording of the session.

Xenography is the writing of an unfamiliar language. I have come across two or three cases of people with only rudimentary education who suddenly produce a page of mediaeval Latin, in one instance after a vivid dream of being in a monastery and having to copy out texts.

REINCARNATION

Reincarnation, the belief that our soul returns to a new body after death, is accepted by about two-thirds of the world's population, mainly in the East, and is thousands of years old. Such philosophies regard progressive lives as lessons that need to be learned, or as righting omissions or sins in past lives. Since the 1960s the belief in reincarnation has increased in the Western world with the growing quest to find enlightenment through Eastern spirituality.

The Origins of and Theories of Reincarnation

According to Hindu beliefs, the human soul is immortal, existing independently of the body, and rebirth is likened to casting off worn clothes and putting on new ones. Buddhism, in contrast, does not see the individual soul as permanent but as a pulsating subconsciousness that passes from life to life in an attempt to attain the necessary detachment from desire and negativity to attain Nirvana or a state of undifferentiated cosmic bliss.

But reincarnation is not just an Eastern concept. In Ancient Greece, both Pythagoras and Plato believed that in each successive incarnation one experienced the consequences of deeds from an earlier life. Early Christian Gnostic (shamanistic and psychic) sects also believed in rebirth, perhaps inheriting the idea from Ancient Egypt, while the Christian missionary St Augustine who lived from AD354–430 declared that the message of Plato's reincarnation is 'the purest and most luminous of all philosophy'.

Although in AD529 Emperor Justinian prohibited such beliefs, adherence to reincarnation survived, and St Francis of Assisi was a believer. In the 12th and 13th centuries, the persecuted Cathars in France also subscribed to the view that we are all reborn many times. Belief in reincarnation re-emerged publicly with the Spiritists (early Spiritualists) in France in the 1850s, and this formed a source for reincarnation theory in the Theosophical Movement. Theosophists believe that reincarnation is part of the continuing evolutionary path of the soul.

Evidence for Reincarnation

Dr Ian Stevenson is Head of the Department of Psychiatric Medicine at the University of Virginia and has studied reincarnation for more than 30 years. Dr Stevenson found that young children gave the most consistent results in past life recollection, but that they lost spontaneous recall of earlier worlds at about the age of seven.

Perhaps the most significant evidence for reincarnation in Stevenson's research is his finding that 35 per cent of 895 children who claimed to remember previous lives possessed either birthmarks of an unusual kind or had birth defects not linked to any apparent genetic or physiological cause. These birth scars correlated with wounds apparently inflicted on the person whose life the child recalled as his or her own in an earlier existence. What is more, medical corroboration, usually in the form of a post-mortem report, was obtained in a significant number of these cases. For example, a Burmese child claimed she was her reincarnated aunt who had died during surgery for congenital heart disease. The child was born with a long, vertical linear birthmark in the same place as her late aunt's surgical incision.

Children who do recall previous lives tend to speak of them almost as soon as they learn to talk, and in some cases may give names and/or events that identify a deceased person either specifically or as coming from a particular place and background. They may also display detailed knowledge of, for example, cooking or animals, or use snatches of a language or dialect, all of which are totally alien to their current home culture but are connected with the past life.

Although children who remember previous lives come from many cultures, the majority of the cases in Stevenson's research were reported in southern Asia, possibly because parents in this area are more willing to take their children seriously on the subject. In the UK especially, a child who talks of a past life at school is likely to be referred to a psychiatrist for therapy rather than investigation, as such claims would be regarded as a symptom of family trauma.

For every case that is verifiable by ongoing or retrospective investigation, a thousand more exist in which the child refers to the past life only once. Psychic researcher Joe Cooper told me of an 18-month-old child seated on a motorbike by an adult, who suddenly announced, 'I was killed on a motorbike when I was seventeen'. At the time the infant could hardly say more than single words and could never be persuaded to repeat the words again.

What is more, many parents are understandably unwilling to allow their children to be investigated by researchers, and from my own research I know that the most dramatic cases will never be spoken of outside the home, apart from a single reference in confidence. Children themselves can also become distressed or genuinely have no recall of their words, which are usually heard by the mother.

The Case of Shanti Devi

Shanti Devi is probably the most famous of all documented cases of childhood past life memories, and dates back to the 1930s. The case was investigated by a committee of prominent men appointed by Mahatma Gandhi. They took Shanti from her home near Delhi to the village where she claimed to have lived in her previous incarnation as Lugdi, wife of Kedarnath Chaube.

From the age of four, Shanti had talked about her husband in Mathura, who, she said, owned a cloth shop. She called herself Chaubine (Chaube's wife) and when Shanti was eight she reluctantly gave her former husband's full name. She described her husband in detail and also mentioned that her husband's shop was located in front of Dwarkadhish Temple, which on her later visit was discovered to be the exact location, but as she predicted closed at that time of day.

When Shanti was six years old, she gave an account of her death following child-birth, including details of the complicated surgical procedures that were used in an attempt to save her. As the girl grew older, she became desperate to be taken to

Mathura, and at last a relative of Kedarnath was sent to visit her. Shanti recognised her husband's cousin instantly, described her former home and mentioned a place she had hidden some money before her death. At last her former husband came to Delhi, but to mislead Shanti he was introduced to the child as his elder brother. Shanti identified him correctly and her earlier description matched precisely, including a wart on the left side of his cheek near his ear. Shanti also described a well in the courtyard of the house at Mathura where she used to take her bath. This was hidden by a stone when Shanti visited her former home accompanied by the committee members, but she nevertheless identified the exact spot.

On the journey from the station, Shanti guided the driver to her former home, pointing out changes made to the area since her death. On the journey she insisted on stopping to greet an elderly person in the crowd, whom she correctly identified as her former father-in-law. At the house Shanti took the committee to the second floor to show them the hiding place for her money. No money was found, but her husband later admitted he had removed the money after his wife's death.

The Case of Adam

The case of Adam is from my own research and has not been formally investigated. Nevertheless, Adam's story has been corroborated by independent witnesses. Pam, who lives in County Durham, wrote to me describing her young son's spontaneous past life recall:

We were travelling to Sunderland one day in June 1996. We were just coming into a small village on the outskirts of Sunderland when our son Adam who was in the back seat of the car, pointed to a spot just before a bridge we were about to go under, saying he had died over there.

A bit further along the road, Adam pointed to the same spot from a different direction and repeated that he had been killed at the place. As Adam was only three and a half it was a shock for us. I asked how he had died. Adam told me that he had been in a plane and that it had crashed. He kept saying that it was not an accident but that he had died on purpose. We let the matter rest for a couple of weeks.

When we questioned Adam again, he repeated to us about the plane, which was a quiet one, not a fast one like a jet, flying round and round.

I wanted to find out more. I telephoned the Sunderland Air Museum and asked them about the crash. The curator told me that it was a British plane during the Second World War and the only person who had been killed was the pilot. The pilot's name was Cyril, and a book had been written about him as he was a hero, because he had lost his own life to avoid crashing on the town. I managed to get hold of the book. As I read it so many of the things confirmed the details Adam was gradually unfolding.

About a month before Christmas, Adam suddenly took the book from my desk and said that the photo of the man on the front was him before he died. Though many of Cyril's friends and family were pictured, Adam always pointed out Cyril among them, even at different ages and insisted that it was himself.

SPIRITUALISM

What is Spiritualism?

Spiritualism is rooted in the belief that life continues after death and that those on the spirit plane can communicate with people still on earth.

Spiritualists regard God as infinite intelligence, and Jesus as one of the greatest mediums that ever lived on the earth plane. The term Spirit is sometimes applied to this infinite source of wisdom and goodness. The God of your understanding, another term for the Godhead, is said to be the highest and purest vibration. Personal vibrations are determined by one's thoughts and actions, and life is regarded as continuous. After death, the essential self, who is no different from the earthly person, continues to live and evolve on the spirit plane.

One of the fundamental beliefs is that spirit people who draw close to an individual on earth will be at the same spiritual level of evolution, according to the Law of Attraction, so the more wise and noble a person in life, the more spiritually evolved will be his or her spirit guides, and the easier the contact with loving relations now on the spirit plane. Conversely, dabbling with ouija boards or summoning up spirits may well attract negative or trickster spirits.

Relatives will still be loving and speak in much the same way as they did when physically present, but may not necessarily know more than they did on earth, especially if newly deceased, though in time they may be able to see further into the future than people on earth. However, Spiritualism is not about predictions, for the fundamental belief is that everyone, on earth and in spirit, has free will and so the responsibility to make choices.

The Spirit World

The spirit world is considered to co-exist with the earth plane, and so spirits are not in a separate dimension but ever-present, though unseen except to children, those in need of comfort from a deceased relation, or those with developed clairvoyant abilities. Trained mediums (see p. 287) are not only able to see, but with the help of their personal spirit guides to intentionally instigate positive two-way contact with spirits, either at a Spiritualist service or in a private sitting for someone who wants to contact a deceased relation.

The spirit plane is said to be very beautiful, with buildings, trees, flowers, music, science, literature, philosophy and schools for children who have died young, who are cared for by grandparents and their spirit guides. Colours are brighter, flowers have richer perfume, and senses are more finely tuned.

This spirit world is created by thought, and so the more spiritually evolved a person, the lovelier the next world they will perceive.

Natural Law

Spiritual evolution depends, according to Spiritualist tenets, on the operation of Natural Law, both on the earth and spirit planes, whereby good and bad deeds and thoughts are returned to the perpetrator either in this lifetime or in the next. Heaven and hell are not separate places of reward and punishment, but are created by a person's own thoughts and deeds. So those who live a materialistic or selfish life will on the spirit plane be with others who have acted similarly.

However, through wise guides and teachers it is always possible to progress. Spirit teachers and guides are attached to a person throughout life on earth and in the next world as well. Many children 'see' an invisible friend who, according to Spiritualists, is a child's first spirit companion. Some guides may remain with a person throughout his or her lifetime, others just for a specific phase or need. Everyone has guardian spirits, though a medium's spirit guides will be especially skilled in communication with the earth plane.

The History of Spiritualism

Both the Old and New Testaments talk of spirit communication, and indeed Jesus appeared 11 times after his death. The Virgin Mary has also appeared many times throughout the world for almost 2,000 years. The 16th-century astrologer Doctor John Dee regularly communicated with spirits through his medium, Edward Kelly, and in many cultures ghosts of ancestors return or remain present to impart wisdom and maintain right conduct.

However, Spiritualism as a religion is dated not from when the first spirit communication took place, but from the point at which the Fox sisters at Hydesville, near Rochester in New York State, deliberately communicated with a ghost on March 31, 1848, so demonstrating the possibility of two-way communication and providing evidence of conscious life after death. What was remarkable was that the communication took place between ordinary people, one of whom was in spirit, that it was not confined to the particular house or spirit of the original haunting, and that what might have been seen as poltergeist activity – i.e. nothing new – was the vehicle through which two untrained girls were able to channel spirit communication in an increasingly controlled manner.

Thus what was originally a haunting/poltergeist phenomenon provided the catalyst for a flood of Spiritualist demonstrations and writings. The time was right and the way had been prepared by a number of philosophical, visionary and trance teachings that were to prove the guiding tracts of the new religion. Above all, the way was opened for ordinary people who previously had not understood or developed their innate spiritual and mediumistic abilities, to find a place – and for some women a new career – in a religion that promised eternal life in a comprehensible form.

Influences on Spiritualist Philosophy

Swedenborg

The scientist Emanuel Swedenborg, who lived during the 18th century, was the first person to set down, as a result of his own spirit communication through dreams and visions, a comprehensive philosophy that recognised connections between the earth and spirit worlds. He saw in operation in the spirit world the power, not of Divine retribution or reward, but of Natural Law and justice that, he believed, governed both planes of existence.

Swedenborg's angels and demons were not a higher order of being, but ordinary people who had begun their respective paths to good or evil in earthly life and created their own heavens and hells. Swedenborg believed that the spirit world is in a number of concentric spheres, each with its own density and inhabitants. After death, the soul rests for a few days and then regains full consciousness. Those who are old or sick regain their youth and health in the spirit world. The impact of his ideas upon Spiritualism was great, though his followers established a different religion, The Church of New Jerusalem.

Andrew Jackson Davis

The American Andrew Jackson Davis, a follower of Swedenborg, predicted in trance the birth of Spiritualism. On March 6, 1844, Davis, a natural clairvoyant and clairaudient, communicated with the spirits of the ancient philosopher Galen and the seer Swedenborg. They revealed many things to him about the universe and the ability of humans to determine their own spiritual as well as earthly destiny. Thereafter, Jackson Davis travelled round the country giving lectures in trance about the nature of the soul and survival after death, and in November 1845 began dictating his great works, *The Principles of Nature: Her Divine Revelations* and *A Voice to Mankind*, both of which became guides for the Spiritualist movement. What is remarkable is that Jackson Davies had little education, yet not only spoke profoundly, but displayed fluency in Hebrew under trance.

The Events at Hydesville

The spirit communications began after John Fox, his wife Margaret and two of their daughters, Catherine (Kate) aged 12 and Margaretta (Maggie) aged 14, moved into a house in Hydesville near Rochester in New York State, that was believed to be haunted.

Three months later, around the middle of March 1848, the family were disturbed by rapping and bangings that were so loud that the beds and walls of the house shook. On March 31, Kate Fox challenged the ghost who seemed to be responsible for the persistent and increasing disturbances to repeat the snaps of her fingers, which it did. The sound stopped when Kate did – and the first display of mediumship had taken place.

Then Maggie told the spirit, 'Now, do just as I do. Count one, two, three, four,' and she struck one hand against the other at the same time. The ghost obliged. Next Mrs

Fox asked the ghost to rap out all the children's ages successively, which the spirit did, even the age of a younger child who had died.

When neighbours were called, one of them, a sceptic by the name of William Duesler, ascertained by raps and knocks that the spirit was a pedlar, Charles B. Rosa, who claimed to have been murdered in the house for $500 he carried. Subsequently, the spirit revealed that his body had been buried in the cellar. It was not, however, until November 1904 when a wall in the cellar collapsed that the skeleton of the pedlar and the pedlar's tin box were recovered, thus confirming the paranormal information as true.

When the children were moved out, the paranormal activity followed them and intensified, especially at Leah, an elder sister's home, to which Kate was temporarily sent. Here a family friend, Isaac Post, recalled that David Fox, the girls' brother, had used an alphabet system to communicate with the Hydesville ghost. Using this method, the spirits told him:

> *Dear Friends, you must proclaim this truth to the world. This is the dawning of a new era; you must not try to conceal it any longer. When you do your duty God will protect you and good spirits will watch over you.*

Although the activity increased, it became controllable, and so the girls were able to demonstrate publicly the power channelled through them in a controlled and there-fore positive way that was qualitatively distinguishable from poltergeist phenomena. Tables moved, rapping with their legs, musical instruments were played with unseen fingers, objects moved round the room. Thus began for the Fox sisters a career of demonstrating physical mediumship that was to end, because of the pressures of sustaining their early gifts, in alcoholism, and at one point in Maggie denying her original powers.

The Development of Spiritualism

On November 14, 1849, the first meeting of a small group of Spiritualists was held in the Corinthian Hall in Rochester. Other people who perhaps already had similar abilities to the Fox sisters but had never talked of them, began to perform mediumistically, in spite of a great deal of hostility, from friends and family as well as the scientific and religious community who found it disturbing that ordinary people were communicating with spirits at will. There were attempts to pass laws to ban Spiritualism.

From these small beginnings, however, the modern Spiritualist movement grew rapidly, attracting millions of followers throughout the USA and Europe. In 1852, Spiritualism arrived in England with the Boston medium Mrs Hayden, who shocked the establishment by charging money for her seances. By 1855, Spiritualism had more than two million followers worldwide. Investigations into mediums inevitably uncov-ered some fraud, and there was great showmanship even among genuine gifted medi-ums, for example the American Davenport brothers who practised escapology and appeared on theatre bills with conjurors and acrobats. These factors served to cast doubt on the spirituality of the Movement that was ultimately to unfairly marginalise Spiritualism.

During this period, however, the home circle became popular, with small groups meeting in private homes, often under the auspices of a trained medium. During the American Civil War, families would meet and seek news of loved ones and numerous accounts of precognition were given as to when and how they would be reunited. The First World War caused a resurgence of popularity in the UK for the same reason, and served to offer comfort to those bereaved by carnage and loss on a scale never before witnessed. Many of the great mediums on both sides of the Atlantic began in home circles. Even Queen Victoria and Albert experimented at Osborne House and saw the table moving. Victoria later communicated with the dead Albert through mediums, and it was rumoured that her Scottish ghillie John Brown wielded so much power because of his mediumistic abilities.

During the 1930s, the American researcher J.B. Rhine took psychical research into the laboratory, thus helping to prove the existence of psychic powers, but causing the separation between the practice of Spiritualism and the research of psychic phenomena. However, Spiritualism has continued to offer, especially to the bereaved, a powerful focus for belief in survival after death, and though the Movement faces a crisis owing to the lack of younger members, it still offers a coherent and moral path by which to live.

SURVIVAL AFTER DEATH

Family Ghosts

The majority of ghostly encounters involve the benign presence of deceased mothers, grandmothers, fathers and children. These experiences can involve perceiving with the physical eye a solid, three-dimensional figure dressed in familiar clothes, who may look younger and in excellent health. This can be comforting to the bereaved if the relative or close friend died after a degenerative illness or an accident. The favourite scent or tobacco of the departed family member may be detected even by a stranger entering the home. A voice may be heard calling downstairs or singing a favourite song, again by a third party. However, the majority of experiences consist of a light touch on the hair or shoulder, described as gossamer, and a sense of peace and being protected. At least a third of the population has either witnessed or been told of such paranormal encounters in their immediate circle of friends and family.

The majority of family apparitions are not open to formal investigation since they occur spontaneously. For this reason their incidence is regarded by many scientists as purely anecdotal. The case studies in this section come from my own research and have been verified by a third party.

Christine, who lives in Cornwall, believes that her teenage son's spirit returned after he had drowned to offer reassurance to his parents that he had survived death.

The last weekend of his life Rufus had gone to stay with friends in St Ives. On Sunday he was not on the last train as usual, and had made no contact.

At 1am we heard a police car. My husband and I went outside. There were three people walking down the path. Between the two policemen, a head taller and looking over the shoulder of the first one, walked Rufus. I was weak with relief – they must have found him walking home. Rufus looked at me without speaking.

I noticed in that split second that he wasn't wearing his usual clothes, black jacket, T-shirt, jeans and boots; he was wearing light coloured trousers and a light khaki shirt. He was totally real and solid and as I went to rush towards him suddenly he wasn't there anymore. Then I knew [he was dead].

Later they took my husband to Penzance to identify Rufus's body. On the Saturday afternoon unknown to us he had bought some new clothes in a shop in Penzance and was wearing them, a khaki shirt and trousers when his body was recovered.

At the time I said nothing but a few days later my husband Brian told me, 'I saw Rufus that night but I didn't like to say anything in case it upset you that you hadn't seen him.'

Brian saw Rufus in exactly the same place and wearing the same clothes as I had done.

Roy who lives in Essex wrote to me after hearing me talk on a radio programme:

Hilda, my mother and Gladys, her sister, are both widows. Gladys's husband died many years ago. They have recently moved to a block of flats. My mother lives on the first floor and Gladys is on the ground floor. One night, my mother was woken during the early hours by someone standing by her bed. It was Leslie, Gladys's deceased husband. My mother was surprised but not frightened. She told him that he was on the wrong floor and that Gladys was in the flat below. She then went back to sleep.

Early next morning, Gladys came up to Mum's and said, 'Who do you think came to see me last night?'

My mother replied to a startled Gladys, 'Les came here first and I told him where you were.'

This account was told to me by both my mother and aunt independently.

Both these cases, as well as hundreds more I have collected, suggest that we do survive death in a form not dissimilar from our earthly one. We do not know why some people more readily receive contact from deceased loved ones across the dimensions, but it has nothing to do with the intensity of the love or the quality of the earthly relationship. Indeed, unfinished business is one reason why ghosts may appear to relatives. Whether or not one does *see* these family apparitions, the evidence offers reassurance that love does not die with the body.

Days of the Dead

Certain periods of the year are traditionally associated with ghosts and magical energies, and these festivals of the dead are the most potent times for seeing family ghosts.

This may be because these festivals focus attention on departed relations or because – as our ancestors believed – they are periods when other dimensions are more accessible because they fall on or close to a seasonal transition point.

Western Festivals of the Dead

In Celtic times, at the festival of Samhain, the beginning of the Celtic New Year, ghosts were believed to return shivering from the fields on All Hallows Eve, October 31, seeking food and shelter in their former homes. The hearth was the central place of the home and on a spiritual level the meeting place for the upper and lower worlds, living and deceased.

Souling

All Saints and All Souls Days were celebrated from about the 3rd century on November 1 and 2, and were officially introduced in the 7th century by Pope Boniface IV. In the early Christian tradition, on All Hallows Eve souls were released from purgatory for 48 hours and soul cakes and wine were left out for them.

All Souls Day on November 2 is a holy day in the later Christian tradition on which prayers are said for souls in purgatory. On All Souls' Night, Soulers, children and young adults, went from door to door singing special Soul songs. In return for the song, the young people would be given hot soul cakes and money to pay for masses for the souls of the departed.

Modern France is one place in which the religious and spiritual aspects of this time remain strong, and on November 1 the churchyards are filled with flowers, and photographs of the deceased are placed on graves. The family visits the cemeteries, dressed in their party clothes. Mont St Michel, the mediaeval fairytale abbey mentioned in the section on Ley Lines (see p. 193), is regarded in old legends as the Celtic Island of the Dead and spirits are said to gather there on November 1.

In Mexico too, people still celebrate Hallowe'en in its traditional sense. *El Dia del Muerte* (the Day of the Dead) is All Souls Day in the Catholic calendar. The feast is spread over two days; on November 1 departed children are remembered, and on November 2 the ghosts of adults are honoured. People in towns, cities and villages make a path with bright yellow flowers from the cemetery to guide the dead to their former homes. The houses are full of ornaments, pictures of the dead, the foods they enjoyed, flowers and incense.

Eastern Festivals of the Dead

In the East, the dates are different but the festivals of the dead are remarkably similar to those held in the West. *Chung Yuan*, the Chinese Festival of All Souls or Hungry Souls, takes place on the fifteenth day of the seventh lunar month. The Chinese New Year is fixed by the first full moon in February.

From *Chung Yuan* until the end of the month, offerings are made to those who died unprepared or homeless or who have no descendants to venerate them. It also commemorates those without a grave because they had drowned. Such offerings include paper houses, money, clothes and food to give the deceased succour in the spirit world. The paper objects are thrown into local fires and rivers.

Chung Yeung, another festival of the dead, is held on the ninth day of the ninth moon, and is celebrated by going to high places and flying kites in the form of dragons, butterflies, birds and centipedes. Graves are visited and gifts taken for the departed. Paper effigies of goods are burned to send them to the next world. The dead are also sent symbols of objects they desired but had not possessed while they were alive.

Do ghosts actually appear on such festivals? In Japan, the Festival of Bon is celebrated in August. Atushi lives not far from Tokyo. He is a retired civil servant in his seventies and lost his wife from breast cancer seven years ago. He told me:

> *Towards the end of her life, my wife was hospitalised. She was unconscious for a few days and passed away without exchanging words with us. Perhaps she did not anticipate leaving us so soon.*
>
> *Two years ago I was making a Bon festival fire in front of my house, to welcome home her departed soul, one of our Buddhist customs on the Festival of the Dead, the Festival of Lanterns.*
>
> *Suddenly my wife was there but she did not look at me. She was heading for the house and disappeared. At that moment I felt something like an electric shock at my back and saw my wife waiting, standing and signalling to me. She had come back home, actually and really, of that I am 100 per cent sure.*

TELEPATHY

What is Telepathy?

Telepathy is defined as the transmission of ideas, thoughts, feelings and sensations from one person to another without words. The word telepathy comes from the Greek *tele* (distant) and *pathe* (occurrence or feeling), and was coined by Frederic W.H. Myers, a psychical researcher, poet, psychologist and inspector of schools, who founded the Society of Psychical Research (SPR) in 1884. A year later the American Society was created and telepathy became the first psychic phenomena to be studied scientifically.

To Myers, the idea of telepathy was 'the inward spiritual aspect of the outward gravitational law', drawing together 'mindstuff' from an individual's psyche, between two human minds and even from the deceased or other discarnate beings.

Indeed, mediumship (see p. 287) is sometimes explained as a form of telepathy whereby the medium extracts information of the dead person from the sitter's mind, albeit unconsciously, or according to Myers' theory directly from the mind of the deceased person.

But for most modern researchers, telepathy is regarded as a natural extension of conventional communication, a theory borne out by the fact that telepathy is still a normal form of contact among indigenous peoples such as the Australian Aborigines, although as the influence of technological societies increases this faculty is in decline.

Testing telepathy under laboratory conditions has always proved difficult. In 1930, the American parapsychologist J.B. Rhine began ESP tests at Duke University in North Carolina using playing cards and Zener or ESP cards on which five different shapes were printed. He concluded that telepathy and clairvoyance were the same psychic function and weren't affected by distance or obstacles, but he found problems getting enough people to score significantly above chance in his card guessing experiments. Biologically, it was discovered that blood volume changes during telepathic sendings and recipients' brainwaves change to match those of the senders. But the actual process still proved elusive to measurement.

In 1971, astronaut Edgar Mitchell aboard Apollo 14 conducted a telepathy experiment with four recipients 150,000 miles (240,000km) below. He concentrated on 25 random numbers and completed 200 sequences. Guessing 40 correctly was regarded as chance. Two recipients guessed 51 correctly, higher than chance but not that high.

Testing children is even harder than testing adults. The only researcher to have had significant success was Ernesto Spinelli working at Surrey University during the 1960s (see Psychic Children, p. 310). So far no one has been able to replicate his results.

Most telepathic experiments with children fail because the child loses interest or feels under too much pressure to succeed. When the teenage Creery sisters were investigated by the SPR in 1888, they scored remarkably well at card guessing. But the results were discounted when they were found to be using secret signals during sessions when they were in the same room. However, the sisters had still been very successful when separated. They said they had not used signals in their most successful experiments and resorted to them only when they could not get results otherwise because they were anxious to avoid upsetting the testers.

Recent experiments with adults have been more encouraging. Psychic ability may be spread throughout the population according to Dr Deborah Delanoy, a senior researcher in the University of Edinburgh's psychology department, Britain's leading research centre into the paranormal. 'It's like music. There would be Mozarts and people with virtually no ability. Most of us would be somewhere in between.'

Experiments around the world found evidence which appeared to show that people were aware of facts which they could not have known through normal perception. Subjects in experiments at Edinburgh University were blindfolded, placed in an easy chair and played a tape of white noise, a formless noise like an untuned radio, to relax them and prepare them for the experiment. A sender in another room then tried to transmit to the volunteer target thoughts of images and sounds while the experimenter monitored and compared the thought patterns of the two. By the law of averages there should have been similarities in about a quarter of the experiments, but the Edinburgh team got a figure nearer to one third.

The most striking examples of telepathy occur spontaneously between close relations, especially mothers and children, but also between fathers and children, grandparents and children, husbands and wives or lovers, siblings, especially twins, and even close friends, especially in crisis situations. I am convinced that the reason for the problems in testing is that telepathy works through the emotions and in an actual need situation, and that even though laboratory testing results are improving, the topics will inevitably remain fairly trivial and mundane.

Spontaneous Telepathy

There are two main kinds of spontaneous telepathy. The first is when one person communicates distress or danger to another unconsciously; the other is a routine nonverbal and usually unconscious bonding between blood relations, partners or those closely linked by love or strong friendship. In both cases there is a wealth of material from case studies.

The most remarkable case I have ever come across is one I found in a pile of old records at the Alister Hardy Research Centre for Religious and Spiritual Experience in Oxford. Adrian had written:

In 1917 I was piloting an Avro aeroplane in the Royal Flying Corps at Dover and I switched off the engine to glide down. The plane entered a strong wind from the sea and was blown into a flat spinning nose-dive, and this I knew to be fatal. I switched on the engine and to my horror it failed to start up. I realised that in another moment the plane would crash and I would become pulp and ashes. I thought of my wife Rose and she loomed up before me and instantly the engine started up again.

The very next morning I received a letter from my wife asking if something terrible had happened to me as she was suddenly moved to go down on her knees and pray for me. The time she mentioned coincided with the time she loomed up before me, when I believed I was about to be killed.

I have come across other cases where telepathic communication seems to transmit help to the person in danger, but it is an area that needs much more research.

The most common telepathic communication is between twins, but it cannot be explained in genetic terms alone. James E. Peron, Director of the Childbirth Education Foundation in the USA, described the experience he witnessed when he was 11 years old with his twin cousins who were eight months older then he was:

We had been playing with neighbouring children in their farm barn, climbing to the upper beams of the barn and jumping into the hayloft.

My cousin Dick and I returned home for the evening meal but Donny remained playing with the neighbour boys on their adjoining farm.

We were sitting down at the dinner table when Dick suddenly bolted in his chair, screamed in pain and yelled: 'Donny's hurt! He fell backwards from the high beam in the barn and hurt his leg.'

Immediately we rushed to the neighbouring farm. Donny had fallen the precise moment Dick had screamed and had broken his leg rather severely.

Most cases of telepathy are more mundane and tend to occur when people are in a relaxed state, so that their conscious thoughts are not predominant and occur often in the early morning or evening. Jim, a European charity official, told me about this experience with his wife:

The phone rang one morning and I remarked to my wife Lydia: 'I wonder who is calling us so early?'

'It's Penny from Heathrow Airport to say she's just arrived,' Lydia replied automatically.

It was, but Lydia hadn't heard from her friend Penny for a couple of years. Penny had gone to Nairobi with her husband and the friends had lost touch. Penny's marriage had gone wrong and she had flown back to England without telling a soul.

VISIONS OF THE VIRGIN MARY

Though in recent years the ancient, exotic and powerful Black Virgin icon has captured the imagination of those seeking to reconnect with the Divine Feminine, the Virgin Mary continues to represent to Christians and non-Christians alike the gentler aspects of the Goddess, pure virgin and ideal mother. The cult of Mary as Queen of Heaven which began in the 6th century, reached its height in mediaeval times. Though Church fathers discouraged direct worship of Mary, it is precisely because Mary was an earthly mother rather than a remote goddess living on a high mountain, that she became a powerful focus for the prayers and troubles of ordinary people worldwide. Unlike the Mother Goddesses and pagan deities, she reveals no cruel or warlike tendencies. Because she lost her son, yet sought no revenge, she is the *Mater Dolorosa*, the grieving mother, who shares the sorrows of all who have lost a loved one.

The History of the Virgin Mary

There are remarkably few references to Mary, mother of Jesus, in the Bible. Those that exist are cameos, like mediaeval pictures, serene and still.

The Renaissance led to the flowering of paintings of the maternal love of Mary for her infant, for example Raphael's *Alba Madonna* (1511) now in the National Gallery of Arts in Washington, and Michelangelo's *Pietà*, a marble statue of Mary cradling her dead son, carved in 1499 and now in St Peter's Basilica in Rome.

In the Biblical representation, Mary reveals nothing of her emotions during the pregnancy or the birth, apart from the enigmatic words, 'But Mary kept all these things, and pondered them in her heart' (Luke 2:19).

Mary's final act of love to her son that is recorded in the Bible is her vigil with him in his death agony. Mary was last seen among the disciples at Pentecost, but little is known of how she spent her last days, or even where she died exactly. Jerusalem and Ephesus both claim to be the place of her death; Jerusalem is considered to be the more likely.

Marian Apparitions

For almost 2,000 years Mary has appeared in visions, witnessed independently by thousands of people in places as diffuse as Vietnam, Russia and South America.

Lourdes

The most famous visions of Mary were seen at Lourdes in the French Pyrenees by Marie Bernadette Soubrious. Born on January 7, 1844, she was the eldest child of François, a poor miller. On February 11, 1858, Bernadette, then 14, experienced a vision of the Virgin Mary while collecting firewood on the banks of the River Gave near Lourdes. This was the first of 18 visions over a period of six months.

Bernadette said she saw:

… a golden coloured cloud, and soon after a Lady, young and beautiful, exceedingly beautiful … placed herself at the entrance of the opening, above the rose bush. She looked at me immediately, smiled at me and signed to me to advance, as if She had been my Mother. She was dressed in a white robe, girdled at the waist with a blue ribbon. She holds on Her right arm a Rosary of white beads with a chain of gold …

On Wednesday April 7, 1858, at six in the morning, Bernadette was kneeling in prayer. Mary was standing in the niche. This vision lasted for almost 45 minutes. Several witnesses described how Bernadette's Rosary was in her left hand and in Bernadette's right hand was a large lighted candle. As her right hand joined her left, the flame of the candle passed between the fingers of the hand. Although fanned by a fairly strong breeze, the flame produced no effect upon the skin it was touching.

This continued for 15 minutes until Bernadette, still in her ecstasy, advanced to the upper part of the Grotto, separating her hands. Bernadette finished her prayer and the wonder left her face.

PSYCHIC POWERS AND STRANGE PHENOMENA

Fatima

Fatima is a village in the centre of Portugal, about 70 miles (112km) north of Lisbon. In 1915 three peasant children, eight-year-old Lucia Santos and her two cousins, Francisco and Jacinta Marto, saw an angel on three separate occasions and, later, the Virgin Mary herself. Portugal's republican government was hostile towards religion and the children were treated very cruelly. They were placed in prison and threatened with torture unless they admitted they had lied. However, the children still insisted they had seen the Virgin.

They said she had appeared to them on Sunday May 13, 1917. As usual, Lucia and her two cousins went to a cave to eat their lunch at noon after tending the sheep. Suddenly a bright shaft of light pierced the air. As the children descended the hill, there was another flash of lightning and standing over the foliage of a small holm oak was a beautiful lady, surrounded by rays of brilliant light, dressed all in white.

She told the children that she had come from heaven and that she wanted them to return on the thirteenth day for six consecutive months at the same hour. The Virgin Mary appeared on the thirteenth of each month and the children kept their promise, except for one month when they were in prison.

At each successive apparition, news of Fatima spread. It was predicted that the October visitation would offer unmistakable evidence that it was the Virgin Mary herself. On October 13, there was a crowd of more than 70,000. At about ten o'clock in the morning it began to rain heavily. At midday the expected time of the apparition passed. As people began to leave, Lucia saw the flash of light that always preceded the vision of Mary.

At this moment, the rain stopped and the sun began to come out. Mary opened her hands, which let forth a flood of light. As she rose into the sky, she pointed towards the sun which began to spin. To the left the children saw Saint Joseph holding in his left arm the child Jesus. Saint Joseph raised his right hand and together with the child Jesus made the sign of the Cross three times over the crowd. Although only the children saw this vision, the crowd were transfixed by the pulsating, spinning sun.

Later, people found that their clothing, which had been soaked in the downpour, was quite dry.

Medjugorje

Since 1981, in a small village in former Yugoslavia named Medjugorje, the Virgin Mary has been appearing to six young people from the village: Ivan, Jakov, Marija, Mirjana, Vicka and Ivanka. Of the original visionaries, Vicka, Ivan, Marija and Jakov still have visions on a daily basis; Mirjana on her birthday; and Ivanka once a year on the anniversary of the first apparition.

On the 25th of each month Mary gives a message through Marija. Marija has described:

… it is magnificent to see Our Lady for Christmas when she appears with baby Jesus in her arms. Two years ago she came with the 'big' Jesus on Good Friday. He was in wounds all over, in torn clothes and with a crown of thorns on the head. Our Lady says, 'I have come for you to see how much Jesus suffered for you.'

Vicka has said of the daily visions:

Each time before Our Lady comes, we see a light three times, which is a sign that she is coming. When she appears, she has a white veil, a crown of stars on her head – she is hovering in the air on a great cloud. For some greater festivities, for example Christmas and Easter, or for her birthday, she wears a robe of gold.

In the first months of the apparitions in Medjugorje, signs or supernatural events were particularly numerous. These signs were witnessed by many people, especially those of the hamlet of Bijakovici, in which all the visionaries were born.

Manifestations of light that assume many forms are one of the most frequent signs witnessed at Medjugorje. The first of these was seen on June 27, 1981. On that day, the Virgin Mary's coming was preceded by a brilliant light that illumined not only the village, but the entire area.

The sign observed on August 2, 1981, was the dancing, spinning sun. At the end of the event, a white cloud was seen moving over the mountain side. It moved towards the sun, which continued to spin briefly, and then returned to its normal state. The entire phenomenon lasted about 15 minutes.

One of the most important signs that has been observed is the word MIR (peace in Croatian), which was written one evening in large bright burning letters in the sky above the Cross on Mount Krizevac. This particular sign has been observed numerous times by the pastor and the people from the village. The village has escaped damage from the war in Croatia, although all the surrounding area was affected.

Suggested Reading

African Magic

Burnham, Owen, *African Wisdom*, Piatkus, 2000

Patrice, Malidoma, *Of Water and the Spirit: Ritual, Magic and Initiation and the Life of an African Shaman*, Penguin USA, 1995

Alchemy

Holyard, E. J., *Alchemy*, Dover Publications, 1990

Jung, Carl Gustav, *Alchemical Studies*, Princetown University Press, Princetown, 1983

Amulets and Talismans

Gonzalez-Wipler, Migene, *Complete Guide to Amulets and Talismans*, Llewellyn, St Paul, Minnesota, 1991

Thomas, Willam and Pavitt, Kate, *The Book of Talismans, Amulets and Zodiacal Gems*, Kessinger, New York, 1998

Angels, Fairies and Nature Spirits

Bloom, William, *Working with Angels, Fairies and Nature Spirits*, Piatkus, 1998

Burnham, Sophie, *A Book of Angels*, Ballantine, New York, 1990

Animals, Psychic

Bardens, Dennis, *Psychic Animals*, Capall Bann, 1995, Robert Hale, 1987

Sheldrake, Rupert, *Dogs That Know When Their Owners Are Coming Home*, Crown Publications, 1999

Astral Projection/Out of Body Experiences

Frost, Yvonne and Gavin, *Astral Travel*, Samuel Weiser, New York, 1986

Tart, Charles, *Out of the Body Experiences*, Putnam, 1994

Astrology

Cornelius, Geoffrey and Hyde, Maggie, *Astrology for Beginners*, Icon Books, 1995

Fenton, Sasha, *Predicting the Future*, Piatkus, 1999

Gettings, Fred, *Arkana Dictionary of Astrology*, Arkana, 1990

Atlantis

Brennan, Herbie, *The Atlantis Enigma*, Piatkus, 2000

Hope, Murry, *Ancient Wisdom of Atlantis*, Thorsons, 1999

Auras

Andrews, Ted, *How to Read and See the Aura*, Llewellyn, St Paul, Minnesota, 1996

Smith, Mark and Moody, Raymond A. Jr, *Auras: see them in only 60 seconds*, Llewellyn, St Paul, Minnesota, 1997

Australian Aboriginal Spirituality

Charlesworth, Max, *Religious Business: Essays on Australian Aboriginal Spirituality*, Cambridge University Press, 1999

Lawlor, Robert, *Voices of the First Day: Awakening in the Aboriginal Dreamtimes*, Inner Traditions, 1991

Buddhism

Bechert, H. and Gombrich, R., *The World of Buddhism*, Thames & Hudson, 1991

Snelling, John, *The Buddhist Handbook*, Rider, 1992

Candle Magic

Buckland, Ray, *Advanced Candle Magic*, Llewellyn, St Paul, Minnesota, 1996

Eason, Cassandra, *Candle Power*, Blandford, 1999

Celtic Spirituality

Anderson, Rosemarie, *Celtic Oracles*, Piatkus, 1999

Green, Miranda, *Dictionary of Celtic Myth and Legend*, Thames & Hudson, 1992

Chakras

Karagulla, Shafica and Van Gelder Kunz, Dora, *Chakras and the Human Energy Field*, Theosophical University Press, 1994

Ozaniec, Naomi, *The Elements of the Chakras*, Element, 1989

Clairvoyance

Evans, Hilary, *Frontiers of Reality: where Science Meets the Paranormal*, Thorsons, 1989

Flora, Mary Ellen, *Clairvoyance: Key to Spiritual Perspective*, CDM Publications, 1993

Colour Magic

Buckland, Ray, *Practical Color Magic*, Llewellyn, St Paul, Minnesota, 1996

Sun, Howard and Dorothy, *Colour Your Life*, Piatkus, 1999

Crop Circles

Noyes, Ralph, *The Crop Circle Enigma*, Gateway Books, 1990

Fuller, Roy and Randles, Jenny, *Crop Circles, a Mystery Solved*, Robert Hale, 1990

Crystals

Bourgault, Luc, *The American Indian Secrets of Crystal Healing*, Quantum, 1997

Cunningham, Scott, *Encyclopedia of Crystal, Gem and Metal Magic*, Llewllyn, St Paul, Minnesota, 1991

Curses/Evil Eye/Psychic Protection

Dundee, Alan, *The Evil Eye: A Folklore Casebook*, Garland Publishing, Inc., New York, 1981

Fortune, Dion, *Psychic Self-Defense*, Aquarian, 1998

Dowsing

Bailey, Arthur, *Anyone can Dowse for Better Health*, Quantum, 1999

Lonegren, Sig, *Spiritual Dowsing*, Gothic Images, 1986

Dreams

Delaney, Gayle, *All About Dreams*, HarperCollins, 1998

Lewis, James R., *The Dream Encyclopedia*, Visible Ink, 1995

Druids

Ellis-Berresford, Peter, *The Druids*, Constable, 1994

Nichols, Ross, *Book of Druidry*, Aquarian/Thorsons, 1990

Earth Energies/Ley Lines

Molyneaux, Brian Leigh, *The Sacred Earth*, Macmillan, 1991

Sullivan, Brian, *Ley Lines*, Piatkus, 2000

Feng Shui

Hobson, Wendy, *Simply Feng Shui*, Quantum, 1999

Kingston, Karen, *Creating Sacred Space with Feng Shui*, Piatkus, 1999

Flowers, Trees and Plants

Tompkins and Bird, *Secret Life of Plants*, Avon Books, New York, 1974

Graves, Robert, *The White Goddess*, Faber and Faber, 1988 (Best book on Tree Alphabet and Tree Lore)

Geomancy

Peek, M. (ed.), *African Divination Systems: Ways of Knowing*, Indiana University Press, 1991

Pennick, Nigel, *Secret Games of the Gods*, Samuel Weiser, Maine, 1992

Ghosts

Eason, Cassandra, *Ghost Encounters*, Blandford, 1997

Spencer, John and Anne, *Encyclopedia of Ghosts and Spirits*, Headline, 1992

Goddess

Gadon, Elinor, *The Once and Future Goddess*, Aquarian/Thorsons, 1990

Budapest, Z., *The Holy Book of Women's Mysteries*, Harper Row, New York, 1990

Grail/Arthurian

Jung, Emma and von Franz, Marie Louise, *The Grail Legend*, Element, 1989

Stewart, R. J., *The Prophetic Vision of Merlin*, Arkana, Penguin, 1986

Healing

Brennan, Barbara, *Hands of Light*, Bantam Books, 1987

Eden, Donna, *Energy Medicine*, Piatkus, 1999

Herbalism

Cunningham, Scott, *Encyclopedia of Herbs*, Llewellyn, St Paul, Minnesota, 1997

Lipp, Frank J., *Herbalism*, Macmillan, 1996

Hinduism

Bowes, Pratima, *The Hindu Religious Tradition*, Routledge and Kagan Paul, 1978

Heiman, Betty, *Facts of Indian Thought*, Allen and Unwin, 1964

I Ching

Wilhelm, Richard and Baynes, Cary, *I Ching*, Arkana, Penguin, 1992

Sherrill, W. A. and Chu, W. K., *The Anthology of the I Ching*, Arkana, 1989

Incenses and Oils

Cunningham, Scott, *Complete Book of Oils, Incenses and Brews*, Llewellyn, St Paul, Minnesota, 1991

Dunwich, Gerena, *Wicca Garden, a Witch's Guide to Magical and Enchanted Herbs and Plants*, Citadel, Carol, New York, 1996

Kabbalah

Fortune, Dion, *The Mystical Qabalah*, Ernest Benn Ltd, 1979

Parfitt, Will, *The Living Qabalah*, Element Books, 1988

Magic

Bowes, Sue, *Woman's Magic*, Piatkus, 2000

Eason, Cassandra, *Complete Guide to Magic and Ritual*, Piatkus, 1999

Maternal Intuition

Eason, Cassandra, *The Mother Link*, Ulysses/Seastone, Berkeley, California, 1999

Eason, Cassandra, *Mother Love*, Robinson, 1998

Mediumship/Spiritualism

Berube, Raymond G. and North, Nancy, *You, the Medium*, Northray Publishing, 1995

Williamson, Linda, *Contacting the Spirit World*, Piatkus, 1998

Megalithic Mysteries/Sacred Sites

Balfour, Michael, *Megalithic Mysteries*, Dragon's World, 1996

Wilson, Colin, *The Atlas of Holy Places and Sacred Sites*, Dorling Kindersley, 1996

Miracles

Eason, Cassandra, *Miracles*, Piatkus, 1996

Price, Hope, *Miracles*, Macmillan, 1995

Mysticism

Willis, Roy, *The Complete Guide to World Mysticism*, Piatkus, 1999

Maxwell, Meg and Tschudin, Verena, *Seeing the Invisible*, Arkana, 1990

Native North America

Meadows, Kenneth, *Earth Medicine*, Element, 1996

Wallace, Black Elk and Lyon, William, *Black Elk: the Sacred Ways of a Lakota*, Harper and Row, New York, 1990

Near Death Experiences

Moody, Raymond, *Life after Life*, Bantam, 1975

Morse, Melvin, *Close to the Light*, Souvenir Press, 1991

Parapsychology

Rattray-Taylor, Gordon, *The Natural History of the Mind*, Secker and Warburg, 1979

Wolman, Benjamin (ed.), *Handbook of Parapsychology*, McFarland Publications, 1977

Past Lives/Reincarnation

Cockell, Jenny, *Yesterday's Children*, Piatkus, 1997

White, Ruth, *Karma and Reincarnation*, Piatkus, 2000

Poltergeists

Gauld, Alan and Cornell, Tony, *Poltergeists*, Routledge and Kagan Paul, 1979

Playfair, Guy Lyon, *This House is Haunted*, Souvenir Press, 1980

Prophecy/Predictions

Lemesurier, Peter, *Nostradamus, the Final Reckoning*, Piatkus, 1999

Snow, Chet B., *Dreams of the Future*, Aquarian/Thorsons, 1991

Psychic Children

Eason, Cassandra, *Psychic Power of Children*, Foulsham, 1994

Williamson, Linda, *Children and the Spirit World*, Piatkus, 1999

Psychic Powers, Psychometry

Eason, Cassandra, *Complete Guide to Psychic Development*, Piatkus, 1997

Shine, Betty, *Mind to Mind*, Corgi, 1989

Pyramid Energies

Lemesurier, Peter, *Gods of the Dawn: The Message of the Pyramids and the True Stargate Mystery*, Thorsons, 1998

Runes

Thorsson, Edred, *At the Well of Wyrd, a Handbook of Runic Divination*, Samuel Weiser, Maine, 1988

Taylor, Paul B. and Auden, W. H. (translators), *The Elder Edda, A Selection from the Icelandic*, Faber and Faber, 1973

Sacred Sound

Hame, Peter Michael, *Through Music to the Self*, Element, 1981

Roden, Shirley, *Sound Healing*, Piatkus, 1999

Seasonal Magic/Old Festivals

Cooper, J. C., *Aquarian Dictionary of Festivals*, Aquarian/Thorsons, 1990

Pegg, Bob, *Rites and Riots, Folk Customs in Britain and Europe*, Blandford, 1981

Shamanism

Castenada, Carlos, *Journey to Ixtlan*, Penguin, 1972

Wahoo, Dhyani, *Voices of our Ancestors*, Shambhala, 1987

Survival after Death

Lorimer, David, *Survival?*, Routledge and Kagan Paul, 1984

Hough, Peter, *Life after Death and the World Beyond*, Piatkus, 1998

Tarot

Eason, Cassandra, *Complete Book of the Tarot*, Piatkus, 1999/Crossing Press, 2000

Nichols, Sallie, *Jung and Tarot*, Samuel Weiser, Maine, 1988

Telepathy/Psychokinesis

Eysenck, Hans and Sargent, Carl, *Explained the Unexplained*, Weidenfeld and Nicolson, 1982

Rhine, Joseph, *The Reach of the Mind*, William Morrow, New York, 1947 (Worth tracking down)

Theosophy

Blavatsky, Helena, *The Key to Theosophy*, Theosophical University Press, 1991

Blavatsky, Helena, *The Secret Doctrine: The Synthesis of Science, Religion and Philosophy*, Theosophical University Press, 1992

Western Magical Tradition/Golden Dawn

Regardie, Israel, *Golden Dawn: A Complete Course in Practical Ceremonial Magic*, Llewellyn, St Paul, Minnesota, 1989

Matthews, Caitlin and John, *The Western Way. A Practical Guide to the Western Mystical Tradition*, Arkana, 1996

Wicca and Witchcraft

Buckland, Raymond, *Buckland's Complete Guide to Witchcraft*, Llewellyn, St Paul, Minnesota, 1997

Crowley, Vivienne, *Wicca, The Old Religion on the New Age*, Aquarian, Thorsons, 1989

Witchcraft, History

Briggs, Robin, *Witches and Neighbours, the Social and Cultural Context of European Witchcraft*, HarperCollins, 1996

Guiley, Rosemary Ellen, *Encyclopedia of Witches and Witchcraft*, Facts on File, New York, 1989

Index

Picture Credits

Marble head of Aristotle, Kunsthistoriches Museum, Vienna, Austria, p. 30, Bridgeman Art Library

Hildegard Von Bingen, Lucca, Biblioteca Governativa Statale, p. 41, photo: AKG, London

Pyramid Mausoleum, Norfolk, p. 55, E. & E. Picture Library

Huichol Indian Shaman, 1998, p. 75, Fortean Picture Library

Curse from late 18th or early 19th century, Hereford Museum, p. 102, Fortean Picture Library

Glastonbury Order of Druids at Stonehenge, p.109, Fortean Picture Library

King Arthur's Knights at the Round Table, painting from Trehorenteuc Church, France, p.117, Andreas Trottmann/Fortean Picture Library

Map of Atlantis, from Athanasius Kircher, *Mundus Subterraneus*, p.131, Fortean Picture Library

Cartomancy, from *The Mystic Test Book*, 1893, p. 134, Fortean Picture Library

Tea Leaf Reading, p. 140, Fortean Picture Library

Black Madonna, Chateau d'Ansony, French 17th century, p. 147, photo: AKG, London, Erich Lessing

The Dryad, Evelyn de Morgan, 1884-5, p. 154, The De Morgan Foundation, London, Bridgeman Art Library

Fairy, drawing by Ethel K. Burgess, c. 1920, p. 158, Fortean Picture Library

Ghostly image photographed in 1995, p. 161, Tony O'Rahilly/Fortean Picture Library

Little Red Riding Hood, children's book illustration, early 19th century, p. 167, Victoria and Albert Museum, Bridgeman Art Library

Crop Circle 23 July 1999, Wiltshire, p. 176, photo: Francine Blake, Bridgeman Art Library

St Lucy, c. 1550, Umbrian School, p. 179, Phillips, The International Fine Art Auctioneers, Bridgeman Art Library

Alfred Watkins, 1926, p. 194, Fortean Picture Library

Avebury, Wiltshire, p. 198, Janet and Colin Bord/Fortean Picture Library

Stonehenge, Wiltshire, p. 199, Janet and Colin Bord/Fortean Picture Library

Gautama the Buddha, Nepalese (Nepalese copper), Christie's Images, London, p. 229, Bridgeman Art Library

Daniel Dunglas Home, p. 289, Fortean Picture Library

Mrs Osborne Leonard, p. 290, Fortean Picture Library

Christ in the Sepulchre, Guarded by Angels, William Blake, Victoria and Albert Museum, London, p. 292, Bridgeman Art Library

Angel, John Melhuish Strudwick, p. 296, Roy Miles Esq., Bridgeman Art Library

North American Indian medicine men, p. 298, Fortean Picture Library

Nostradamus, woodcut c., 1850, p. 304, private collection, photo: AKG, London

The Cumaean Sibyl, Agostino Musi, 1516, p. 308, private collection, Elizabeth Harvey-Lee, Bridgeman Art Library

Carl Jung, p. 320, Fortean Picture Library

Portrait of John Dee, English School, 17th century, Ashmolean Museum, Oxford, p. 327, Bridgeman Art Library

Triptych 1934-6, Julius Paul Junghanns, p. 332, Bridgeman Art Library, Gemalde Mensing

The Madonna Conestabile, Raphael, 1502-3, p. 338, Hermitage, St Petersburg, Bridgeman Art Library

Colour Plates

'The Anatomy of Man', French book illumination, c. 1416, Germanisches Nationalmuseum, Nuremberg, photo: AKG, London

'Pisces', Turkish 16th century miniature, Bibliothèque Nationale, Paris, photo: AKG, London

'Senior and Adept under the Tree of Life', decorative script, c. 16th century, photo: AKG, London

Three Angels (panel), Ridolfo Ghirlandaio (1483-1561), Galleria dell'Accademia, Florence, Bridgeman Art Library

Titania, 1866 (w/c and gouache), John Simmons, Bristol City Museum and Art Gallery, Bridgeman Art Library

'Vision of St. Hildegard', pictography, c.1230, Biblioteca Governitva Stutale, Lucca, photo: AKG, London

'Seti makes an incense offering to Horus', relief, Temple of Seti I, photo: AKG, London

Black Madonna, 17th century, Aurillac, France, photo: AKG, London

'The Wheel of Fortuna', French book illumination, 1503, photo: AKG, London

'Crowning of the great goddess', Indian miniature, 17th century, photo: AKG, London

Ivory figure of the Hindu Goddess Kali, ivory, private collection, Bridgeman Art Library

Wooden roof boss depicting the green man, St Andrews Church, Sampford Courtney, Devon, E.& E. Picture Library

The stag god Cerunnos, detail from the Gundestrop cauldron, 1st century AD, Jutland, photo: AKG, London

Spiral formation crop circle, 4 July 1999, Hackpen Hill near Avebury, Wiltshire, photo: Francine Blake, Bridgeman Art Library

Fourteen-pointed star crop circle, 31 July 1999, Roundway, Devizes, Wiltshire, photo: Francine Blake, Bridgeman Art Library

Janus figure, Fermanagh, Northern Ireland, E. & E. Picture Library, Ring of Brodgar, Orkney, Scotland, E. & E. Picture Library

Sigurd's Stone, Upland, Sweden, photo: AKG, London

Stonehenge, Wiltshire, E. & E. Picture Library

'The six stages of reincarnation', wall painting in the Hemis Monastery, Ladakh, photo: AKG, London

Sleeping Buddha, Polonnaruwa, Sri Lanka, photo: AKG, London, Jean-Louis Nou

Thangka of Mandala of Chakrasamvara, 19th – 20th century, Durham University, Bridgeman Art Library

'Lohan, a student of Buddha', brush painting from the Sung Dynasty (AD960-1279), photo: AKG, London

Censer with representation of a priest, Mayan, AD 500-600, Museu Popul Vah, photo: AKG, London

Aboriginal bark painting, Bridgeman Art Library

Kirlian photograph of a fossilised ammonite, Garion Hutchings, Science Photo Library

Kirlian photograph showing the electromagnetic 'aura' around the human body, Garion Hutchings, Science Photo Library